the baking bible

the baking bible

with more than 300 recipes

MURDOCH BOOKS

contents

Of all the culinary skills, the ability to bake reaps the biggest accolades. Some people have a knack with pastry, producing the most ethereal layers of puffed golden crust seemingly with ease. Others are the champions of the feather-light sponge, and yet more can whip up a delicious slice that turns the morning-tea break into a special occasion. All these pinnacles of baking glory are, in fact, within everyone's reach and this book shows you how. Baking has a comfort factor built right in. The act of making the dough, icing the cake and looking admiringly at the finished tart are satisfying and positive experiences. And then there's the pleasure of sharing your handiwork, savouring the flavours and basking in the compliments. With a broad range of recipes and a fund of how-to-get-it-right information, *The Baking Bible* will turn each and every person into a star with the eggs, flour, butter and sugar. Start stirring now.

basics

Beautiful baking

There is nothing quite as comforting, or irresistible, as the delicious smells of home baking—the rewards of taking a tray of freshly cooked delights from the oven are many. Whoever first came up with the idea of combining these three essentially simple ingredients—butter, sugar and flour—to make batters and doughs, was onto a very good thing.

There are two things you need to know about baking before you begin. One—it's a miracle that a pile of flour, some shortening and a good blast of heat can form the base for such a varied and scrumptious array of food. Two—the sum of these raw materials can be temperamental, moody and difficult, and will drive you mad if your first attempts at baking are not as successful as you'd hoped. If this does happen to you, try not to feel discouraged. As well as making sure our recipe methods are clear and informative, we've given a lot of thought to the some of the problems you might encounter along the way, and have put together a series of 'what went wrong?' and 'hints and tips' pages to help you with your next baking adventure.

For centuries, people have been turning flour into food with the help of little more than water. Today, baking remains a pleasure and a passion for many of us who have fallen in love with this fascinating and age-old tradition.

In this book you will find classic recipes from granny's day alongside refreshing takes on all-time favourites and fabulous contemporary recipes. Some recipes are purely indulgent—making the most of luscious ingredients such as cream and chocolate, fresh dates and burstingly ripe berries. The ingredients in others—oats, seeds, semolina, dried fruits and nuts—are healthy enough to make them ideal for wholesome snacks or nutritious lunch box additions. Some are so simple they'll be a cinch to make with the kids, while others may be a little more time-consuming, and take a bit more of your patience and concentration—but the impression they will leave on your guests will be well worth your efforts.

There should be something for all tastes in this book. But it could be difficult deciding between making your own breakfast banana bread, or taking on the culinary adventure of turning out pumpernickel or some pissaladière. You can opt for the decadence of those delicious perennials—chocolate mud cake or black forest cake, or turn out a batch of comparatively understated yet no less scrumptious chocolate hazelnut friands. Will you choose the lightness of a classic sponge for afternoon tea or the rich indulgence of a Devil's food cake, which could easily double as a dessert? Or perhaps you will discover the joy that comes from baking your own bread.

When it comes to filling the cookie jar, there's a tantalizing range from traditional shortbread to macaroons and mouthwatering peanut butter cookies. Sometimes only a slice will suffice—peach crumble slice or walnut brownies perhaps? And you'll no longer need to head to your nearest bakery, café or pizzeria if you have a sudden urge for quiche lorraine, chicken and leek pie, chapattis, pizza margharita, Portuguese custard tarts, lemon meringue pie, baklava or tarte tatin—all your essential baking recipes are right here.

In short, baking is back. And the range and quality of kitchen equipment now available makes the once arduous tasks of beating, whipping and kneading a breeze. Buy the best quality ingredients you can afford, borrow baking pans and beaters if you need to, and make a beeline for the kitchen!

It really is worth taking the time to learn the art of baking, and once you've mastered it, you'll be so proud of yourself, you'll wonder why you didn't get started years ago.

Baking hints and tips

1 Make sure your ingredients are fresh and not past their use-by date. This is especially important for bicarbonate of soda (baking soda) and yeast, which lose their effectiveness (or die, in the case of yeast) if stored for too long.

2 Before you start baking, read the recipe thoroughly and check you have the correct quantity of ingredients and the necessary equipment. Most baking recipes will require standard measuring cups and spoons and an accurate set of kitchen scales.

3 An accurate oven temperature is vital so invest in an oven thermometer. The recipes in this book have all been tested in a conventional (not fan-forced) oven. Preheat the oven to the required temperature—all ovens vary but this will take at least 10 minutes.

4 Bring chilled ingredients, such as butter and eggs, to room temperature, unless specified otherwise.

5 Always use the shape and size of tin or tray specified in each recipe, so as to ensure cooking times are accurate. Line the tin(s) or tray(s) as specified in the recipe, or grease or dust with flour.

6 Position a shelf in the centre of the oven for most baking; this will ensure even baking. For cakes, position the shelf on the bottom third of the oven so the top of the cake is in the middle of the oven. Remember to allow enough room above it to allow room for the cake to rise.

7 Always weigh and measure ingredients accurately, either with scales or cup measures (although cup measures are never as accurate as weighing the ingredients). A set of digital scales is the most accurate method of measuring ingredients.

8 If melting ingredients in a saucepan, never allow the mixture to boil unless specified in the recipe.

9 Eggs or egg yolks should always be added to a creamed mixture one at a time or little by little, beating well after each addition.

10 If a creamed mixture of sugar and egg looks like it may be starting to curdle, sift in a little of the flour alternately with each egg to prevent this occuring.

11 Any raising agent should always be sifted into the bowl with the flour so that it is evenly dispersed.

12 When whisking egg whites, ensure the bowl and beaters (or whisk) are clean and dry before you start, or the egg whites won't whisk properly. The egg whites should always be at room temperature before whisking.

13 Dry ingredients should always be folded into a whisked egg and sugar mixture with a large metal spoon. Fold lightly and gently from the centre of the bowl outwards, turning the bowl a little with each fold. Fold whisked egg whites into the other ingredients (not the other way round), so as to retain as much aeration as possible.

14 Spoon thick batters into a tin. Gently pour thinner batters into a tin. If necessary, smooth the surface of the batter using a spatula to ensure even cooking and browning.

15 Never open the oven door during the first half of cooking time. After the halfway point, if you do need to open the door, open and close it gently.

16 If you are cooking more than one tin or tray at a time, swap their position halfway through the baking time.

17 If the finished product is stuck to the tin, run a palette knife gently around the outside of the tin before unmoulding.

18 Allow baked goods to cool a little before inverting onto a wire rack to cool. When inverting cakes or slices, place another wire rack on the base of the cake and invert the cake onto the second rack so it is right side up—this will prevent any marks on top of the cake or slice.

19 If you intend to ice your baked good, allow it to cool completely first. If you intend to drizzle it with hot syrup, however, do this while still hot.

Cakes

BUTTER CAKES

If you follow our hints you will have no trouble making a delicious butter cake that can be stored for a couple of days, wrapped in plastic wrap.

Fundamentals

It is crucial to use the correct-sized tin. Lightly grease the base and side of the tin with melted unsalted butter or oil. Use a pastry brush to apply an even layer. Line the tin (see pages 14–15) with baking paper or greaseproof and brush the paper with melted unsalted butter or oil.

In addition to the standard baking equipment, you will also need a small and large mixing bowl, a metal spoon, a sieve, a spatula and an electric mixer. If the quantities are not too great, adequate results can be obtained using a hand-held electric beater or mixing by hand, but the mixing time will increase.

The butter, eggs and liquid should be at room temperature. The butter should be malleable, not melted or very soft. Preheat the oven to the correct temperature.

The creaming method

The creaming method is the most frequently used technique in cake-making. The first step is to sift the flours to aerate and separate the particles. Cream the butter and sugar in a small bowl by beating at speed until light and fluffy. The mixture will almost double in volume and should have no trace of the sugar granules. Scrape the side of the bowl with a spatula several times to make sure the butter and sugar are well incorporated. This process can take up to 8 minutes.

With the beaters still running, gradually add the egg, a little at a time, beating thoroughly after each addition. Add any flavourings or essences and beat well to combine.

Transfer the mixture to a large mixing bowl. Using a metal spoon, gently fold in the sifted flour and the liquid (often milk). Stir until just combined and almost smooth. Take care with this final stage, mixing the ingredients lightly. Over-enthusiastic beating can produce a heavy, coarse-textured cake.

Next, gently spoon or pour the mixture into the tin, spread out evenly and smooth the surface. Check the oven temperature. Position an oven rack in the lower third of the oven so the top of the cake is in the middle of the oven. Centre the cake tin on the oven rack and bake for the required time.

When is it ready?

The cake is cooked when it begins to shrink from the side of the tin and is lightly golden. If gently pressed with a finger, it should spring back into shape. As a final check, insert a fine skewer in the centre—it should come out clean, without any moisture. Avoid opening the oven door until at least two-thirds of the way through baking.

A cake is fragile when removed from the oven, so leave in the tin for 10 minutes before turning out onto a wire rack to cool. If the cake is stuck to the tin, gently run a flat-bladed knife around the side to release it. Remove the lining immediately.

FRUIT CAKES

With a little careful attention to the lining of the tin, you will be assured of that special feeling of fulfilment when lifting a freshly baked fruit cake out of the oven.

Fundamentals

Fruit cakes are generally made by the creaming method so it is recommended you read the detailed description of creaming butter and sugar in the opposite column.

Before you begin, read through your recipe, checking you have all the right equipment and ingredients at hand. Leave plenty of time as fruit cakes take a little longer to prepare than simple cakes and also take a few hours to cook.

Before you mix your cake, line the tin and make sure the oven rack is positioned so the cake will sit in the centre of the oven, then preheat the oven.

Lining the tin

Lightly grease the cake tin. Fruit cakes need a double layer of baking paper for the collar and base. Cut two circles of baking paper, using the base as a guide.

To make the collar, cut a double strip of baking paper long enough to fit around the outside of the tin and tall enough to extend 5 cm (2 inch) above the top of the tin. Fold a 2 cm (¾ inch) deep cuff along the length of the strip, then make diagonal cuts up to the fold line about 1 cm (½ inch) apart. Fit in the tin, with the cuts on the base, pressing them out at right angles so they sit flat around the base. Place the circles of baking paper over the cuts. (See pages 14–15 for more information.)

Because of the long cooking time, fruit cakes require extra protection, both around the side and under the base. This is why we wrap layers of newspaper around the outside of the tin, and sit the tin on layers of newspaper in the oven. Because the oven temperature is low, this is quite safe.

Making the cake

Weigh all the ingredients in your recipe and complete preparations such as softening butter, sifting flour and spices, blanching nuts, tossing fruit in flour or marinating fruit, if required. Dates and prunes may have stones that need to be removed. Glacé (candied) fruit such as cherries, pineapple or ginger are better if cut into small pieces. If mixed peel (mixed candied citrus peel) pieces are large, chop into smaller pieces.

Following the methods described in making a creamed butter cake, beat the butter and sugar with electric beaters until light and fluffy. Gradually add the eggs, beating thoroughly after each addition. Add any essences, rind, juice, jam, syrup or molasses as specified. Transfer to a large bowl and add the specified dried or glacé fruit. Mix the batter with a large metal spoon until combined.

Next, using a metal spoon, fold in the sifted dry ingredients. Alcohol, if specified, can also be added at this time. Stir until just combined and almost smooth. Spoon the batter evenly into the tin, spread into the corners of square tins, and smooth the top. Some fruit cakes are decorated at this stage by placing blanched almonds in a pattern on the top. Check that the oven temperature is correct. Wrap layers of newspaper around the tin, coming up as high as the collar, and secure with string or paper clips. Place a few layers of newspaper on the rack in the oven and place the tin on top. If the cake starts to brown before it is cooked, cover it loosely with a piece of foil.

When is it ready?

As ovens vary, check the cake 20 minutes before the specified time. If it is cooked, a skewer should come out clean when inserted into the centre. The cake should shrink from the side of the tin. Cool the cake completely in the tin, preferably overnight, before removing.

Storage

Fruit cakes improve if kept for a few weeks wrapped in baking paper and foil, or kept in an airtight container, before decorating or cutting. Un-iced fruit cakes can be refrigerated for up to 3 months. They can be fed alcohol by inserting holes with a skewer and pouring in brandy or whisky.

What went wrong?

Butter cake

Perfect The texture is light, moist and even, with a golden brown crust. When a skewer is inserted into the centre of the cake, it comes out clean. The cake springs back when pressed lightly with a fingertip.

Overcooked The top of the cake is very dark and the texture of the cake crumb quite dry. The cooking time may have been too long or the cooking temperature too high. It's also possible that the tin was the wrong size or that the cake was placed too high in the oven.

Undercooked and sunken The centre of the cake is sunken and when a skewer is inserted into the centre, it comes out sticky. The cake has a soggy, dense texture. The cooking time may have been too short or the oven temperature too low. Too little flour or too much butter may have been used in the recipe. The oven door may have been opened during the early stages of cooking.

Fruit cake

Perfect The crust is an even, deep golden brown. When a skewer is inserted into the centre of the cake, it comes out clean. The texture of the cake is moist and the fruit is evenly distributed.

Overcooked The oven temperature may have been too high or the cooking time too long. The mixture might have had too little fat or too much raising agent. Too much sugar may cause a dark crust. If the cake is colouring too quickly and the oven temperature is correct, then the top can be protected by covering with foil or a double layer of baking paper.

Undercooked and sunken The baking time may have been too short or the oven temperature too low. There might be too much fruit or too little raising agent. The cake may have been placed too low in the oven. The tin needs to be placed in the middle of the oven.

Cake tins and linings

Cakes can be an easy way to impress, but don't let your masterpiece be spoiled at the last minute as you struggle to turn it out of the tin. Follow these simple instructions for preparing your cake tin to ensure perfect results every time.

Fundamentals

Cake tins are greased and lined to prevent the mixture from sticking to the tin. Always prepare the tin according to the instructions before preparing the cake as different types of cakes require different tin sizes and preparation.

Check the size of your cake tin by measuring the diameter or width and length of the base. It is important to use the tin size specified in the recipe or at least one of the same cup capacity—you can check this by filling the tin with water and measuring the volume.

Aluminium cake tins give consistently good results, with even cooking. Avoid using dark-coloured tins as they may brown the cake before it cooks through. Cake tins that have a non-stick coating on them tend to cook the cake more rapidly. If you are using these tins, experiment with reducing the cooking time by 10 minutes or so, or reducing the oven temperature a little to avoid overcooking your cake. When choosing a cake tin for delicate sponge cakes, choose one with deep sides to protect the mixture.

Remember—when you start to make your cake, it is very important to read through the recipe first to be sure you have all the necessary ingredients and equipment. Preheat the oven and put the cake on the middle shelf once it has reached the correct temperature.

Greasing and lining the cake tin

Once you have chosen the correct cake tin for the recipe, grease the tin using melted unsalted butter or a mild-flavoured oil. Apply just enough to evenly coat the base and sides of the tin using a pastry brush, making sure there is no excess dripping back to the base of the tin. A relatively recent invention—oil spray—is a quick and easy alternative to the more traditional greasing method; just make sure to spray away from the heat source in a well-ventilated area. The greasing also helps if you then line the cake tin—the grease will help the paper adhere to the tin.

Lining the tin

After greasing, some cake tins are also lined. Average-sized cakes generally only need the base of the tin to be lined, not the side(s). This is because they don't have a particularly long cooking time. Simply place the tin on top of a piece of baking paper, draw around it and cut out the traced shape to fit the base of the tin. Use a good-quality baking paper, making sure that it is free of any wrinkles that could spoil your cake's smooth finish.

Other cakes, such as fruit cake, which are cooked for a much longer time or those with a high sugar content, require extra protection, both around the side and under the base. Generally, with these cakes the oven temperature will be quite low so the best way to do it will be to tie a few layers of newspaper in a cuff around the outside of the tin, and to sit the tin on a wad of newspaper in the oven in addition to greasing and lining it as described before. Because the oven temperature stays low, this is quite safe.

Making a collar

Some of the cakes in this book are cooked with a collar. This extends the height of the cake, giving a more dramatic result. Collars can also give extra protection during cooking. In general, a collar is recommended for cakes that have a baking time in excess of 1 hour.

As a general rule a single layer of baking paper is enough for a collar on an average-sized cake. Larger cakes and fruit cakes will need a double layer of baking paper to make the collar and line the base.

To make a collar, lightly grease the cake tin. Cut a strip of paper long enough to fit around the outside of the tin and tall enough to extend 5 cm (2 inches) above the top of the tin. Fold down one cuff, about 2 cm (¾ inch) deep, along the length of the strip.

Make diagonal cuts up to the fold line about 1 cm (½ inch) apart. Fit the collar around the inside edge of the tin, with the cuts in the base of the tin, pressing them out at right angles so they sit flat around the bottom edge of the tin. Cut a circle of baking paper using the bottom of the tin as a guide. Place the circle of paper in the base of the tin, over the cuts in the collar. Make sure that the paper is smooth and crease-free before pouring in your cake batter or the base and side of your cake will come out with the creases baked into them. (See steps 1 and 2 of Lining a round cake tin on the opposite page.)

Lining a round cake tin

Step 1: To make a collar for a round cake tin, cut a strip of baking paper long enough to cover the outside of the tin (with a little extra for overlapping) and up to 6 cm (2½ inches) wider than the height. Fold down a 2 cm (¾ inch) cuff along the length of the paper, then cut slits into the cuff on the diagonal at 1–2 cm (½–¾ inch) intervals.

Step 2: Grease the inside of the tin and place the strip of baking paper against the inside edge with the cut cuff sitting neatly on the base. Press the cuff out so the paper pieces sit flat—the cut cuff will act like pleats, ensuring that the paper sits snug against the side of the pan.

Step 3: Place the cake tin on a sheet of baking paper and trace around the outside, then cut out with a pair of scissors. Place, pencil-side down, onto the base of the tin over the pleats and smooth out any bubbles or creases.

Note: If just lining the base of the tin, complete Step 3 only.

Lining a square cake tin

Step 1: Place the cake tin on a sheet of baking paper and trace around the outside with a pencil.

Step 2: Cut out the paper. Grease the inside of the tin and place the paper, pencil-side down, onto the base of the tin, smoothing out any air bubbles.

Step 3: If lining the sides of the tin as well, cut a strip of baking paper the same length as the outside of the tin and 1 cm (½ inch) wider than the height. Place against the inside around the sides, smoothing out any bubbles or creases.

Lining a loaf (bar) cake tin

Step 1: Cut a strip of baking paper long enough to cover the base and two long sides of the loaf tin, allowing extra to overhang the sides—these will act as handles when it comes to removing the cake from the tin.

Step 2: Grease the tin and place the paper into the tin, smoothing out any bubbles or creases.

Lining a round cake tin

Fold down a cuff on one edge of the baking paper and cut the cuff up to the fold line.

Place the baking paper along the greased side of the tin, with the cut cuff sitting on the base.

Cut a circle of baking paper to fit into the base of the tin and put it in place.

Lining a square cake tin

Use the base of the cake tin to accurately trace the shape onto the baking paper.

Grease the tin, then fit the paper into the base, eliminating any air bubbles as you go.

Cut a strip of baking paper to fit the sides of the tin and smooth them into place.

Muffin and scone basics

MUFFIN BASICS

Wonderfully simple, muffins can be plain, sweet or savoury. Master the basic muffin, then experiment with different flavour combinations and enjoy them for breakfast, snacks, lunch or dinner.

Perfect muffins

Follow these simple instructions to make twelve delicious muffins. You will need 310 g (11 oz/2½ cups) self-raising flour, 125 g (4½ oz/½ cup) caster (superfine) sugar, 375 ml (13 fl oz/ 1½ cups) milk, 2 lightly beaten eggs, 1 teaspoon natural vanilla extract and 150 g (5½ oz) unsalted butter that has been melted and cooled.

Here we have used the regular (100 ml/3½ fl oz) size American-style non-stick tins but muffin tins are also available in mini and Texan sizes, and some recipes in the book will specify these other tin sizes. Even though most muffin tins have non-stick surfaces, it is worth greasing the holes, especially when making sweet muffins, as the sugar can make them very sticky and difficult to remove once cooked.

Assemble your ingredients and utensils and preheat the oven to 200°C (400°F/Gas 6). Sift the flour into a bowl to aerate the flour and ensure a light muffin. Add the sugar to the bowl and stir through the flour. Make a well in the centre.

In a jug, mix together the milk, eggs and natural vanilla extract. Pour the liquid into the well in the flour and add the cooled butter. Melted butter doesn't always combine well with other liquids so it is often added separately. Fold the mixture gently with a metal spoon until just combined. Be careful not to overbeat or the muffins will become tough and rubbery. The mixture should still be lumpy at this stage.

Divide the mixture evenly among the holes using two metal spoons—fill each hole to about three-quarters full. Always try to use the hole size indicated in the recipe because if you use a different size the cooking time changes.

Cooking

Bake the muffins for 20–25 minutes, or until they are risen, golden and come away slightly from the sides of the holes. Test if the muffins are ready by pressing lightly with your fingertips—they are cooked when they feel firm, and spring back. Another test is to insert a skewer into the centre— if it comes out clean they are ready.

Most muffins should be left in the tin for a couple of minutes once out of the oven, but don't leave them too long or trapped steam will make the bases soggy.

Using a flat-bladed knife, loosen the muffins and transfer to a wire rack. They can be eaten warm or cool and can be decorated or iced—most cake toppings or icings are also suitable for muffins.

Simple muffin variations

The basic muffin recipe can be adapted to add many flavours. You can use the same tin but the muffin holes will be quite full.

Banana Add an extra 60 g (2¼ oz/¼ cup) caster (superfine) sugar and ½ teaspoon mixed spice to the flour and 240 g (8½ oz/1 cup) mashed ripe bananas to the butter. Use only 250 ml (9 fl oz/1 cup) milk. Proceed with the recipe.

Pecan Replace the caster (superfine) sugar with 140 g (5 oz/ ¾ cup) soft brown sugar. Add 90 g (3¼ oz/¾ cup) chopped pecans with the flour. Mix to distribute evenly, then proceed with the recipe.

Storage

Cold muffins can be frozen for 3 months. When required, thaw, wrap in foil, then reheat in a 180°C (350°F/Gas 4) oven for about 8 minutes, or until heated through.

SCONE SECRETS

Scones are so easy—they can be mixed and baked in no time at all. For perfect scones, handle them quickly and lightly and cook in a hot oven.

Light and easy

All scones are made according to the same principles: add the wet ingredients to the dry and mix the dough as briefly and lightly as possible. Because the moisture content of flour varies, you may not need all the liquid stated in your recipe. The amount of liquid the flour absorbs can also change according to the room temperature and even the altitude. Although our recipe uses self-raising flour, some people prefer to use plain (all-purpose) flour and add more raising agents such as baking powder. Salt is added to enhance the flavour of all scones, even sweet ones, and the taste is not noticeable.

Making perfect scones

Follow these simple directions to achieve a good batch of high, light and golden scones. Remember that unlike bread, which requires vigorous kneading, scone dough just needs quick light handling.

To make 10–12 scones, you will need 310 g (11 oz/2½ cups) self-raising flour, 1 teaspoon baking powder, a pinch of salt, 40 g (1½ oz) chilled unsalted butter, cut into small cubes, and 250 ml (9 fl oz/1 cup) milk. Assemble all the ingredients as well as a large bowl, a flat-bladed metal spatula or knife, a round scone or cookie cutter, a pastry brush and a baking tray. You will also need a cloth to wrap the scones.

Before you begin mixing, preheat the oven to 220°C (425°F/Gas 7) and lightly grease the baking tray or line it with baking paper. Sift the flour, baking powder and salt into a bowl. Sifting aerates the dry ingredients and helps achieve lighter scones. Many bakers sift the flour twice. Rub in the butter briefly with your fingertips until the mixture is crumbly and resembles fine breadcrumbs. Mixing in 1 tablespoon of sugar at this stage will lessen any floury taste. Make a well in the centre.

Pour in almost all the milk and mix with a flat-bladed knife, using a cutting action, until the dough comes together in clumps. Rotate the bowl as you work. Use the remaining milk if the mixture seems dry. Handle the mixture with care and a light hand. If you are heavy-handed and mix too much, your scones will be tough. The dough should feel slightly wet and sticky.

With floured hands, gently gather the dough together, lift onto a lightly floured surface and pat into a smooth ball. Do not knead. Pat or lightly roll the dough out to 2 cm (¾ inch) thick. Using a floured 6 cm (2½ inch) cutter, cut into rounds. Don't pat out too thinly or the scones will not be a good height. Gather the scraps together and, without handling too much, press out as before and cut out more rounds. Place close together on the baking tray and lightly brush the tops with milk. Bake in the top half of the oven for 12–15 minutes, or until risen and golden. It is important to cook scones at a high temperature, otherwise the raising agents will not work. If you aren't sure they are cooked, break one open. If still doughy in the centre, cook for a few more minutes. For soft scones, wrap them in a dry tea towel (dish towel) while hot. For scones with a crisp top, transfer to a wire rack to cool slightly before wrapping. Serve warm, or at room temperature, with butter or jam and whipped or clotted cream.

Storage

As scones contain little fat, they dry out quickly so are best eaten soon after baking. They freeze successfully—they can be frozen for 3 months. When required, thaw, wrap in foil, then reheat in a 180°C (350°F/Gas 4) oven for about 8 minutes, or until heated through.

What went wrong?

Muffins

Perfect The texture of the muffin is even with a nicely risen centre and good golden colouring. The muffin has started to come away from the side of the holes.

Undercooked The muffin is moist in the centre with insufficient peaking. The oven wasn't hot enough, or the cooking time may have been too short.

Poorly risen The texture is heavy and dense. This can be caused by insufficient raising agent or a missing ingredient.

Scones

Perfect The scone is evenly risen, has a soft crust and soft inside texture and is light golden.

Poorly risen If the scone texture feels heavy and dense, the dough may have been either too dry or too wet, or the dough may have been mixed too much.

Undercooked The scone is pale, sticky in the centre and has a dense texture. The cooking time was too short or the oven temperature too low.

Small cakes and slices

FRIANDS AND CUPCAKES

These delightful little treats are just the thing to satisfy those afternoon sweet cravings. The only problem is that it can be almost impossible to stop at just one …

Afternoon tea time

Teatime gives us the chance to enjoy delicious baked goodies, such as delicate little friands and cupcakes, washed down with a perfectly brewed cup of tea.

For the delightful custom of afternoon tea, we must thank Anna, wife of the seventh Duke of Bedford. In the 19th century, lunch was a very light meal, and dinner was not served until eight o'clock. Not happy with this arrangement, the Duchess of Bedford asked that tea and cakes be served mid-afternoon because, to quote herself, she had 'a sinking feeling'. She invited friends to join her and in no time at all this became a fashionable thing to do!

In an arguably more civilized age, the world stopped for a mid-morning snack—and perhaps even for an afternoon one as well. Home baking was a regular activity, deliciously warm aromas permeated the kitchen and cake tins were filled for another week. Now, it seems, we're all far too busy to enjoy even a half-hour's pause over a cup of tea or freshly brewed coffee. Let alone devote time to baking 'from scratch'. Before we completely relinquish the joys of snack-time though, it's good to remind ourselves that, in an increasingly frantic world, it makes sense to pause from life's demands and take time for an energizing drink and a nibble of some delectable morsel.

Kitchen teas, baby showers, birthday celebrations, anniversaries and pre-Christmas get-togethers are also excellent opportunities to buff up silver teapots, dust off fine, bone china and pass around plates of gorgeous sweet and savoury goodies.

Fundamentals

One of the most attractive characteristics of cupcakes and friands is that they are easily portable and can be made in advance, which makes them ideal for picnics, lunch boxes or parties. Cupcakes are simply a small cake and are usually made with a standard cake batter. In this book we use standard muffin tins for cupcakes—you can choose whether or not to line the tin with a case or not. There is a range of paper cases available from supermarkets and specialist food stores to fit the cupcake and add a decorative touch.

Friands are very dense and moist and are easily recognizable by their oval shape. In the past, friand tins were only available in single tins but now they are available in trays with multiple holes, similar to muffin trays. However, if you don't have a friand tray, you can use a muffin tray.

SLICE SECRETS

The slice or bar cookie has long been a favourite accompaniment for morning coffee or afternoon tea. Most slices are quick and easy to cook and for the beginner, slices are a dream come true: less daunting to prepare than a cake, but more exciting than a batch of cookies.

Equip yourself

We've used an assortment of baking tins in our recipes to suit both the flavour and richness of each slice, giving a selection of shapes, sizes and thicknesses. Don't forget: always measure your tins across the base. Obviously we don't expect everyone to have the full array of tins in their kitchen, so if you don't have the exact size specified, use the closest you have and adjust the cooking time accordingly. If you have the choice, use a slightly larger tin—your mixture will be spread a little more thinly and so will take less time to cook. If you use a smaller tin than we have specified, your mixture is likely to bubble up over the top. Bear in mind that using a smaller tin may take slightly longer to cook than the recipe states. Using a non-stick tin means your slice will cook slightly faster and brown more—check it about 5 minutes earlier than the cooking time given in the recipe.

Basic metric cup and spoon measures and scales will help you measure your ingredients accurately and appliances such as electric beaters and food processors will help minimize preparation time.

Tin talk

Lining the tin has a dual purpose—it prevents the slice sticking to the tin but also means you can lift your slice out of the tin after cooking. Line the tin before you start any mixing. Lightly grease the base and sides with butter or oil spray, then line the base with a piece of non-stick baking paper. The paper should fit the base of the tin neatly, without creases, but should be wide so that it overhangs the two long sides of the tin. This creates the simple handles that enable you to lift your slice out of the tin. Some recipes may only require the base to be lined. To do this, draw around the base onto paper, then cut it out. If all four sides of the tin need to be lined, simply line the base, overhanging two sides, then lay another piece of paper over the top, overhanging the other two sides.

In the oven

If the top of the slice starts to over-brown while it is cooking, cover it loosely with foil or baking paper—not tightly or the slice will become soggy. For best results cook the slice on the middle rack in the centre of the oven. In some recipes you'll need to check if the slice is cooked by inserting a skewer into the centre. The skewer should come out clean, without sticky crumbs on it. If it doesn't, bake the slice for a further 5 minutes and retest. This doesn't apply to all slices as many have soft fillings. With many slices you will find they are soft when removed from the oven and then firm up a little as they cool. This is why the recipe will often state 'leave to cool in the tin for 5 minutes'.

Cutting

Use the baking paper 'handles' to lift the whole slice out of the tin. It is much easier to cut the slice into neat squares, fingers or even diamonds if you use a ruler as a guide. For clean edges, wipe the blade of the knife with a damp cloth between each cut. Use a sawing action with a serrated knife for cakey slices. If you have cut the slice in the tin, remove the corner piece with a palette knife—this makes it easier to lift out the other pieces.

Storage

Most slices can be stored in an airtight container, or in the fridge in warm weather, for between 3 and 7 days.

SLICE HINTS AND TIPS

1 Buy good quality, sturdy, non-stick baking tins. Always use the size of tin recommended in the recipe to ensure the cooking times are accurate.

2 Line trays or tins with baking paper so that the paper extends over the two long sides. This makes it easier to lift the cooled mixture out of the tin to cut into slices.

3 If you use a food processor to make the pastry, use it only to rub the fat into the flour. After adding the liquid, pulse briefly until the mixture just comes together, then turn out onto a work surface and gently shape the dough into a ball. It is important not to overwork pastry dough or it will be tough when cooked.

4 A soft pastry dough can be rolled out between two sheets of baking paper to prevent it from sticking to the work surface.

5 If the dough is too soft to be rolled out, it may be necessary to press it into the tin. Once pressed well into the base and edges of the tin, use the back of a spoon to smooth the surface as flat and evenly as possible.

6 Use the back of a spoon to press the slice mixture evenly into the tin.

7 If you are baking two slices at once, swap the tins halfway through the cooking time so they brown evenly.

8 When bars and slices are made with several layers, it is important that each layer is completely cold before adding the next one.

9 If short on time, the slice can be made in two stages. After lining the tin with pastry, chill overnight, wrapped loosely in plastic wrap, ready to finish the next day.

10 Slices should only be iced when completely cooled.

11 Allow the cooked mixture to cool before slicing it, unless specified.

12 If the slice is quite sticky and difficult to cut, run the blade of the knife under hot or boiling water before cutting.

13 Cut chocolate-topped slices with a hot knife. Dip the knife in boiling water, then wipe dry before cutting.

14 Decorate slices by dusting with icing sugar or cocoa. Dust half the slice, or make decorative templates, using baking paper. You can also dip whole pieces of slice, or the corners, in melted chocolate.

15 Wrap plain, un-iced pieces of slice in plastic or foil and freeze for up to 2–3 months. Pop a frozen piece into a lunchbox to thaw out by lunch time.

16 To grate citrus zest, place a piece of baking paper over the grater. This will prevent zest getting caught in the holes.

17 Toasting nuts and coconut before use enhances their flavour. Spread on a baking tray and toast in the oven for 5–8 minutes at 180°C (350°F/Gas 4).

Cookies

Nothing beats the heavenly aroma of freshly baked cookies. Cookies are made using several methods, each giving special characteristics to the cookies.

Fundamentals

When making cookies, it is important to use the right type of tray. Choose a baking tray that has either very short or no sides—this will aid even heat circulation. It is fine to cook two trays of cookies at the same time as long as the trays don't touch. If they are on different shelves, swap them around halfway through the baking time.

Perfect cookies using the creaming method

With the following recipe, you can make a basic butter cookie and variations. To make about 30 cookies, line two baking trays with baking paper or lightly grease with melted butter. Soften 125 g (4½ oz) butter, then cut into cubes.

Preheat the oven to 210°C (415°F/Gas 6–7). Cream the softened butter with 125 g (4½ oz/½ cup) caster (superfine) sugar in a bowl using electric beaters until light and fluffy. The mixture should be pale and smooth. The sugar should be almost dissolved. Add 60 ml (2 fl oz/¼ cup) milk and ¼ teaspoon natural vanilla extract and beat until combined. Add 185 g (6 oz/1½ cups) self-raising flour and 60 g (2¼ oz/ ½ cup) custard powder (instant vanilla pudding mix) and use a flat-bladed knife to bring to a soft dough. Rotate the bowl as you work and use a cutting motion to incorporate the dry ingredients. Don't overwork the dough.

Roll level teaspoonfuls into balls and place on the trays, leaving 5 cm (2 inch) between each cookie. Flatten the balls lightly with your fingertips, then press with a fork. The cookies should be about 5 cm (2 inch) in diameter. Bake for 15–18 minutes, until lightly golden. Cool on the trays for 3 minutes before transferring to a wire rack to cool completely.

Plain cooked cookies can be decorated with icing (confectioners') sugar just before serving. Or they can be iced (see a range of cookie icings and toppings on page 31), or drizzled with melted chocolate.

Storage

Cookies can be stored in an airtight container for up to a week. They also freeze well. To freeze, place in freezer bags and seal, label and date. Unfilled and un-iced cooked cookies can be frozen for up to two months. After thawing, refresh them in a 180°C (350°F/Gas 4) oven for a few minutes, then cool and decorate, as desired, before serving.

Uncooked cookie dough freezes well. To do this, wrap it in plastic wrap, place in a plastic bag and seal. When ready to use, thaw at room temperature and bake as directed.

Simple cookie variations

The basic cookie recipe is very versatile and can be adapted.

Citrus Omit the natural vanilla extract, and instead add 2 teaspoons orange or lemon zest to the creamed butter and sugar and proceed with the recipe. When the cookies are cool, make an icing: combine 250 g (9 oz/ 2 cups) sifted icing (confectioners') sugar, 20 g (¾ oz) softened butter and 1 tablespoon lemon or orange juice in a bowl. Ice the cookies with the icing.

Nutty Mix 55 g (2 oz/½ cup) finely chopped walnuts, pecans or macadamia nuts into the basic mixture before adding the flour. Press a nut onto each cookie, instead of pressing with a fork, and bake as described in the opposite column.

Melt and mix method

This quick method involves mixing the dry ingredients, then mixing in the melted butter (and any other ingredients in the recipe) with a wooden spoon until the dry ingredients are well moistened.

Rubbing in method

This involves cutting cold butter into pieces and rubbing it into the flour with your fingertips until the mixture is crumbly and resembles fine breadcrumbs. Then almost all the liquid is added and cut into the dry ingredients with a knife, adding the remaining liquid if necessary to bring the mixture together. Do not add the liquid all at once as flour varies a great deal so the full amount of liquid may not be required.

What went wrong?

Drop cookies

Perfect The cookie has even golden colouring on both the top and base and has even thickness.

Undercooked, sticking These cookies are pale and the tops soft to touch. This indicates that the cooking time may have been too short, leaving the mixture undercooked and sticky. Alternatively, the oven temperature may have been too low or the oven insufficiently preheated before baking the cookies.

Overcooked The oven temperature may have been too high or the cooking time may have been too long. Be sure to only rest the cookies for a couple of minutes on the tray after cooking because they will continue to cook if left on the hot tray.

Mixture rolled out and cut into shapes

Perfect The cookie has a light golden colouring and even thickness.

Thin, overcooked The mixture may have been rolled too thinly or the oven may have been too hot, or perhaps the cookies cooked too long.

Too thick The mixture was rolled and cut too thickly. This cookie, although probably too thick, would need extra baking time.

Mixture shaped by hand or piped

Perfect The cookie has even, golden colouring on both the top and base. It is also the correct thickness.

Undercooked The cookie is a pale colour. The oven temperature may have been too low, the oven not preheated, or the cookies not cooked long enough.

Overcooked and spread too much The oven may have been too hot or the cookies cooked too long.

basics

Perfect pastry

What does 'rub in the butter' mean? How do you 'line the tin with pastry'? Why are some pastry cases baked blind before they are filled? These are some of the questions that can vex newcomers to pastry-making. Take a little time to read the following hints and all will be clear.

Which pastry?

For most of the recipes in this book, you can make your own pastry or buy ready-made. If we specify a home-made pastry it is because the taste is better in that particular pie. We have used only a few types of pastry throughout this book. Beginners should probably choose recipes using the easiest pastries, such as shortcrust (pie) pastry. Instead of, or as well as, butter, some pastries use olive oil and others lard. Some shortcrusts have sugar or an egg added—you could use bought shortcrust, but the pastry won't be quite as rich. Plain shortcrust can be used for sweet pies but sweet pastry is most commonly used.

Ingredients

Pastry at its simplest is flour mixed with half its weight in some form of fat, then bound with water.

Flour Plain (all-purpose) white flour is the one most commonly used for pastry. For a slightly different texture, a combination of wholemeal (whole-wheat) plain and plain white flour can be used. Store your flour in an airtight container.

Fat Butter is the most commonly used fat for making pastry and gives a wonderful colour to the pastry. Use real butter, not margarine or softened butter blends. Sometimes a mixture of butter and lard is used, sometimes all lard. Lard gives a good flaky texture. Butter and lard are usually chilled and cut into cubes to make it easier to incorporate them into the flour, keeping the pastry cooler and more manageable. Generally, unsalted butter should be used for sweet and salted butter for savoury recipes. Olive oil is sometimes used to give pastries a different texture, for example in a traditional spinach pie.

Salt Salt can be added to both sweet and savoury pastry to add flavour.

Sugar Caster (superfine) sugar is used in sweet shortcrust pastry as its fine texture ensures that it blends well.

Liquid The usual binding liquid in pastry-making is iced water, but sometimes an egg or an egg yolk will be used to enrich the dough. You will find that most pastry recipes only give an approximate liquid measure because the amount will vary according to the flour, the temperature, the altitude and the humidity. Add a little at a time and work it in until the pastry 'starts to come together' in clumps that can then be pressed together with your hands.

Tools of the trade

Food processor While not essential, a food processor can make pastry-making easy. Pastry should be kept cool and a processor means you don't need to touch the dough as you mix. If you prefer, you can use the processor just to combine the butter and flour before continuing to mix by hand.

Marble pastry board Although not strictly necessary, marble boards are favoured by pastry-makers for their cool and hygienic surface. If you don't have one, place a roasting tin full of iced water on your work surface for a while to cool the surface before rolling your pastry.

Rolling pins An essential tool in pastry-making. They are now available in traditional wood, marble, plastic and stainless steel. Lightly sprinkle your rolling pin with flour to prevent the pastry sticking. You can also use the rolling pin to lift the pastry into the tin and then trim away the excess pastry by rolling over the top.

Baking paper Very useful when rolling out pastry. The dough is rolled out between two sheets of paper, the top sheet is removed and the pastry is inverted into the tin before removing the other sheet. A crumpled sheet of baking paper is also used to line pastry shells when blind baking.

Baking beads Reusable baking beads (also known as pie weights) are spread in a layer over baking paper to weigh down pastry during blind baking. They are available in kitchenware shops and department stores. Dried beans or uncooked rice can also be used and stored in a jar for re-use.

Cutters Available in all shapes and sizes. They are used to cut bases and tops for small pies and to cut out pieces of dough to decorate pies. Cutters may need to be dusted lightly with flour to prevent them from sticking to the pastry. If you don't have a pastry cutter, a fine-rimmed glass, turned upside down, is a good substitute.

Pie tins and dishes Available in many styles. While testing the pies for this book we baked with metal, glass and ceramic pie dishes. We found the crispest base crusts were achieved in the metal tins.

Pastry brushes Used for glazing. A glaze gives the pastry crispness and colour. Pastry can also be sealed and joined by brushing the edges with milk or beaten egg. Use only a small amount of liquid or your pastry may become soggy.

PASTRY HINTS AND TIPS

1 Dough must be kept cool. Work in a cool kitchen if possible. If you are baking in summer, chill your work surface by leaving a tin of iced water on it before you start rolling or shaping. Make sure all the ingredients are as cool as possible and that they stay cool during the preparation.

2 Because your hands are warm, try to handle the pastry as little as possible. Cool your hands under cold water. Good pastry-makers work quickly—too much handling will cause the cooked pastry to toughen and shrink.

3 Flours vary in their moisture content. Because of this, the liquid is not added all at once. Test the dough by pinching a little piece together. If it holds together and doesn't crumble, you don't need more liquid. If the pastry is too dry, it will be difficult to put into tins; if too wet it will shrink when cooked.

4 Pastry should be wrapped in plastic wrap and put in the fridge for 20–30 minutes before rolling or shaping. In hot weather, refrigerate the pastry for at least 30 minutes.

5 For ease of rolling, roll out dough between two sheets of baking paper.

6 Pies with a bottom crust benefit from being cooked on a heated metal baking tray. Put the tray in the oven as the oven warms up.

7 Pastry can be stored in the fridge for 2 days or frozen for up to 3 months. Ensure that it is well sealed in plastic wrap. Thaw on a wire rack to let the air circulate.

8 Pastry should always be cooked in a preheated oven, never one that is still warming up. It is a good idea to use an oven thermometer.

9 Pies can be frozen as long as the filling is suitable (don't freeze creamy, egg fillings) and the pastry has not already been frozen. For best results, reheat in a slow oven.

10 To test if a pie is cooked, poke a metal skewer into the centre. If the skewer comes out cold, the pie needs to be baked for longer.

What went wrong?

Shortcrust (pie) pastry

Perfect Pastry is even and lightly golden. The sides are cooked evenly and shrunk slightly from the sides of the tin. The base is crisp, golden and dry.

Stuck to base The pastry may have had too much liquid added, or may not have been chilled before rolling.

Undercooked The cooking temperature was too low, or the cooking time not long enough. The pastry case may have been rolled out too thickly.

Overcooked The cooking time was too long, or the oven too hot. The pastry may have been placed either too high or too low in the oven.

Pastry shrunk too much The pastry was overworked or not chilled before baking. The weights may have been pressed too firmly against the sides of the pastry case.

Other problems If there are holes in the pastry case, the pastry was rolled out too thinly or the pastry case has shrunk and split during cooking due to being overworked or not being chilled before cooking. If the fork marks are too large, this can cause holes.

If the pastry is tough, the pastry dough may have been overworked during mixing or rolling, or there may have been too much liquid added to the pastry dough.

Ready-made pastry

For busy cooks, there is a large range of ready-made frozen or refrigerated pastries available. Standard puff and shortcrust (pie) pastries are available in blocks, and puff, butter puff and shortcrust pastries also come as ready-rolled sheets. The recipe will simply say '2 sheets puff pastry' or '250 g shortcrust pastry' and these should be thawed. Thaw frozen block pastry for 2 hours. Sheets take only 5–10 minutes to thaw.

Lining the tin

Roll out the dough between two sheets of baking paper, or on a lightly floured surface. Always roll from the centre outwards, rotating the dough, rather than rolling backwards and forwards. Reduce the pressure towards the edges of the dough. If you used baking paper, remove the top sheet and invert the pastry over the tin, then peel away the other sheet. Centre the pastry as it can't be moved once in place. Quickly lift up the sides so they don't break over the edges of the tin. Use a small ball of dough to press the pastry into the side of the tin. Trim away the excess pastry with a small, sharp knife or by rolling the rolling pin over the top. However gently you handle the dough it is bound to shrink slightly, so let it sit a little higher above the side of the tin. Chill the pastry in the tin for 20 minutes or as specified in the recipe to relax it and minimize shrinkage.

Blind baking

If a pie or tart is to have a liquid filling, the pastry usually requires blind baking to partially cook it before filling.

When blind baking, the pastry needs to be weighted down to prevent it rising. Cover the base and side with a crumpled piece of baking paper. Pour in a layer of baking beads (also called pie weights), dried beans or uncooked rice and spread out over the paper to cover the pastry base. Bake for the recommended time (usually about 10 minutes), then remove the paper and beads. Return the pastry to the oven for 10–15 minutes, or as specified in the recipe, until the base is dry with no greasy patches. Let the pastry cool completely.

The filling should also be completely cooled before filling the shell—filling a cold shell with a hot mixture can also cause the pastry to become soggy.

Decorative edges

There are many decorative edges to pastry to make the pie look attractive. The simplest is fork pressed, which simply involves pressing a lightly floured fork around the edge of the pie crust. If you are feeling more inventive, you can crimp the pastry edge with your thumb and forefinger or create ropes or plaits with excess pastry and adhere these to the edge.

Decorative tops

There are endless shapes you can use to decorate pies, from stars to abstract patterns. Alternatively, you can buy small cookie cutters in various shapes. When rolling out the pastry trimmings, don't make the shapes too thick or they won't cook through. To attach them, first brush the pie lid with an egg glaze, then arrange the decorations and glaze them as well.

CHOUX PASTRY

This is best known as the pastry used for eclairs and profiteroles.

Fundamentals

Always preheat the oven before beginning to make choux pastry because it is cooked immediately after it is shaped or piped. Likewise, prepare your equipment before you start. Lightly grease or line the baking tray with baking paper. If piping the dough, fit a large plain nozzle to the piping bag.

Spraying the inside of the oven with water, as well as sprinkling the baking tray with water, helps create steam which aids in the rising of choux pastry.

Making choux pastry

Add the flour to the boiling butter and water mixture in one go. Immediately beat the mixture with a wooden spoon to prevent lumps forming. Stop beating as soon as the soft dough comes away from the side of the pan and remove from the heat. Allow the hot mixture to cool for 2–3 minutes before adding eggs or they can start to cook. Beat in the eggs one at a time, making sure they are completely beaten in before adding the next egg. The dough is ready when it is smooth and glossy. It should be piped or shaped while still warm. Leave about 4 cm (1½ inch) between the piped dough because it will spread once cooked.

FILO PASTRY

This is most often used to make a variety of pies and pastries or to wrap fillings in.

About filo pastry

Filo pastry is a paper-thin pastry made with flour and water. Filo means 'leaf' in Greek, and is used widely in the Middle East, Turkey, Greece and Europe for making a variety of pastries and pies such as spanokopita and baklava, or to wrap seafood or vegetable fillings. The dough for filo is simple enough to make, but stretching it until it is tissue-thin requires great skill and patience. For this reason, commercially made filo, which is available fresh or frozen, is often used.

Cooking with filo pastry

Allow frozen filo to thaw in the packet, then take out the sheets and stack them on a cloth. Cover the sheets with a dry cloth and use them one at a time as they dry out quickly when exposed to air. Brush each sheet with a little oil or melted butter to make them crisp when cooked. Filled filo parcels can be frozen and then cooked when frozen.

Problem solving

If the filling leaks, there may be too much filling, or not enough filo layers. The oven may have been too hot or the filling too moist. Otherwise, the parcels were not shaped and secured well enough or were rolled too tightly.

What went wrong?

Puff pastry

Perfect The pastry is well and evenly risen with pastry layers visible. The pastry is deep golden brown and the texture is light and flaky.

Overcooked The oven may have been too hot, or the cooking time too long, or the pastry may have been placed too high.

Unevenly risen when cooked The edges were not trimmed with a sharp knife. The glaze has dripped down the sides, gluing the layers together.

Choux pastry

Perfect The choux pastry is crisp and puffy, hollow inside and has a deep golden colour. To assist in drying and to release steam, make a small hole in the base of each pastry puff with a skewer.

Poorly risen The pastry is not puffed and dense inside. Too little egg was added (the more eggs you add the more the dough will puff). Otherwise, the oven temperature was not hot enough or the oven was opened too soon during baking. Also, the cooking time may have been too short.

Filo pastry

Perfect The filo pastry is dry, crisp, flaky, puffed and golden brown.

Overcooked The pastry is unevenly coloured. The oven temperature may have been too high or the layers unevenly brushed with butter.

Undercooked The pastry is pale and soggy. The filling may be heavy and too moist or there may be too many layers of filo. The oven temperature may have been too low or the cooking time too short.

ALL ABOUT DOUGH

When you master the techniques described here, in no time you will be delighted by the wonderful aroma of freshly baked bread all over the house. The general principles are the same for breads, pizzas and foccacia dough.

Fundamentals

Once you have an understanding of some of the important elements of dough making, such as working with yeast, and kneading techniques, you will find that delicious bread, pizza or focaccia is simple to make.

Make sure you read the recipe thoroughly, carefully weigh all the ingredients and assemble the equipment you need.

Mysteries of yeast solved

Working with yeast, probably the most important ingredient in bread and pizza dough, is not as difficult as you may think. Yeast is available dried or fresh. Dried yeast, available at supermarkets, generally comes in a box containing 7 g (¼ oz) sachets, one of which is enough for a standard loaf or four small pizza bases. Fresh yeast, sometimes harder to obtain, is available at some health food shops and bakeries. It has quite a short storage life.

About 15 g (½ oz) of fresh yeast is equivalent to a 7 g (¼ oz) sachet of dried. We used dried yeast in our recipes as it is readily available, can be stored in the pantry and carries a use-by date.

The mixture above looks frothy and has doubled in size.

Types of flour

The type and quality of flour you use is vital. Many recipes call for the use of flour that is labelled as bread or strong flour. This is high in protein and will form gluten, which helps the bread or pizza dough rise and bake well. For most breads, if you use a regular flour the loaf will not rise well, gluten will not form and the loaf will be heavy and dense.

To make your loaf

This recipe will make one plain white loaf. The principles are the same for pizza dough although the quantities will be different. Put a 7 g (¼ oz) sachet of dried yeast, 125 ml (4 fl oz/½ cup) warm water and 1 teaspoon caster (superfine) sugar in a bowl and stir to combine. Leave in a warm, draught-free place for 10 minutes, or until bubbles appear on the surface. The mixture should be frothy and slightly increased in volume. If it isn't, discard it and start again. Sift 500 g (1 lb 2 oz/4 cups) white bread flour, 1 teaspoon salt, 2 tablespoons dried whole milk powder and 1 tablespoon caster sugar into a large bowl. Make a well in the centre, add the yeast mixture, 60 ml (2 fl oz/¼ cup) vegetable oil and 250 ml (9 fl oz/1 cup) warm water. Mix to a soft dough using a large metal spoon. The moisture content of flour can vary greatly between brands and even between batches so add extra water or flour, 1 tablespoon at a time, if the dough is too dry or sticky. Do not add too much flour because the dough will absorb more flour during kneading.

Kneading the dough

The dough is then formed into a ball on a lightly floured surface and kneaded. Don't be tempted to cut short the kneading time as it affects the texture of the finished bread or pizza dough. Kneading distributes the yeast evenly throughout the dough and allows the flour's protein to develop into gluten. Gluten gives the dough elasticity, strength and the ability to expand, as it traps the carbon dioxide gas created by the yeast and this allows the bread to rise.

The kneading action is simple and it is quite easy to get into a rhythm. Hold one end of the dough down with one hand, and stretch it away from you with the other hand. Fold the dough back together, make a quarter turn and repeat the action. Knead for 10 minutes, or until smooth and elastic.

For pizzas, the dough does not have to be kneaded as well as it does for bread as it will be rolled out thinly and doesn't need to rise. About 5 minutes kneading should be enough.

Proving

After kneading, put the dough into a lightly greased bowl. Cover loosely with plastic wrap or a damp cloth. Leave the bowl in a warm place (around 30°C is ideal) to allow the dough to rise—this stage is called proving. When the dough is ready it should be doubled in volume and not spring back when touched with a fingertip. This will take about an hour. Lightly grease a bread tin that measures 22 x 9 x 9 cm (9 x 3½ x 3½ inch) with melted butter or oil. If you are making pizzas, grease a pizza tray.

Punching down

After proving, punch down the dough to expel the air, and knead again for 1 minute, or until smooth. The dough is now ready for shaping. Shape the loaf to fit into the prepared tin, placing it in with any seam at the base. Cover with plastic wrap or a damp tea towel (dish towel) and place the tin in a warm, draught-free place until the dough is well risen and doubled in size. This will take about 45–60 minutes. This is the final rise for the dough.

Baking

Preheat the oven to 210°C (415°F/Gas 6–7). To glaze, beat 1 egg with 1 tablespoon milk and brush over the top of the dough with a pastry brush. Place the bread in the middle of the hot oven and bake for 10 minutes. Don't open the oven during the first 10 minutes of baking as intense heat is needed during this time. Reduce the oven temperature to 180°C (350°F/Gas 4) and bake for a further 30–40 minutes. At the end of the cooking time, test for doneness by turning the loaf out of the tin and tapping the base. The bread will sound hollow when cooked. If it is not cooked, return it to the tin and bake for a further 5–10 minutes. Remove from the tin and cool on a wire rack.

Other bread shapes

Bread dough can be made into many shapes and does not have to be baked in a bread or loaf tin.

Bloomer At the shaping stage, roll out the dough on a lightly floured surface to a rectangle about 2.5 cm (1 inch) thick. Starting from the short end, roll up the dough like you would a swiss roll. Roll firmly to make a short, rather thick loaf. Place with the seam underneath on the baking tray. Cover the dough with a cloth and leave in a warm, draught-free place for an hour, or until doubled in size. Using a sharp knife, make six evenly spaced slashes across the top of the dough. Spray the loaf with water and place in a hot 220°C (425°F/Gas 7) oven for 10 minutes. Reduce to 200°C (400°F/Gas 6) and bake for 30 minutes, or until the loaf is golden brown and sounds hollow when tapped underneath. Cool on a wire rack.

Plaited loaf After knocking back, divide the dough into three. Roll each portion into a 30 cm (12 inch) sausage, then transfer to a greased baking tray. Arrange next to one another on the tray, then join the strands at one end and start plaiting them together. Pinch and tuck under at both ends to seal the plait. Cover with a tea towel and set aside in a warm, draught-free place for 1 hour, or until doubled in size. Brush with milk and bake in a 220°C (425°F/Gas 7) oven for 10 minutes. Reduce the oven to 200°C (400°F/Gas 6) and cook for 30 minutes, or until the loaf is golden brown and sounds hollow when tapped underneath. Cool on a wire rack.

Bread storage

Home-baked bread is best eaten on the day of baking. Because it has no preservatives it doesn't keep as long as commercial bread, but it can be wrapped and frozen for up to 3 months. When required, thaw at room temperature, then refresh in a 180°C (350°F/Gas 4) oven for 10 minutes.

Pizza storage

Untopped pizza bases can be frozen for up to 3 months. Freeze each base separately. Once the bases are hard and solid, you can stack them on top of each other, separated by layers of baking paper or plastic wrap.

Problem solving

Dead yeast If your yeast mixture has not risen and is not frothy, the yeast is dead. If this happens, you will have to throw away the mixture and start again. Take care when measuring the yeast. The temperature of the water should be tepid, not too warm, or you may kill the yeast. If using dry yeast, check the expiry date on the back of the packet before you start.

Strong smell and taste of yeast If there is a strong smell and taste of yeast, the bread or pizza dough was undercooked or there was too much yeast used in proportion to the amount of flour.

Loaf didn't rise or rose poorly If the loaf didn't rise or rose poorly, the yeast was old or dead. The liquid may have been too hot and killed the yeast. The yeast may have worked itself out too early by being placed to rise in a spot that was too warm. It may have been left too long to prove.

Loaf over-risen and puffy If there are large holes in the loaf and it has risen too much and is puffy, the dough may have been insufficiently kneaded during the first kneading stage. The rising time for the dough may have too long, or the dough may not have been correctly knocked backed before being shaped.

Loaf crust and crumb separate If the crumb and crust separate from one another, the bread dough was not properly knocked back before shaping the loaf.

Loaf rose unevenly If the loaf rises unevenly, or is cracked along one side, the oven temperature was uneven or the bread was not placed in the centre of the oven or was too close to the heating elements. The baking tin may have been too small.

Loaf has uneven colour If the bread is unevenly coloured, the oven temperature was uneven, too high or the bread was placed too low in the oven. A hard crust forms if the dough is not covered during the rising stage, allowing the surface to dry out and thus form a crust.

BREAD HINTS AND TIPS

1 When adding water to yeast (or a yeast and flour mixture), warm it first until tepid or hand hot. Do not use water that is too hot to touch or it will kill the yeast.

2 If dissolving yeast first, leave it in a warm place for at least 10 minutes, or until a good foam appears on the surface. If it does not foam, the yeast is dead and you will have to start again with a new batch.

3 If mixing dough by hand use a wooden spoon to bring the ingredients together. The dough should feel sticky when it first comes together. If it feels dry, add a little more water, a tablespoon at a time.

4 If using an electric stand mixer always use the dough attachment, unless otherwise specified. Stand the mixer well away from the edge of the work surface because it may move as it is mixing the dough.

5 Always start with the electric mixer on its lowest setting to first mix the ingredients, then increase the speed to medium to knead the dough.

6 When leaving dough to rise, use a large bowl at least twice the size of the dough so it has plenty of room to expand.

7 Lightly oil both the bowl and the surface of the dough before leaving the dough to rise. The dough should be covered with plastic wrap to prevent it forming a skin, which prevents it from rising properly.

8 To test if a dough has risen sufficiently, press a finger into the surface. The fingerprint should remain indented and should not spring back.

9 Draughts can cause dough to deflate, so make sure the room is draught-free.

10 Doughs will rise too fast if the room is overly hot, which will give an unpleasant smell and flavour to the bread. If this happens, deflate the dough and leave to rise again in a cool place (for at least 1 hour to develop flavour).

11 If leaving bread dough overnight in the refrigerator, allow time for it to return to room temperature so it can begin to rise. This should take 45–60 minutes.

12 Always grease the tin with spray oil or melted butter. Baking trays should be lightly greased or dusted with flour.

13 When pressing dough into a tin it should reach to 1.5 cm (½ inch) below the top of the tin. After rising, the centre of the dough should protrude about 2.5 cm (1 inch) above the top of the tin. The dough is then ready to be baked.

14 Never open the oven door during the first half of the total baking time or the bread can collapse. If you do need to turn the bread to get even browning, do this after the halfway point.

15 To test if a bread is cooked, gently remove it from the tray or tin and tap it on the bottom—it should sound hollow. If it doesn't, return it to the oven for a further 5 minutes, then test again.

16 Store bread in a paper or cloth bag for up to 24 hours in a cool place. Do not refrigerate bread as this makes it become stale more quickly. If keeping bread longer, store in a plastic bag or a zip lock bag.

17 To freeze bread, wrap it in plastic wrap and then place inside a freezer bag. Defrost to room temperature before use. Bread that is allowed to defrost slowly, at room temperature, will retain its freshness for longer.

PIZZA HINTS AND TIPS

1 If you want a pizza with a thin crust you will need to roll the base very thinly because bread dough rises in the oven. Leave a small ridge around the edge to stop the filling running out.

2 A pizza stone gives great results. Make sure your stone has time to heat up properly before baking the pizza.

3 Spread the topping on the base on a work surface and then slide the whole thing onto a hot stone or baking tray already in the oven. This will give a crisp base. If you're not confident doing this, you can construct and bake the pizza on a cold tray but the base won't be as crispy.

What went wrong?

Bread

Perfect The bread has a good even crumb and the loaf has risen evenly and well. It has even spring on the sides and sounds hollow when tapped. The crust is coloured to a golden brown.

Undercooked The crumb is damp and sticky and the crust soft and pale. If very under-baked, the loaf may not hold its shape and may be wet or have wet holes. If the loaf does not sound hollow when tapped, bake it for another 10 minutes. Check that the oven has reached the correct temperature before putting the dough in the oven.

Overcooked The crust is too dark and is cracked on top. The crumb is dry. The oven may have been too hot or the cooking time too long or there may have been too much sugar in the mix. The bread may have been placed too high in the oven.

Focaccia

Perfect The bread is evenly and well risen and has coloured to a golden brown. The crust is crisp but not hard.

Soggy, under-baked The crust is soft and pale and the crumb is dense and wet. The bread may not have been cooked long enough, or the oven temperature may have been too low.

Uneven rising, puffy The dough was not rolled evenly. Also the dough may not have been sufficiently kneaded. The rising time for the dough may have been too long or too much yeast was used.

Pizza

Perfect The dough is well risen and lightly browned. It is crisp but not tough. The topping is evenly spread and light golden brown.

Risen too much The dough is unevenly risen and may be dry with a yeasty taste. Too much yeast may have been used or the dough allowed to prove to quickly (too warm) or for too long.

Uneven rising, puffy The dough is not evenly rolled and the topping not even. The oven heat may have been uneven or the shelf placed too low or too high.

Your favourite carrot cake just isn't the same without that delicious cream cheese icing, chocolate cake loses a little of its allure without its rich chocolate topping and a simple butter cake gains five-star standing when partnered with coffee buttercream. The icing (frosting) on the cake can make all the difference.

Ginger and lemon glacé icing

Sift 40 g (1½ oz/⅓ cup) icing (confectioners') sugar into a small heatproof bowl. Add ½ teaspoon ginger, 20 g (¾ oz) melted unsalted butter, 2 teaspoons milk and 1 teaspoon lemon juice and mix to form a paste. Place the bowl over a saucepan of simmering water, making sure the base does not touch the water, and stir until the icing is smooth and glossy. Remove the bowl from the heat. Spread with a knife dipped in hot water for even covering. Do not reheat.

Lemon cream cheese icing

Place 60 g (2¼ oz/¼ cup) softened cream cheese and 30 g (1 oz) unsalted butter in a small mixing bowl. Using electric beaters, beat until combined. Add 1 tablespoon lemon juice and 185 g (6 oz/ 1½ cups) sifted icing (confectioners') sugar and beat until smooth.

Butterscotch frosting

Chop 20 g (¾ oz) unsalted butter into small pieces and place in a saucepan with 95 g (3¼ oz/½ cup) lightly packed brown sugar. Stir constantly over low heat until the mixture boils and the sugar dissolves. Simmer for 3 minutes. Remove from the heat, add 90 g (3¼ oz/⅓ cup) sour cream and stir. Leave to cool. Place 100 g (3½ oz) softened cream cheese in a mixing bowl and beat with electric beaters until light and creamy. Add the cooled butterscotch mixture, a little at a time, beating well after each addition.

Chocolate ganache

Combine 60 ml (2 fl oz/¼ cup) cream and 150 g (5½ oz) dark chocolate in a small saucepan. Stir over low heat until the chocolate has melted and the mixture is smooth. Remove from the heat and allow to cool. Pour the ganache on to the cake, then smooth the top and around the side with a flat-bladed knife or palette knife.

Caramel icing

Place 185 g (6½ oz/¾ cup) icing (confectioners') sugar, 1 tablespoon milk, 2 tablespoons golden syrup and 30 g (1 oz) softened unsalted butter in a bowl and beat with a wooden spoon until smooth.

Coffee buttercream

Dissolve 3 teaspoons instant coffee in 2 tablespoons boiling water. Place 125 g (4½ oz) unsalted butter and 185 g (6½ oz/ ¾ cup) icing (confectioners') sugar in a mixing bowl. Using electric beaters, beat until pale and creamy. Add ½ teaspoon natural vanilla extract, the coffee mixture and 2 teaspoons milk and beat for 2 minutes, or until smooth and fluffy.

Lime icing

Place 250 g (9 oz/1 cup) sifted icing (confectioners') sugar, 80 g (2¾ oz) softened unsalted butter and 2 tablespoons lime juice in a mixing bowl and beat with a wooden spoon until smooth, adding 1–2 tablespoons water, if necessary.

Chocolate fudge icing

Coarsely chop 150 g (5½ oz) dark chocolate and place in a small saucepan with 90 g (3¼ oz) unsalted butter and 160 g (5½ oz/ ½ cup) condensed milk. Stir over low heat until the chocolate and butter have melted and the mixture is smooth. Remove from the heat. Allow to cool until thick and spreadable.

Orange glacé icing

Sift 125 g (4½ oz/½ cup) icing (confectioners') sugar into a heatproof bowl. Add 10 g (¼ oz) softened unsalted butter, 1 teaspoon grated orange zest and enough orange juice to make a soft pouring consistency. Place the bowl, making sure the base does not touch the water, over a saucepan of simmering water and stir until the icing is smooth and glossy. Remove from the heat. Drizzle over the cake.

Cookie icings and toppings

These delicious toppings will add a special touch to even a basic cookie. Just remember to cool the cookies before adding the icing (frosting) or topping. Choose a topping that complements the cookie. A zesty citrus or passionfruit topping would go beautifully with a simple citrus cookie and a chocolate topping is best with a chocolate chip or nutty cookie.

Maple syrup icing

Mix 125 g (4½ oz/½ cup) sifted icing (confectioners') sugar, 2 tablespoons maple syrup and 1 tablespoon softened unsalted butter in a small, heatproof bowl. Stir the mixture over a saucepan of simmering water until the mixture softens and is smooth and easy to spread.

Passionfruit glacé icing

Mix 2 tablespoons fresh passionfruit pulp and 155 g (5½ oz) sifted icing (confectioners') sugar in a small, heatproof bowl. Stir the mixture over a saucepan of simmering water until it becomes smooth and glossy. You can use tinned pulp if fresh passionfruit is not in season.

Coconut ice topping

Mix 155 g (5½ oz/1¼ cups) sifted icing (confectioners') sugar, 1 tablespoon softened unsalted butter, 45 g (1½ oz/½ cup) desiccated coconut, ½ teaspoon natural vanilla extract and a few drops pink food colouring in a bowl. Add 6–8 teaspoons boiling water to make a thick, spreadable mixture.

Vanilla icing

Sift 155 g (5½ oz/1¼ cups) icing (confectioners') sugar into a small bowl. Add 1 tablespoon cubed and softened unsalted butter, ½ teaspoon natural vanilla extract and 1–2 tablespoons boiling water. Stir until the mixture is smooth and spreadable.

Citrus fruit icing

Put 2 teaspoons each of finely shredded lime, lemon and orange zest, 60 g (2¼ oz/½ cup) sifted icing (confectioners') sugar and 60 ml (2 fl oz/¼ cup) water in a saucepan. Stir constantly over low heat until the sugar dissolves. Simmer, without stirring, for 5 minutes. Remove the zest and drain on a wire rack. Mix together 155 g (5½ oz/1¼ cups) sifted icing (confectioners') sugar, 1 tablespoon softened butter, 2 teaspoons lemon juice, 3 teaspoons lime juice, 2 teaspoons orange juice and the drained zests in a bowl until spreadable.

Choc and nut topping

Sift 155 g (5½ oz/1¼ cups) icing (confectioners') sugar and 1 tablespoon cocoa powder into a bowl. Add 1 tablespoon softened unsalted butter, 1–2 tablespoons boiling water and mix together until smooth. Spread the cookies with the topping, then sprinkle with chopped, roasted hazelnuts or almonds. The nuts can be replaced by coloured sprinkles for a more colourful effect.

Marshmallow topping

Mix 125 g (4½ oz/½ cup) sifted icing (confectioners') sugar, 1 tablespoon softened unsalted butter and 1 tablespoon boiling water in a bowl until smooth. Add 25 g (1 oz/½ cup) mini marshmallows. Stir over a saucepan of simmering water for 1 minute, or until the marshmallows have just melted. Spread quickly onto the cookies.

Chocolate fleck icing

Sift 155 g (5½ oz/1¼ cups) icing (confectioners') sugar into a bowl. Add 1 tablespoon softened unsalted butter, ½ teaspoon natural vanilla extract and 5 teaspoons boiling water. Stir until smooth. Gently mix in 2 tablespoons grated dark chocolate, then spread on the cookies.

Basic utensils

Lattice cutters For topping pies and tarts, these simplify cutting a lattice pattern into rolled out pastry.

Rolling pins These should be big enough to roll out a full sheet of pastry. Good-quality rolling pins are made from hardwood with a close grain and smooth finish.

Flour sieves and dredgers These are ideal for incorporating air into flour or dusting flour onto work surfaces. They can also be used when decorating or dusting with icing sugar or cocoa.

Baking beads Reusable ceramic or metal beads used when blind baking pastry. Dried beans or uncooked rice can be used instead.

Wooden spoons These are useful for beating, mixing and stirring because they do not conduct heat or scratch non-stick surfaces. Choose spoons made from hard, close-grained wood.

Metal spoons Large metal spoons are best for folding in dry ingredients, or combining one mixture with another without losing too much air.

Piping bags and nozzles Piping bags of different sizes accommodate metal or plastic nozzles with various shaped openings.

Graters Graters with perforations of different sizes are designed for specific functions, from grating cheese to citrus zest. Nutmeg graters are small and concave.

Dough scrapers These are used to divide, separate and scrape dough on a work surface. They are used mainly for pastry and bread doughs.

Cutters These come in a various shapes and sizes, ranging from plain and fluted rounds to hearts and gingerbread people. Metal cutters have a better edge than plastic.

Cooling racks These footed metal grids enable air to circulate around baked food during cooling.

Citrus juicers These are available in glass, ceramic, plastic and wood, as well as electric.

Oven thermometers These stand or hang in the oven. Always check the accuracy of the oven temperature when baking to achieve the best results.

Whisks Whisks beat air into ingredients and remove any lumps from the mixture.

Apple corers These have a blade that fits around an apple core and removes it without damaging the shape of the fruit.

Citrus zesters Zesters have a row of holes with sharp edges running across the top. They peel off the zest in thin shreds.

Metal skewers Long and thin with a sharp, pointed edge, these are useful for testing to see if a cake is cooked through.

Pastry brushes Made with nylon or natural bristles, these can be flat or round and are used for glazing.

Pastry wheels These are metal or plastic wheels used for cutting fluted edges on pastry.

Scales Essential for weighing ingredients, kitchen scales vary from balance scales to digital display.

Measuring cups and spoons All spoon and cup measures in this book are level. Dry ingredients should be levelled off.

Sifters A hand sifter is used to aerate lumpy flour.

Palette knives These are available in various sizes and degrees of flexibility. The blade is thin and flat with a rounded end and is useful for transferring cookies and for spreading decorative icings.

Paring knives With a short blade, these are a handy all-purpose knife. They are perfect for cutting fruit.

Serrated knives These are best for slicing through bread and cakes neatly and evenly.

Spatulas These are useful for scraping a bowl clean.

Mixers These can be hand-held or table models. They make creaming mixtures, mixing batters and whisking whites easier.

Mixing bowls Stainless steel bowls are durable and are good conductors of heat and cold. Heatproof bowls are essential for slow heating over a water bath.

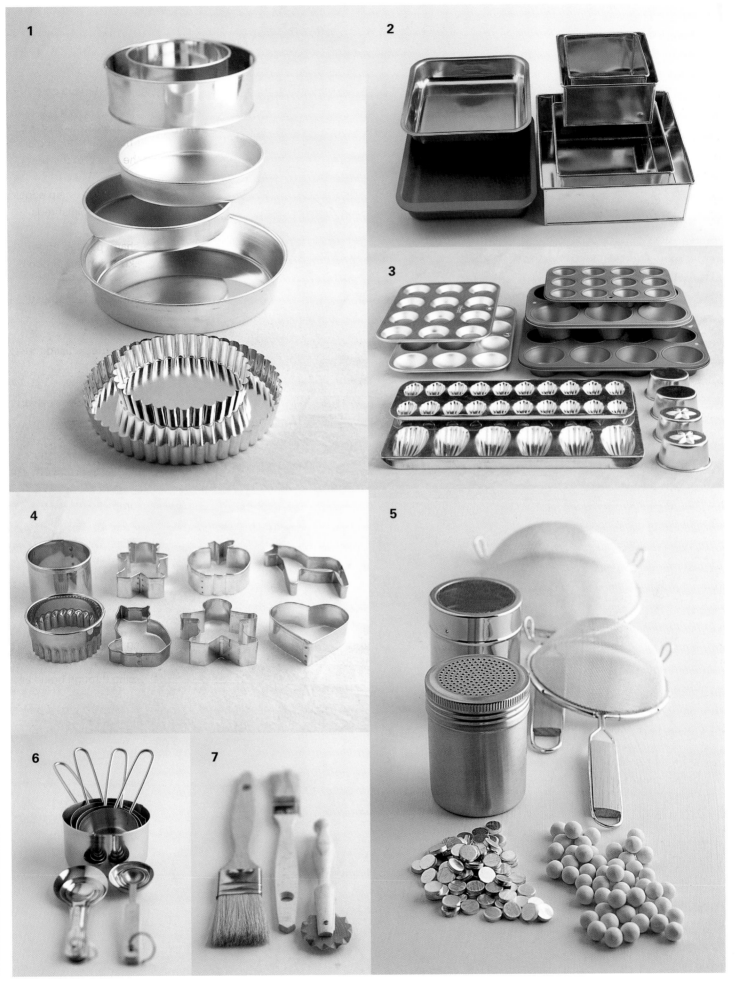

1. Round tins. 2. Cake and slab tins. 3. Muffin and small cake tins. 4. Cutters. 5. Flour sieves, dredgers and baking beads. 6. Measuring cups and spoons. 7. Pastry brushes and pastry wheel.

basics

small cakes
and slices

Butterfly chocolate cakes

preparation 20 minutes
cooking 20 minutes
makes 24

60 g (2¼ oz) unsalted butter, softened
80 g (2¾ oz/⅓ cup firmly packed) soft brown sugar
½ teaspoon natural vanilla extract
1 egg, at room temperature
60 g (2½ oz/¼ cup) self-raising flour
30 g (1 oz/¼ cup) unsweetened cocoa powder
2 tablespoons milk
60 g (2 oz/¼ cup) thick (double/heavy) cream
80 g (2¾ oz/¼ cup) raspberry jam
icing (confectioners') sugar, to dust

Preheat the oven to 180°C (350°F/Gas 4). Line two 12-hole muffin trays with paper cases.

Using electric beaters, beat the butter, sugar and vanilla until pale and creamy. Add the egg and beat well. Sift together the flour and cocoa. Add half the flour mixture to the butter and whisk gently, then add the milk and mix together. Add the rest of the flour and mix well.

Divide the mixture evenly among the paper cases. Bake for 15–20 minutes, or until a skewer inserted into the centre of a cake comes out clean. Transfer to a wire rack to cool.

Cut shallow rounds from the centre of each cake with the point of a sharp knife, then cut the rounds in half. Fill the centres of the cakes with a little cream and some raspberry jam. Position the two cake wedges on the cream, pressing them down very gently to resemble butterfly wings. Dust with sifted icing sugar.

Ginger cakes with chocolate centres

preparation 15 minutes + refrigeration
cooking 35 minutes
makes 12

100 g (3½ oz) unsalted butter, softened
125 g (4½ oz/⅔ cup lightly packed) soft brown sugar
115 g (4 oz/⅓ cup) treacle or dark corn syrup
2 eggs, at room temperature
125 g (4½ oz/1 cup) self-raising flour
85 g (3 oz/⅔ cup) plain (all-purpose) flour
2 teaspoons ground cinnamon
1 tablespoon ground ginger
60 ml (2 fl oz/¼ cup) buttermilk

chocolate ganache
100 g (3½ oz/⅓ cup) chopped dark chocolate
60 ml (2 fl oz/¼ cup) cream
1 tablespoon finely chopped glacé (candied) ginger

Preheat the oven to 180°C (350°F/Gas 4). Line a 12-hole muffin tray with paper cases.

To make the chocolate ganache, place the chocolate in a heatproof bowl. Heat the cream in a saucepan until almost boiling. Pour over the chocolate and leave for 1 minute, then stir until it has melted and the mixture is smooth. Stir in the glacé ginger. Cool to room temperature, then chill in the refrigerator until firm. Divide the mixture into 12 equal portions and roll each into a ball. Freeze until required.

Using electric beaters, cream the butter, sugar and treacle in a large bowl until the mixture is light and creamy. Add the eggs one at a time, beating well after each addition. Sift the flours and spices on top of the mixture, then fold in alternately with the buttermilk.

Divide three-quarters of the mixture among the paper cases. Top each with a ball of frozen ganache, then cover the ganache with the rest of the mixture. Bake for 25–30 minutes, or until the cakes are deep golden (the cakes cannot be tested with a skewer as the centres will be molten). Leave to cool for 5 minutes. Remove the paper cases and serve warm.

Use a small sharp knife to cut small rounds from the cakes, then cut in half.

Bottom: Ginger cakes with chocolate centres. Top: Butterfly chocolate cakes.

Rum baba with figs

preparation 40 minutes + 2 hours standing
cooking 35 minutes
serves 10

185 g (6½ oz/1½ cups) plain (all-purpose) flour
2 teaspoons dried yeast
¼ teaspoon salt
2 teaspoons sugar
80 ml (2½ fl oz/⅓ cup) lukewarm milk
80 g (2¾ oz) unsalted butter
3 eggs, lightly beaten
375 g (13 oz/1½ cups) caster (superfine) sugar
80 ml (2½ fl oz/⅓ cup) dark rum
240 g (8½ oz/¾ cup) apricot jam
2 tablespoons dark rum, extra
5 figs

Lightly brush ten 125 ml (4 fl oz/½ cup) dariole moulds with oil. Place 1 tablespoon of the flour and the yeast, salt, sugar and milk in a small bowl. Cover with plastic wrap and leave in a warm place until foamy. Using your fingertips, rub the butter into the remaining flour in a large mixing bowl, until it resembles fine breadcrumbs.

Add the yeast mixture and eggs to the flour mixture. Beat with a spoon for 2 minutes, until smooth and glossy. Scrape the mixture down the side of the bowl. Cover and leave in a warm place for 1½ hours, until well risen.

Preheat the oven to 210°C (415°F/Gas 6–7). Using a wooden spoon, beat the mixture for 2 minutes, then divide between the prepared tins. Set aside, covered with plastic wrap, until the dough is well risen. Bake for 20 minutes.

Meanwhile, combine 500 ml (17 fl oz/2 cups) water and the caster sugar in a saucepan. Stir over medium heat without boiling until the sugar is dissolved. Bring to the boil then reduce the heat and simmer, without stirring, for 15 minutes. Remove from the heat, cool slightly and add the rum.

Turn the babas out onto a wire rack placed over a shallow oven tray. Brush them with the warm rum syrup until well soaked. Strain the excess syrup to remove any crumbs; reserve the syrup.

Heat the jam in a small saucepan and strain. Add the extra rum, stir to combine, then brush over the babas to glaze. Place the babas on a serving plate, then drizzle the reserved syrup around them. Cut the figs in half and serve one piece with each baba.

The yeast mixture will become foamy after sitting in a warm place for 10 minutes.

Pour the mixture into the prepared tins and set aside again to allow the dough to rise.

Chocolate hazelnut friands

preparation 20 minutes
cooking 40 minutes
makes 12

200 g (7 oz) whole hazelnuts
185 g (6½ oz) unsalted butter
6 egg whites
155 g (5½ oz/1¼ cups) plain (all-purpose) flour
30 g (1 oz/¼ cup) unsweetened cocoa powder
250 g (9 oz/2 cups) icing (confectioners') sugar
icing (confectioners') sugar, extra, to dust

Preheat the oven to 200°C (400°F/Gas 6). Lightly grease twelve 125 ml (4 fl oz/½ cup) friand or muffin tins.

Spread the hazelnuts on a baking tray and bake for about 7 minutes, or until lightly browned. Remove from the oven and, while they are still hot, wrap them in a tea towel (dish towel) and rub away the skins. Cool, then process in a food processor until finely ground.

Place the butter in a small pan and melt over medium heat, then cook for 3–4 minutes, or until the butter turns a deep golden colour. Strain any dark solids and set aside to cool (the colour will become deeper on standing).

Lightly whisk the egg whites in a clean, dry bowl until frothy but not firm. Sift the flour, cocoa and icing sugar into a large mixing bowl and stir in the ground hazelnuts. Make a well in the centre and add the egg whites and butter and mix until combined.

Spoon the mixture into the prepared tins until three-quarters filled. Bake for 20–25 minutes, or until a skewer inserted into the centre comes out clean. Leave in the tin for a few minutes, then cool on a wire rack. Dust with sifted icing sugar, to serve.

Butterfly cupcakes

preparation 10 minutes
cooking 30 minutes
makes 12

125 g (4½ oz) unsalted butter, softened
160 g (5¾ oz/⅔ cup) caster (superfine) sugar
285 g (10 oz) self-raising flour
125 ml (4 fl oz/½ cup) milk
2 eggs, at room temperature
125 ml (4 fl oz/½ cup) thick (double/heavy) cream
80 g (2¾ oz/¼ cup) strawberry jam
icing (confectioners') sugar, to dust

Preheat the oven to 180°C (350°F/Gas 4). Line a flat-bottomed 12-hole mini muffin tray with paper cases.

Place the butter, caster sugar, flour, milk and eggs in a large mixing bowl. Using electric beaters, beat on low speed then increase the speed and beat until the mixture is smooth and pale. Divide the mixture evenly among the cases and bake for 30 minutes, or until a skewer inserted into the centre comes out clean. Transfer to a wire rack to cool.

Cut shallow rounds from the centre of each cake using the point of a sharp knife, then cut the rounds in half. Spoon 2 teaspoons of cream into each cavity, top with 1 teaspoon of jam and position two halves of the cake tops in the jam to resemble butterfly wings. Dust with icing sugar.

Note *If you use foil paper cases instead of the standard paper ones, the size and number of butterfly cakes may vary.*

Spoon the friand mixture into the greased tins until three-quarters full.

Once you have cut the rounds from the cakes, cut them in half to form two wedges.

Bottom: Butterfly cupcakes. Top: Chocolate hazelnut friands.

Chocolate beetroot cakes

preparation 20 minutes
cooking 20 minutes
makes 8

cooking oil spray
125 g (4½ oz/1 cup) plain (all-purpose) flour
40 g (1½ oz/⅓ cup) unsweetened cocoa powder
1½ teaspoons bicarbonate of soda (baking soda)
½ teaspoon baking powder
1 teaspoon mixed (pumpkin pie) spice
230 g (8 oz/1 cup firmly packed) soft brown sugar
75 g (2½ oz/¾ cup) walnut halves, chopped
170 ml (5½ fl oz/⅔ cup) canola or vegetable oil
2 eggs, at room temperature
225 g (8 oz) beetroot (beet), finely shredded

chocolate drizzle icing
195 g (6¾ oz/1¼ cups) icing (confectioners') sugar
30 g (1 oz/¼ cup) unsweetened cocoa powder

Preheat the oven to 180°C (350°F/Gas 4). Spray eight ramekins with oil and place on a large baking tray.

Sift together the flour, cocoa, bicarbonate of soda, baking powder and mixed spice into a large bowl. Stir in the sugar and walnuts, then make a well in the centre.

Whisk together the oil and eggs. Add the shredded beetroot and stir together.

Pour the beetroot mixture into the well in the dry ingredients and, using a large metal spoon, fold them together. Divide the mixture among the ramekins and smooth the surfaces with a spatula.

Bake for 20 minutes, or until a skewer inserted into the centre of a cake comes out clean. Leave the cakes in the ramekins for 5 minutes before turning out onto a wire rack to cool.

To make the chocolate drizzle icing, sift together the icing sugar and cocoa. Add 60 ml (2 fl oz/¼ cup) boiling water and mix until smooth.

Drizzle the cakes with the icing in a decorative pattern. Set aside for 30 minutes, or until the icing is set. Serve with thick cream or ice cream.

Individual white chocolate-chip cakes

preparation 15 minutes
cooking 20 minutes
makes 12

110 g (3¾ oz) unsalted butter, softened
185 g (6½ oz/¾ cup) caster (superfine) sugar
2 eggs, lightly beaten
1 teaspoon natural vanilla extract
290 g (10¼ oz) self-raising flour
125 ml (4 fl oz/½ cup) buttermilk
250 g (9 oz) white chocolate chips
200 g (7 oz) white chocolate melts (buttons)
12 yellow sugar flowers, to decorate, optional

Preheat the oven to 170°C (325°F/Gas 3). Lightly grease a 12-hole 125 ml (4 fl oz/½ cup) muffin tray.

Using electric beaters, beat the butter and sugar in a large mixing bowl until the mixture is light and creamy. Add the egg, a little at a time, beating well after each addition. Add the vanilla and beat until well combined. Sift the flour into the bowl, then fold in alternately with the buttermilk. Stir in the chocolate chips.

Fill each muffin hole three-quarters full with the mixture. Bake for 20 minutes, or until a skewer comes out clean when inserted into the centre of each cake. Leave in the tin for 5 minutes before turning out onto a wire rack to cool completely. Use a flat-bladed knife to loosen around the edges of the cakes if they stick.

Place the chocolate melts in a heatproof bowl and sit it over a saucepan of barely simmering water, making sure the base of the bowl does not touch the water. Stir until the chocolate has melted. Using a flat-bladed knife, spread the chocolate over the cooled muffins and decorate with sugar flowers, if you like. Let set.

Fold the chocolate chips into the batter, making sure they are evenly distributed.

Mini mango cakes with lime syrup

preparation 25 minutes
cooking 35 minutes
makes 4

425 g (15 oz) tinned mango slices in syrup, drained
90 g (3¼ oz) unsalted butter, softened
185 g (6½ oz/¾ cup) caster (superfine) sugar
2 eggs, lightly beaten
60 g (2¼ oz/½ cup) self-raising flour
2 tablespoons ground almonds
2 tablespoons coconut milk
2 tablespoons lime juice

Preheat the oven to 200°C (400°F/Gas 6). Lightly grease a 4-hole 250 ml (9 fl oz/1 cup) muffin tray and line with mango slices.

Using electric beaters, beat the butter and 125 g (4½ oz/½ cup) of the sugar in a large mixing bowl until the mixture is light and creamy. Add the egg, a little at a time, beating well after each addition. Sift the flour into the bowl, then fold into the mixture. Stir in the almonds and coconut milk.

Divide the mixture among the muffin holes. Bake for 25 minutes, or until a skewer comes out clean when inserted into the centre of each cake.

To make the lime syrup, place the lime juice, the remaining sugar and 125 ml (4 fl oz/½ cup) water in a small saucepan and stir over low heat until the sugar is dissolved. Increase the heat and simmer for 10 minutes.

Pierce holes in each cake with a skewer. Drizzle the syrup over the top and allow to stand for 5 minutes to soak up the liquid. Turn out and serve.

The skewer holes in each cake will help the syrup be absorbed into the cakes.

Bottom: Mini mango cakes with lime syrup. Top: Individual white chocolate-chip cakes.

White chocolate and almond cakes

preparation 30 minutes
cooking 30 minutes
makes 12

140 g (5 oz/1 cup) chopped white chocolate
85 g (3 oz) unsalted butter, chopped
125 ml (4 fl oz/½ cup) milk
115 g (4 oz/½ cup) caster (superfine) sugar
1 egg, at room temperature
115 g (4 oz/¾ cup) self-raising flour, sifted
55 g (2 oz/½ cup) ground almonds
12 raspberries
icing (confectioners') sugar, to dust

white chocolate ganache
400 g (15½ oz) white chocolate, finely chopped
170 ml (5½ fl oz/⅔ cup) cream

Preheat the oven to 190°C (375°F/Gas 5). Line a 12-hole muffin tray with paper cases.

Mix together the chocolate, butter and milk in a saucepan. Stir over low heat until melted and smooth. Transfer the mixture to a bowl and set aside to cool a little. Whisk in the sugar and egg.

Mix together the flour and ground almonds, then add to the chocolate mixture and mix well. Spoon into the muffin holes and bake for 20 minutes, or until a skewer inserted into the centre of a cake comes out clean. Leave in the tray for 5 minutes before transferring to a wire rack to cool.

Meanwhile, to make the white chocolate ganache, place the chocolate in a heatproof bowl. Heat the cream in a saucepan until almost boiling. Pour over the chocolate and leave for 1 minute, then stir until it has melted and the mixture is smooth. Cool in the fridge, stirring occasionally, until the ganache has a thick, spreadable consistency.

To serve, spread the ganache over the cakes. Top each one with a raspberry and dust with a little sifted icing sugar.

Cheesecakes with mixed berries

preparation 20 minutes + 1 hour refrigeration
cooking 30 minutes
serves 4

4 butternut biscuits (cookies)
85 g (2 oz/½ cup) white chocolate chips
250 g (9 oz/1 cup) cream cheese, at room temperature
60 ml (2 fl oz/¼ cup) cream, for whipping
115 g (4 oz/½ cup) caster (superfine) sugar
1 egg, at room temperature
250 g (9 oz/1½–2 cups) mixed berries, such as raspberries, blueberries and sliced strawberries
Framboise or Cointreau

Preheat the oven to 160°C (315°F/Gas 2–3). Grease a four-hole muffin tray and line each with two strips of baking paper to make a cross pattern.

Put a biscuit in the base of each hole. Place the chocolate in a heatproof bowl and sit it over a saucepan of barely simmering water, making sure the base of the bowl does not touch the water. Stir until the chocolate has melted.

Using electric beaters, beat the cream cheese, cream and half the sugar until thick and smooth. Beat in the egg and then the melted chocolate. Pour evenly into the muffin holes and bake for 25 minutes, or until set. Cool completely in the tray, then carefully run a small spatula or flat-bladed knife around the edge and lift out of the holes using the paper strips as handles. Refrigerate for 1 hour, or until ready to serve.

Meanwhile, place the berries in a bowl and fold in the remaining sugar. Leave for 10–15 minutes, or until juices form. Flavour with a little liqueur. Serve the cheesecakes topped with the berries.

Bottom: Cheesecakes with mixed berries. Top: White chocolate and almond cakes.

Coffee cupcakes

preparation 15 minutes
cooking 30 minutes
makes 24

185 g (6½ oz) unsalted butter, softened
125 g (4½ oz/⅔ cup lightly packed) soft brown sugar
2 eggs, at room temperature
3 teaspoons coffee and chicory essence
155 g (5½ oz/1¼ cups) self-raising flour
100 ml (3½ fl oz) buttermilk
chocolate-coated coffee beans, to decorate, optional

icing
125 g (4½ oz/1 cup) icing (confectioners') sugar
10 g (¼ oz) unsalted butter
1 teaspoon coffee and chicory essence
1½ tablespoons boiling water

Preheat the oven to 150°C (300°F/Gas 2). Line two 12-hole mini muffin trays with paper cases.

Using electric beaters, beat the butter and brown sugar in a mixing bowl until the mixture is light and creamy. Add the eggs one at a time, beating well after each addition. Add the coffee and chicory essence and beat until well combined. Sift the flour and a pinch of salt into the bowl, then fold in alternately with the buttermilk.

Spoon the mixture evenly into the paper cases and bake for 25–30 minutes, or until just springy to the touch. Leave to cool in the tins.

To make the icing (frosting), combine the icing sugar, butter, coffee and chicory essence and boiling water in a small mixing bowl. Spread a little icing over each cupcake with a flat-bladed knife. If you like, decorate each cake with a chocolate-coated coffee bean.

Individual sticky date cakes

preparation 10 minutes
cooking 30 minutes
makes 8

270 g (9½ oz/1⅔ cups) stoned dates, chopped
1 teaspoon bicarbonate of soda (baking soda)
150 g (5½ oz) unsalted butter, chopped
185 g (6½ oz/1½ cups) self-raising flour
265 g (9¼ oz) soft brown sugar
2 eggs, lightly beaten
2 tablespoons golden syrup (if unavailable, substitute with half
honey and half dark corn syrup)
185 ml (6 fl oz/¾ cup) cream

Preheat the oven to 180°C (350°F/Gas 4). Grease six 250 ml (9 fl oz/1 cup) muffin holes.

Place the dates and 250 ml (9 fl oz/1 cup) water in a saucepan, bring to the boil, then remove from the heat and stir in the bicarbonate of soda. Add 60 g (2¼ oz) of the butter and stir until completely dissolved.

Sift the flour into a large mixing bowl, add 125 g (4½ oz/⅔ cup) of the sugar and stir. Make a well in the centre, add the date mixture and egg and stir until just combined. Spoon the mixture evenly into the prepared holes and bake for 20 minutes, or until a skewer comes out clean when inserted into the centre of the cake.

To make the sauce, place the golden syrup and cream with the remaining butter and sugar in a small saucepan and stir over low heat for 3–4 minutes, or until the sugar has dissolved. Bring to the boil, then reduce the heat and simmer, stirring the sauce occasionally, for 2 minutes. To serve, turn the cakes out onto serving plates, pierce the tops a few times with a skewer and drizzle with the sauce.

Using electric beaters, cream the butter and sugar before adding the eggs.

Bring the dates and water to the boil, then stir in the bicarbonate of soda and butter.

Bottom: Individual sticky date cakes. Top: Coffee cupcakes.

Ginger and macadamia squares

preparation 20 minutes
cooking 35 minutes
makes 20 pieces

125 g (4½ oz) unsalted butter
185 g (6½ oz/1 cup lightly packed) soft brown sugar
2 eggs, lightly beaten
175 g (6 oz/1¼ cups) self-raising flour
4 teaspoons ground ginger

white chocolate icing
150 g (5½ oz) white chocolate, chopped
60 ml (2 fl oz/¼ cup) cream
2 tablespoons chopped glacé (candied) ginger
2 tablespoons chopped macadamia nuts

Preheat the oven to 180°C (350°F/Gas 4). Lightly grease a 27 x 18 cm (10¾ x 7 inch) shallow baking tin. Cover the base with baking paper, making sure the paper overhangs on two opposite sides, then grease the paper.

Using electric beaters, beat the butter and sugar in a small mixing bowl until light and creamy. Add the eggs a little at a time, beating well after each addition. Transfer the mixture to a large mixing bowl, then sift in the flour and ginger. Using a metal spoon, fold in the flour and ginger until just combined.

Spread the mixture into the prepared baking tin. Bake for 30 minutes, or until golden and firm in the centre. Leave to cool in the tin.

To make the white chocolate icing (frosting), combine the chocolate and cream in a small saucepan. Stir over low heat until the chocolate has melted and the mixture is smooth. Leave to cool. Using a flat-bladed knife, spread the icing evenly over the slice. Sprinkle with the glacé ginger and macadamia nuts. Allow the icing to set and then cut into squares to serve.

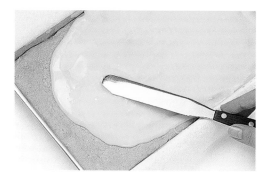

While the slice is still in the tin, spread the icing over the top with a flat-bladed knife.

Vanilla and passionfruit slice

preparation 35 minutes + 2 hours refrigeration
cooking 20–25 minutes
makes 12 pieces

2 sheets frozen puff pastry, thawed

custard
30 g (1 oz/¼ cup) custard powder (if unavailable, substitute with instant vanilla pudding mix)
60 g (2¼ oz/¼ cup) caster (superfine) sugar
250 ml (9 fl oz/1 cup) cream
375 ml (13 fl oz/1½ cups) milk
½ teaspoon natural vanilla extract

icing
60 g (2¼ oz/¼ cup) passionfruit pulp
25 g (1 oz) unsalted butter
185 g (6½ oz/1½ cups) icing (confectioners') sugar

Preheat the oven to 210°C (415°F/Gas 6–7). Line two baking trays with baking paper.

Place the pastry on the trays and prick all over with a fork. Bake for 10–15 minutes, or until golden. Cool on a wire rack.

To make the custard, combine the custard powder, sugar and cream in a medium-sized heavy-based saucepan. Gradually stir in the milk and stir constantly over medium heat until the custard boils and thickens. Remove from the heat. Stir in the vanilla. Place plastic wrap onto the surface of the custard to prevent a skin forming. Cool.

Place one sheet of pastry onto a board. Spread the custard evenly over the surface. Top with the remaining pastry sheet upside down.

To make the icing (frosting), combine the passionfruit pulp, butter and icing sugar in a medium heatproof bowl. Stand over a saucepan of simmering water and stir until the icing is smooth and glossy. Remove from the heat. Spread the icing evenly over the pastry sheet, using a flat-bladed knife. Refrigerate for several hours or until the pastry softens slightly. Cut the slice into 12 squares using a serrated knife.

Finish the slice off with a layer of passionfruit icing before chilling for several hours.

Bottom: Vanilla and passionfruit slice. Top: Ginger and macadamia squares.

Tipsy currant slice

preparation 20 minutes + 15 minutes standing
cooking 25 minutes
makes 16 pieces

75 g (2½ oz/½ cup) currants
60 ml (2 fl oz/¼ cup) brandy
125 g (4½ oz/1 cup) plain (all-purpose) flour
175 g (6 oz/1 cup) rice flour
1 teaspoon baking powder
1 teaspoon mixed (pumpkin pie) spice
185 g (6½ oz/¾ cup) caster (superfine) sugar, plus
extra to sprinkle
125 g (4½ oz) unsalted butter, melted
170 ml (5½ fl oz/⅔ cup) milk
2 eggs, lightly beaten
1 egg white, lightly beaten

Preheat the oven to 180°C (350°F/Gas 4). Lightly grease a
28 x 18 cm (11¼ x 7 inch) shallow baking tin and line with
baking paper, making sure the paper overhangs on two
opposite sides.

Soak the currants in the brandy, covered, for 15 minutes.

Sift the flours, baking powder and mixed spice into a large
bowl. Stir in the sugar. Make a well in the centre, then add
the melted butter, milk and egg. Add the currants and mix
together gently.

Spoon the mixture evenly into the tin and smooth the
surface. Brush with the egg white and sprinkle with sugar.
Bake for 25 minutes, or until a skewer inserted into the
slice comes out clean. Leave to cool in the tin, then lift out.
Sprinkle again with sugar, then cut into pieces and serve.

Caramel pecan squares

preparation 25 minutes + 3 hours refrigeration
cooking 35 minutes
makes 16 pieces

250 g (9 oz) plain chocolate biscuits (cookies)
1 tablespoon drinking chocolate
150 g (5½ oz/1½ cups) pecans
110 g (3¾ oz) unsalted butter, melted
icing (confectioners') sugar, to dust
drinking chocolate, to dust

caramel topping
90 g (3¼ oz/½ cup lightly packed) soft brown sugar
60 g (2¼ oz) unsalted butter
400 g (14 oz) tin sweetened condensed milk

Preheat the oven to 180°C (350°F/Gas 4). Lightly grease a
28 x 18 cm (11¼ x 7 inch) shallow baking tin and line with
baking paper, making sure the paper overhangs on two
opposite sides.

Finely crush the biscuits, drinking chocolate and one-third
of the pecans in a food processor. Transfer to a mixing bowl
and add the melted butter. Mix well and press firmly into
the prepared tin. Press the rest of the pecans gently over
the top.

To make the caramel topping, place the brown sugar and
butter in a saucepan over low heat. Stir until the butter
melts and the sugar dissolves. Add the condensed milk and
cook, stirring, until thicker and slightly darker. Pour over the
biscuit base.

Bake for 25–30 minutes, or until the caramel is firm and
golden—the edges will bubble and darken. Cool, then
refrigerate for at least 3 hours. Trim off the crusty edges and
cut the slice into squares. Hold a piece of paper over the
squares to help you create a neat edge and dust one side
with icing sugar and the other with drinking chocolate.

Smooth the surface of the mixture, then brush
lightly with the beaten egg white.

Arrange the rest of the pecans in the base, pressing
them in lightly.

53

Bottom: Caramel pecan squares. Top: Tipsy currant slice.

Brandy mocha bars

preparation 45 minutes + overnight refrigeration
cooking 15 minutes
makes 15 pieces

1 tablespoon instant coffee
1 tablespoon boiling water
280 g (10 oz/2¼ cups) icing (confectioners') sugar
110 g (3¾ oz/1 cup) full-cream milk powder
60 g (2¼ oz/½ cup) unsweetened cocoa powder
2 eggs, at room temperature
60 ml (2 fl oz/¼ cup) brandy
375 g (13 oz) white vegetable shortening, melted
125 g (4½ oz/1¼ cups) flaked almonds, toasted, plus
extra, to decorate

base
125 g (4½ oz) unsalted butter
60 g (2¼ oz/¼ cup) caster (superfine) sugar
155 g (5½ oz/1¼ cups) plain (all-purpose) flour

chocolate topping
250 g (9 oz/1⅔ cups) dark chocolate, chopped
50 g (1¾ oz) white vegetable shortening, chopped

Preheat the oven to 180°C (350°F/Gas 4). Lightly grease a 23 cm (9 inch) square shallow baking tin and line with baking paper, making sure the paper overhangs on two opposite sides.

To make the base, beat the butter and sugar in a mixing bowl until just combined. Stir in the flour, then press into the prepared tin. Bake for 10 minutes, or until lightly browned. Cool.

Dissolve the coffee in the boiling water. Using electric beaters, beat the icing sugar, milk powder, cocoa, coffee, eggs and brandy until well combined. Gradually add the shortening and mix until well combined. Stir in the almonds then pour the mixture over the base. Refrigerate overnight, or until the topping is firm. Cut into small pieces.

To make the chocolate icing (frosting), place the chocolate and shortening in a heatproof bowl. Place the bowl over a saucepan of barely simmering water, making sure the base of the bowl does not touch the water. Stir until the chocolate has melted. Dip the bars into the icing until coated and place on a wire rack over baking paper. Leave to set. Decorate with toasted flaked almonds.

Cappuccino slice

preparation 30 minutes + cooling
cooking 55 minutes
makes 16 pieces

40 g (1½ oz/⅓ cup) self-raising flour
30 g (1 oz/¼ cup) plain (all-purpose) flour
1 tablespoon unsweetened cocoa powder
60 g (2¼ oz/¼ cup) caster (superfine) sugar
1 egg, lightly beaten
1 teaspoon natural vanilla extract
65 g (2¼ oz) unsalted butter, melted
60 ml (2 fl oz/¼ cup) milk
50 g (1¾ oz) dark chocolate, grated

cappuccino filling
350 g (12 oz) cream cheese
100 g (3½ oz) mascarpone cheese
90 g (3¼ oz/⅓ cup) sour cream
90 g (3¼ oz/⅓ cup) caster (superfine) sugar
3 eggs, lightly beaten
1 tablespoon instant coffee
1 tablespoon warm water

Preheat the oven to 180°C (350°F/Gas 4). Lightly grease a 19 cm (7½ inch) square cake tin and line with baking paper, making sure the paper overhangs on two opposite sides.

Sift the flours and cocoa into a large mixing bowl. Add the sugar and make a well in the centre of the dry ingredients. In a separate bowl, mix the egg, vanilla, butter and milk until well combined. Pour the egg mixture into the dry ingredients and stir until just combined. Spoon into the prepared tin and bake for 10–15 minutes and then cool completely. Reduce the oven to 160°C (315°F/Gas 2–3).

To make the filling, beat the cream cheese, mascarpone cheese and sour cream with electric beaters for 3 minutes, or until smooth. Add the sugar in batches and beat for another 3 minutes. Add the eggs gradually, beating well after each addition.

Dissolve the coffee in the warm water, add to the filling and beat until well combined. Pour over the base. Bake for 40 minutes, or until set. Leave in the tin to cool completely. Cut into slices, top with grated chocolate and serve.

54

55

Bottom: Cappuccino slice. Top: Brandy mocha bars.

Wholemeal lemon and walnut slice

preparation 30 minutes
cooking 25 minutes
makes 16 pieces

2 teaspoons finely grated lemon zest
40 g (1½ oz/⅓ cup) icing (confectioners') sugar
110 g (3¾ oz/¾ cup) wholemeal (whole-wheat) flour
30 g (1 oz/¼ cup) plain (all-purpose) flour
125 g (4½ oz/½ cup) raw (demerara) sugar
150 g (5½ oz/1¼ cups) walnuts, roughly chopped
90 g (3¼ oz/½ cup) mixed peel (mixed candied citrus peel),
finely chopped
115 g (4 oz/⅓ cup) golden syrup (if unavailable, substitute with
half honey and half dark corn syrup)
125 g (4½ oz) unsalted butter, chopped

Put the lemon zest and icing sugar in a small bowl and rub gently to just combine. Spread the mixture out on a plate and leave to dry.

Preheat the oven to 180°C (350°F/Gas 4). Lightly grease a 27 x 18 cm (10¾ x 7 inch) shallow baking tin and line with baking paper, making sure the paper overhangs on two opposite sides.

Sift the flours into a large mixing bowl, returning any husks to the bowl. Stir in the raw sugar, walnuts and mixed peel.

Put the syrup and butter in a saucepan and stir over low heat until melted. Add to the bowl and mix well. Spread into the prepared tin and bake for 20–25 minutes, or until golden brown and a skewer inserted into the centre comes out clean. Leave to cool completely in the tin. Put the lemon sugar in a sieve and sprinkle over the slice before cutting into fingers or squares.

Berry almond slice

preparation 25 minutes
cooking 1 hour 5 minutes
makes 15 pieces

1 sheet frozen puff pastry, thawed
150 g (5½ oz) unsalted butter
185 g (6½ oz/¾ cup) caster (superfine) sugar
3 eggs, lightly beaten
2 tablespoons grated lemon zest
125 g (4½ oz/1¼ cups) ground almonds
2 tablespoons plain (all-purpose) flour
150 g (5½ oz) fresh raspberries
150 g (5½ oz) fresh blackberries
icing (confectioners') sugar, to dust

Preheat the oven to 200°C (400°F/Gas 6). Lightly grease a 23 cm (9 inch) square shallow baking tin and line with baking paper, making sure the paper overhangs on two opposite sides.

Place the pastry on a baking tray lined with baking paper. Prick all over with a fork and bake for 15 minutes, or until golden. Ease the pastry into the prepared tin, trimming the edges if necessary. Reduce the oven to 180°C (350°F/Gas 4).

Using electric beaters, beat the butter and sugar in a mixing bowl until light and creamy. Add the egg, a little at a time, beating after each addition, then add the lemon zest. Fold in the ground almonds and flour. Spread the mixture over the pastry base. Scatter the fruit on top and bake for 45–50 minutes, or until lightly golden. Cool in the tin before lifting out to cut. Dust with icing sugar and serve.

Sift the flours into a bowl, returning any husks from the wholemeal flour to the bowl.

Fold the ground almonds and flour into the beaten mixture, then spread over the base.

Bottom: Berry almond slice. Top: Wholemeal lemon and walnut slice.

Plum and almond slice

preparation 30 minutes
cooking 1 hour 10 minutes
makes 9 pieces

160 g (5½ oz) unsalted butter
160 g (5½ oz/⅔ cup) caster (superfine) sugar
2 eggs, at room temperature
60 g (2¼ oz/½ cup) plain (all-purpose) flour
40 g (1½ oz/⅓ cup) cornflour (cornstarch)
2 tablespoons rice flour
1½ tablespoons thinly sliced glacé (candied) ginger
825 g (1 lb 13 oz) tinned plums in syrup, drained and halved
(see Note)
100 g (3½ oz/1 cup) flaked almonds
1 tablespoon honey, warmed

Preheat the oven to 180°C (350°F/Gas 4). Lightly grease a
20 cm (8 inch) square cake tin and line with baking paper,
making sure the paper overhangs on all sides.

Using electric beaters, beat the butter and sugar in a mixing
bowl until light and creamy. Add the eggs one at a time,
beating well after each addition. Sift the flour into the bowl,
then fold in along with the ginger. Spread into the tin.
Arrange the plums on top, pressing them in. Scatter with
the almonds, pressing in gently, then drizzle with the honey.

Bake for 1 hour 10 minutes, or until firm and golden (cover
with foil if the almonds are over-browning). Cool in the tin
before cutting.

Note *If in season, use 7 ripe blood plums instead of tinned.
They might bleed more than the tinned variety.*

Peach crumble slice

preparation 30 minutes
cooking 1 hour
makes 9 pieces

60 g (2¼ oz/½ cup) self-raising flour
90 g (3¼ oz/¾ cup) plain (all-purpose) flour
60 g (2¼ oz/1 cup) shredded coconut
50 g (1¾ oz/½ cup) rolled (porridge) oats
95 g (3¼ oz/½ cup lightly packed) soft brown sugar
160 g (5¾ oz) unsalted butter, melted
1 teaspoon natural vanilla extract
2 x 415 g (14¾ oz) tinned peaches
2 tablespoons honey
60 g (2¼ oz/½ cup) sultanas (golden raisins)
¼ teaspoon ground cinnamon

Preheat the oven to 180°C (350°F/Gas 4). Lightly grease a
28 x 18 cm (11¼ x 7 inch) shallow baking tin and line with
baking paper, making sure the paper overhangs on two
opposite sides.

Sift the flours into a mixing bowl. Stir in the coconut, rolled
oats and brown sugar. Mix in the butter and vanilla.

Set aside one-third of the mixture and press the rest
into the prepared tin. Smooth the surface and bake for
15–20 minutes. Leave to cool in the tin.

Mix the peaches, honey and sultanas in a bowl and spread
over the cooked base. Mix the cinnamon into the reserved
crumble mixture and sprinkle over the top. Bake for
35–40 minutes, or until golden. Leave to cool, then cut into
pieces to serve.

Arrange the plum halves on top, pressing them into
the filling mixture.

Sprinkle the remaining crumble mixture over the top,
then bake until golden.

Bottom: Peach crumble slice. Top: Plum and almond slice.

Choc-raspberry cheesecake slice

preparation 1 hour + overnight refrigeration
cooking 5 minutes
makes 16 pieces

150 g (5½ oz) plain sweet biscuits (cookies), crushed
80 g (2¾ oz) unsalted butter, melted
½ teaspoon mixed (pumpkin pie) spice
1 tablespoon powdered gelatine
100 g (3½ oz) white chocolate
125 g (4½ oz) cream cheese, softened
90 g (3¼ oz/⅓ cup) caster (superfine) sugar
1 egg, at room temperature
250 ml (9 fl oz/1 cup) cream
1 teaspoon natural vanilla extract
300 g (10½ oz) fresh or frozen raspberries (see Note)

Lightly grease a 20 cm (8 inch) square cake tin and line with baking paper, making sure the paper overhangs on all sides.

Mix together the biscuit crumbs, melted butter and mixed spice and press evenly into the prepared tin. Refrigerate until set.

Dissolve the gelatine in 2 tablespoons hot water, then leave to cool slightly. Place the chocolate in a heatproof bowl and sit over a saucepan of barely simmering water, making sure the base of the bowl does not touch the water. Stir the chocolate until melted. Leave to cool.

Using electric beaters, beat the cream cheese and sugar in a mixing bowl until light and creamy. Beat in the egg, cream and vanilla until just combined. With the beaters running at low speed, add the cooled gelatine and melted chocolate to the mixture and mix until just combined. Do not overmix.

Pour the mixture over the set biscuit base, then scatter with the raspberries, gently pressing them down. Refrigerate overnight to set. Using a sharp knife dipped in hot water, cut the slice into small squares.

Note *If you are using frozen raspberries, defrost and drain them well on paper towels before using.*

Hint *Make sure the melted chocolate and gelatine have cooled before beating them into the cream cheese mixture or they'll become lumpy.*

Walnut brownies

preparation 20 minutes
cooking 35 minutes
makes 20 diamonds

100 g (3½ oz) unsalted butter
125 g (4½ oz/⅔ cup lightly packed) soft brown sugar
40 g (1½ oz/⅓ cup) sultanas (golden raisins), chopped
125 g (4½ oz/1 cup) self-raising flour
125 g (4½ oz/1 cup) plain (all-purpose) flour
1 teaspoon ground cinnamon
1 tablespoon unsweetened cocoa powder
60 g (2¼ oz/½ cup) chopped walnuts
90 g (3¼ oz) dark chocolate chips
20 walnut halves

icing
60 g (2¼ oz) unsalted butter
90 g (3¼ oz/¾ cup) icing (confectioners') sugar
1 tablespoon unsweetened cocoa powder
1 tablespoon milk

Preheat the oven to 180°C (350°F/Gas 4). Lightly grease a 27 x 18 cm (10¾ x 7 inch) shallow rectangular baking tin and line with baking paper, making sure the paper overhangs on the two longer sides. Grease the paper.

Combine the butter, sugar, sultanas and 185 ml (6 fl oz/¾ cup) water in a small saucepan. Constantly stir over low heat for 5 minutes, or until the butter is melted and the sugar is dissolved. Remove from the heat.

Sift the flour, cinnamon and cocoa into a large mixing bowl and add the chopped nuts and chocolate chips. Make a well in the centre of the dry ingredients and add the butter mixture. Using a wooden spoon, stir until just combined. Do not overmix.

Spoon the mixture into the prepared tin and smooth the surface. Bake for 25–30 minutes, or until a skewer comes out clean when inserted in the centre of the slice. Leave in the tin for 20 minutes before turning onto a wire rack to cool completely.

To make the icing (frosting), beat the butter with electric beaters until light and creamy. Add the icing sugar, cocoa and milk. Beat until smooth. Spread the icing over the brownie. Cut into diamonds and top with the walnut halves.

Bottom: Walnut brownies. Top: Choc-raspberry cheesecake slice.

Choc-caramel slice

preparation 40 minutes + refrigeration
cooking 30 minutes
makes 24 triangles

125 g (4½ oz) plain sweet biscuits (cookies), crushed
80 g (2¾ oz) unsalted butter, melted
2 tablespoons desiccated coconut
400 g (14 oz) tin sweetened condensed milk
125 g (4½ oz) unsalted butter
90 g (3¼ oz/⅓ cup) caster (superfine) sugar
115 g (4 oz/⅓ cup) golden syrup (if unavailable, substitute with
half honey and half dark corn syrup)
250 g (9 oz/1⅔ cups) chocolate melts (buttons)
1 tablespoon vegetable oil

Lightly grease a 30 x 20 cm (12 x 8 inch) shallow baking tin and line with foil. Grease the foil.

Combine the crushed biscuits, butter and coconut in a medium-sized mixing bowl. Press the mixture evenly into the prepared tin and smooth the surface.

Combine the condensed milk, butter, sugar and golden syrup in a small saucepan. Stir over low heat for 25 minutes or until the sugar has dissolved and the mixture is smooth, thick and lightly browned. Remove the pan from the heat and leave to cool slightly. Pour over the biscuit base and smooth the surface.

Place the milk chocolate melts and oil in a small heatproof bowl and sit it over a saucepan of barely simmering water, making sure the base of the bowl does not touch the water. Stir until the chocolate has melted. Spread the chocolate mixture over the caramel. Allow to partially set before marking into 24 triangles. Refrigerate until firm, then cut into triangles.

Using a ruler and a sharp knife, mark the 24 triangles before chilling and then cutting.

Brandy Alexander slice

preparation 20 minutes + overnight refrigeration
cooking 5 minutes
makes 12 pieces

80 g (2¾ oz) unsalted butter, chopped
60 g (2¼ oz) dark cooking chocolate, chopped
250 g (9 oz) packet plain chocolate biscuits (cookies),
finely crushed
300 g (10½ oz) ricotta cheese
60 ml (2 fl oz/¼ cup) cream
40 g (1½ oz/⅓ cup) icing (confectioners') sugar, sifted
60 g (2¼ oz/½ cup) grated milk chocolate
1 tablespoon brandy
1 tablespoon crème de cacao liqueur
½ teaspoon freshly grated nutmeg
60 g (2¼ oz) dark chocolate melts (buttons)

Lightly grease a 30 x 20 cm (12 x 8 inch) shallow baking tin and line with baking paper, making sure the paper overhangs on two opposite sides.

Place the butter and dark chocolate in a small heatproof bowl. Stand over a saucepan of simmering water and stir until the chocolate is melted and the mixture is smooth. Remove from the heat. Using a flat-bladed knife, mix the chocolate mixture with the biscuit crumbs in a small bowl.

Press the biscuit mixture evenly over the base of the tin.

Using electric beaters, beat the ricotta, cream and icing sugar in a small mixing bowl on medium speed for 3 minutes, or until the mixture is light and creamy. Add the grated chocolate, brandy and crème de cacao and beat until combined.

Spread the cheese mixture over the prepared base and sprinkle with the nutmeg. Refrigerate for several hours or overnight. Cut into 12 pieces. Place the chocolate melts in a small heatproof bowl and stand over simmering water until melted. Place in a small piping (icing) bag and pipe a design on top of each bar.

Storage *Store this slice in the refrigerator for up to 2 days.*

Press the biscuit mixture firmly into the tin, making sure it is evenly distributed.

Bottom: Brandy Alexander slice. Top: Choc-caramel slice.

Lemon and almond slice

preparation 25 minutes
cooking 1 hour
makes 18 pieces

60 g (2¼ oz/½ cup) plain (all-purpose) flour
40 g (1½ oz/⅓ cup) self-raising flour
2 tablespoons icing (confectioners') sugar
60 g (2¼ oz) unsalted butter, chopped
1 egg, lightly beaten
lemon zest, to garnish

almond cream

3 eggs, at room temperature
125 g (4½ oz/½ cup) caster (superfine) sugar
2 teaspoons grated lemon zest
125 ml (4 fl oz/½ cup) lemon juice
80 g (2¾ oz/¾ cup) ground almonds
250 ml (9 fl oz/1 cup) cream

Preheat the oven to 190°C (375°F/Gas 5). Lightly grease a 23 cm (9 inch) square shallow baking tin and line with baking paper, making sure the paper overhangs on two opposite sides.

Put the flours, sugar and butter in a food processor and process until the mixture resembles fine breadcrumbs. Add the egg and process briefly, until the dough just comes together, adding a small amount of water if necessary.

Press the dough into the base of the prepared tin and prick well with a fork. Bake for 10–12 minutes, or until golden. Allow to cool. Reduce the oven to 170°C (325°F/Gas 3).

To make the almond cream, beat the eggs and sugar with a wooden spoon. Stir in the lemon zest, lemon juice, ground almonds and cream. Pour over the pastry and bake for 35–40 minutes, or until lightly set. Leave to cool in the tin. Slice into pieces and garnish with lemon zest. Serve with whipped cream.

Fruity chews

preparation 30 minutes + cooling
cooking 25 minutes
makes 16 pieces

2 eggs, at room temperature
230 g (8½ oz/1 cup firmly packed) soft brown sugar
90 g (3¼ oz) unsalted butter, melted
1 teaspoon natural vanilla extract
185 g (6½ oz/1½ cups) plain (all-purpose) flour
1 teaspoon baking powder
140 g (5 oz/¾ cup) chopped dates
90 g (3¼ oz/¾ cup) chopped walnuts or pecans
110 g (3¾ oz/½ cup) chopped glacé (candied) ginger
50 g (1¾ oz/½ cup) rolled (porridge) oats

lemon icing

60 g (2¼ oz) unsalted butter
1 teaspoon grated lemon zest
125 g (4½ oz/1 cup) icing (confectioners') sugar
2 teaspoons lemon juice
75 g (2½ oz/⅓ cup) finely chopped glacé (candied) ginger

Preheat the oven to 180°C (350°F/Gas 4). Lightly grease a 28 x 18 cm (11¼ x 7 inch) shallow baking tin and line with baking paper, making sure the paper overhangs on two opposite sides.

Using electric beaters, beat the eggs and brown sugar in a large mixing bowl for 1 minute, or until well combined. Stir in the melted butter and vanilla. Sift the flour and baking powder and fold into the mixture with a metal spoon until just combined. Do not overmix.

Stir in the dates, nuts, glacé ginger and oats until well combined. Spread into the prepared tin and smooth the surface. Bake for 25 minutes, or until lightly browned. Leave to cool in the tin.

To make the lemon icing (frosting), place the butter and lemon zest in a small bowl and beat with electric beaters until creamy. Gradually add the sifted icing sugar, beating well after each addition. Add enough lemon juice to make a spreadable icing. Spread the lemon icing over the cold slice, sprinkle with the ginger and cut into pieces to serve.

Once the dough has been pressed into the tin, prick it all over with a fork.

Bottom: Fruity chews. Top: Lemon and almond slice.

Continental slice

preparation 25 minutes + 4 hours refrigeration
cooking 10 minutes
makes about 24 pieces

125 g (4½ oz) unsalted butter
125 g (4½ oz/½ cup) caster (superfine) sugar
30 g (1 oz/¼ cup) unsweetened cocoa powder
250 g (9 oz) shredded wheat biscuits (cookies), crushed
75 g (2½ oz/¾ cup) desiccated coconut
30 g (1 oz/¼ cup) chopped hazelnuts
60 g (2¼ oz/¼ cup) chopped glacé (candied) cherries
1 egg, lightly beaten
1 teaspoon natural vanilla extract

topping
60 g (2¼ oz) unsalted butter
220 g (7¾ oz/1¾ cups) icing (confectioners') sugar
2 tablespoons custard powder (if unavailable, substitute
with instant vanilla pudding mix)
1 tablespoon hot water
1 tablespoon Grand Marnier
125 g (4½ oz) dark chocolate
60 g (2¼ oz) white vegetable shortening

Line the base and sides of a 28 x 18 cm (11¼ x 7 inch) shallow baking tin with foil.

Combine the butter, sugar and cocoa in a small saucepan. Stir over low heat until the butter melts and the mixture is well combined. Cook, stirring, for 1 minute. Remove from the heat and cool slightly. Combine the biscuit crumbs, coconut, hazelnuts and cherries in a large mixing bowl. Make a well in the centre and add the butter mixture, egg and vanilla and stir well. Press the mixture firmly into the prepared tin. Refrigerate until firm.

To make the topping, beat the butter with electric beaters until creamy. Gradually add the icing sugar and custard powder, alternately with the hot water and Grand Marnier. Beat the mixture until light and fluffy. Spread evenly over the base. Refrigerate until set.

Place the chocolate and shortening in a heatproof bowl and set over a saucepan of simmering water. Stir over low heat until the chocolate melts and the mixture is smooth. Spread over the slice. Refrigerate until firm. Cut into small squares to serve.

Hazelnut truffle slice

preparation 30 minutes + 2 hours refrigeration
cooking 40 minutes
makes 24 pieces

100 g (3½ oz) hazelnuts
80 g (2¾ oz) unsalted butter
90 g (3¼ oz/⅓ cup) caster (superfine) sugar
90 g (3¼ oz/¾ cup) plain (all-purpose) flour
1½ tablespoons unsweetened cocoa powder

chocolate brandy icing
200 g (7 oz) dark chocolate, chopped (see Note)
125 ml (4 fl oz/½ cup) cream
2 teaspoons brandy or rum

Preheat the oven to 180°C (350°F/Gas 4). Lightly grease a 21 x 11 cm (8¼ x 4¼ inch) loaf (bar) tin and line with baking paper, making sure the paper overhangs on two opposite sides.

Spread the hazelnuts on a baking tray and bake for about 7 minutes, or until lightly browned. Remove from the oven and, while they are still hot, wrap them in a tea towel (dish towel) and rub away the skins. Cool, then chop roughly.

Beat the butter and sugar with electric beaters until light and creamy. Sift the flour and cocoa powder into a bowl, then stir into the butter mixture. Press evenly over the base of the tin and bake for 25–30 minutes, or until firm. Leave to cool completely.

To make the chocolate brandy icing (frosting), place the chocolate and cream in a small saucepan. Stir over low heat until the chocolate has melted and the mixture is very smooth. Do not overheat. Leave the mixture to cool slightly, then add the brandy or rum and stir until well combined.

Stir the hazelnuts into the icing, then pour over the cooled pastry base. Refrigerate for several hours, or until the topping is firm. The slice is very rich, so cut into small pieces to serve.

Storage In warm weather, store this slice in the fridge.

Note Use the best quality eating or cooking chocolate that you can afford for this recipe.

Bottom: Hazelnut truffle slice. Top: Continental slice.

Lime custard slice

preparation 30 minutes + 3 hours refrigeration
cooking 10 minutes
makes 12 pieces

250 g (9 oz) plain sweet biscuits (cookies), crushed
120 g (4¼ oz) unsalted butter, melted
40 g (1½ oz/⅓ cup) custard powder (if unavailable,
substitute with instant vanilla pudding mix)
250 g (9 oz/1 cup) caster (superfine) sugar
60 g (2¼ oz/½ cup) cornflour (cornstarch)
750 ml (26 fl oz/3 cups) milk
250 ml (9 fl oz/1 cup) lime juice
60 g (2¼ oz) unsalted butter, extra
3 egg yolks
lime zest, cut into strips, to garnish

Lightly grease a 30 x 20 cm (12 x 8 inch) shallow baking
tin and line with baking paper, making sure the paper
overhangs on two opposite sides.

Combine the biscuit crumbs and melted butter. Press firmly
into the prepared tin and refrigerate.

Put the custard powder, sugar and cornflour in a saucepan.
Mix the milk, lime juice and 185 ml (6 fl oz/¾ cup) water in
a separate bowl and gradually stir into the custard mixture.
Stir over medium heat for 5 minutes, or until the custard
thickens. Remove and cool a little. Whisk in the extra butter
and egg yolks.

Pour over the base and chill for 2–3 hours. Cut the slice into
12 pieces and garnish each piece with strips of lime zest.

Mixed nut slice

preparation 25 minutes + 30 minutes refrigeration
cooking 50 minutes
makes 20 pieces

215 g (7½ oz) plain (all-purpose) flour
2 tablespoons icing (confectioners') sugar
125 g (4½ oz) unsalted butter, chopped
1–2 tablespoons lemon juice or water
80 g (2¾ oz/½ cup) macadamia nuts
80 g (2¾ oz/½ cup) whole unblanched almonds
75 g (2½ oz/½ cup) pistachio nuts
70 g (2½ oz/½ cup) hazelnuts
2 eggs, lightly beaten
50 g (1¾ oz) unsalted butter, melted
60 g (2¼ oz/⅓ cup lightly packed) soft brown sugar
80 ml (2½ fl oz/⅓ cup) dark corn syrup
1 teaspoon natural vanilla extract
2 tablespoons cream

Lightly grease a 28 x 18 cm (11¼ x 7 inch) shallow baking
tin and line with baking paper, making sure the paper
overhangs on two opposite sides.

Process the flour, icing sugar and butter in a food processor
until crumbs form. Add the lemon juice or water and
process until the mixture just comes together. Wrap in
plastic wrap and refrigerate for 30 minutes. Preheat the
oven to 180°C (350°F/Gas 4). Roll the pastry out between
two sheets of baking paper and fit to the base and sides of
the tin. Trim away the excess pastry.

Cover the pastry with baking paper and fill with baking
beads or uncooked rice. Bake for 10 minutes. Remove the
paper and beads and bake the pastry base for 5–10 minutes
longer, or until lightly golden. Cool completely.

Mix together the nuts and scatter over the pastry base.

Whisk together the remaining ingredients, pour over the
nuts, then bake the slice for 25–30 minutes, or until set.
Cool completely in the tin before lifting out to cut and serve.

Using a wooden spoon, stir the custard mixture over
medium heat until it boils and thickens.

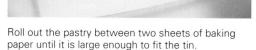

Roll out the pastry between two sheets of baking
paper until it is large enough to fit the tin.

Bottom: Mixed nut slice. Top: Lime custard slice.

Apple and cinnamon slice

preparation 15 minutes
cooking 35 minutes
makes about 20 slices

125 g (4½ oz) unsalted butter
125 g (4½ oz/½ cup) caster (superfine) sugar
2 eggs, at room temperature
250 g (9 oz/2 cups) self-raising flour, sifted
300 g (10½ oz/1¼ cups) sour cream
2 green apples, peeled, cored and sliced
60 g (2¼ oz/½ cup) finely chopped pecans
2 tablespoons caster (superfine) sugar
1 teaspoon ground cinnamon

Preheat the oven to 180°C (350°F/Gas 4). Lightly grease a 30 x 20 cm (12 x 8 inch) shallow baking tin and line with baking paper, making sure the paper overhangs on two opposite sides.

Using electric beaters, beat the butter and sugar in a large mixing bowl until the mixture is light and creamy. Add the eggs one at a time, beating well after each addition. Sift the flour into the bowl, then fold in. Add the sour cream and stir to combine. Spoon the mixture into the prepared tin.

Arrange the apples over the base. Sprinkle with the combined pecans, sugar and cinnamon. Bake for 30–35 minutes. Leave to cool in the tin. Cut into pieces.

White chocolate and mango slice

preparation 25 minutes
cooking 45 minutes
makes 10 pieces

100 g (3½ oz) unsalted butter
125 g (4½ oz/½ cup) caster (superfine) sugar
2 eggs, lightly beaten
1 teaspoon natural vanilla extract
185 g (6½ oz/1½ cups) self-raising flour
125 ml (4 fl oz/½ cup) buttermilk
100 g (3½ oz) white chocolate, grated
2 x 425 g (15 oz) tinned mango slices, drained, or 2 large fresh mangoes, sliced
60 g (2¼ oz/¼ cup) caster (superfine) sugar, extra

Preheat the oven to 180°C (350°F/Gas 4). Lightly grease a 28 x 18 cm (11¼ x 7 inch) shallow baking tin and line with baking paper, making sure the paper overhangs on two opposite sides.

Using electric beaters, beat the butter and sugar in a mixing bowl until the mixture is light and creamy. Gradually add the egg and vanilla, beating until well combined.

Sift the flour into the bowl, then fold in alternately with the buttermilk. Add the grated chocolate. Pour into the prepared tin and smooth the surface. Arrange the mango over the top. Place the tin on an oven tray to catch any drips. Bake for 35–40 minutes, or until golden brown.

Put the extra sugar in a small saucepan with 1 tablespoon water and stir over low heat until dissolved. Bring to the boil, then simmer for 1–2 minutes. Brush the syrup over the hot slice. Cut into pieces and serve hot.

Passionfruit marshmallow slice

preparation 25 minutes + overnight refrigeration
cooking 30 minutes
makes 16 pieces

150 g (5½ oz) unsalted butter
60 g (2¼ oz/¼ cup) caster (superfine) sugar
½ teaspoon natural vanilla extract
125 g (4½ oz/1 cup) plain (all-purpose) flour
60 g (2¼ oz/½ cup) self-raising flour

marshmallow topping
125 ml (4 fl oz/½ cup) passionfruit pulp
250 g (9 oz) white marshmallows
125 ml (4 fl oz/½ cup) milk
2 tablespoons caster (superfine) sugar
2 teaspoons lemon juice
315 ml (10¾ fl oz/1¼ cups) whipping cream, lightly whipped

Preheat the oven to 180°C (350°F/Gas 4). Lightly grease a 28 x 18 cm (11¼ x 7 inch) shallow baking tin and line with baking paper, making sure the paper overhangs on two opposite sides.

Using electric beaters, beat the butter and sugar in a mixing bowl until the mixture is light and creamy. Stir in the vanilla. Sift the flours into the bowl, then fold in and mix to a soft dough. Knead gently to bring together.

Press the dough into the prepared tin and smooth with the back of a spoon. Lightly prick the dough and bake for 25 minutes, or until golden. Leave to cool completely.

Put the passionfruit, marshmallows, milk and sugar in a saucepan and stir over low heat until the marshmallows melt. Stir in the juice and transfer to a bowl. Refrigerate, stirring occasionally, for 30 minutes, or until slightly thickened. Working quickly, fold in the cream, then pour over the slice and refrigerate overnight. Cut into pieces.

Top left: Apple and cinnamon slice. Top right: White chocolate and mango slice. Bottom right: Passionfruit marshmallow slice.

Pear and macadamia fingers

preparation 25 minutes + 30 minutes refrigeration
cooking 55 minutes
makes 20 pieces

90 g (3¼ oz/¾ cup) plain (all-purpose) flour
25 g (1 oz) unsalted butter, chopped
1½ tablespoons ground almonds
1½ tablespoons icing (confectioners') sugar
1 egg yolk
¼ teaspoon natural vanilla extract

macadamia topping
100 g (3½ oz/¾ cup) macadamia nuts, roughly chopped
185 g (6½ oz/1 cup lightly packed) soft brown sugar
150 g (5½ oz) unsalted butter, chopped
1 teaspoon natural vanilla extract
100 g (3½ oz) dried pears, chopped
50 g (1¾ oz) dark chocolate chips

Place the flour, butter, ground almonds and icing sugar in a food processor and process until the mixture is crumbly. Add the egg yolk, vanilla and 1–2 teaspoons cold water to make the dough just come together. Turn out, gather into a ball and cover with plastic wrap. Refrigerate for 30 minutes.

Preheat the oven to 180°C (350°F/Gas 4). Lightly grease a 20 cm (8 inch) square cake tin and line the base and sides with baking paper.

Roll out the dough to fit the base of the tin. Bake for 15 minutes, or until lightly browned. Leave to cool.

To make the macadamia topping, spread the macadamias on a baking tray and roast for 7 minutes, or until golden.

Put the brown sugar and butter in a saucepan and stir over low heat until the butter is melted and the sugar is dissolved. Bring to the boil, reduce the heat to low and cook for 1 minute, stirring. Remove from the heat and add the vanilla, pears, chocolate chips and macadamia nuts.

Spread the mixture over the pastry and bake for 30 minutes, or until bubbling all over. Leave the slice to cool completely in the tin before cutting into fingers.

Add the nuts, pears and chocolate chips and stir them into the caramel mixture.

Fruit and oat slice

preparation 20 minutes + 10 minutes standing
cooking 1 hour
makes 24 pieces

125 g (4½ oz) unsalted butter
95 g (3¼ oz/½ cup lightly packed) soft brown sugar
2 eggs, separated
160 g (5½ oz/1 cup) wholemeal (whole-wheat) self-raising flour
25 g (1 oz/¼ cup) wheatgerm

topping
35 g (1¼ oz) dried apricots, finely chopped
60 ml (2 fl oz/¼ cup) boiling water
425 g (15 oz) tinned pie apples (see Note)
1 small zucchini (courgette), grated
45 g (1½ oz) rolled (porridge) oats
45 g (1½ oz/½ cup) desiccated coconut
2 tablespoons honey

Preheat the oven to 180°C (350°F/Gas 4). Lightly grease a 30 x 20 cm (12 x 8 inch) shallow baking tin and line the base and sides with baking paper.

Using electric beaters, beat the butter and sugar in a large bowl until light and creamy. Add the egg yolks and beat until combined. Sift the flour into the mixture, return the husks to the bowl, and mix with a flat-bladed knife. Add the wheatgerm and mix until a soft dough forms. Press the mixture over the base of the prepared tin and smooth the surface. Bake for 12–15 minutes, or until golden.

Soak the apricots in the boiling water for 10 minutes, or until almost all the liquid is absorbed.

Spread the apple over the base. Combine the undrained apricots with the zucchini, oats, coconut and honey in a mixing bowl. Using electric beaters, beat the egg whites in a clean, dry mixing bowl until stiff peaks form, then gently fold into the mixture.

Spoon the mixture over the apples. Bake for 40–45 minutes, or until golden. Leave to cool in the tin, then cut into slices.

Note *Freshly cooked apples may be used instead of tinned apples, if you prefer.*

Bottom: Fruit and oat slice. Top: Pear and macadamia fingers.

Cherry slice

preparation 15 minutes
cooking 35 minutes
makes about 15 pieces

250 g (9 oz/2 cups) plain (all-purpose) flour
60 g (2¼ oz/½ cup) icing (confectioners') sugar
250 g (9 oz) unsalted butter, chopped

topping
30 g (1 oz) unsalted butter
90 g (3¼ oz/⅓ cup) caster (superfine) sugar
1 tablespoon milk
2 teaspoons natural vanilla extract
90 g (3¼ oz/¾ cup) chopped hazelnuts
150 g (5½ oz) sliced red glacé (candied) cherries

Preheat the oven to 210°C (415°F/Gas 6–7). Lightly grease a 28 x 18 cm (11¼ x 7 inch) shallow baking tin. Line the base with baking paper, making sure the paper overhangs on two opposite sides.

Sift the flour and icing sugar into a mixing bowl. Add the butter and, using your fingertips, rub in until a dough forms. Press into the prepared tin. Bake for 15 minutes, or until light golden brown.

To make the topping, melt the butter in a small saucepan and add the sugar, milk and vanilla. Stir, without boiling, until the sugar dissolves, then bring to the boil. Remove from the heat. Add the hazelnuts and cherries and stir.

Spread the topping over the base. Bake for 15–20 minutes, or until golden. Cut the slice into squares while still warm and cool before serving.

Apple crumble slice

preparation 20 minutes
cooking 40 minutes
makes 15 pieces

90 g (3¼ oz/¾ cup) self-raising flour
90 g (3¼ oz/¾ cup) plain (all-purpose) flour
90 g (3¼ oz/1 cup) desiccated coconut
250 g (9 oz) unsalted butter
140 g (5 oz/¾ cup lightly packed) soft brown sugar
410 g (14½ oz) tinned pie apples
35 g (1¼ oz/⅓ cup) rolled (porridge) oats
35 g (1¼ oz/¼ cup) currants
¼ teaspoon ground cinnamon

Preheat the oven to 180°C (350°F/Gas 4). Lightly grease a 27 x 18 cm (10¾ x 7 inch) shallow baking tin and line with baking paper, making sure the paper overhangs on two opposite sides.

Sift the flours into a large mixing bowl and add the coconut. Combine 200 g (7 oz) of the butter and the sugar in a small saucepan. Stir over low heat until the butter is melted and the sugar is dissolved. Remove from the heat and pour the mixture into the dry ingredients. Using a wooden spoon, stir until well combined.

Reserve 1 cup of the mixture. Press the remaining mixture into the prepared tin. Bake for 10 minutes and leave to cool completely.

Spread the pie apple over the base. Combine the reserved mixture, remaining butter, oats and currants. Using fingertips, crumble the mixture over the apple. Dust with the cinnamon. Bake for 20 minutes, or until the crumble is golden brown. Cool, lift from tin and cut into squares.

Remove the slice from the baking tin and cut into squares while it is still warm.

Using a wooden spoon, stir the melted butter and sugar into the sifted flour.

Bottom: Apple crumble slice. Top: Cherry slice.

Coconut pineapple squares

preparation 20 minutes
cooking 20 minutes
makes 12 squares

250 g (9 oz) oatmeal biscuits (cookies), crushed
90 g (3¼ oz/1½ cups) shredded coconut
250 g (9 oz) chopped glacé (candied) pineapple
90 g (3¼ oz/1 cup) flaked almonds
200 ml (7 fl oz) sweetened condensed milk
100 g (3½ oz) unsalted butter, melted

coconut icing
60 g (2¼ oz) unsalted butter, softened
few drops coconut essence
90 g (3¼ oz/¾ cup) icing (confectioners') sugar, sifted
1 tablespoon milk
90 g (3¼ oz) toasted flaked coconut (see Hint)

Preheat the oven to 180°C (350°F/Gas 4). Lightly grease a 27 x 18 cm (10¾ x 7 inch) shallow baking tin and line with baking paper, making sure the paper overhangs on two opposite sides.

Combine the crushed biscuits, coconut, pineapple and almonds in a large mixing bowl. Make a well in the centre of the ingredients and pour in the condensed milk and butter. Stir until well combined.

Press the mixture firmly into the prepared tin. Bake for 20 minutes, or until the top is lightly golden. Leave to cool in the tin.

To make the coconut icing (frosting), beat the butter and coconut essence with electric beaters in a mixing bowl until light and creamy. Add the icing sugar and milk. Beat until smooth and fluffy. Spread the icing evenly over the slice and sprinkle with the toasted coconut. Cut into squares.

Hint *Toast the coconut by simply spreading it on a baking tray and baking for 5 minutes, or until golden.*

This slice needs to be cooled in the baking tin rather than on a wire rack.

Raspberry linzer slice

preparation 30 minutes
cooking 45 minutes
makes 20 pieces

90 g (3¼ oz) unsalted butter
125 g (4½ oz/½ cup) caster (superfine) sugar
1 teaspoon natural vanilla extract
1 egg, lightly beaten
85 g (3 oz/⅔ cup) plain (all-purpose) flour
40 g (1½ oz/⅓ cup) self-raising flour
240 g (8½ oz/¾ cup) raspberry jam, warmed
icing (confectioners') sugar, to dust

hazelnut topping
125 g (4½ oz) unsalted butter
90 g (3¼ oz/⅓ cup) caster (superfine) sugar
1 egg, lightly beaten
60 g (2¼ oz/½ cup) plain (all-purpose) flour
1 tablespoon custard powder (if unavailable, substitute with instant vanilla pudding mix)
1 teaspoon baking powder
120 g (4¼ oz) plain cake crumbs
60 g (2¼ oz) ground hazelnuts
80 ml (2½ fl oz/⅓ cup) milk

Preheat the oven to 180°C (350°F/Gas 4). Lightly grease a 30 x 20 cm (12 x 8 inch) shallow baking tin and line with baking paper, making sure the paper overhangs on two opposite sides.

Using electric beaters, beat the butter, sugar and vanilla in a mixing bowl until light and creamy. Add the egg to the mixture, a little at a time, beating well after each addition.

Sift the flours and fold into the mixture with a metal spoon. Spread into the prepared tin and spread evenly with the raspberry jam.

To make the hazelnut topping, beat the butter and sugar with electric beaters until light and creamy. Add the egg gradually, beating well. Sift the flour, custard powder and baking powder and fold into the mixture with the cake crumbs and ground hazelnuts. Fold in the milk.

Spread the topping over the jam. Bake for 45 minutes, or until firm and golden brown. Leave to cool in the tin before cutting into pieces.

Bottom: Raspberry linzer slice. Top: Coconut pineapple squares.

Lamingtons

preparation 40 minutes + 1 hour standing
cooking 20 minutes
makes 60

4 eggs, at room temperature, separated
145 g (5 oz/⅔ cup) caster (superfine) sugar
2 tablespoons unsweetened cocoa powder
30 g (1 oz/¼ cup) plain (all-purpose) flour
30 g (1 oz/¼ cup) cornflour (cornstarch)
40 g (1½ oz/⅓ cup) self-raising flour

chocolate icing

375 g (13 oz/3 cups) icing (confectioners') sugar
60 g (2¼ oz/½ cup) unsweetened cocoa powder
90 g (3¼ oz) butter, chopped
185 ml (6 fl oz/¾ cup) boiling water
1 tablespoon instant coffee powder
270 g (9 ½ oz/3 cups) desiccated coconut

Preheat the oven to 180°C (350°F/Gas 4). Lightly grease a 30 x 20 cm (12 x 8 inch) shallow baking tin and line with baking paper, making sure the paper overhangs on two opposite sides.

Using electric beaters, beat the egg whites until soft peaks form. Add the sugar gradually, beating well after each addition. Beat until the sugar dissolves and the mixture is thick and glossy. Add the egg yolks and beat well. Gently fold through the sifted cocoa and flours.

Pour into the tin and smooth the surface. Bake for about 20 minutes, or until the cake is springy to the touch. Stand in the tin for 5 minutes before turning out onto a wire rack to cool. Cut into 3 cm (1¼ inch) squares.

To make the chocolate icing (frosting), sift together the icing sugar and cocoa. Stir in the butter, boiling water and coffee. Mix until smooth. Place the coconut on a large plate. Using two forks, dip the cake squares, one at a time, into the chocolate icing, toss in coconut and then place on a wire rack. Repeat until all the cake squares have been coated. Allow to stand at least 1 hour before serving.

Chocolate peanut slice

preparation 35 minutes + 15 minutes refrigeration
cooking 20 minutes
serves 8–10

250 g (9 oz) chocolate chip biscuits (cookies), finely crushed
130 g (4½ oz) unsalted butter, melted
45 g (1½ oz/¼ cup lightly packed) soft brown sugar
2 eggs, at room temperature
60 ml (2 fl oz/¼ cup) sweetened condensed milk
250 g (9 oz/1 cup) smooth peanut butter
150 g (5½ oz/1 cup) chopped dark chocolate, melted

Preheat the oven to 180°C (350°F/Gas 4). Lightly grease a 28 x 18 cm (11¼ x 7 inch) shallow baking tin and line with baking paper, making sure the paper overhangs on the two longest sides.

Combine the biscuit crumbs and half the melted butter. Press firmly into base of the tin. Refrigerate for 10–15 minutes, or until the mixture is firm.

Using electric beaters, beat the rest of butter and sugar until light and creamy. Add the eggs, condensed milk and peanut butter and mix until smooth. Spread evenly over the biscuit base. Bake for 15–20 minutes, or until lightly golden. Leave in the tin to cool.

Spread the melted chocolate over the cooled slice. Allow the chocolate to set, then remove the slice from the tin. Cut into bars.

Note *When melting the chocolate, take care not to let water come into contact with the melting mixture or it will begin to seize and start to harden immediately.*

78

Bottom: Chocolate peanut slice. Top: Lamingtons.

cookies

Chocolate meringue kisses

preparation 20 minutes
cooking 40 minutes
makes 25

2 egg whites, at room temperature
115 g (4 oz/½ cup) caster (superfine) sugar
¼ teaspoon ground cinnamon

filling
125 g (4½ oz) dark chocolate melts (buttons)
90 g (3¼ oz/⅓ cup) sour cream

Preheat the oven to 150°C (300°F/Gas 2). Lightly grease two baking trays and line with baking paper.

Using electric beaters, beat the egg whites in a clean, dry mixing bowl until soft peaks form. Gradually add the sugar, beating well after each addition. Beat until the sugar has dissolved and the mixture is thick and glossy. Add the cinnamon and beat well.

Transfer to a piping (icing) bag fitted with a 1 cm (½ inch) fluted nozzle. Pipe small stars of 1.5 cm (⅝ inch) diameter onto the trays 3 cm (1¼ inches) apart. Bake for 30 minutes, or until pale and crisp. Turn the oven off and cool with the door ajar.

To make the chocolate filling, put the chocolate and sour cream in a small heatproof bowl. Sit the bowl over a saucepan of simmering water. Stir until the chocolate has melted and the mixture is smooth. Remove from the heat and cool slightly.

Sandwich the meringues together with the filling.

Florentines

preparation 15 minutes
cooking 15 minutes
makes 12

55 g (2 oz) unsalted butter
45 g (1½ oz/¼ cup) soft brown sugar
2 teaspoons honey
25 g (1 oz/¼ cup) roughly chopped flaked almonds
2 tablespoons chopped dried apricots
2 tablespoons chopped glacé cherries
2 tablespoons mixed peel
40 g (1½ oz/⅓ cup) plain (all-purpose) flour, sifted
110 g (3¾ oz/¾ cup) dark chocolate

Preheat the oven to 180°C (350°F/Gas 4). Lightly grease two baking trays and line with baking paper.

Melt the butter, sugar and honey in a saucepan until the butter has melted and all the ingredients are combined. Remove from the heat and add the almonds, apricots, glacé cherries, mixed peel and the flour. Mix well.

Place level tablespoons of the mixture on the trays, allowing room for spreading. Reshape and flatten the biscuits into 5 cm (2 inch) rounds before cooking.

Bake for 10 minutes, or until lightly browned. Cool on the trays, then allow to cool completely on a wire rack.

Place the chocolate in a heatproof bowl and sit it over a saucepan of barely simmering water, making sure the base of the bowl does not touch the water. Stir until the chocolate has melted.

Spread the melted chocolate on the bottom of each florentine and, using a fork, make a wavy pattern in the chocolate before it sets. Let the chocolate set.

Crackle cookies

preparation 20 minutes + 3 hours refrigeration
cooking 25 minutes per batch
makes about 60

125 g (4½ oz) unsalted butter, softened
370 g (13 oz/2 cups firmly packed) soft brown sugar
2 eggs, at room temperature
1 teaspoon natural vanilla extract
60 g (2¼ oz) dark chocolate, melted
80 ml (2¾ fl oz/⅓ cup) milk
340 g (12 oz/2¾ cups) plain (all-purpose) flour
2 tablespoons unsweetened cocoa powder
2 teaspoons baking powder
¼ teaspoon ground allspice
85 g (3 oz/⅔ cup) chopped pecans
icing (confectioners') sugar, to coat

Lightly grease two baking trays and line with baking paper. Using electric beaters, beat the butter and sugar in a mixing bowl until the mixture is light and creamy. Add the eggs one at a time, beating well after each addition. Add the vanilla, chocolate and milk and beat until well combined.

Sift the flour, cocoa, baking powder, allspice and a pinch of salt into the bowl and mix well. Stir the pecans through. Refrigerate for at least 3 hours, or overnight.

Preheat the oven to 180°C (350°F/Gas 4). Roll tablespoons of the mixture into balls and roll each in sifted icing sugar. Place well apart on the trays to allow for spreading. Bake for 20–25 minutes, or until lightly browned and just firm. Leave on the trays for 4 minutes, then cool on a wire rack.

Note When melting the chocolate, take care not to let water come into contact with the mixture or it will begin to seize.

Top left: Chocolate meringue kisses. Top right: Florentines. Bottom right: Crackle cookies.

Choc-dipped macaroons

preparation 25 minutes
cooking 15–18 minutes
makes about 32

1 egg white
90 g (3¼ oz/⅓ cup) caster (superfine) sugar
2 teaspoons cornflour (cornstarch)
90 g (3¼ oz/1 cup) desiccated coconut
65 g (2¼ oz) dark chocolate

Preheat the oven to 160°C (315°F/Gas 2–3). Lightly grease two baking trays and line with baking paper.

Using electric beaters, beat the egg whites in a clean, dry mixing bowl until firm peaks form. Gradually add the sugar, beating well after each addition. Beat until the sugar has dissolved and the mixture is thick and glossy. Add the cornflour and beat until the ingredients are just combined.

Add the coconut to the egg white mixture. Using a metal spoon, stir until just combined. Roll heaped teaspoons of the mixture into balls and place on the prepared trays. Bake for 15–18 minutes, or until the macaroons are lightly golden. Remove from the oven and leave the macaroons to cool on the tray.

Place the chocolate in a heatproof bowl and sit it over a saucepan of barely simmering water, making sure the base of the bowl does not touch the water. Stir until the chocolate has melted. Dip the macaroons into the chocolate and allow the excess to drain. Place on a foil-lined tray and leave to set. Dust with cocoa powder if desired.

Hint *These are delicious served with a soft, creamy dessert.*

84

Roll the macaroon mixture into balls and place on the prepared trays.

Amaretti

preparation 15 minutes + 1 hour standing
cooking 20 minutes
makes 30

1 tablespoon plain (all-purpose) flour
1 tablespoon cornflour (cornstarch)
1 teaspoon ground cinnamon
160 g (5½ oz/⅔ cup) caster (superfine) sugar
95 g (3¼ oz/1 cup) ground almonds
1 teaspoon grated lemon zest
2 egg whites
30 g (1 oz/¼ cup) icing (confectioners') sugar

Lightly grease two baking trays and line with baking paper. Sift the flour, cornflour, cinnamon and half the caster sugar into a large bowl, then stir in the ground almonds and lemon zest.

Using electric beaters, beat the egg whites in a clean, dry mixing bowl until firm peaks form. Gradually add the remaining caster sugar, beating well after each addition. Beat until the sugar has dissolved and the mixture is thick and glossy. Using a metal spoon, fold the egg white mixture into the dry ingredients and stir until the ingredients are just combined.

Roll 2 level teaspoons of mixture at a time with oiled or wetted hands into balls and arrange on the trays, allowing room for spreading. Set the trays aside, uncovered, for 1 hour.

Preheat the oven to 180°C (350°F/Gas 4). Sift the icing sugar liberally over the uncooked biscuits, then bake for 15–20 minutes, or until crisp and lightly browned. Transfer to a wire rack and leave to cool completely.

Using a metal spoon, gently fold the egg white mixture into the dry ingredients.

Bottom: Amaretti. Top: Choc-dipped macaroons.

Vanilla custard kisses

preparation 15 minutes
cooking 12 minutes
makes 26

125 g (4½ oz) unsalted butter
125 g (4½ oz/½ cup) caster (superfine) sugar
2 egg yolks, lightly beaten
2 teaspoons natural vanilla extract
60 g (2¼ oz/½ cup) custard powder (if unavailable,
substitute with instant vanilla pudding mix)
250 g (9 oz/2 cups) plain (all-purpose) flour

vanilla cream
40 g (1½ oz) unsalted butter, softened
1 teaspoon natural vanilla extract
90 g (3¼ oz/¾ cup) icing (confectioners') sugar
1 tablespoon milk

Preheat the oven to 180°C (350°F/Gas 4). Lightly grease two baking trays and line with baking paper.

Using electric beaters, beat the butter and sugar in a small mixing bowl until the mixture is light and creamy. Add the egg yolks gradually, beating the mixture thoroughly after each addition. Add the vanilla and beat until combined.

Transfer the mixture to a large mixing bowl. Using a metal spoon, fold in the sifted custard powder and flour. Stir until the ingredients are just combined and the mixture is almost smooth. Press the mixture together with fingertips to form a soft dough.

Roll 1 level teaspoon of mixture at a time into balls. Arrange about 5 cm (2 inches) apart on the prepared trays. Flatten lightly with the base of a glass into 2.5 cm (1 inch) rounds. Bake for 12 minutes, or until golden.

To make the vanilla cream, beat the butter and vanilla in a small bowl with a wooden spoon until smooth. Add the sifted icing sugar and milk gradually, stirring until the mixture is smooth. Leave the biscuits on the trays for 5 minutes then transfer to a wire rack to cool. Spread half the biscuits with vanilla cream and sandwich together with the remaining biscuits.

Peanut butter cookies

preparation 25 minutes
cooking 10 minutes
makes about 40

185 g (6½ oz/1½ cups) plain (all-purpose) flour
75 g (2½ oz/½ cup) self-raising flour
90 g (3¼ oz/1 cup) rolled (porridge) oats
125 g (4½ oz) unsalted butter
110 g (3¾ oz/½ cup) caster (superfine) sugar
120 g (4¼ oz/⅓ cup) honey
2 tablespoons peanut butter

topping
120 g (4¼ oz/¾ cup) icing (confectioners') sugar
25 g (1 oz) unsalted butter, softened
1 tablespoon warm water
150 g (5½ oz/1 cup) roasted unsalted peanuts, finely chopped

Preheat the oven to 180°C (350°F/Gas 4). Lightly grease two baking trays and line with baking paper.

Sift the flours into a large mixing bowl and stir in the oats.

Combine the butter, sugar, honey and peanut butter in a saucepan and stir over medium heat until melted. Add to the flour mixture. Using a metal spoon, stir to just combine the ingredients. Roll heaped teaspoons of mixture into balls. Arrange on the prepared trays and press lightly to flatten. Bake for 10 minutes, or until golden. Cool the cookies on the trays.

To make the topping, combine the icing sugar, butter and water in a small bowl. Stir until smooth. Dip the tops of the cookies into the topping, then into the nuts.

Pour the melted honey–peanut butter mixture into the dry ingredients.

Bottom: Peanut butter cookies. Top: Vanilla custard kisses.

Jam drops

preparation 20 minutes
cooking 10–12 minutes
makes 26

80 g (2¾ oz) unsalted butter, softened
90 g (3¼ oz/⅓ cup) caster (superfine) sugar
2 tablespoons milk
½ teaspoon natural vanilla extract
175 g (6 oz/1½ cups) plain (all-purpose) flour
40 g (1½ oz/⅓ cup) custard powder (if unavailable,
substitute with instant vanilla pudding mix)
105 g (3½ oz/⅓ cup) raspberry jam

Preheat the oven to 180°C (350°F/Gas 4). Lightly grease two baking trays and line with baking paper.

Using electric beaters, beat the butter and sugar in a mixing bowl until the mixture is light and creamy. Add the milk and vanilla and beat until well combined. Add the sifted flour and custard powder and mix with a flat-bladed knife to form a soft dough.

Roll heaped teaspoons of the mixture into balls and place on the prepared trays.

Make an indentation in each ball using the end of a wooden spoon. Fill each hole with a little jam.

Bake the biscuits for 10–12 minutes, or until lightly golden. Cool slightly on the trays, then transfer to a wire rack to cool completely.

Pecan maple shortbreads

preparation 30 minutes
cooking 20 minutes
makes about 20

125 g (4½ oz/1 cup) plain (all-purpose) flour
60 g (2¼ oz/½ cup) ground pecans
2 tablespoons icing (confectioners') sugar
90 g (3¼ oz) unsalted butter, chopped
2 tablespoons maple syrup
50 g (1¾ oz/⅓ cup) white chocolate melts (buttons), melted

Preheat the oven to 180°C (350°F/Gas 4). Lightly grease a baking tray and line with baking paper.

Place the flour, pecans, icing sugar and butter in a food processor and process for 1 minute or until the mixture comes together.

Turn onto a lightly floured surface, and press together to form a smooth dough. Roll out on a sheet of baking paper

to a thickness of 5 mm (¼ inch). Using a 4 cm (1½ inch) heart-shaped cutter, cut out shapes.

Transfer to the prepared tray, bake for 10 minutes and remove from the oven. Brush each shortbread generously with the maple syrup and bake for another 8–10 minutes. Transfer to a wire rack to cool completely. Spoon the white chocolate into a small piping (icing) bag and pipe around the edge of the biscuits.

Note *When melting the chocolate, take care not to let water come into contact with the melting mixture or it will begin to seize and start to harden immediately.*

Chocolate butter fingers

preparation 30 minutes
cooking 15 minutes
makes 40

125 g (4½ oz) unsalted butter
40 g (1½ oz/⅓ cup) icing (confectioners') sugar
½ teaspoon natural vanilla extract
½ teaspoon grated lemon zest
1 teaspoon cream
60 g (2¼ oz/½ cup) cornflour (cornstarch)
80 g (2¾ oz/⅔ cup) plain (all-purpose) flour
60 g (2¼ oz) chocolate melts (buttons), melted

Preheat the oven to 180°C (350°F/Gas 4). Lightly grease two baking trays and line with baking paper.

Using electric beaters, beat the butter and sugar until light and creamy. Add the vanilla, lemon zest and cream, and beat until combined. Add the sifted flours and beat until the mixture is smooth enough for piping.

Spoon the mixture into a piping (icing) bag fitted with a 1.5 cm (⅝ inch) star nozzle. Pipe 4 cm (1½ inch) lengths onto the prepared trays. Bake the biscuits for 15 minutes, or until lightly golden. Cool the biscuits on the trays before transferring to a wire rack.

Place the melted chocolate into a small paper piping (icing) bag and snip off the tip. Drizzle diagonally over the fingers. Allow to set.

Storage *These biscuits can be made up to 3 days in advance. Store in an airtight container in a cool, dark place.*

Notes *Decorate with dark or white chocolate, or dust with combined icing sugar and cocoa.*

When melting the chocolate, take care not to let water come into contact with the melting mixture or it will begin to seize and start to harden immediately.

Top left: Jam drops. Top right: Pecan maple shortbreads. Bottom right: Chocolate butter fingers.

Monte creams

preparation 30 minutes
cooking 20 minutes
makes 13

125 g (4½ oz) unsalted butter
125 g (4½ oz/½ cup) caster (superfine) sugar
60 ml (2 fl oz/¼ cup) milk
220 g (7¾ oz/1¾ cups) plain (all-purpose) flour
30 g (1 oz/¼ cup) custard powder (if unavailable,
substitute with instant vanilla pudding mix)
30 g (1 oz/⅓ cup) desiccated coconut

filling
75 g (2½ oz) unsalted butter, softened
90 g (3¼ oz/¾ cup) icing (confectioners') sugar
2 teaspoons milk
105 g (3½ oz/⅓ cup) strawberry jam

Preheat the oven to 180°C (350°F/Gas 4). Lightly grease two baking trays and line with baking paper.

Using electric beaters, beat the butter and sugar in a mixing bowl until the mixture is light and creamy. Add the milk and beat until combined. Sift the flour and custard powder together and add to the bowl with the coconut. Mix to form a soft dough.

Roll the mixture into balls using 1 heaped teaspoon at a time. Place on the prepared trays, making sure they are spaced enough to allow for spreading during baking, and press with a fork. Dip the fork in custard powder occasionally to prevent it from sticking. Bake for 15–20 minutes, or until just golden. Transfer the biscuits to a wire rack to cool completely before filling.

For the filling, beat the butter and icing sugar in a small bowl with electric beaters until light and creamy. Beat in the milk. Spread one biscuit with ½ teaspoon of the filling and one with ½ teaspoon of jam, then press them together.

Two-tone biscuits

preparation 30 minutes + 20 minutes refrigeration
cooking 10–12 minutes
makes about 25

125 g (4½ oz) unsalted butter
90 g (3¼ oz/¾ cup) icing (confectioners') sugar
1 egg, at room temperature
200 g (7 oz/1⅔ cups) plain (all-purpose) flour
1 tablespoon cornflour (cornstarch)
2 tablespoons unsweetened cocoa powder
50 g (1¾ oz) dark chocolate, melted

Preheat the oven to 180°C (350°F/Gas 4). Lightly grease two baking trays and line with baking paper.

Using electric beaters, beat the butter and icing sugar in a large mixing bowl until light and creamy. Add the egg and beat until smooth. Add the sifted plain flour and cornflour and mix with a flat-bladed knife until well combined.

Divide the mixture evenly between two bowls. Only add the cocoa powder and melted chocolate to one portion, then mix both until well combined. Wrap the dough portions separately in plastic wrap and refrigerate for 20 minutes, or until firm.

Roll the dough portions separately between sheets of baking paper until 5 mm (¼ inch) thick. Use two sizes of cookie cutter of the same shape. Cut large shapes from each sheet of dough, then take the smaller cutter and cut a shape from inside the larger dough shape; swap inner shapes and assemble to make two-tone biscuits. Place on the prepared trays and bake for 10–12 minutes, or until just golden. Cool on the tray.

Note *When melting the chocolate, take care not to let water come into contact with the melting mixture or it will begin to seize and start to harden immediately.*

Sandwich the cooled biscuits together with the jam and butter mixture.

Assemble the biscuits by placing smaller shapes inside bigger pieces of a different colour.

Bottom: Two-tone biscuits. Top: Monte creams.

Lebkuchen

preparation 25 minutes
cooking 30 minutes
makes 40

350 g (12 oz/2¾ cups) plain (all-purpose) flour
60 g (2¼ oz/½ cup) cornflour (cornstarch)
2 teaspoons unsweetened cocoa powder
1 teaspoon mixed (pumpkin pie) spice
1 teaspoon ground cinnamon
½ teaspoon freshly grated nutmeg
100 g (3½ oz) unsalted butter, cubed
260 g (9¼ oz/¾ cup) golden syrup (if unavailable, substitute with half honey and half dark corn syrup)
2 tablespoons milk
150 g (5½ oz/1 cup) white chocolate melts (buttons)
¼ teaspoon mixed (pumpkin pie) spice, extra, to sprinkle

Preheat the oven to 180°C (350°F/Gas 4). Lightly grease two baking trays and line with baking paper.

Sift the plain flour, cornflour, cocoa and spices into a large bowl and make a well in the centre.

Place the butter, golden syrup and milk in a small saucepan, and stir over low heat until the butter has melted and the mixture is smooth. Remove from the heat and add to the dry ingredients. Mix with a flat-bladed knife until the ingredients come together in small beads. Gather together with your hands and turn out onto a sheet of baking paper.

Roll the dough out to about 7 mm (⅜ inch) thick. Cut into heart shapes using a 6 cm (2½ inch) cookie cutter. Place on

the prepared trays and bake for 20 minutes, or until lightly browned. Cool slightly, then transfer to a wire rack until the biscuits are completely cool.

Place the chocolate in a heatproof bowl and sit it over a saucepan of barely simmering water, making sure the base of the bowl does not touch the water. Stir until the chocolate has melted.

Dip one half of each biscuit into the chocolate and place on a sheet of baking paper until set. Sprinkle with mixed spice.

Storage *These biscuits can be stored in an airtight container for up to 5 days.*

Carefully transfer the dough shapes to the prepared baking trays using a flat-bladed knife.

Dip one half of each biscuit into the melted chocolate and place on a sheet of baking paper.

Chocolate tuiles

preparation 15 minutes
cooking 35 minutes
makes 12

1 egg white, at room temperature
60 g (2¼ oz/¼ cup) caster (superfine) sugar
2 tablespoons plain (all-purpose) flour
30 g (1 oz) unsalted butter, melted
1 teaspoon natural vanilla extract
60 g (2 oz) dark chocolate melts (buttons), melted

Preheat the oven to 180°C (350°F/Gas 4). Lightly grease two baking trays and line with baking paper. Draw two 10 cm (4 inch) circles on each sheet of paper.

Combine the egg white, sugar, flour, butter and vanilla until a paste forms. Place the chocolate in a paper piping (icing) bag, seal the end and snip off the tip. Drizzle the chocolate over the baking paper in swirls, following the marked circles. Allow the chocolate to set.

Spread 1½ teaspoons of the egg mixture over the circles. Bake the tuiles, one tray at a time, for 4–6 minutes, or until the edges are just turning golden.

Remove from the oven and quickly shape each circle over a rolling pin. Repeat until you have finished with all of the mixture. Cool the tuiles until crisp.

Note When melting the chocolate, take care not to let water come into contact with the melting mixture or it will begin to seize and start to harden immediately.

Brazil nut and coffee biscotti

preparation 20 minutes
cooking 45 minutes
makes 40 pieces

3 teaspoons instant coffee powder
1 tablespoon dark rum, warmed
2 eggs, at room temperature
125 g (4½ oz/½ cup) caster (superfine) sugar
155 g (5½ oz/1¼ cups) plain (all-purpose) flour
60 g (2¼ oz/½ cup) self-raising flour
1 teaspoon ground cinnamon
105 g (3½ oz/¾ cup) Brazil nuts, roughly chopped
1 tablespoon caster (superfine) sugar, extra

Preheat the oven to 180°C (350°F/Gas 4). Lightly grease a baking tray and line with baking paper.

Dissolve the coffee in the rum. Beat the eggs and sugar until thick and creamy, then beat in the coffee. Sift the flours and cinnamon into a bowl, then stir in the nuts. Mix in the egg mixture.

Divide the mixture into two rolls, each about 28 cm (11¼ inches) long. Put the rolls on the tray and press lightly to flatten to about 6 cm (2½ inches) across. Brush lightly with water and sprinkle with the extra sugar. Bake for 25 minutes, or until firm and light brown. Cool until warm on the tray. Reduce the oven temperature to 160°C (315°F/Gas 2–3).

Cut into 1 cm (½ inch) thick diagonal slices. Bake in a single layer on the lined tray for 20 minutes, or until dry, turning once. Cool on a rack.

Storage These biscuits store for a long time: 2–3 weeks if kept in an airtight container.

Sultana and chocolate cornflake cookies

preparation 30 minutes
cooking 15 minutes
makes 40

60 g (2¼ oz/⅓ cup) dark chocolate chips
60 g (2¼ oz/½ cup) sultanas (golden raisins)
30 g (1 oz/¼ cup) roughly chopped walnuts
1 teaspoon grated orange zest
125 g (4½ oz) unsalted butter, chopped
80 g (2¾ oz/⅓ cup) caster (superfine) sugar
1 egg, at room temperature
125 g (4½ oz/1 cup) self-raising flour, sifted
80 g (2¾ oz/2⅔ cups) cornflakes, lightly crushed
80 g (2⅔ oz/½ cup) dark chocolate, melted

Preheat the oven to 180°C (350°F/Gas 4). Lightly grease two baking trays and line with baking paper.

Combine the chocolate chips, sultanas, chopped walnuts and orange zest.

Using electric beaters, beat the butter and sugar until very light and creamy. Add the egg and beat well. Transfer to a large bowl. Using a metal spoon, fold in the flour. Add the sultana mixture and stir well.

Roll 2 level teaspoons of the mixture in the crushed cornflakes to coat. Bake for 15 minutes, or until golden and crisp. Transfer to a wire rack to cool. To serve, drizzle melted chocolate over the cooled cookies.

Note When melting the chocolate, take care not to let water come into contact with the melting mixture or it will begin to seize and start to harden immediately.

Top left: Chocolate tuiles. Top right: Brazil nut and coffee biscotti. Bottom right: Sultana and chocolate cornflake cookies.

Coconut macaroons

preparation 15 minutes
cooking 15–20 minutes
makes 45

3 egg whites
250 g (9 oz/1 cup) caster (superfine) sugar
½ teaspoon coconut essence
1 teaspoon grated lemon zest
2 tablespoons cornflour (cornstarch), sifted
180 g (6 oz/2 cups) desiccated coconut

Preheat the oven to 180°C (350°F/Gas 4). Lightly grease two baking trays and line with baking paper.

Using electric beaters, beat the egg whites in a clean, dry mixing bowl until firm peaks form. Gradually add the sugar, beating well after each addition. Beat until the sugar has dissolved and the mixture is thick and glossy. Add the coconut essence and lemon zest and beat until just combined.

Transfer the mixture to a large mixing bowl and add the cornflour and coconut. Using a metal spoon, stir until just combined.

Drop 2 level teaspoons of mixture onto the prepared trays about 3 cm (1¼ inch) apart. Bake on the top shelf of the oven for 15–20 minutes, or until golden. Leave the macaroons to cool completely on the trays.

Hints: *Sprinkle biscuits with shredded coconut before baking. Drizzle with melted chocolate before serving.*

Chocolate lemon swirls

preparation 12 minutes
cooking 12–15 minutes
makes about 40

125 g (4½ oz) unsalted butter
85 g (3 oz/⅔ cup) icing (confectioners') sugar
1 egg, lightly beaten
2 teaspoons finely grated lemon zest (see Variation)
155 g (5½ oz/1¼ cups) plain (all-purpose) flour
25 g (1 oz/¼ cup) unsweetened cocoa powder
2 tablespoons mixed peel (mixed candied citrus peel)

Preheat the oven to 180°C (350°F/Gas 4). Lightly grease two baking trays and line with baking paper.

Using electric beaters, beat the butter and icing sugar until light and creamy. Add the egg and lemon zest, and beat until well combined.

Add the flour and cocoa. Using a metal spoon, stir until the ingredients are just combined.

Spoon the mixture into a piping (icing) bag fitted with a fluted 1 cm (½ inch) piping nozzle and pipe swirls about 3 cm (1¼ inch) in diameter onto the prepared trays. Top each swirl with a few pieces of the mixed peel. Bake for 12–15 minutes. Leave the biscuits to cool on the trays.

Variation *You can use orange zest in place of the lemon zest, if you prefer.*

Scottish shortbread

preparation 25 minutes + 20 minutes refrigeration
cooking 30–35 minutes
makes two 20 cm (8 inch) rounds

275 g (9¾ oz/2¼ cups) plain (all-purpose) flour
125 g (4½ oz/⅔ cup) rice flour
250 g (9 oz) unsalted butter, softened
125 g (4½ oz/½ cup) caster (superfine) sugar
1 teaspoon sugar, to decorate

Preheat the oven to 160°C (315°F/Gas 2–3). Lightly grease two baking trays and line with baking paper. Mark a 20 cm (8 inch) circle on each piece of baking paper and turn the paper over.

Sift the flours into a large mixing bowl and add the butter and sugar. Using your fingertips, rub the butter into the flour mixture until a soft dough forms. Add a pinch of salt and gather together. Divide the dough into two portions, then wrap in plastic wrap and refrigerate for 20 minutes.

Place one dough portion on each tray and press into a round, using the drawn circle as a guide. Pinch and flute the edges decoratively and prick the surface with a fork. Use a knife to mark each circle into 12 segments. Sprinkle with the sugar and bake for 30–35 minutes, until firm and pale golden. Leave to cool on the trays then break into scored wedges to serve.

Note *Usually no liquid is used, but if the dough is very crumbly, add not more than 1 tablespoon of milk or cream.*

Top left: Coconut macaroons. Top right: Chocolate lemon swirls. Bottom right: Scottish shortbread.

Jaffa rings

preparation 30 minutes
cooking 20 minutes
makes about 45

180 g (6 oz) unsalted butter
125 g (4½ oz/½ cup) caster (superfine) sugar
1 egg, lightly beaten
1½ teaspoons finely grated orange zest
50 g (1¾ oz) milk chocolate, grated
125 g (4½ oz/1 cup) self-raising flour
250 g (9 oz/2 cups) plain (all-purpose) flour
100 g (3½ oz) milk chocolate melts (buttons) (see Hint)

Preheat the oven to 180°C (350°F/Gas 4). Lightly grease two baking trays and line with baking paper.

Using electric beaters, beat the butter, sugar and egg in a large mixing bowl until light and creamy. Add the orange zest and grated chocolate and beat until well combined.

Sift in the flours and use a flat-bladed knife to mix into a soft dough. Turn onto a lightly floured surface and knead for 30 seconds or until the dough is smooth.

Roll 3 teaspoonfuls of mixture into small oblongs. Continue rolling into lengths of 20 cm (8 inch). Carefully fold in half and twist. Form the twisted rope into a ring. Place on the prepared trays. Bake for 12–15 minutes and transfer to a wire rack to cool.

Place the chocolate melts in a heatproof bowl and sit it over a saucepan of barely simmering water, making sure the base of the bowl does not touch the water. Stir until the chocolate has melted. Cool slightly. Dip bases of the biscuits into the melted chocolate. Stand the biscuits on a wire rack to set.

Hint *To decorate these biscuits quickly, the melted chocolate can be simply drizzled off the end of the prongs of a fork.*

Orange and almond tuiles

preparation 30 minutes
cooking 10 minutes
makes about 15

90 g (3¼ oz) unsalted butter
90 g (3¼ oz/⅓ cup) caster (superfine) sugar
30 g (1 oz/¼ cup) plain (all-purpose) flour
25 g (1 oz/¼ cup) flaked almonds, crushed slightly
1 tablespoon finely chopped mixed peel (mixed candied citrus peel)

Preheat the oven to 180°C (350°F/Gas 4). Lightly grease a large baking tray and dust lightly with flour.

Using electric beaters, beat the butter and sugar in a small mixing bowl until light and creamy. Add the flour and stir until combined. Add the flaked almonds and mixed peel. Stir until well combined.

Cook in batches. Place heaped teaspoonfuls of the mixture about 10 cm (4 inches) apart on the prepared tray. Spread each spoonful of the mixture out into a 5 cm (2 inch) circle. Bake for 10 minutes or until golden.

Remove the tray from the oven and stand for 1 minute. Carefully lift each circle off the tray with a flat-bladed knife and drape immediately over a rolling pin to curl. Leave to cool on the rolling pin. Repeat with the remaining circles.

Hint *Cook only about 4–6 tuiles at a time, as they cool and harden very quickly. Grease and flour the tray again before baking each batch.*

Roll the dough into lengths before folding in half and plaiting together.

Leave the tuiles to cool on the rolling pin and they will retain their curled shape.

Bottom: Orange and almond tuiles. Top: Jaffa rings.

Afghans

preparation 20 minutes
cooking 20 minutes.
makes 25

150 g (5½ oz) unsalted butter, softened
60 g (2¼ oz/⅓ cup lightly packed) soft brown sugar
1 egg, lightly beaten
1 teaspoon natural vanilla extract
125 g (4½ oz/1 cup) plain (all-purpose) flour
2 tablespoons unsweetened cocoa powder
30 g (1 oz/⅓ cup) desiccated coconut
45 g (1½ oz/1½ cups) cornflakes, lightly crushed
90 g (3¼ oz/½ cup) dark chocolate chips

Preheat the oven to 180°C (350°F/Gas 4). Lightly grease two baking trays and line with baking paper.

Using electric beaters, beat the butter and sugar in a mixing bowl until the mixture is light and creamy. Add the egg and vanilla and beat well.

Sift the flour and cocoa powder into the bowl, then add the coconut and cornflakes. Stir with a metal spoon until the ingredients are just combined. Put level tablespoons of mixture on the prepared trays, allowing room for spreading. Bake for 20 minutes, or until lightly browned, then leave on the tray to cool completely.

Place the chocolate chips in a heatproof bowl and sit it over a saucepan of barely simmering water, making sure the base of the bowl does not touch the water. Stir until the chocolate has melted. Spread the top of each biscuit thickly with the melted chocolate and allow to set.

Orange poppy seed cookies

preparation 30 minutes
cooking 10 minutes
makes 30

75 g (2½ oz) unsalted butter
185 g (6½ oz/¾ cup) caster (superfine) sugar
1 egg, at room temperature
1½ teaspoons finely grated orange zest
2 teaspoons orange juice
200 g (7 oz/1⅔ cups) plain (all-purpose) flour
35 g (1¼ oz/¼ cup) cornflour (cornstarch)
¼ teaspoon bicarbonate of soda (baking soda)
1 tablespoon buttermilk
2 tablespoons poppy seeds
185 g (6½ oz/1¼ cups) white chocolate melts (buttons)

Preheat the oven to 180°C (350°F/Gas 4). Lightly grease two baking trays and line with baking paper.

Using electric beaters, beat the butter and sugar in a small mixing bowl until the mixture is light and creamy. Add egg and orange zest and juice and beat until combined. Transfer the mixture to a medium bowl.

Sift the flour, cornflour and bicarbonate of soda into the bowl, then add the buttermilk and poppy seeds. Using a metal spoon, mix to a soft dough.

Drop the mixture, 2 teaspoons at a time, onto the prepared trays. Press a white chocolate melt into the centre of each cookie. Bake for 10 minutes, or until just golden. Cool the cookies on trays for 5 minutes before transferring to a wire rack to cool completely.

Hint *These cookies are also delicious if topped with an orange glaze icing, if desired.*

Drop level tablespoons of the mixture onto the prepared baking trays.

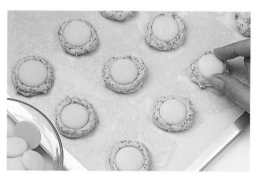

Firmly press a white chocolate melt into the centre of each cookie before baking.

Bottom: Orange poppy seed cookies. Top: Afghans.

Choc-vanilla creams

preparation 45 minutes
cooking 10 minutes
makes 10

125 g (4½ oz) unsalted butter
40 g (1½ oz/⅓ cup) icing (confectioners') sugar
175 g (6 oz/1½ cups) plain (all-purpose) flour
2 tablespoons unsweetened cocoa powder
120 g (4¼ oz/⅔ cup) chocolate sprinkles
icing (confectioners') sugar, to dust

vanilla cream
75 g (2½ oz) unsalted butter
85 g (3 oz/⅔ cup) icing (confectioners') sugar
1 teaspoon natural vanilla extract

Preheat the oven to 180°C (350°F/Gas 4). Lightly grease a baking tray and line with baking paper.

Using electric beaters, beat the butter and sugar in a small mixing bowl until light and creamy. Sift the flour and cocoa into the bowl and, using a metal spoon, mix to a soft dough. Roll the mixture into balls using 2 teaspoons at a time. Using the base of a glass, press into 4 cm (1½ inch) rounds. Place on the prepared tray. Bake for 10 minutes. Transfer to a wire rack to cool before decorating.

To make the vanilla cream, beat the butter and sugar until light and creamy. Add the vanilla and beat until well combined.

To assemble the biscuits, spread one biscuit with the vanilla cream and place another on top. Spread vanilla cream around the join.

Place the chocolate sprinkles on a plate and roll each biscuit on the side to coat the join. Dust with sifted icing sugar.

Choc-hazelnut scrolls

preparation 25 minutes + 30 minutes refrigeration
cooking 15 minutes
makes 35

250 g (9 oz/2 cups) plain (all-purpose) flour
60 g (2¼ oz/½ cup) ground hazelnuts
100 g (3½ oz) unsalted butter
125 g (4½ oz/½ cup) caster (superfine) sugar
1 egg, lightly beaten
2 tablespoons iced water
80 g (2¾ oz/¼ cup) chocolate hazelnut spread

Lightly grease two baking trays and line with baking paper. Place the flour and hazelnuts in a food processor and add the butter and sugar. Process until the mixture resembles fine breadcrumbs. Add the combined egg and water and process until the mixture forms a dough. Turn out onto a lightly floured surface and knead for 30 seconds or until the dough is smooth.

Place the dough onto a large sheet of baking paper and roll out into a 25 x 35 cm (10 x 14 inch) rectangle. Trim the edges. Spread the dough evenly with the chocolate hazelnut spread. Using the baking paper to lift the dough, roll up from the long side in Swiss-roll style. Wrap tightly in baking paper and refrigerate for 30 minutes.

Preheat the oven to 180°C (350°F/Gas 4). Cut the roll into 1 cm (½ inch) slices, wiping the knife's blade clean between each cut. Place the slices on the prepared baking trays and bake for 15 minutes or until golden. Transfer the biscuits to a wire rack to cool.

Roll the assembled biscuit in chocolate sprinkles, making sure the join is well covered.

Cut the roll into neat slices, making sure to wipe the blade clean between each cut.

Bottom: Choc-hazelnut scrolls. Top: Choc-vanilla creams.

Gingerbread people

preparation 40 minutes + 15 minutes refrigeration
cooking 10 minutes
makes 8

125 g (4½ oz) unsalted butter, softened
60 g (2¼ oz/⅓ cup lightly packed) soft brown sugar
90 g (3¼ oz/¼ cup) golden syrup (if unavailable, substitute with half honey and half dark corn syrup)
1 egg, lightly beaten
300 g (10½ oz/2½ cups) plain (all-purpose) flour
1 tablespoon ground ginger
1 teaspoon bicarbonate of soda (baking soda)
1 tablespoon currants

icing
1 egg white
½ teaspoon lemon juice
155 g (5½ oz/1¼ cups) icing (confectioners') sugar
assorted food colourings

Preheat the oven to 180°C (350°F/Gas 4). Lightly grease two baking trays and line with baking paper.

Using electric beaters, beat the butter, sugar and golden syrup in a large mixing bowl until the mixture is light and creamy. Add the egg gradually, beating well after each addition.

Sift the dry ingredients over the butter mixture and mix with a flat-bladed knife until just combined. Combine the dough with your hands. Turn onto a well-floured surface and knead for 1–2 minutes, or until smooth. Roll out on a board, between two sheets of baking paper, to 5 mm (¼ inch) thick. Refrigerate on the board for 15 minutes to firm.

Cut the dough into shapes with a 13 cm (5 inch) gingerbread person cutter. Press the remaining dough together and re-roll. Cut out shapes and place the biscuits on the trays. Place the currants as eyes and noses. Bake for 10 minutes, or until lightly browned. Cool on the trays.

To make the icing (frosting), beat the egg white with electric beaters in a small, clean, dry bowl until foamy. Gradually add the lemon juice and icing sugar and beat until thick. Divide the icing among several bowls and add the food colourings. Spoon into small paper piping (icing) bags. Seal the ends, snip the tips off the bags and pipe on faces and clothing as desired.

Use a cookie cutter to cut out the gingerbread person shape from the dough.

Snip the tip off the piping (icing) bag to decorate the gingerbread people.

Citrus cookies

preparation 20 minutes
cooking 15 minutes
makes about 30

125 g (4½ oz) unsalted butter
90 g (3¼ oz/¾ cup) icing (confectioners') sugar, sifted
185 g (6½ oz/1½ cups) plain (all-purpose) flour
2 teaspoons finely grated lime zest
2 teaspoons finely grated lemon zest
80 g (2¾ oz/⅓ cup) sour cream
1 tablespoon lemon juice

orange icing
150 g (5½ oz/1¼ cups) icing (confectioners') sugar
2 teaspoons finely grated orange zest
2 tablespoons orange juice

Preheat the oven to 180°C (350°F/Gas 4). Lightly grease two baking trays and line with baking paper.

Place the butter, icing sugar, flour and lime and lemon zest in a food processor. Process for 10 seconds or until the mixture resembles fine breadcrumbs. Add the sour cream and lemon juice and process for 10 seconds or until the mixture is well combined.

Drop level tablespoons of mixture onto the prepared trays, allowing room for spreading. Bake for 15 minutes, or until lightly golden. Cool completely on a wire rack.

To make the orange icing (frosting), combine the icing sugar, zest and juice in a bowl. Stand the bowl over a saucepan of simmering water, stirring until the icing is smooth and glossy. Spread the icing over the cookies with a flat-bladed knife.

Storage *These biscuits will store for up to 2 months in the freezer, without icing.*

Cornflake cookies

preparation 15 minutes
cooking 20 minutes
makes 36

125 g (4½ oz) unsalted butter, softened
185 g (6½ oz/¾ cup) sugar
2 eggs, lightly beaten
1 teaspoon natural vanilla extract
2 tablespoons currants
135 g (4¾ oz/1½ cups) desiccated coconut
½ teaspoon bicarbonate of soda (baking soda)
½ teaspoon baking powder
250 g (9 oz/2 cups) plain (all-purpose) flour
90 g (3¼ oz/3 cups) cornflakes, lightly crushed (see Note)

Preheat the oven to 180°C (350°F/Gas 4). Lightly grease two baking trays and line with baking paper.

Using electric beaters, beat the butter and sugar in a mixing bowl until the mixture is light and creamy. Add the eggs a little at a time, beating well after each addition. Add the vanilla and beat until well combined.

Transfer the mixture to a large bowl and stir in the currants and desiccated coconut. Fold in the sifted bicarbonate of soda, baking powder and flour with a metal spoon and stir until the mixture is almost smooth. Put the cornflakes in a shallow dish, drop level tablespoons of mixture onto the cornflakes and roll into balls. Arrange on the trays, allowing room for spreading.

Bake for 15–20 minutes, or until crisp and golden. Cool slightly on the tray, then transfer to a wire rack to cool. When completely cold, store in an airtight container.

Note *A mess-free method for crushing cornflakes is to put them in a plastic bag and lightly crush with your hands or a rolling pin.*

Remove the cookies from the oven and set on a wire rack to cool.

Roll balls of the mixture in the crushed cornflakes on a piece of baking paper.

Bottom: Cornflake cookies. Top: Citrus cookies.

Hazelnut coffee biscuits

preparation 1 hour + 20 minutes refrigeration
cooking 25–35 minutes
makes 60

125 g (4½ oz) unsalted butter
125 g (4½ oz/½ cup) caster (superfine) sugar
1 teaspoon grated lemon zest
1 egg yolk
1 teaspoon lemon juice
125 g (4½ oz/1 cup) hazelnuts, ground
155 g (5½ oz/1¼ cups) plain (all-purpose) flour

icing
125 g (4½ oz/1 cup) icing (confectioners') sugar, sifted
30 g (1 oz) unsalted butter, melted
3–4 teaspoons lemon juice

coffee cream
125 g (4½ oz/½ cup) caster (superfine) sugar
1 tablespoon instant coffee
80 g (2¾ oz) unsalted butter

Preheat the oven to 180°C (350°F/Gas 4). Lightly grease two baking trays and line with baking paper.

Using electric beaters, beat the butter and sugar in a mixing bowl until the mixture is light and creamy. Add the zest, egg yolk, juice and nuts. Beat until well combined. Using a metal spoon, stir in the sifted flour. Shape the dough into a smooth ball and cover in plastic wrap. Refrigerate for 20 minutes.

Divide the mixture in half. Roll one portion between two sheets of baking paper until 5 mm (¼ inch) thick. Using a 3 cm (1¼ inch) fluted cutter, cut out rounds and place on the prepared trays. Repeat with remaining dough. Bake for 10 minutes, or until biscuits are golden. Remove from the oven and transfer to wire racks to cool.

To make the icing (frosting), combine the icing sugar and butter. Add enough lemon juice to form a smooth mixture. Place into a paper piping (icing) bag, snip off the tip, and pipe icing onto each biscuit.

To make the coffee cream, combine the sugar, 60 ml (2 fl oz/¼ cup) water and coffee in a saucepan. Stir over low heat, without boiling, until the sugar dissolves. Bring to the boil, reduce the heat and simmer, uncovered, without stirring for 4–5 minutes. Using electric beaters, beat the butter in a mixing bowl until light and creamy. Pour the cooled syrup into the bowl in a thin stream, beating constantly until the mixture is thick and glossy.

Spoon the coffee cream into a paper piping (icing) bag, then snip off the tip to an inverted 'V'. Pipe small rosettes on top of the iced biscuits.

Storage *You can make the biscuits up to a week in advance but decorate them just before serving.*

Cut out the biscuits using a small fluted or straight-edged cutter.

Pipe icing (frosting) onto each biscuit and top with a small rosette of coffee cream.

Cats' tongues

preparation 20 minutes
cooking 8 minutes
makes 40

80 g (2¾ oz) unsalted butter, chopped
80 g (2¾ oz/⅔ cup) icing (confectioners') sugar
2 egg whites
2 tablespoons caster (superfine) sugar
90 g (3¼ oz/¾ cup) plain (all-purpose) flour
icing sugar, extra, to dust

Preheat the oven to 180°C (350°F/Gas 4). Lightly grease a baking tray and line with baking paper. Use a ruler to draw lines at 8 cm (3¼ inch) intervals on the paper, then turn it over. Grease the top of the baking paper.

Using electric beaters, beat the butter and sifted icing sugar in a small mixing bowl until the mixture is light and creamy. Transfer the mixture to a large bowl.

In a separate clean, dry mixing bowl, use electric beaters to beat the egg whites until firm peaks form. Gradually add the sugar, beating well after each addition. Beat until the sugar has dissolved and the mixture is thick and glossy. Using a metal spoon, fold the egg mixture into the butter mixture. Sift in the flour and fold in quickly and lightly, making sure not to overmix.

Spoon the mixture into a piping (icing) bag fitted with a 1 cm (½ inch) piping nozzle. Pipe the mixture into 8 cm (3¼ inch) lengths onto the prepared tray, allowing room for spreading.

Bake for 8 minutes, or until lightly golden. Leave the biscuits to stand on the tray for 1 minute, then cool completely on a wire rack. Dust with icing sugar.

Variation *Add ½ teaspoon finely grated orange or lemon zest to the mixture, if desired.*

Sugar and spice palmiers

preparation 20 minutes + 15 minutes refrigeration
cooking 20 minutes
makes 32

2 tablespoons raw (demerara) sugar
1 teaspoon mixed (pumpkin pie) spice
1 teaspoon ground cinnamon
1 sheet frozen puff pastry, thawed
40 g (1½ oz) unsalted butter, melted

Preheat the oven to 210°C (415°F/Gas 6–7). Lightly grease two baking trays and line with baking paper.

Combine the sugar and spices in a small mixing bowl. Cut the pastry sheet in half and brush with the melted butter. Sprinkle with the sugar and spice mixture until the pastry sheet is well covered, reserving 2 teaspoons.

Fold the long edges of the pastry inwards, then fold again so that the edges almost meet in the centre. Fold once more, place the pastry on a baking tray and refrigerate for 15 minutes. Using a small, sharp knife, cut the pastry pieces into 32 slices.

Arrange the palmiers cut side up onto the prepared trays, brush with butter and sprinkle lightly with the reserved sugar and spice mixture. Bake for 20 minutes, or until golden. Transfer to a wire rack to cool completely.

Storage *Palmiers will only keep for up to a day in an airtight container. They may be re-crisped in a 180°C (350°F/Gas 4) oven for 5 minutes before serving.*

Draw guide lines on the baking paper, then turn the paper over before piping the mixture onto the tray.

Fold the side edges of the pastry inwards and then again so that they almost meet in the centre.

Bottom: Sugar and spice palmiers. Top: Cats' tongues.

Frosted crescents

preparation 30 minutes
cooking 12 minutes
makes 45

60 g (2¼ oz) roasted macadamia nuts or almonds
125 g (4½ oz/1 cup) plain (all-purpose) flour
60 g (2¼ oz/¼ cup) sugar
½ teaspoon grated orange zest (see Variation)
125 g (4½ oz) unsalted butter, chopped
1 egg yolk
icing (confectioners') sugar, to dust

Preheat the oven to 170°C (325°F/Gas 3). Lightly grease two baking trays or line with baking paper.

Place the macadamia nuts or almonds in a food processor and process until finely crushed. Sift the flour into a medium bowl and add the sugar, orange zest and butter. Using your fingertips, rub the butter into the flour mixture for 5 minutes, or until the mixture is fine and crumbly. Add the egg yolk and ground nuts. Mix until well combined and the mixture forms a soft dough.

Shape level teaspoonfuls of the dough into small crescents and place on the prepared trays. Bake for 12 minutes or until pale golden in colour.

While the crescents are still warm, sift a generous amount of icing sugar over them. Stand the crescents for 2 minutes. Transfer to wire racks to cool completely.

Storage *You can make the crescents 1 week in advance. Store in an airtight container in a cool, dry place.*

Variation *Use lemon zest instead of the orange zest, if desired. Add ¼ teaspoonful of orange-flower water to the dough for extra flavour.*

Mixed nut biscotti

preparation 30 minutes
cooking 45 minutes
makes about 50

25 g (1 oz) almonds (see Variation)
25 g (1 oz) hazelnuts
75 g (2½ oz) unsalted pistachios
3 egg whites
125 g (4½ oz/½ cup) caster (superfine) sugar
100 g (3½ oz/¾ cup) plain (all-purpose) flour

Preheat the oven to 180°C (350°F/Gas 4). Lightly grease a 26 x 8 x 4.5 cm (10½ x 3¼ x 1¾ inch) loaf (bar) tin and line the base and sides with baking paper.

Spread the almonds, hazelnuts and pistachios onto a flat baking tray and place in the oven for 2–3 minutes, until the nuts are just toasted. Leave to cool.

Using electric beaters, beat the egg whites in a clean, dry mixing bowl until firm peaks form. Gradually add the sugar, beating well after each addition. Beat until the sugar has dissolved and the mixture is thick and glossy. Transfer the mixture to a large mixing bowl. Add the sifted flour and nuts. Using a metal spoon, gently fold the ingredients together until well combined. Spread into the prepared tin and smooth the surface with a spoon. Bake for 25 minutes, or until set. Leave to cool completely in the tin.

Preheat the oven to 160°C (315°F/Gas 2–3). Using a sharp, serrated knife, cut the baked loaf into 5 mm (¼ inch) slices. Spread the slices onto prepared baking trays and bake for about 15 minutes, turning once halfway through cooking, until slices are lightly golden and crisp.

Variation *Use any combination of nuts, or a single variety, to the weight of 125 g (4½ oz).*

Shape the dough into crescent shapes and place on the prepared trays.

Using a metal spoon, fold the flour and nuts through the beaten egg whites.

Bottom: Mixed nut biscotti. Top: Frosted crescents.

Cinnamon pecan biscuits

preparation 20 minutes
cooking 15 minutes
makes 50

100 g (3½ oz) dark chocolate, chopped
125 g (4½ oz) unsalted butter
125 g (4½ oz/½ cup) caster (superfine) sugar
1 egg, lightly beaten
75 g (2½ oz) finely chopped pecans
200 g (7 oz/1⅔ cups) plain (all-purpose) flour
2 teaspoons ground cinnamon (see Variation)
100 g (3½ oz/1 cup) whole pecans, for decoration (see Hint)
icing (confectioners') sugar, to dust

Preheat the oven to 180°C (350°F/Gas 4). Lightly grease two baking trays and line with baking paper.

Place the chocolate in a heatproof bowl and sit it over a saucepan of barely simmering water, making sure the base of the bowl does not touch the water. Stir until the chocolate has melted. Allow to cool but not to reset.

Using electric beaters, beat the butter and sugar in a small mixing bowl until the mixture is light and creamy. Add the egg gradually, beating thoroughly. Add the cooled melted chocolate and beat until combined.

Transfer the mixture to a large bowl and add the chopped pecans. Using a metal spoon, fold in the sifted flour and cinnamon. Stir until the ingredients are combined but do not overbeat. Lightly roll 2 teaspoons of the mixture into oval shapes with floured hands, place on the prepared trays and press a pecan onto each. Bake for 10 minutes or until well coloured and firm.

Transfer to a wire rack to cool completely. Lightly dust each biscuit with icing sugar.

Variation Use allspice in place of the cinnamon.

Hint If preferred, bake the biscuits without the pecan on top. When baked and cooled, dip the top of each biscuit in melted chocolate and press a pecan on top.

Gingernuts

preparation 25 minutes
cooking 15 minutes
makes 30

250 g (9 oz/2 cups) plain (all-purpose) flour
½ teaspoon bicarbonate of soda (baking soda)
1 tablespoon ground ginger
½ teaspoon mixed (pumpkin pie) spice
125 g (4½ oz) unsalted butter, chopped
185 g (6½ oz/1 cup lightly packed) soft brown sugar
60 ml (2 fl oz/¼ cup) boiling water
1 tablespoon golden syrup (if unavailable, substitute with half honey and half dark corn syrup)

Preheat the oven to 180°C (350°F/Gas 4). Lightly grease two baking trays and line with baking paper.

Sift the flour, bicarbonate of soda, ginger and mixed spice into a large mixing bowl. Add the butter and sugar and rub into the flour with your fingertips until the mixture resembles fine breadcrumbs.

Pour the boiling water into a small heatproof bowl, add the golden syrup and stir until dissolved. Add to the flour mixture and mix to a soft dough with a flat-bladed knife.

Roll into balls using 2 heaped teaspoons of mixture at a time. Place on the prepared trays, allowing enough room for spreading, and flatten out slightly with your fingertips. Bake for 15 minutes, or until well coloured and firm. Leave to cool on the trays for 10 minutes before transferring to a wire rack to cool. Repeat with the remaining mixture.

Variation If you want to dress the biscuits up, make icing by combining 2–3 teaspoons lemon juice, 60 g (2¼ oz/½ cup) sifted icing (confectioners') sugar and 10 g (¼ oz) melted butter in a small bowl. Mix until smooth, then spread over the biscuits and allow to set.

Roll the mixture into oval shapes, place on the prepared tray and press pecans on top.

Place the balls of dough on the prepared trays and press with your fingertips to flatten.

Bottom: Gingernuts. Top: Cinnamon pecan biscuits.

Chocolate chip cookies

preparation 20 minutes
cooking 15 minutes
makes 40

185 g (6½ oz/1½ cups) plain (all-purpose) flour
90 g (3¼ oz/¾ cup) unsweetened cocoa powder
280 g (10 oz/1½ cups) soft brown sugar
180 g (6½ oz) unsalted butter, cubed
150 g (5 oz/1 cup) chopped dark chocolate
3 eggs, lightly beaten
265 g (9¼ oz/1½ cups) chocolate chips

Preheat the oven to 180°C (350°F/Gas 4). Lightly grease two baking trays and line with baking paper.

Sift the flour and cocoa into a large bowl, add the sugar and make a well in the centre.

Put the butter and chocolate in a small heatproof bowl. Bring a saucepan of water to the boil, then remove the pan from the heat. Sit the bowl over the saucepan. Stir occasionally until the chocolate and butter have melted and are smooth.

Add the butter and chocolate mixture and the eggs to the dry ingredients. Mix well with a wooden spoon, but do not overmix. Stir in the chocolate chips. Drop tablespoons of the mixture onto the trays, allowing room for spreading. Bake for 7–10 minutes, or until firm to touch. Cool on the trays for 5 minutes before transferring to a wire rack.

Chocolate fudge cookies

preparation 15 minutes + 1 hour refrigeration
cooking 12 minutes
makes 30

150 g (5½ oz/1¼ cups) plain (all-purpose) flour
125 g (4½ oz/1 cup) chopped walnuts
90 g (3¼ oz/½ cup) chocolate chips
125 g (4½ oz) unsalted butter, chopped
200 g (7 oz) dark chocolate, chopped
2 tablespoons golden syrup (if unavailable, substitute with half honey and half dark corn syrup)
2 eggs, lightly beaten

Lightly grease two baking trays and line with baking paper. Sift the flour into a large mixing bowl. Add the walnuts and chocolate chips and make a well in the centre.

Combine the butter and dark chocolate in a small saucepan. Stir over low heat for 5 minutes, or until the chocolate has melted and the mixture is smooth. Remove the pan from the heat, add the syrup and beaten eggs, mixing well.

Pour the chocolate mixture into a large mixing bowl with the dry ingredients. Using a metal spoon, stir until just combined. Cover with plastic wrap and refrigerate for 1 hour.

Preheat the oven to 180°C (350°F/Gas 4). Roll 1 level tablespoon of mixture at a time into a ball. Arrange the balls on the prepared trays and bake for 12 minutes. (The biscuits will still be soft at this stage, but they will become firm on standing.) Remove the biscuits from the oven and transfer to a wire rack to cool completely.

Note These rich, chocolate cookies have a delicious fudge-like texture. Sprinkle them with chocolate sprinkles before baking, if desired. This mixture can also be baked in a tin as a slice and cut into fingers when cooked. Spread with your favourite rich chocolate icing before cutting, if desired.

Tollhouse cookies

preparation 20 minutes
cooking 10 minutes
makes 40

180 g (6½ oz) unsalted butter, cubed and softened
140 g (5 oz/¾ cup) soft brown sugar
110 g (3¾ oz/½ cup) sugar
2 eggs, lightly beaten
1 teaspoon natural vanilla extract
280 g (10 oz/2¼ cups) plain (all-purpose) flour
1 teaspoon bicarbonate of soda (baking soda)
350 g (12 oz/2 cups) dark chocolate chips
100 g (3½ oz/1 cup) pecans, roughly chopped

Preheat the oven to 190°C (375°F/Gas 5). Lightly grease two baking trays and line with baking paper.

Using electric beaters, beat the butter and sugars in a large mixing bowl until the mixture is light and creamy. Add the egg, a little at a time, beating well after each addition. Add the vanilla and beat until well combined. Sift the flour into the bowl, then fold in alternately with the buttermilk. Stir in the chocolate chips and pecans.

Drop tablespoons of mixture onto the trays, leaving room for spreading. Bake the cookies for 8–10 minutes, or until lightly golden. Cool slightly on the trays before transferring to a wire rack to cool completely. When completely cold, store in an airtight container.

Top left: Chocolate chip cookies. Top right: Chocolate fudge cookies. Bottom right: Tollhouse cookies.

cakes

Chocolate mud cake

preparation 30 minutes
cooking 1 hour 30 minutes
serves 8–10

250 g (9 oz) unsalted butter
250 g (9 oz) dark chocolate, chopped
2 tablespoons instant coffee
185 ml (6 fl oz/¾ cup) hot water
150 g (5½ oz/1¼ cups) self-raising flour
150 g (5½ oz/1¼ cups) plain (all-purpose) flour
½ teaspoon bicarbonate of soda (baking soda)
60 g (2¼ oz/½ cup) unsweetened cocoa powder
550 g (1 lb 4 oz/2¼ cups) caster (superfine) sugar
4 eggs, lightly beaten
2 tablespoons vegetable oil
125 ml (4 fl oz/½ cup) buttermilk

icing
150 g (5½ oz) unsalted butter, chopped
150 g (5½ oz) dark chocolate, chopped

Preheat the oven to 160°C (315°F/Gas 2–3). Lightly grease a deep 22 cm (8½ inch) round cake tin and line with baking paper, making sure the paper around the side extends at least 5 cm (2 inches) above the top edge.

Put the butter, chocolate, coffee and water in a saucepan and stir over low heat until smooth. Remove from the heat.

Sift the flours, bicarbonate of soda and cocoa into a large mixing bowl. Stir in the sugar and make a well in the centre. Place the eggs, oil and buttermilk in a separate mixing bowl and mix until combined. Pour into the dry ingredients and mix together with a whisk. Gradually add the chocolate mixture, a little at a time, whisking well after each addition.

Pour the mixture (it will be quite wet) into the prepared tin and bake for 1¼ hours. Test the centre with a skewer—the skewer may be slightly wetter than normal. Remove the cake from the oven. If the top looks raw, bake for another 5–10 minutes, then remove. Leave in the tin until cold, then turn out and wrap in plastic wrap.

For the icing (frosting), combine the butter and chocolate in a saucepan and stir over low heat until the butter and chocolate are melted. Remove and cool slightly. Pour over the cake and allow it to run down the side.

Storage *Keep in the fridge in an airtight container for 3 weeks or in a cool dry place for 1 week. Can be frozen for up to 2 months.*

Gradually whisk the chocolate mixture into the well in the dry ingredients.

Pour the cooled chocolate icing over the upside down cake.

Classic sponge

preparation 20 minutes
cooking 25 minutes
serves 8

75 g (2½ oz/½ cup) plain (all-purpose) flour
150 g (5½ oz/1¼ cups) self-raising flour
6 eggs, at room temperature
220 g (7¾ oz/1 cup) caster (superfine) sugar
2 tablespoons boiling water
whipping cream, whipped, optional
jam, for filling, optional

Preheat the oven to 180°C (350°F/Gas 4). Lightly grease two deep 22 cm (8½ inch) round cake tins and line the bases with baking paper. Dust the tins lightly with a little extra flour, shaking off the excess.

Sift the flours three times onto baking paper. Beat the eggs in a large mixing bowl with electric beaters for 7 minutes, or until thick and pale.

Gradually add the sugar to the eggs, beating well after each addition. Using a metal spoon, fold in the sifted flour and boiling water. Spread evenly into the prepared tins and bake for 25 minutes, or until each sponge is lightly golden and shrinks slightly from the side of the tin. Leave the sponges in their tins for 5 minutes before turning out onto a wire rack to cool. Slice cake in half and fill with whipped cream and jam, if desired.

Storage *This sponge is best eaten on the day it is made. It won't keep well as it only contains a very small amount of fat. Unfilled sponges can be frozen for up to 1 month—make sure you freeze the cakes in separate freezer bags. Thaw at room temperature for about 20 minutes.*

Notes *The secret to making the perfect sponge lies in the folding technique. A beating action, or using a wooden spoon, will cause loss of volume in the egg mixture and result in a flat, heavy cake. Another very important factor is the amount of air incorporated in the flour. To make a light-textured sponge, you must sift the flour several times. Sifting not only removes any lumps in the flour but incorporates air. The final tip is to take the eggs out of the fridge at least an hour before required so they are at room temperature before adding them to the mixture.*

Madeira cake

preparation 10 minutes
cooking 50 minutes
serves 6

180 g (6 oz) unsalted butter, softened
185 g (6½ oz/¾ cup) caster (superfine) sugar
3 eggs, beaten
155 g (5½ oz/1¼ cups) self-raising flour, sifted
125 g (4½ oz/1 cup) plain (all-purpose) flour, sifted
2 teaspoons finely grated lemon zest
2 tablespoons milk
2 teaspoons caster (superfine) sugar, to sprinkle
icing (confectioners') sugar, to dust, optional

Preheat the oven to 160°C (315°F/Gas 2–3). Lightly grease and flour a deep 18 cm (7 inch) round cake tin, shaking out any excess flour. Beat the butter and sugar with electric beaters until pale and creamy. Add the eggs a little at a time, beating well after each addition. Fold in the flours, zest and milk until combined. When smooth, spoon into the tin and level the surface. Sprinkle with the caster sugar.

Bake for 50 minutes, or until a skewer comes out clean when inserted into the centre of the cake. Allow to cool for 15 minutes in the tin before turning out onto a wire rack to cool completely. If desired, dust with sifted icing sugar.

Zesty olive oil cake

preparation 15 minutes
cooking 40 minutes
serves 8

2 eggs, at room temperature
160 g (5½ oz/⅔ cup) caster (superfine) sugar
2 teaspoons finely grated orange zest
2 teaspoons finely grated lemon zest
125 ml (4 fl oz/½ cup) olive oil
185 g (6½ oz/1½ cups) self-raising flour
60 ml (2 fl oz/¼ cup) milk
60 ml (2 fl oz/¼ cup) orange juice

Preheat the oven to 180°C (350°F/Gas 4). Lightly grease a shallow 20 cm (8 inch) round cake tin and line the base with baking paper. Whisk the eggs and sugar in a large mixing bowl until well combined. Add the zest, then stir in the oil.

Stir in the sifted flour alternately with the milk and orange juice. Stir the mixture gently for 30 seconds with a wooden spoon. Pour into the prepared tin. Bake for 40 minutes, or until a skewer comes out clean when inserted into the centre of the cake. Leave to cool in the tin for 5 minutes before turning out onto a wire rack.

Top left: Classic sponge. Top right: Madeira cake. Bottom right: Zesty olive oil cake.

Chocolate cake

preparation 25 minutes
cooking 1 hour 15 minutes
serves 10

185 g (6½ oz) unsalted butter
330 g (11½ oz) caster (superfine) sugar
2½ teaspoons natural vanilla extract
3 eggs, at room temperature
75 g (2½ oz) self-raising flour, sifted
225 g (8 oz) plain (all-purpose) flour, sifted
1½ teaspoons bicarbonate of soda (baking soda)
90 g (3¼ oz/¾ cup) unsweetened cocoa powder
280 ml (9½ fl oz) buttermilk
125 ml (4 fl oz/½ cup) whipped cream
50 g (1¾ oz) almond flakes, roasted

icing
150 g (5½ oz) unsalted butter, chopped
150 g (5½ oz) dark chocolate, chopped

Preheat the oven to 180°C (350°F/Gas 4). Lightly grease a deep 20 cm (8 inch) round cake tin and line the base with baking paper.

Beat the butter and sugar with electric beaters until light and creamy. Beat in the vanilla. Add the eggs, one at a time, beating well after each addition.

Using a metal spoon, fold in the combined sifted flours, bicarbonate of soda and cocoa alternately with the buttermilk. Stir until the mixture is just smooth.

Spoon the mixture into the prepared tin and smooth the surface. Bake for 1 hour 15 minutes, or until a skewer comes out clean when inserted into the centre of the cake. Leave the cake to cool in the tin for at least 5 minutes before turning out onto a wire rack to cool completely. Cut the cake in half horizontally and fill with the whipped cream before placing the top back on.

For the icing (frosting), combine the butter and chocolate in a saucepan and stir over low heat until the butter and chocolate are melted. Remove and cool slightly. Pour over the cake and allow it to run down the side. While the icing is still soft sprinkle with the almond flakes.

Strawberry mousse sponge

preparation 35 minutes + 2–3 hours refrigeration
cooking 30 minutes
serves 8

510 g (1 lb 2 oz) packet French vanilla cake mix
3 eggs, at room temperature
80 ml (2½ fl oz/⅓ cup) vegetable oil
500 g (1 lb 2 oz) fresh strawberries, hulled
60 g (2¼ oz/¼ cup) caster (superfine) sugar
2 teaspoons powdered gelatine
125 ml (4 fl oz/½ cup) cream
1 egg white

Preheat the oven to 180°C (350°F/Gas 4). Lightly grease two shallow 20 cm (8 inch) round cake tins and line each base with baking paper.

Using electric beaters, beat the cake mix, eggs, oil and 290 ml (10 fl oz) water on low speed for 30 seconds. Increase to medium speed and continue beating for 2 minutes, or until well combined. Evenly divide the mixture into the prepared tins and bake for 25–30 minutes, or until a skewer comes out clean when inserted into the centre of each cake. Leave in the tins for 5 minutes before turning out onto a wire rack to cool completely.

Place 250 g (9 oz) of the strawberries in a food processor and blend until smooth. Stir in the sugar. Pour the strawberry mixture into a saucepan and bring to the boil, then take off the heat. Sprinkle in the gelatine, whisking until dissolved. Transfer to a bowl and set aside to cool. Slice half of the remaining strawberries and set aside the remaining whole strawberries to serve with the cake. Beat the cream until soft peaks form. Using electric beaters, beat the egg white in a clean, dry bowl until soft peaks form. Fold one-third of the cream into the cooled strawberry mixture, then fold in the egg white until combined. Refrigerate for 20 minutes.

Trim the top off one of the cakes to level the surface, then place on a serving plate. Fill with three-quarters of the mousse and arrange the sliced strawberries on top. Spread the underside of the other cake with the remaining mousse so it will stick and place it on top. Refrigerate the cake for 2½ hours before serving with the remaining cream and whole strawberries.

Bottom: Strawberry mousse sponge. Top: Chocolate cake.

Angel food cake with chocolate sauce

preparation 30 minutes
cooking 50 minutes
serves 8

125 g (4½ oz/1 cup) plain (all-purpose) flour
230 g (8 oz/1 cup) caster (superfine) sugar
10 egg whites, at room temperature
1 teaspoon cream of tartar
½ teaspoon natural vanilla extract

chocolate sauce
250 g (9 oz/1⅔ cups) chopped dark chocolate
185 ml (6 fl oz/¾ cup) cream
50 g (1¾ oz) chopped unsalted butter

Preheat the oven to 180°C (350°F/Gas 4). Have an ungreased angel cake tin ready. Sift the flour and half the sugar four times into a large bowl. Set aside.

Beat the egg whites, cream of tartar and ¼ teaspoon salt with electric beaters until soft peaks form. Gradually add the remaining sugar and beat until thick and glossy. Add the vanilla extract.

Sift half the flour and sugar mixture over the meringue and gently fold in with a metal spoon. Do the same with the rest of the flour and sugar. Spoon into the tin and bake for 45 minutes, or until a skewer inserted into the centre comes out clean. Gently loosen around the side of the cake with a spatula, then turn the cake out onto a wire rack to cool completely.

To make the chocolate sauce, put the chocolate, cream and butter in a saucepan. Stir over low heat until the chocolate has melted and the mixture is smooth. Drizzle over the cake and serve.

Devil's food cake

preparation 15 minutes
cooking 50 minutes
serves 8–10

165 g (5¾ oz/1⅓ cups) plain (all-purpose) flour
85 g (3 oz/⅔ cup) unsweetened cocoa powder
1 teaspoon bicarbonate of soda (baking soda)
250 g (9 oz/1 cup) sugar
250 ml (9 fl oz/1 cup) buttermilk
2 eggs, lightly beaten
125 g (4½ oz) unsalted butter, softened
125 ml (4 fl oz/½ cup) whipped cream
icing (confectioners') sugar, to dust

Preheat the oven to 180°C (350°F/Gas 4). Lightly grease a deep 20 cm (8 inch) round cake tin and line the base with baking paper. Sift the flour, cocoa and bicarbonate of soda into a large bowl.

Add the sugar to the bowl. Combine the buttermilk, eggs and butter in a separate bowl, then pour onto the dry ingredients. Using electric beaters, beat on low speed for 3 minutes, or until just combined. Increase the speed to high and beat for another 3 minutes, or until the mixture is free of any lumps and increased in volume.

Spoon the mixture into the prepared tin and smooth the surface. Bake for 40–50 minutes, or until a skewer inserted into the centre comes out clean. Leave the cake in the tin for at least 15 minutes before turning out onto a wire rack to cool completely. Cut the cake in half horizontally and fill with the whipped cream. Dust with sifted icing sugar and serve with fresh berries.

Storage *Unfilled, the cake will keep for 3 days in an airtight container or up to 3 months in the freezer.*

The cake batter needs to be beaten for about 6 minutes until it is smooth and thick.

Bottom: Devil's food cake. Top: Angel food cake with chocolate sauce.

Marble cake

preparation 20 minutes
cooking 1 hour
serves 6

1 vanilla bean or 1 teaspoon natural vanilla extract
185 g (6½ oz) chopped unsalted butter, softened
30 g (8 oz/1 cup) caster (superfine) sugar
3 eggs, at room temperature
280 g (10 oz/2¼ cups) self-raising flour
185 ml (6 fl oz/¾ cup) milk
2 tablespoons unsweetened cocoa powder
1½ tablespoons warm milk

Preheat the oven to 200°C (400°F/Gas 6). Lightly grease a 25 x 11 x 7.5 cm (10 x 4¼ x 3 inch) loaf (bar) tin and line the base with baking paper.

Split the vanilla bean down the middle and scrape out the seeds. Put the seeds (or vanilla extract) in a bowl with the butter and sugar and, using electric beaters, cream the mixture until pale and fluffy. Add the eggs one at a time, beating well after each addition. Sift the flour, then fold it into the creamed mixture alternately with the milk until they are combined. Put half the mixture into another bowl.

Mix the cocoa and warm milk until smooth, then add to one of the bowls and mix well. Spoon the plain mixture and chocolate mixture into the tin in alternating spoonfuls. Use a metal skewer to gently cut through the mixture a few times to create a marbled effect. Bake for 50–60 minutes, or until a skewer inserted into the centre comes out clean. Leave in the tin for 5 minutes before turning out onto a wire rack to cool. Cut into slices and serve.

Walnut and chocolate plum torte

preparation 30 minutes
cooking 1 hour 10 minutes
serves 8–10

200 g (7 oz/2 cups) walnuts
200 g (7 oz/1⅓ cups) chopped dark chocolate
2 teaspoons instant coffee
100 g (3½ oz/heaped ¾ cup) cornflour (cornstarch)
200 g (7 oz) unsalted butter, softened
185 g (6½ oz/1 cup) raw caster (superfine) sugar
4 eggs, at room temperature, separated
2 teaspoons coffee liqueur
450 g (1 lb) small firm plums (angelina or sugar plums are ideal) or 800 g (1 lb 12 oz) medium to large plums, halved and stoned
2 tablespoons dark brown sugar
20 g (¾ oz) unsalted butter, extra

Preheat the oven to 170°C (325°F/Gas 3). Lightly grease a 25 cm (10 inch) spring-form cake tin and line the base with baking paper.

In a food processor, grind the walnuts and chocolate until finely processed. Add the coffee granules and cornflour and process briefly.

Cream the butter and sugar with electric beaters until pale. Add the egg yolks, one at a time, alternately with some of the walnut mixture, beating well after each addition. Stir in the liqueur.

Whisk the egg whites until soft peaks form. Fold a large spoonful into the walnut mixture, then gently fold the rest of the egg white through. Spoon into the tin and smooth the surface. Bake for 30 minutes.

Remove from the oven and arrange the plums, cut side up, on top of the cake. Scatter the brown sugar over the plums and dot the extra butter over the sugar. Return the torte to the oven and bake for another 40 minutes, or until a skewer comes out clean when poked into the centre.

Remove the torte from the oven and cool for 1 minute, then carefully run a knife around the edge to prevent any toffee sticking to the tin. Leave in the tin for 15 minutes before turning out onto a wire rack. Serve warm in slices, accompanied with vanilla ice cream or whipped cream.

Bottom: Walnut and chocolate plum torte. Top: Marble cake.

Caramel peach cake

preparation 25 minutes + 30 minutes standing
cooking 1 hour 25 minutes
serves 8–10

250 g (9 oz) unsalted butter, softened
60 g (2¼ oz/⅓ cup lightly packed) soft brown sugar
1½ x 825 g (1 lb 13 oz) tinned peach halves in natural juice,
drained
250 g (9 oz/1 cup) caster (superfine) sugar
3 teaspoons finely grated lemon zest
3 eggs, lightly beaten
385 g (13½ oz/2⅔ cups) self-raising flour, sifted
250 g (9 oz/1 cup) plain yoghurt

Preheat the oven to 180°C (350°F/Gas 4). Lightly grease a deep 23 cm (9 inch) round cake tin and line the base with baking paper.

Melt 50 g (1¾ oz) of the butter and pour on the base of the tin. Evenly sprinkle the brown sugar on top. Drain the peaches, reserving 1 tablespoon of the liquid. Arrange the peach halves, cut side up, over the sugar mixture.

Beat the caster sugar, lemon zest and remaining butter with electric beaters for 5–6 minutes, or until pale and creamy. Add the egg a little at a time, beating well after each addition. The mixture may look curdled but it will come together once the flour is added.

Using a metal spoon, fold in the flour alternately with the yoghurt (in two batches) then the reserved peach liquid. Spoon the mixture over the peaches in the tin and smooth the surface. Bake for 1 hour 25 minutes, or until a skewer inserted into the centre comes out clean. Leave to cool in the tin for 30 minutes before carefully turning out onto a large serving plate.

Swiss roll

preparation 25 minutes
cooking 12 minutes
serves 10

90 g (3¼ oz/¾ cup) self-raising flour
3 eggs, at room temperature
185 g (6½ oz/¾ cup) caster (superfine) sugar
160 g (5½ oz/½ cup) strawberry jam (see Hint)

Preheat the oven to 210°C (415°F/Gas 6–7). Lightly grease a 30 x 25 x 2 cm (12 x 10 x ¾ inch) Swiss roll (jelly roll) tin. Line the base with baking paper, extending over the two long sides. Sift the flour three times on a large sheet of baking paper.

Using electric beaters, beat the eggs in a mixing bowl until thick and pale. Add 125 g (4½ oz/½ cup) of the sugar gradually, beating constantly until the mixture is pale and glossy.

Transfer to a large mixing bowl. Using a metal spoon, fold in the flour quickly and lightly. Spread into the tin and smooth the surface. Bake for 10–12 minutes, or until lightly golden and springy to touch. Meanwhile, place a clean tea towel (dish towel) on a surface, cover with baking paper and lightly sprinkle with the remaining caster sugar. Turn the cooked cake out immediately onto the sugar.

Using the tea towel as a guide, carefully roll the cake up from the short side, rolling the paper inside the roll. Stand the rolled cake on a wire rack for 5 minutes, then carefully unroll and allow the cake to cool to room temperature. Remove the paper, spread with the jam and re-roll. Trim the ends so they are neat.

Hint *Beat the jam with a spatula for 30 seconds before applying to the cake. This makes it easier to spread. Any type of jam can be used.*

Make sure you place the peaches closely together over the sugar mixture.

Turn the cake out onto baking paper sprinkled with sugar and roll up. Set aside for 5 minutes.

Bottom: Swiss roll. Top: Caramel peach cake.

Apple and spice teacake

preparation 35 minutes
cooking 45–50 minutes
serves 10

180 g (6 oz) unsalted butter
95 g (3¼ oz/½ cup lightly packed) soft brown sugar
2 teaspoons finely grated lemon zest
3 eggs, lightly beaten
250 g (9 oz/1 cup) self-raising flour
75 g (2½ oz/½ cup) wholemeal (whole-wheat) flour
½ teaspoon ground cinnamon
250 ml (9 fl oz/1 cup) milk
410 g (14½ oz) tinned pie apples
¼ teaspoon mixed (pumpkin pie) spice
1 tablespoon soft brown sugar, extra
25 g (1 oz/¼ cup) flaked almonds

Preheat the oven to 180°C (350°F/Gas 4). Lightly grease a 20 cm (8 inch) spring-form cake tin and line the base with baking paper.

Using electric beaters, beat the butter and sugar until light and creamy. Beat in the lemon zest. Add the egg gradually, beating well.

Fold the sifted flours and cinnamon into the mixture alternately with the milk. Spoon half the mixture into the prepared tin, top with three-quarters of the pie apple then top with the remaining cake batter. Press the remaining pie apple around the edge of the top. Combine the mixed spice, extra sugar and flaked almonds and sprinkle them over the cake batter.

Bake for 45–50 minutes, or until a skewer inserted into the centre comes out clean. Remove from the tin and allow to cool completely on a wire rack.

The cake is cooked when a skewer inserted into the middle comes out clean.

Flourless orange and almond cake

preparation 15 minutes
cooking 1 hour 20 minutes
serves 8–10

2 small oranges
280 g (10 oz) ground almonds
250 g (9 oz/1 cup) caster (superfine) sugar
1 teaspoon baking powder
1 teaspoon natural vanilla extract
1 teaspoon Cointreau (orange liquor)
6 eggs, lightly beaten
icing (confectioners') sugar, to dust

Wash the oranges to remove any sprays or waxes. Place the whole oranges in a large saucepan, add enough water to cover them and place a small plate on top to keep the oranges submerged. Gradually bring the water to the boil, then reduce the heat and leave to simmer for 40 minutes, or until the oranges are very soft. Preheat the oven to 180°C (350°F/Gas 4). Line the base of a 24 cm (9½ inch) spring-form cake tin with baking paper.

Cut each of the oranges into quarters and leave the pieces to cool. Remove any pips, then place the oranges in a food processor and blend until they form a very smooth pulp. Add the ground almonds, sugar, baking powder, vanilla and Cointreau and, using the pulse button, process until combined. Add the egg and process again until just combined—take care not to over-process. Pour the orange mixture into the prepared tin and bake for 40 minutes, or until the cake is firm and leaves the side of the tin. Leave to cool completely in the tin. Dust with icing sugar to serve.

Variation Try this cake with an orange syrup. Pour 500 ml (17 fl oz/2 cups) fresh orange juice in a pan with 185 g (6½ oz/¾ cup) caster (superfine) sugar and 60 ml (2 fl oz/¼ cup) Sauternes. Put the pan over medium heat and stir until the sugar has dissolved. Reduce the heat and simmer until the liquid is reduced and syrupy. Skim any scum off the surface. Drizzle the syrup over the cake and dust with icing sugar.

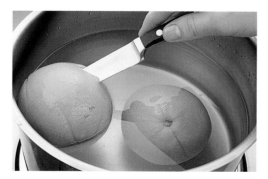

The oranges should be quite soft; if a sharp knife cuts into them easily, they are done.

Bottom: Flourless orange and almond cake. Top: Apple and spice teacake.

Sour cherry cake

preparation 20 minutes
cooking 40–45 minutes
serves 8–10

125 g (4½ oz) unsalted butter, softened
185 g (6½ oz/¾ cup) caster (superfine) sugar
2 eggs, lightly beaten
95 g (3¼ oz) ground almonds
125 g (4½ oz/1 cup) self-raising flour
60 g (2¼ oz/½ cup) plain (all-purpose) flour
125 ml (4 fl oz/½ cup) milk
680 g (1 lb 8 oz) jar pitted morello cherries, well drained
icing (confectioners') sugar, to dust

Preheat the oven to 180°C (350°F/Gas 4). Lightly grease and flour a 20 cm (8 inch) fluted baba or ring tin, shaking out any excess flour.

Using electric beaters, beat the butter and sugar in a mixing bowl until the mixture is light and creamy. Add the beaten egg a little at a time, beating well after each addition.

Stir in the ground almonds, then fold in the sifted flours alternately with the milk. Gently fold in the cherries. Spoon the mixture into the prepared tin and smooth the surface. Bake for 40–45 minutes, or until a skewer inserted into the centre comes out clean. Leave to cool in the tin for 10 minutes before turning out onto a wire rack to cool. Dust with sifted icing sugar before serving.

Note *This cake is best eaten on the day it is made.*

Date chocolate torte

preparation 20 minutes
cooking 35 minutes
serves 6

100 g (3½ oz/¾ cup) slivered almonds
150 g (5½ oz/1 cup) chopped dark chocolate
120 g (4¼ oz/⅔ cup) pitted dried dates
3 egg whites, at room temperature
115 g (4 oz/½ cup) caster (superfine) sugar
125 ml (4 fl oz/½ cup) cream, for whipping
2 teaspoons caster (superfine) sugar, extra
grated dark chocolate, to serve

Preheat the oven to 180°C (350°F/Gas 4). Lightly grease a 22 cm (8½ inch) spring-form cake tin and line with foil.

Finely chop the almonds and chocolate in a food processor. Use a knife to finely chop the dates.

Beat the egg whites with electric beaters until soft peaks form. Slowly add the sugar and continue beating until the sugar dissolves. Fold in the almond and chocolate mixture, then the dates. Spoon into the tin and smooth the surface. Bake for 30–35 minutes, or until a skewer inserted in the centre comes out clean. Leave in tin to cool a little before turning out onto a serving plate.

To serve, whip the cream and extra sugar until soft peaks form. Spread the cream over the cake, then sprinkle with the grated chocolate.

Pistachio, yoghurt and cardamom cake

preparation 25 minutes
cooking 55 minutes
serves 8–10

150 g (5½ oz/1 cup) unsalted pistachio nuts
½ teaspoon ground cardamom
150 g (5½ oz) unsalted butter, chopped
185 g (6½ oz/1½ cups) self-raising flour
310 g (10 oz/1¼ cups) caster (superfine) sugar
3 eggs, at room temperature
125 g (4½ oz/½ cup) plain yoghurt
1 lime

Preheat the oven to 180°C (350°F/Gas 4). Lightly grease a deep 20 cm (8 inch) round cake tin and line the base with baking paper.

Place the pistachio nuts and cardamom in a food processor and process until just chopped. Add the butter, flour and 185 g (6½ oz/¾ cup) of the caster sugar and process for 20 seconds, or until the mixture is crumbly. Add the combined eggs and yoghurt and process for another 10 seconds, or until everything is just combined.

Spoon the mixture into the prepared tin and smooth the surface. Bake for 45–50 minutes, or until a skewer inserted into the centre comes out clean. Leave the cake in the tin for 5 minutes before turning out onto a wire rack to cool completely.

To make the syrup, peel the skin off the lime with a vegetable peeler and make sure the white pith is removed. Place the remaining caster sugar and 100 ml (3½ fl oz) water in a small saucepan and stir over low heat until the sugar has dissolved. Bring to the boil, then add the lime peel and cook for 5 minutes. Strain and cool slightly. Pierce the cake several times with a skewer then pour the hot syrup over.

Top left: Sour cherry cake. Top right: Date chocolate torte. Bottom right: Pistachio, yoghurt and cardamom cake.

Coffee syrup cake

preparation 45 minutes
cooking 45–50 minutes
serves 8–10

185 g (6½ oz) unsalted butter
185 g (6½ oz/¾ cup) caster (superfine) sugar
3 eggs, separated
1 teaspoon grated lemon zest
250 g (9 oz/1 cup) sour cream
60 g (2¼ oz/¼ cup) plain yoghurt
235 g (8½ oz/1⅔ cups) self-raising flour
25 g (1 oz/¼ cup) ground almonds
chocolate curls, to serve

syrup
250 ml (9 fl oz/1 cup) strong coffee
125 g (4½ oz/½ cup) caster (superfine) sugar
2 tablespoons cognac

Preheat the oven to 180°C (350°F/Gas 4). Lightly grease a 23 cm (9 inch) fluted ring tin. Dust the tin with flour, shaking out any excess.

Using electric beaters, beat the butter and sugar in a mixing bowl until light and creamy. Add the egg yolks one at time, beating after each addition. Add the zest and beat well. Add the combined sour cream and yoghurt alternately with the sifted flour. Stir in the ground almonds.

Using electric beaters, beat the egg whites until stiff peaks form. Using a metal spoon, fold the egg whites into the flour mixture. Spoon into the prepared tin and bake for 5 minutes. Reduce the temperature to 160°C (315°F/Gas 2–3). Bake for

another 40 minutes, or until a skewer inserted into the centre comes out clean. Stand the cake in the tin for 5 minutes before turning out onto a wire rack to cool completely.

To make the syrup, combine the coffee, sugar and cognac in a saucepan over low heat without boiling until the sugar is dissolved. Bring to the boil, then simmer for 3 minutes to reduce. Remove from the heat and cool slightly.

Stand the cake on a wire rack over a baking tray and skewer random holes on top. Spoon the syrup over and collect any excess syrup from the tray to spoon over again. Cool. Serve the cake with whipped cream and chocolate curls.

Make the coffee syrup by heating the syrup until the sugar has dissolved.

Skewer random holes on top, then spoon the syrup over several times so it is well soaked.

cakes

Charlotte Malakoff

preparation 1 hour + 8 hours refrigeration
cooking nil
serves 8–12

250 g (9 oz) savoiardi (lady finger) biscuits
125 ml (4 fl oz/½ cup) Grand Marnier
500 g (1 lb 2 oz) strawberries, hulled and halved

almond cream
125 g (4½ oz) unsalted butter
80 g (2¾ oz/⅓ cup) caster (superfine) sugar
60 ml (2 fl oz/¼ cup) Grand Marnier
¼ teaspoon almond essence
185 ml (6 fl oz/¾ cup) cream, whipped
140 g (5 oz/1⅓ cups) ground almonds

Brush a deep 1–1.5 litre (35–52 fl oz/4–6 cup) soufflé dish with melted butter or oil. Line the base with baking paper and grease the paper. Trim the biscuits to fit the height of the dish.

Combine the liqueur with 125 ml (4 fl oz/½ cup) water. Quickly dip the biscuits into the liqueur mixture and arrange upright around the side of the dish, rounded side down.

To make the almond cream, using electric beaters, beat the butter and sugar until light and creamy. Add the liqueur and almond essence. Continue beating until the mixture is smooth and the sugar has dissolved. Using a metal spoon, fold in the whipped cream and ground almonds.

Place the strawberry halves, cut side down, into the base of the dish. Spoon one-third of the almond cream over the strawberries. Top with a layer of dipped biscuits. Continue layering, finishing with a layer of biscuits, then press down.

Cover with foil and place a small plate and weight on top. Refrigerate for 8 hours, or overnight. Remove the plate and foil and turn onto a chilled serving plate. Remove the baking paper. Decorate with whipped cream and strawberries.

Pavlova with fresh fruit

preparation 20 minutes
cooking 40 minutes
serves 8

4 egg whites
230 g (8 oz/1 cup) caster (superfine) sugar
375 ml (13 fl oz/1½ cups) cream, whipped
1 banana, sliced
125 g (4½ oz) raspberries
125 g (4½ oz) blueberries

Preheat the oven to 150°C (300°F/Gas 2). Line a baking tray with baking paper. Mark a 20 cm (8 inch) circle on the paper as a guide for the pavlova base if you find it easier.

Put the egg whites in a large, very clean, dry stainless steel or glass bowl—any hint of grease will prevent the egg whites foaming. Leave the whites for a few minutes to reach room temperature, then, using electric beaters, beat slowly until the whites start to become a frothy foam, then increase the speed until the bubbles in the foam have become small and even-sized. When the foam forms stiff peaks, add the sugar gradually, beating constantly after each addition, until the mixture is thick and glossy and all the sugar has dissolved. Don't overbeat or the mixture will become grainy.

Spread the mixture on the paper and shape it evenly into a circle, running a flat-bladed knife or spatula around the edge and over the top. Run the knife up the edge of the mixture, all the way around, to make furrows. This will strengthen the pavlova and give it a decorative finish.

Bake for 40 minutes, or until pale and crisp, then turn off the oven and cool the pavlova in the oven with the door ajar. When cold, decorate with whipped cream, banana, raspberries and blueberries.

Note *The meringue can be cooked in advance and kept overnight in an airtight container. Serve within 1 hour of decorating.*

Bottom: Pavlova with fresh fruit. Top: Charlotte Malakoff.

Coconut syrup cake

preparation 20 minutes + 2 hours soaking
cooking 50 minutes
serves 12

200 g (7 oz) unsalted butter, softened
375 g (13 oz/1½ cups) caster (superfine) sugar
6 eggs, at room temperature
185 g (6½ oz/1½ cups) self-raising flour
270 g (9½ oz/3 cups) desiccated coconut

syrup
1 tablespoon lemon zest
375 g (13 oz/1½ cups) sugar

Preheat the oven to 180°C (350°F/Gas 4). Lightly grease and flour a 2 litre (70 fl oz/8 cup) fluted baba or ring tin, shaking out any excess flour.

Using electric beaters, beat the butter and sugar for 5 minutes, or until light and creamy. Add the eggs one at a time, beating well after each addition, until combined. Fold in the flour and coconut and mix well.

Spoon the mixture into the prepared tin and bake for 45 minutes, or until a skewer inserted into the centre comes out clean. Cool slightly in the tin, then turn out onto a wire rack to cool completely.

To make the syrup, place the zest, sugar and 250 ml (9 fl oz/ 1 cup) water in a small saucepan. Stir over medium heat until the sugar is dissolved. Cool to room temperature. Pierce the cake all over with a skewer, pour the syrup over the cake and leave for 2 hours to soak up the syrup.

Lemon semolina cake

preparation 25 minute
cooking 45 minutes
serves 8–10

6 eggs, separated
310 g (11 oz/1¼ cups) caster (superfine) sugar
2 teaspoons finely grated lemon zest
80 ml (2½ fl oz/⅓ cup) lemon juice
90 g (3¼ oz/¾ cup) semolina
95 g (3¼ oz) ground almonds
2 tablespoons self-raising flour

Preheat the oven to 170°C (325°F/Gas 3). Lightly grease a 24 cm (9½ inch) spring-form cake tin and line the base with baking paper.

Using electric beaters, beat the egg yolks, 250 g (9 oz/1 cup) of the sugar, the zest and 2 tablespoons of the lemon juice in a mixing bowl for 8 minutes, or until thick and pale and the mixture leaves a trail when the beaters are lifted.

Beat the egg whites in a clean bowl with electric beaters until firm peaks form. Gently fold the whites with a metal spoon into the egg yolk mixture alternately with the combined semolina, ground almonds and flour. Take care not to overmix. Carefully pour the mixture into the prepared tin and smooth the surface. Bake for 35–40 minutes, or until a skewer comes out clean when inserted into the centre of the cake. Leave the cake in the tin for 5 minutes then turn out onto a wire rack to cool completely. Pierce a few holes in the cake with a skewer.

Place the remaining lemon juice and sugar in a saucepan with 125 ml (4 fl oz/½ cup) water. Stir over low heat until the sugar is dissolved. Increase the heat and simmer for 3 minutes, or until thick and syrupy. Pour the hot syrup over the cooled cake. Serve with thick (double/heavy) cream.

Spoon the cake mixture into the prepared tin, making sure it is evenly distributed.

Simmer the sugar mixture until it is thick and syrupy. Take care as it will be very hot.

Bottom: Lemon semolina cake. Top: Coconut syrup cake.

Rich dark chocolate cake

preparation 35 minutes
cooking 1 hour 40 minutes
serves 10–12

185 g (6½ oz) unsalted butter, chopped
250 g (9 oz) dark chocolate chips
220 g (7¾ oz/1¾ cups) self-raising flour
40 g (1½ oz/⅓ cup) unsweetened cocoa powder
375 g (13 oz/1½ cups) caster (superfine) sugar
3 eggs, lightly beaten

chocolate topping
20 g (¾ oz) unsalted butter, chopped
125 g (4½ oz) dark chocolate, chopped

Preheat the oven to 160°C (315°F/Gas 2–3). Lightly grease a 22 cm (8½ inch) spring-form cake tin and line the base with baking paper.

Place the butter and chocolate chips in a small heatproof bowl. Place the bowl over a saucepan of simmering water, making sure the base does not touch the water, and stir frequently until melted.

Sift the flour and cocoa into a large mixing bowl. Combine the chocolate mixture, sugar and egg, then add 250 ml (9 fl oz/1 cup) of water and mix well. Add to the flour and cocoa and stir until well combined. Pour the mixture into the prepared tin and bake for 1 hour 30 minutes, or until a skewer inserted into the centre comes out clean. Leave the cake in the tin for 15 minutes before turning out onto a wire rack to cool completely.

To make the topping, place the butter and chocolate in a small heatproof bowl. Place the bowl over a saucepan of simmering water, making sure the base does not touch the water. Spread over the cooled cake in a swirl pattern.

Prune and ricotta cheesecake

preparation 30 minutes
cooking 2 hours
serves 8–10

150 g (5½ oz) pitted prunes, chopped
2 tablespoons Marsala
500 g (1 lb 2 oz) dry ricotta cheese
250 g (9 oz/1 cup) caster (superfine) sugar
3 eggs, lightly beaten
125 ml (4 fl oz/½ cup) cream
60 g (2¼ oz/½ cup) cornflour (cornstarch), sifted
60 g (2¼ oz/½ cup) grated chocolate
icing (confectioners') sugar, to dust

Preheat the oven to 160°C (315°F/Gas 2–3). Lightly grease a deep 23 cm (9 inch) round cake tin and line the base with baking paper.

Combine the chopped prunes and Marsala in a small saucepan. Bring to the boil, reduce the heat and then simmer for 30 seconds, or until the Marsala is absorbed. Allow to cool.

Using electric beaters, beat the ricotta and sugar in a large mixing bowl for 4 minutes, or until light and creamy. Add the egg, a little at a time, beating well after each addition. Add the cream and beat for 2 minutes. Gently fold in the cornflour, prune mixture and chocolate with a metal spoon.

Spoon the mixture into the prepared tin and bake for 1¾–2 hours, or until a skewer inserted into the centre comes out clean. Leave in the tin for 15–20 minutes before gently turning out onto a wire rack to cool. Dust with sifted icing sugar and serve.

Using a flat-bladed knife, spread the chocolate topping over the cooled cake.

Place the ricotta and sugar in a mixing bowl, add the egg and cream then beat until light and creamy.

Bottom: Prune and ricotta cheesecake. Top: Rich dark chocolate cake.

Fruit mince and nut cake

preparation 40 minutes + 3 hours standing
cooking 2½–3 hours
serves 10

185 g (6½ oz/1½ cups) plain (all-purpose) flour
60 g (2¼ oz/½ cup) self-raising flour
1 teaspoon mixed (pumpkin pie) spice
140 g (5 oz/¾ cup lightly packed) soft brown sugar
170 g (5¾ oz) raisins
160 g (5½ oz) sultanas (golden raisins)
200 g (7 oz/2 cups) pecans
100 g (3½ oz) mixed raw nuts, chopped
250 g (9 oz) unsalted butter, melted and cooled
425 g (15 oz) ready-made fruit mince (mincemeat)
1 green apple, peeled and grated
2 tablespoons orange marmalade
2 tablespoons rum
2 eggs, lightly beaten

Preheat the oven to 160°C (315°F/Gas 2–3). Lightly grease a deep 20 cm (8 inch) round cake tin and line the base and side with baking paper. Line the outside of the tin with a double thickness of brown paper and secure with string.

Sift the flours and mixed spice into a large bowl. Add the sugar, raisins, sultanas and nuts, reserving half of the pecans. Make a well in the centre of the dry ingredients. Add the butter, fruit mince, grated apple, marmalade, rum and egg and stir until well combined.

Spoon the mixture evenly into the prepared tin and smooth the surface. Decorate with the reserved pecans. Bake for 2½–3 hours, or until a skewer inserted into the centre comes out clean. Allow the cake to cool in the tin overnight before turning out.

Butter cake

preparation 20 minutes
cooking 1 hour 15 minutes
serves 8

280 g (10 oz) unsalted butter
225 g (8 oz/1 cup) caster (superfine) sugar
1½ teaspoons natural vanilla extract
4 eggs, at room temperature
225 g (8 oz/1¾ cups) self-raising flour
150 g (5½ oz/1¼ cups) plain (all-purpose) flour
185 ml (6 fl oz/¾ cup) milk

Preheat the oven to 180°C (350°F/Gas 4). Lightly grease a deep 20 cm (8 inch) round cake tin and line the base with baking paper.

Using electric beaters, beat the butter and sugar in a mixing bowl until the mixture is light and creamy. Add the vanilla, then the eggs one at a time, beating well after each addition.

Sift the flours together into a mixing bowl. Using a large metal spoon, add the combined flours alternately with the milk into the butter mixture, folding until smooth. Spoon into the prepared tin and smooth the surface. Bake for 1¼ hours, or until a skewer inserted into the centre comes out clean.

Leave the cake in the tin for 5 minutes before turning out onto a wire rack to cool completely.

Storage *This butter cake can be kept in an airtight container in the fridge for up to 1 week, or for 3–4 days in an airtight container in a cool dry place. It can be frozen for up to 2 months.*

Variations *To make a 22 cm (8½ inch) round cake, bake for 1 hour 5 minutes. To make a 20 cm (8 inch) square cake, bake for 55 minutes. To make a 23 cm (9 inch) square cake, bake for 55 minutes.*

Once all the ingredients have been added, stir well to combine.

Place the butter and sugar in a mixing bowl and beat until light and creamy.

Bottom: Butter cake. Top: Fruit mince and nut cake.

Chocolate cherry cake

preparation 30 minutes
cooking 1 hour 10 minutes
serves 8

200 g (7 oz) dark chocolate, chopped
250 g (9 oz) unsalted butter, chopped
230 g (8 oz/1 cup firmly packed) soft brown sugar
1 teaspoon natural vanilla extract
155 g (5½ oz/1¼ cups) self-raising flour
45 g (1½ oz/½ cup) desiccated coconut
2 eggs, at room temperature
180 g (6 oz) pitted sour cherries, drained
icing (confectioners') sugar, to dust, optional
fresh cherries, to garnish, optional

Preheat the oven to 160°C (315°F/Gas 2–3). Lightly grease
a deep 23 cm (9 inch) round cake tin and line the base with
baking paper. Grease the paper.

Place the chocolate, butter, sugar and vanilla in a heatproof
bowl. Sit the bowl, making sure the base does not touch
the water, over a saucepan of simmering water. Stir
occasionally until the chocolate has melted and the mixture
is smooth. Remove the saucepan from the heat and sit the
bowl in a sink of cold water until cooled.

Combine the flour and coconut in a food processor. Add
the chocolate mixture and eggs and process in short bursts
until the mixture is just combined. Add the cherries and
process until they are just chopped.

Pour the mixture into the prepared tin and bake for 1 hour
10 minutes, or until a skewer inserted into the centre comes
out clean. Leave the cake in the tin for 15 minutes before
carefully turning out onto a wire rack to cool completely.
If desired, dust with sifted icing sugar and decorate with
fresh cherries.

Chocolate ginger and fig cake

preparation 15 minutes
cooking 1 hour
serves 8–10

125 g (4½ oz) unsalted butter, softened
230 g (8 oz/1 cup firmly packed) soft brown sugar
2 eggs, lightly beaten
185 g (6½ oz/1½ cups) self-raising flour
40 g (1½ oz/⅓ cup) unsweetened cocoa powder
185 ml (6 fl oz/¾ cup) milk
125 g (4½ oz/⅔ cup) dried figs, chopped
75 g (2½ oz/⅓ cup) glacé (candied) ginger, chopped

Preheat the oven to 180°C (350°F/Gas 4). Lightly grease a
22 x 12 cm (8½ x 4½ inch) loaf (bar) tin and line the base
with baking paper.

Using electric beaters, beat the butter and sugar in a mixing
bowl until the mixture is light and creamy. Add the egg, a
little at a time, beating well after each addition. Sift the flour
and cocoa into the bowl, then fold in alternately with the
milk to make a smooth batter. Fold in the chopped figs and
half the ginger.

Spoon the mixture into the prepared tin and smooth the
surface. Scatter the remaining ginger over the top. Bake for
1 hour, or until a skewer inserted into the centre comes out
clean. Leave to cool in the tin for 5 minutes before turning
out onto a wire rack to cool.

Leave the cake in the tin before turning out onto a
wire rack to cool.

Scatter the remaining chopped ginger over the top
after you have smoothed the surface of the mixture.

Bottom: Chocolate ginger and fig cake. Top: Chocolate cherry cake.

Hawaiian macadamia cake

preparation 10 minutes
cooking 1 hour
serves 10–12

375 g (13 oz/3 cups) self-raising flour
1 teaspoon ground cinnamon
185 g (6½ oz/1½ cups) caster (superfine) sugar
90 g (3¼ oz/1 cup) desiccated coconut
5 eggs, lightly beaten
440 g (15½ oz) tinned crushed pineapple in syrup
375 ml (13 fl oz/1½ cups) vegetable oil
100 g (3½ oz/¾ cup) chopped macadamia nuts

Preheat the oven to 180°C (350°F/Gas 4). Lightly grease a deep 23 cm (9 inch) round cake tin. Line the base and side with two sheets of baking paper, cutting it to make a collar that sits 2–3 cm (¾–1¼ inches) above the side of the tin.

Sift the flour and cinnamon into a mixing bowl, add the sugar and coconut and stir to combine. Add the eggs, pineapple and oil and mix well. Stir in the chopped macadamia nuts.

Spoon the mixture into the prepared tin and level the surface. Bake for 1 hour, or until a skewer inserted into the centre comes out clean. Cover the top of the cake with a layer of foil if it is browning too much. Leave in the tin for 30 minutes before turning out onto a wire rack to cool completely.

Storage *Store this cake in the fridge—it will keep for 1 week in an airtight container.*

Rum and raisin cake

preparation 15 minutes + 10 minutes soaking
cooking 45 minutes
serves 8

160 g (5½ oz) raisins
60 ml (2 fl oz/¼ cup) dark rum
185 g (6½ oz/1½ cups) self-raising flour
60 g (2¼ oz/½ cup) plain (all-purpose) flour
150 g (5½ oz) unsalted butter, chopped
140 g (5 oz/¾ cup lightly packed) soft brown sugar
3 eggs, lightly beaten

Preheat the oven to 180°C (350°F/Gas 4). Lightly grease a deep 20 cm (8 inch) round cake tin and line the base with baking paper. Soak the raisins and rum in a small bowl for 10 minutes. Sift the flours into a large mixing bowl and make a well in the centre.

Melt the butter and sugar in a small saucepan over low heat, stirring until the sugar is dissolved. Remove from the heat. Combine with the rum and raisin mixture and add to the flour with the egg. Stir, making sure not to overbeat, with a wooden spoon until just combined.

Spoon the mixture into the prepared tin and smooth the surface. Bake for 40 minutes, or until a skewer comes out clean when inserted into the centre of the cake. Serve with ice cream.

Blueberry shortcake

preparation 15 minutes
cooking 1 hour
serves 8–10

100 g (3½ oz) whole hazelnuts
280 g (10 oz/2¼ cups) self-raising flour
1½ teaspoons ground cinnamon
165 g (5¾ oz/¾ cup) raw (demerara) sugar
150 g (5½ oz) unsalted butter, chopped
2 eggs, at room temperature
165 g (5¾ oz) blueberry jam
1 tablespoon raw (demerara) sugar, extra

Preheat the oven to 180°C (350°F/Gas 4). Lightly grease a deep 20 cm (8 inch) round cake tin and line the base with baking paper.

Spread the hazelnuts on a baking tray and bake for 5–10 minutes. Place in a clean tea towel (dish towel) and rub together to remove the skins, then roughly chop.

Process the flour, cinnamon, sugar, butter and half the hazelnuts in a food processor until finely chopped. Add the eggs and process until combined. Press half the mixture onto the base of the prepared tin, then spread the jam evenly over the mixture.

Lightly knead the remaining hazelnuts into the remaining dough, then press evenly over the jam layer. Sprinkle the extra sugar over the top and bake for 50 minutes, or until a skewer inserted into the centre comes out clean. Leave in the tin for 15 minutes before turning out onto a wire rack to cool completely. Serve with whipped cream.

Top left: Hawaiian macadamia cake. Top right: Rum and raisin cake. Bottom right: Blueberry shortcake.

Honey and coconut cake

preparation 40 minutes
cooking 30–35 minutes
serves 16

125 g (4½ oz) unsalted butter, softened
140 g (5 oz/⅔ cup) raw (demerara) sugar
2 large eggs, lightly beaten
1 teaspoon natural vanilla extract
90 g (3¼ oz/¼ cup) honey
45 g (1½ oz/½ cup) desiccated coconut
220 g (7¾ oz/1¾ cups) self-raising flour
1 teaspoon freshly grated nutmeg
¼ teaspoon ground cinnamon
¼ teaspoon ground allspice
125 ml (4 fl oz/½ cup) milk

honey and cream cheese icing
125 g (4½ oz) cream cheese, softened
60 g (2¼ oz/½ cup) icing (confectioners') sugar
1 tablespoon honey

Preheat the oven to 180°C (350°F/Gas 4). Lightly grease a 28 x 18 x 3 cm (11¼ x 7 x 1¼ inch) cake tin. Line with baking paper, then lightly grease the paper.

Using electric beaters, beat the butter and sugar in a small mixing bowl until light and creamy. Add the eggs, a little at a time, beating thoroughly after each addition. Add the vanilla and honey. Beat until well combined.

Transfer the mixture to a large mixing bowl and add the desiccated coconut. Using a metal spoon, fold in the sifted flour and spices alternating with the milk. Stir until just combined and the mixture is almost smooth. Spoon into the prepared tin and smooth the surface.

Bake for 30–35 minutes, or until a skewer inserted into the centre comes out clean. Leave the cake in the tin for 10 minutes before turning out onto a wire rack to cool. Remove the baking paper.

To make the icing (frosting), beat the cream cheese with electric beaters in a small mixing bowl until creamy. Add the sifted icing sugar and the honey, beating until the mixture is smooth and fluffy. Spread evenly over the cake using a flat-bladed knife.

Custard butter cake

preparation 30 minutes
cooking 40 minutes
serves 8–10

250 g (9 oz/2 cups) self-raising flour
110 g (3¾ oz) custard powder (if unavailable,
    substitute with instant vanilla pudding mix)
½ teaspoon bicarbonate of soda (baking soda)
185 g (6½ oz) unsalted butter, chopped
275 g (9¾ oz) caster (superfine) sugar
4 eggs, lightly beaten
1 teaspoon natural vanilla extract
90 ml (3 fl oz) buttermilk

icing
100 g (3½ oz) white chocolate
60 ml (2 fl oz/¼ cup) cream
200 g (7 oz) cream cheese, softened
40 g (1½ oz/⅓ cup) icing (confectioners') sugar
silver cachous and crystallised violets, to decorate

Preheat the oven to 180°C (350°F/Gas 4). Lightly grease a deep 20 cm (8 inch) square cake tin and line the base with baking paper.

Sift the flour, custard powder and bicarbonate of soda into a bowl and make a well in the centre.

Melt the butter and sugar in a heavy-based saucepan over low heat, stirring until the sugar is dissolved. Remove from the heat. Add the butter mixture and combined egg, vanilla and buttermilk to the dry ingredients and stir until just combined. Spoon into the prepared tin. Bake for 35 minutes, or until a skewer inserted into the centre comes out clean. Leave in the tin to cool.

To make the icing, melt the white chocolate and cream in a saucepan over low heat. Cool and add to the cream cheese and icing sugar. Beat until smooth. Spread the cake with the icing and decorate with silver cachous and crystallised violets before it sets.

Make a well in the centre of the sifted dry ingredients in preparation for adding the wet ingredients.

Bottom: Custard butter cake. Top: Honey and coconut cake.

Walnut cake with chocolate icing

preparation 25 minutes
cooking 40 minutes
serves 6

185 g (6½ oz) unsalted butter
95 g (3¼ oz/½ cup lightly packed) soft brown sugar
2 eggs, at room temperature
185 g (6½ oz/1½ cups) self-raising flour
60 g (2¼ oz/½ cup) chopped walnuts,
plus 30 g (1 oz/¼ cup) for decoration
80 ml (2½ fl oz/⅓ cup) milk

chocolate icing
20 g (¾ oz) unsalted butter
125 g (4½ oz) good-quality dark chocolate, chopped

Preheat the oven to 180°C (350°F/Gas 4). Lightly grease a 20 cm (8 inch) spring-form cake tin and line the base with baking paper.

Using electric beaters, beat the butter and sugar in a large mixing bowl for 5 minutes, or until thick and creamy. Add the eggs one at a time, beating well after each addition. Using a metal spoon, fold in the sifted flour and 60 g (2¼ oz/½ cup) of the walnuts alternately with the milk until just combined.

Spoon the mixture into the prepared tin and smooth the surface. Bake for 35 minutes, or until a skewer inserted into the centre comes out clean. Remove from the oven and leave the cake in the tin for 5 minutes before turning out onto a wire rack to cool completely.

To make the icing (frosting), place the butter and chocolate in a heatproof bowl. Bring a saucepan of water to the boil, then reduce the heat to a gentle simmer. Sit the bowl over the saucepan, making sure the base of the bowl does not touch the water. Stir occasionally until melted and smooth. Remove from the heat and leave to cool slightly. Spread the icing over the cake with a flat-bladed knife. Sprinkle with the remaining walnuts.

Orange poppy seed cake

preparation 25 minutes + 15 minutes soaking
cooking 50 minutes
serves 8

50 g (1¾ oz/⅓ cup) poppy seeds
185 ml (6 fl oz/¾ cup) warm milk
250 g (9 oz/1 cup) caster (superfine) sugar
3 eggs, at room temperature
250 g (9 oz/2 cups) self-raising flour
210 g (7½ oz) unsalted butter, softened
1½ tablespoons finely grated orange zest
250 g (9 oz/2 cups) icing (confectioners') sugar
60 ml (2 fl oz/¼ cup) boiling water

Preheat the oven to 180°C (350°F/Gas 4). Lightly grease and flour a 23 cm (9 inch) fluted baba or ring tin, shaking out any excess flour.

Combine the poppy seeds and milk in a mixing bowl and set aside for at least 15 minutes.

Place the caster sugar, eggs, sifted flour, 185 g (6½ oz) of the butter and 3 teaspoons of the grated orange zest in a large mixing bowl. Add the poppy seed mixture and beat with electric beaters on low speed until just combined. Increase to medium speed and beat for another 3 minutes, or until the mixture is thick and pale. Pour evenly into the prepared tin. Bake for 50 minutes, or until a skewer inserted into the centre comes out clean. Leave in the tin for 5 minutes then turn out onto a wire rack.

To make the icing, melt the remaining butter, then place in a bowl with the icing sugar, remaining zest and the boiling water. Mix together to make a soft icing, then spread over the warm cake.

Melt the butter and chocolate in a heatproof bowl over a saucepan of simmering water.

Make the icing by combining the melted butter, icing sugar, orange zest and boiling water.

Bottom: Orange poppy seed cake. Top: Walnut cake with chocolate icing.

Date and walnut loaf

preparation 25 minutes
cooking 1 hour
serves 9–12

125 g (4½ oz) unsalted butter
350 g (12 oz/½ cup) honey (see Hint)
55 g (2 oz/¼ cup firmly packed) soft brown sugar
2 tablespoons milk
280 g (10 oz/1½ cups) chopped stoned dates
¼ teaspoon bicarbonate of soda (baking soda)
250 g (9 oz/2 cups) plain (all-purpose) flour
½ teaspoon freshly grated nutmeg
125 g (4½ oz/1 cup) chopped walnuts
2 eggs, lightly beaten

Preheat the oven to 180°C (350°F/Gas 4). Lightly grease a 21 x 14 x 8 cm (8¼ x 5½ x 3¼ inch) loaf (bar) tin and line with baking paper. Grease the baking paper.

Combine the butter, honey, brown sugar and milk in a medium saucepan. Stir over low heat until the butter has melted and the sugar has dissolved. Remove from the heat. Stir in the dates and bicarbonate of soda, then set aside to cool. Sift the flour and nutmeg into a large mixing bowl. Add the chopped walnuts and stir. Make a well in the centre of the dry ingredients.

Pour the butter mixture and the eggs into the dry ingredients. Using a wooden spoon, stir until well combined but do not overbeat. Spoon evenly into the prepared tin and smooth the surface. Bake for 55 minutes, or until a skewer inserted into the centre comes out clean. Leave the cake in the tin for 15 minutes, then turn out onto a wire rack. Remove the baking paper. Serve the loaf with extra butter, if desired.

Hint *Cakes that are made with honey will stay moist for longer than those made with sugar.*

Constantly stir over a low heat until the butter has melted and the sugar has dissolved.

Fruit cake

preparation 20 minutes
cooking 3 hours 30 minutes
makes 1

250 g (9 oz) softened unsalted butter
230 g (8 oz/1 cup firmly packed) soft brown sugar
2 teaspoons finely grated orange zest
2 teaspoons finely grated lemon zest
4 eggs, at room temperature
250 g (9 oz/2 cups) plain (all-purpose) flour, sifted
60 g (2¼ oz/½ cup) self-raising flour, sifted
whole blanched almonds, to decorate

Fruit mix

800 g (1 lb 12 oz) sultanas (goldern raisins)
320 g (11¼ oz) raisins, chopped
185 g (6½ oz/1¼ cups) currants
155 g (5½ oz) glacé cherries, quartered
250 g (9 oz) pitted prunes, quartered
125 g (4½ oz) mixed peel
250 ml (9 fl oz/1 cup) brandy
55 g (2 oz/¼ cup) soft brown sugar
80 g (2¾ oz) sweet orange marmalade
1 tablespoon cocoa powder
½ teaspoon ground cinnamon
1 teaspoon ground ginger
1 teaspoon mixed spice

Preheat the oven to 150°C (300°F/Gas 2). Lightly grease a deep 23 cm (9 inch) round or square cake tin and line the base with baking paper.

Beat the butter, sugar and zests in a bowl with electric beaters until just combined. Add the eggs, one at a time, beating well after each addition. Transfer to a bowl and stir in half of the soaked fruit mix alternately with the plain flour and the self-raising flour. Mix well, then spread evenly into the tin and tap the tin on the bench to remove any air bubbles. Dip your fingers in water and level the surface.

Decorate the top of the cake with the almonds. Sit the cake on several layers of newspaper on the oven shelf and bake for 3¼–3½ hours, or until a skewer inserted into the centre comes out clean. Cover the top with baking paper, seal firmly with foil, then wrap the cake and tin in a clean kitchen towel and leave to cool.

Bottom: Fruit cake. Top: Date and walnut loaf.

Honey, nut and fruit loaf

preparation 20 minutes
cooking 1 hour 5 minutes
serves 10

350 g (12 oz/1 cup) honey
45 g (1½ oz) unsalted butter
1 egg, at room temperature
310 g (11 oz/2½ cups) self-raising flour
½ teaspoon bicarbonate of soda (baking soda)
½ teaspoon ground cinnamon
185 ml (6 fl oz/¾ cup) milk
80 g (2¾ oz) chopped pecans
40 g (1½ oz/¼ cup) chopped almonds
60 g (2¼ oz) chopped pitted prunes
45 g (1½ oz/¼ cup) chopped dried apricots
30 g (1 oz/¼ cup) raisins

Preheat the oven to 180°C (350°F/Gas 4). Lightly grease a 23 x 15 cm (9 x 6 inch) loaf (bar) tin and line the base with baking paper. Using electric beaters, beat the honey and butter until well combined. Add the egg and beat well. Transfer the mixture to a large mixing bowl. Fold the sifted flour, bicarbonate of soda and cinnamon into the creamed mixture alternately with the milk. Fold in the nuts and fruit.

Spoon the cake mixture into the prepared tin and smooth the surface. Bake for 45 minutes, then cover the cake with foil and bake for another 20 minutes, or until a skewer inserted into the centre comes out clean. Let the cake cool in the tin for 10 minutes before turning out onto a wire rack to cool completely before serving.

Light fruit cake

preparation 30 minutes
cooking 2 hours
makes 1

185 g (6½ oz) unsalted butter, softened
115 g (4 oz/½ cup) caster (superfine) sugar
3 eggs, at room temperature
160 g (5½ oz/1 cup) sultanas (golden raisins)
100 g (3½ oz/⅔ cup) currants
60 g (2¼ oz/¼ cup) chopped glacé (candied) apricots
45 g (1½ oz/¼ cup) chopped glacé (candied) figs
240 g (7½ oz/1 cup) chopped glacé (candied) cherries, plus extra to decorate
80 g (2¾ oz/½ cup) macadamia nuts, coarsely chopped
185 g (6½ oz/1½ cups) plain (all-purpose) flour
60 g (2¼ oz/½ cup) self-raising flour
125 ml (4 fl oz/½ cup) milk
1 tablespoon sweet sherry

Preheat the oven to 160°C (315°F/Gas 2–3). Grease and line a deep 20 cm (8 inch) round or 18 cm (7 inch) square cake tin.

Using electric beaters, beat the butter and sugar in a mixing bowl until the mixture is light and creamy. Add the eggs, one at a time, beating well after each addition. Transfer the mixture to a bowl and stir in the fruit and nuts. Sift in half the flours and half the milk, stir to combine, then stir in the remaining flours and milk, and the sherry. Spoon into the prepared tin and tap it on the bench to remove any air bubbles. Smooth the surface with wet fingers and decorate the top with nuts or cherries, or both. Wrap the outside of the tin. Sit the tin on layers of newspaper in the oven and bake for 1¾–2 hours, or until a skewer inserted into the centre comes out clean. The top may need to be covered with baking paper if it colours too much.

Remove from the oven, remove the top baking paper and wrap the tin in a kitchen towel until cool. Remove the lining and store in an airtight container.

Carrot cake

preparation 20 minutes
cooking 1 hour 15 minutes
makes 14 slices

310 g (11 oz/2½ cups) self-raising flour
1 teaspoon bicarbonate of soda (baking soda)
2 teaspoons ground cinnamon
1 teaspoon mixed (pumpkin pie) spice
95 g (3¼ oz/½ cup lightly packed) soft brown sugar
60 g (2¼ oz/½ cup) sultanas (golden raisins)
2 eggs, lightly beaten
2 tablespoons vegetable oil
80 ml (2½ fl oz/⅓ cup) low-fat milk
140 g (5 oz) apple purée
300 g (10½ oz) carrot, coarsely grated

ricotta topping
125 g (4½ oz/½ cup) ricotta cheese
30 g (1 oz/¼ cup) icing (confectioners') sugar
½ teaspoon grated lime zest

Preheat the oven to 180°C (350°F/Gas 4). Lightly grease an 18 x 10 cm (7 x 4 inch) loaf (bar) tin and line the base with baking paper.

Sift the flour, bicarbonate of soda and spices into a large bowl. Stir in the sugar and sultanas. Mix the eggs, oil, milk and apple purée and stir into the dry ingredients. Stir in the carrot. Spread into the tin and bake for 1¼ hours, or until a skewer inserted into the centre comes out clean. Cool in the tin for 5 minutes, then cool completely on a wire rack. To make the topping, beat the ingredients together until smooth. Spread over the cake.

Top left: Honey, nut and fruit loaf. Top right: Light fruit cake. Bottom right: Carrot cake.

muffins
and **scones**

Plain muffins

preparation 15 minutes
cooking 25 minutes
makes 12

310 g (11 oz/2½ cups) self-raising flour
60 g (2¼ oz/¼ cup) caster (superfine) sugar
2 teaspoons baking powder
2 eggs, lightly beaten
310 ml (10¾ fl oz/1¼ cups) milk
160 g (5½ oz) unsalted butter, melted

Preheat the oven to 210°C (415°F/Gas 6–7). Lightly grease a 12-hole muffin tray. Sift the flour, sugar and baking powder into a large mixing bowl. Make a well in the centre.

Combine the egg, milk and butter in a separate mixing bowl and add to the flour mixture all at once. Stir gently with a fork or spatula until the mixture is just moistened. (Do not overmix as the batter should look quite lumpy.)

Spoon the mixture evenly into the prepared muffin holes until two-thirds full. Bake for 20–25 minutes, or until golden brown. Loosen the muffins with a flat-bladed knife and transfer to a wire rack to cool.

Blueberry muffins

preparation 20 minutes
cooking 20 minutes
makes 12

375 g (13 oz/3 cups) plain (all-purpose) flour
1 tablespoon baking powder
165 g (5¾ oz/¾ cup firmly packed) soft brown sugar
2 eggs, lightly beaten
250 ml (9 fl oz/1 cup) milk
125 g (4½ oz) unsalted butter, melted
185 g (6½ oz) fresh or thawed frozen blueberries

Preheat the oven to 210°C (415°F/Gas 6–7). Lightly grease a 12-hole muffin tray. Sift the flour and baking powder into a large mixing bowl and stir in the sugar. Make a well in the centre.

Combine the egg, milk and butter in a separate mixing bowl and add to the flour mixture all at once. Stir gently with a fork or spatula until the mixture is just moistened. (Do not overmix as the batter should look quite lumpy.)

Fold in the blueberries. Spoon the mixture evenly into the prepared muffin holes until two-thirds full. Bake for 20 minutes, or until golden brown. Loosen the muffins with a flat-bladed knife and transfer to a wire rack to cool.

Chocolate muffins

preparation 15 minutes
cooking 25 minutes
makes 12

310 g (11 oz/2½ cups) self-raising flour
40 g (1½ oz/⅓ cup) unsweetened cocoa powder
½ teaspoon bicarbonate of soda (baking soda)
145 g (5 oz/⅔ cup) caster (superfine) sugar
375 ml (13 fl oz/1½ cups) buttermilk
2 eggs, at room temperature
160 g (5½ oz) unsalted butter, melted and cooled

Preheat the oven to 200°C (400°F/Gas 6). Lightly grease a 12-hole muffin tray. Sift the flour, cocoa powder and bicarbonate of soda into a large mixing bowl and add the sugar. Make a well in the centre.

Combine the buttermilk and eggs in a separate mixing bowl and add to the flour mixture all at once. Stir gently with a fork or spatula until the mixture is just moistened. (Do not overmix as the batter should look quite lumpy.)

Spoon the mixture evenly into the prepared muffin holes until two-thirds full. Bake for 20–25 minutes, or until golden brown. Loosen the muffins with a flat-bladed knife and transfer to a wire rack to cool.

Banana muffins

preparation 15 minutes
cooking 15 minutes
makes 12

250 g (9 oz/2 cups) self-raising flour
75 g (2½ oz/1 cup) oat bran
185 g (6½ oz/¾ cup) caster (superfine) sugar
2 eggs, lightly beaten
170 ml (5½ fl oz/⅔ cup) milk
60 g (2¼ oz) unsalted butter, melted
2 ripe medium bananas, mashed

Preheat the oven to 210°C (415°F/Gas 6–7). Lightly grease a 12-hole muffin tray. Sift the flour into a large mixing bowl and add the oat bran and sugar. Make a well in the centre.

Combine the egg, milk, butter and banana in a separate bowl and add to the flour mixture all at once. Stir gently with a fork or spatula until the mixture is just moistened. (Do not overmix as the batter should look quite lumpy.)

Spoon the mixture evenly into the prepared muffin holes until two-thirds full. Bake for 15 minutes, or until puffed and golden brown. Transfer the muffins to a wire rack to cool.

Top left: Plain muffins. Top right: Blueberry muffins. Bottom right: Chocolate muffins. Bottom left: Banana muffins.

Baby coffee and walnut sour cream muffins

preparation 15 minutes
cooking 20 minutes
makes 24

75 g (2½ oz) walnuts
155 g (5½ oz/⅔ cup firmly packed) soft brown sugar
125 g (4½ oz) unsalted butter, softened
2 eggs, lightly beaten
125 g (4½ oz/1 cup) self-raising flour
80 g (2¾ oz/⅓ cup) sour cream
1 tablespoon coffee and chicory essence

Preheat the oven to 160°C (315°F/Gas 2–3). Lightly grease two 12-hole 30 ml (1 fl oz) mini muffin trays. Process the walnuts and 45 g (1½ oz/¼ cup) of the brown sugar in a food processor until the walnuts are roughly chopped into small pieces. Transfer to a mixing bowl.

Cream the butter and remaining sugar together in the food processor until pale and creamy. With the motor running, gradually add the egg and process until smooth. Add the flour and blend until well mixed. Add the sour cream and essence and process until thoroughly mixed.

Spoon ½ teaspoon of the walnut and sugar mixture into the base of each muffin hole, followed by a heaped teaspoon of the cake mixture. Sprinkle a little more walnut mixture over the top, add another heaped teaspoon of the cake mixture and top with the remaining walnut mixture. Bake for 20 minutes, or until risen and springy to the touch. Leave in the tins for 5 minutes. Loosen the muffins with a flat-bladed knife and transfer to a wire rack to cool completely.

Orange poppy seed muffins

preparation 20 minutes
cooking 12 minutes
serves 12

215 g (7½ oz/1¾ cups) self-raising flour
1 tablespoon caster (superfine) sugar
1 teaspoon baking powder
¼ teaspoon bicarbonate of soda (baking soda)
1 tablespoon poppy seeds
90 g (3¼ oz) unsalted butter
160 g (5½ oz/½ cup) orange marmalade
1 egg, lightly beaten
185 ml (6 fl oz/¾ cup) milk

Preheat the oven to 210°C (415°F/Gas 6–7). Lightly grease a 12-hole muffin tray. Sift the flour, sugar, baking powder and bicarbonate of soda into a large mixing bowl. Add the poppy seeds and stir. Make a well in the centre.

Combine the butter and marmalade in a small saucepan and stir over low heat until the marmalade becomes runny and the butter has melted. Add the butter mixture and combined egg and milk to the flour mixture, and stir until just combined. (Do not overmix as the batter should look quite lumpy.)

Spoon the batter into the prepared muffin holes and cook for 10–12 minutes or until golden. Loosen the muffins with a flat-bladed knife and transfer to a wire rack.

Variation Beat 60 g (2¼ oz) soft butter, 2 tablespoons icing (confectioners') sugar and 1 teaspoon grated orange zest until light and creamy. Cut a small section from the top of the muffin, fill with mixture and replace the tops.

Process the remaining ingredients until smooth and thoroughly combined.

Add the butter mixture and combined egg and milk to the flour mixture.

163

Bottom: Orange poppy seed muffins. Top: Baby coffee and walnut sour cream muffins

White chocolate mango muffins

preparation 10 minutes
cooking 20 minutes
makes 12

340 g (11¾ oz/2¾ cups) self-raising flour
95 g (3¼ oz/½ cup lightly packed) soft brown sugar
130 g (4½ oz) chopped white chocolate
185 g (6½ oz/1 cup) chopped fresh mango flesh (2 medium) or
440 g (15½ oz) tinned mango pieces, well drained
1 egg, lightly beaten
125 ml (4 fl oz/½ cup) milk
60 ml (2 fl oz/¼ cup) cream
90 g (3¼ oz) unsalted butter, melted

Preheat the oven to 180°C (350°F/Gas 4). Line a 12-hole muffin tray with paper cases. Sift the flour into a large mixing bowl. Stir in the sugar and chopped chocolate and mix well. Fold in the chopped mango gently. Make a well in the centre.

Combine the egg, milk, cream and butter in a separate mixing bowl and add to the flour all at once. Stir gently with a fork or spatula until the mixture is just moistened. (Do not overmix as the batter should look quite lumpy.)

Spoon the mixture evenly into the paper cases. Bake for 20 minutes, or until lightly golden. Loosen the muffins with a flat-bladed knife and transfer to a wire rack to cool.

Note *Serve these muffins warm with whipped cream. They also make an unusual, but delicious, dessert, topped with large shavings of white chocolate or served split with stewed apples.*

Muesli muffins

preparation 15 minutes + 20 minutes standing
cooking 25 minutes
makes 6 large muffins

95 g (3¼ oz) dried apricots, chopped
125 ml (4 fl oz/½ cup) orange juice
2 teaspoons finely grated orange zest
150 g (5½ oz/1 cup) wholemeal (whole-wheat) self-raising flour
60 g (2¼ oz/½ cup) self-raising flour
½ teaspoon baking powder
45 g (1½ oz/¼ cup lightly packed) soft brown sugar
75 g (2½ oz) toasted muesli (granola)
185 ml (6 fl oz/¾ cup) milk
60 g (2¼ oz) unsalted butter, melted

topping
1 tablespoon plain (all-purpose) flour
½ teaspoon ground cinnamon
45 g (1½ oz/¼ cup lightly packed) soft brown sugar
35 g (1¼ oz) toasted muesli (granola)
20 g (¾ oz) unsalted butter, melted

Preheat the oven to 210°C (415°F/Gas 6–7). Lightly grease a 6-hole large muffin tray. Combine the apricots, orange juice and zest in a mixing bowl. Set the mixture aside for 20 minutes.

Sift the flours and baking powder into a large mixing bowl. Stir in the sugar and muesli and make a well in the centre. Combine the milk, butter and undrained apricot mixture in a separate mixing bowl and add to the flour mixture all at once. Stir gently with a fork or spatula until the mixture is just moistened. (Do not overmix as the batter should look quite lumpy.) Spoon the mixture evenly into the prepared muffin holes.

To make the topping, place all ingredients in a bowl and stir to combine. Sprinkle the topping over the muffins.

Bake for 20–25 minutes, or until golden brown. Loosen the muffins with a flat-bladed knife and turn out onto a wire rack to cool completely. Serve with butter, if desired.

Stir in the sugar and chopped white chocolate and mix well.

Spoon the topping over the tops of the muffins before baking for 20–25 minutes.

Bottom: Muesli muffins. Top: White chocolate mango muffins.

Berry cheesecake muffins

preparation 15 minutes
cooking 30 minutes
makes 6 large muffins

215 g (7½ oz/1¾ cups) self-raising flour
2 eggs, lightly beaten
60 ml (2 fl oz/¼ cup) vegetable oil
2 tablespoons raspberry jam
60 g (2¼ oz/¼ cup) mixed berry yoghurt
125 g (4½ oz/½ cup) caster (superfine) sugar
50 g (1¾ oz) cream cheese (see Note)
1 tablespoon raspberry jam, extra, for filling
icing (confectioners') sugar, sifted, to dust

Preheat the oven to 180°C (350°F/Gas 4). Lightly grease a 6-hole muffin tray. Sift the flour into a large mixing bowl and make a well in the centre.

Combine the egg, oil, jam, yoghurt and sugar in a separate bowl and add to the sifted flour all at once. Stir gently with a fork or spatula until the mixture is just moistened. (Do not overmix as the batter should look quite lumpy.)

Spoon three-quarters of the mixture into the prepared muffin holes. Cut the cream cheese into six equal portions and place a portion on the centre of each muffin. Spread the tops of the cheese with jam and cover with the remaining muffin batter.

Bake for 25–30 minutes, or until the muffins are golden. Loosen the muffins with a flat-bladed knife and transfer to a wire rack to cool. Dust with icing sugar.

Note *These muffins are best eaten as soon as they are cool enough. The cream cheese filling will melt slightly as the muffins cook and provide a delicious 'surprise' centre.*

Place a portion of cream cheese in the centre of each muffin.

Strawberry and passionfruit muffins

preparation 20 minutes
cooking 15 minutes
makes 12

215 g (7½ oz/1¾ cups) self-raising flour
pinch of salt
1 teaspoon baking powder
½ teaspoon bicarbonate of soda (baking soda)
60 g (2¼ oz/¼ cup) caster (superfine) sugar
175 g (6 oz/1 cup) fresh strawberries, hulled and chopped
1 egg
185 ml (6 fl oz/¾ cup) milk
125 g (4½ oz/½ cup) passionfruit pulp, tinned or fresh
60 g (2¼ oz) unsalted butter, melted
whipping cream, whipped, to serve
fresh strawberries, hulled and halved, extra
icing (confectioners') sugar, to dust, optional

Preheat the oven to 210°C (415°F/Gas 6–7). Lightly grease a 12-hole muffin tray. Sift the flour, salt, baking powder, bicarbonate of soda and sugar into a mixing bowl. Add the strawberries and stir to combine. Make a well in the centre.

Place the egg and milk in a separate mixing bowl. Combine and add the passionfruit pulp and egg mixture to the flour mixture. Pour the melted butter all at once and lightly stir with a fork until just combined. (Do not overmix as the batter should look quite lumpy.)

Spoon the mixture into the prepared muffin holes and bake for 10–15 minutes, or until golden brown. Loosen the muffins with a flat-bladed knife and transfer to a wire rack to cool. Top with whipped cream and fresh strawberry halves and sprinkle with icing sugar, if desired.

Note *Folding the fruit through the dry mixture helps it to be evenly distributed throughout.*

Bottom: Strawberry and passionfruit muffins. Top: Berry cheesecake muffins.

Coffee pecan streusel muffins

preparation 20 minutes
cooking 12 minutes
makes 9

215 g (7½ oz/1¾ cups) self-raising flour
1 teaspoon baking powder
60 g (2¼ oz/¼ cup) caster (superfine) sugar
60 g (2¼ oz/½ cup) finely chopped pecans
1 tablespoon instant coffee
1 tablespoon boiling water
1 egg
170 ml (5½ fl oz/⅔ cup) milk
80 ml (2½ fl oz/⅓ cup) vegetable oil

streusel topping
30 g (1 oz/¼ cup) self-raising flour
30 g (1 oz) unsalted butter
2 tablespoons soft brown sugar
1 teaspoon ground cinnamon
2 tablespoons finely chopped pecans

Preheat the oven to 210°C (415°F/Gas 6–7). Lightly grease nine holes of a 12-hole muffin tray. Sift the flour and baking powder into a mixing bowl. Add the sugar and pecans. Make a well in the centre.

Combine the instant coffee with the boiling water and stir until dissolved. Cool and add to the flour mixture. In a separate bowl, combine the egg, milk and oil. Add to the flour mixture all at once. Stir gently with a fork or spatula until the mixture is just moistened. (Do not overmix as the batter should look quite lumpy.)

To make the topping, place the flour into a mixing bowl. Rub the butter into the flour until the mixture resembles coarse breadcrumbs. Add the sugar, cinnamon and pecans and mix until well combined.

Spoon the mixture evenly into the prepared muffin holes. Sprinkle with the topping and bake for 10–12 minutes, or until golden. Loosen the muffins with a flat-bladed knife and transfer to a wire rack to cool.

Add the sugar, cinnamon and chopped pecans to the topping mixture.

Double choc muffins

preparation 25 minutes
cooking 12–15 minutes
makes 6 large muffins

250 g (9 oz/2 cups) plain (all-purpose) flour
2½ teaspoons baking powder
30 g (1 oz/¼ cup) unsweetened cocoa powder
2 tablespoons caster (superfine) sugar
130 g (4½ oz) dark chocolate chips
1 egg, lightly beaten
125 g (4½ oz/½ cup) sour cream
185 ml (6 fl oz/¾ cup) milk
90 g (3¼ oz) unsalted butter, melted

topping
50 g (1¾ oz) dark chocolate, chopped
1 tablespoon cream
10 g (¼ oz) butter

Preheat the oven to 180°C (350°F/Gas 4). Brush a 6-hole large muffin tin with melted butter or oil. Sift the flour, baking powder and cocoa into a large mixing bowl. Add the sugar and the chocolate chips and mix. Make a well in the centre.

Combine the egg, sour cream, milk and melted butter in a separate mixing bowl and add to the flour mixture all at once. Stir gently with a fork or spatula until the mixture is just moistened. (Do not overmix as the batter should look quite lumpy.)

Spoon the mixture into the prepared muffin holes. Bake for 12–15 minutes, or until firm. Loosen the muffins with a flat-bladed knife and transfer to a wire rack to cool completely.

Combine the chocolate, cream and butter in a saucepan. Stir over low heat until smooth. Refrigerate until firm but not set. Spread the topping over the muffins using a flat-bladed knife, or put it in a piping (icing) bag with a large fluted piping tip and pipe the chocolate topping on top of the muffins.

Make a well in the flour mixture and fold in the combined butter, eggs and milk.

Bottom: Double choc muffins. Top: Coffee pecan streusel muffins.

Oat and date muffins

preparation 20 minutes
cooking 18 minutes
makes 12

125 g (4½ oz/1 cup) self-raising flour
150 g (5½ oz/1 cup) wholemeal (whole-wheat) self-raising flour
½ teaspoon bicarbonate of soda (baking soda)
100 g (3½ oz/1 cup) quick rolled (porridge) oats
55 g (1¾ oz/¼ cup firmly packed) soft brown sugar
185 g (6½ oz) chopped dates
1 egg
2 tablespoons vegetable oil
90 g (3¼ oz/¼ cup) golden syrup
310 ml (10¾ fl oz/1¼ cups) skim milk
cooking oil spray

Preheat the oven to 200°C (400°F/Gas 6). Lightly grease a 12-hole 125 ml (4 fl oz/½ cup) muffin tray. Sift the self-raising, wholemeal self-raising flour and bicarbonate of soda into a large mixing bowl. Return the husks to the bowl. Stir in the quick rolled oats, brown sugar and chopped dates. Make a well in the centre.

Combine the egg, oil, golden syrup and skim milk in a separate mixing bowl and add to the flour mixture all at once. Stir gently with a fork or spatula until the mixture is just moistened. (Do not overmix as the batter should look quite lumpy.)

Spoon the mixture evenly into the prepared muffin holes. Bake for 18 minutes, or until well risen and golden. Leave in the tins for 5 minutes. Loosen the muffins with a flat-bladed knife and transfer to a wire rack to cool completely.

Raisin, banana and apple muffins

preparation 20 minutes
cooking 20 minutes
makes 12

200 g (7 oz/1¼ cups) chopped raisins
125 g (4½ oz/1 cup) self-raising flour
150 g (5½ oz/1 cup) wholemeal (whole-wheat) self-raising flour
1 teaspoon ground cinnamon
95 g (3¼ oz/½ cup lightly packed) soft brown sugar
135 g (4¾ oz/½ cup) apple sauce
1 egg
250 ml (9 fl oz/1 cup) skim milk
2 tablespoons vegetable oil
1 ripe banana, mashed
cooking oil spray
2 tablespoons rolled (porridge) oats
1 tablespoon soft brown sugar, extra

Preheat the oven to 200°C (400°F/Gas 6). Lightly grease a 12-hole 125 ml (4 fl oz/½ cup) muffin tray. Place the raisins in a bowl, cover with boiling water, set aside for 30 minutes, then drain.

Sift the self-raising, wholemeal self-raising flour and cinnamon into a large mixing bowl. Add the sugar and make a well in the centre.

Combine the apple sauce, egg and skim milk in a separate mixing bowl. Stir in the oil, mashed banana and drained raisins. Add to the flour mixture all at once. Stir gently with a fork or spatula until the mixture is just moistened. (Do not overmix as the batter should look quite lumpy.)

Spoon the mixture evenly into the prepared muffin holes and sprinkle with the rolled oats combined with the sugar. Bake for 20 minutes, or until cooked through. Leave in the tins for 5 minutes. Loosen the muffins with a flat-bladed knife and transfer to a wire rack to cool completely.

Wholemeal flour usually contains husks. Return these to the bowl.

Use a light touch to stir the banana–apple mixture into the well in the dry ingredients.

Bottom: Raisin, banana and apple muffins. Top: Oat and date muffins.

Sultana scones

preparation 20 minutes
cooking 12 minutes
makes 12

280 g (10 oz/2¼ cups) self-raising flour
pinch of salt
30 g (1 oz) unsalted butter, cut into small pieces
90 g (3¼ oz/⅓ cup) caster (superfine) sugar
30 g (1 oz/¼ cup) sultanas (golden raisins) (see Variation)
1 egg, lightly beaten
170 ml (5½ fl oz/⅔ cup) milk
extra milk, to glaze
unsalted butter, to serve

Preheat the oven to 210°C (415°F/Gas 6–7). Lightly grease a baking tray. Sift the flour and salt into a large mixing bowl. Add the butter and rub in lightly with fingertips.

Add the sugar and sultanas and stir to combine. Make a well in the centre of the mixture. Add the egg and almost all the milk. Mix quickly, with a flat-bladed knife, to a soft dough, adding more milk if necessary. Turn out onto a lightly floured surface and knead briefly until smooth. Press or roll out to form a round about 2 cm (¾ inch) thick.

Cut the dough into rounds using a floured plain 5 cm (2 inch) cutter or cut into squares or diamonds using a floured knife. Place the rounds close together on the prepared tray and brush with extra milk. Bake for 10–12 minutes, or until golden brown. Serve with butter.

Variation *Use any type of dried fruit in this recipe, for example, currants, raisins, or chopped and stoned dates or prunes.*

Strawberry shortcakes

preparation 20 minutes
cooking 18 minutes
makes 8

30 g (1 oz) unsalted butter
2 tablespoons caster (superfine) sugar
1 egg
185 g (6½ oz/1½ cups) self-raising flour
pinch of salt
80 ml (2½ fl oz/⅓ cup) milk
1 tablespoon milk, extra
1 tablespoon caster (superfine) sugar, extra
fresh strawberries, hulled and halved, to serve
whipping cream, whipped, to serve

Preheat the oven to 210°C (415°F/Gas 6–7). Lightly grease a baking tray. Place the butter and sugar in a mixing bowl. Using electric beaters, beat the butter and sugar until light and fluffy. Add the egg and mix well.

Sift the flour and salt into another mixing bowl. Make a well in the centre of the dry ingredients. Add the butter, sugar and egg mixture and almost all of the milk. Using a flat-bladed knife, lightly mix until a soft dough forms, adding more milk if necessary. Knead the dough briefly on a lightly floured surface until smooth. Press out dough to a 2 cm (¾ inch) thickness. Using a floured plain 5 cm (2 inch) cutter, cut 12 rounds from the dough and place on the prepared baking tray.

Brush the rounds with the extra milk and top with a sprinkling of caster sugar. Bake for 15–18 minutes, or until lightly golden. Remove and place on a wire rack. When the shortcakes are cool, split and serve with strawberries and whipped cream.

Add the sugar and sultanas and stir to combine with a wooden spoon.

Cream the butter and sugar with electric beaters, then add the egg.

Bottom: Strawberry shortcakes. Top: Sultana scones.

Plain scones

preparation 20 minutes
cooking 12 minutes
makes 12

250 g (9 oz/2 cups) self-raising flour
pinch of salt, optional (see Note)
30 g (1 oz) unsalted butter, cut into small pieces
125 ml (4 fl oz/½ cup) milk
milk, extra, to glaze
jam, to serve
whipped cream, to serve

Preheat the oven to 210°C (415°F/Gas 6–7). Lightly grease a baking tray. Sift the flour and salt, if using, into a large mixing bowl. Add the butter and rub it into the flour lightly using your fingertips.

Make a well in the centre of the flour. Add almost all of the combined milk and 80 ml (2½ fl oz/⅓ cup) water. Mix with a flat-bladed knife to a soft dough, adding a little more liquid, if necessary.

Turn the dough out onto a lightly floured surface (use self-raising flour). Knead the dough briefly and lightly until smooth. Press or roll out the dough to form a round about 1–2 cm (½–¾ inch) thick.

Cut the dough into rounds using a floured round 5 cm (2 inch) cutter. Place the rounds on the prepared tray and glaze with the milk. Bake for 10–12 minutes, or until golden brown. Serve with jam and whipped cream.

Storage *Best eaten on the day of making.*

Note *Add a pinch of salt to your scones, even the sweet ones. Salt acts as a flavour enhancer and will not be tasted in the cooked product.*

Honey, date and ginger scones

preparation 25 minutes
cooking 15 minutes
makes 10

90 g (3¼ oz/½ cup) stoned dates
55 g (2 oz/¼ cup) glacé (candied) ginger
250 g (9 oz/2 cups) self-raising flour
½ teaspoon ground ginger
pinch of salt
1 tablespoon honey
125 ml (4 fl oz/½ cup) milk
60 ml (2 fl oz/¼ cup) cream

honey glaze
1 tablespoon milk
1 teaspoon honey

Preheat the oven to 210°C (415°F/Gas 6–7). Lightly grease a baking tray. Chop the dates and the glacé ginger into small chunks. Sift the flour, ground ginger and salt into a mixing bowl. Add the dates and glacé ginger. Stir to combine.

Combine the honey, milk and cream in a small saucepan and stir over low heat until combined. Add to the flour and mix lightly, with a flat-bladed knife, to form a soft dough, adding more milk if necessary. (The dough should have just lost its stickiness but not become dried or tough.)

Knead the dough briefly on a lightly floured surface until smooth, then press out to 2 cm (¾ inch) thickness. Cut out 10 rounds with a floured plain 5 cm (2 inch) cutter. Place the rounds on the prepared tray and brush with the honey glaze (see next step). Cook for 12–15 minutes, or until lightly golden.

To make the honey glaze, gently warm the milk and honey in a saucepan, stirring constantly until well combined.

Note *Use self-raising flour on your hands and work surfaces.*

Mix the mixture with a flat-bladed knife to form a soft dough, adding more liquid if necessary.

Add the cream mixture to the flour and mix lightly, with a flat-bladed knife, to form a soft dough.

Bottom: Honey, date and ginger scones. Top: Plain scones.

Wholemeal date scones

preparation 20 minutes
cooking 20 minutes
makes 12

185 g (6½ oz/1½ cups) self-raising flour
225 g (8 oz/1½ cups) wholemeal (whole-wheat)
self-raising flour
½ teaspoon baking powder
¼ teaspoon salt
60 g (2¼ oz) unsalted butter, cut into small pieces
2 tablespoons caster (superfine) sugar
185 g (6½ oz) stoned dates, chopped
315 ml (10¾ fl oz/1¼ cups) buttermilk
125 ml (4 fl oz/½ cup) water
buttermilk, extra, to glaze
butter or whipped cream, to serve, optional

Preheat the oven to 210°C (415°F/Gas 6–7). Lightly grease
a baking tray. Sift the flours, baking powder and salt into
a large mixing bowl, returning the husks to the bowl. Add
the butter and rub in lightly using your fingertips. Stir in the
sugar and the dates.

Make a well in the centre of the flour mixture. Add the
buttermilk and almost all of the water. Mix quickly, using a
flat-bladed knife, to form a soft dough, adding more water
if necessary. (The dough should have lost its stickiness but
not become too dry or tough.)

Knead dough briefly on a lightly floured surface until
smooth. Press out the dough with floured hands to form
a 2 cm (¾ inch) thick square. Cut into 12 smaller squares.
Place the squares on the prepared tray, leaving a 2 cm
(¾ inch) gap in between each. Brush with extra buttermilk.

Bake the scones for 18–20 minutes, or until golden brown.
Serve straight from the oven with butter or whipped cream,
if desired.

Note *These scones are more heavily textured than the
traditional recipe. Returning the flour husks to the mixture will
contribute to this texture, however it is still necessary to sift the
flours as this introduces air through the dry ingredients.*

Place the dough squares on the prepared tray,
making sure they are well spread.

Raspberry bun scones

preparation 20 minutes
cooking 12 minutes
makes 8

250 g (9 oz/2 cups) self-raising flour
pinch of salt
2 tablespoons caster (superfine) sugar
125 ml (4 fl oz/½ cup) milk
30 g (1 oz) unsalted butter, melted
80 ml (2½ fl oz/⅓ cup) water
1 tablespoon raspberry jam
1 tablespoon milk, extra
caster (superfine) sugar, extra
unsalted butter, to serve

Preheat the oven to 210°C (415°F/Gas 6–7). Lightly grease a
baking tray. Sift the flour and salt into a large mixing bowl.
Add the sugar and stir to combine.

Make a well in the centre of the flour. Place the milk and
melted butter in a separate bowl and combine. Add to
the flour mixture all at once, reserving a teaspoonful for
glazing. Add almost all of the water. Mix quickly, using a
flat-bladed knife, to form a soft dough, adding more water
if necessary.

Knead the dough briefly on a lightly floured surface until
smooth. Roll out the dough to a 1 cm (½ inch) thickness,
then cut the dough into 8 rounds using a floured 7 cm
(2¾ inch) cutter. Turn each of the scones over and make
an indentation in the centre with your thumb. Place
½ teaspoon of jam in the indentation and fold over dough.
Place the rounds, well apart, on the prepared tray and
flatten tops. Brush with the milk and sprinkle with the extra
caster sugar. Bake for 10–12 minutes, or until golden.
Serve warm with butter.

Spoon the jam into the indentation, then fold the
dough over.

Bottom: Raspberry bun scones. Top: Wholemeal date scones.

Capsicum and corn muffins

preparation 15 minutes
cooking 20 minutes
makes 12

125 g (4½ oz/1 cup) plain (all-purpose) flour
1 tablespoon baking powder
150 g (5½ oz/1 cup) fine polenta
1 tablespoon caster (superfine) sugar
1 egg
170 ml (5½ fl oz/⅔ cup) milk
¼ teaspoon Tabasco sauce, optional
60 ml (2 fl oz/¼ cup) oil
½ red capsicum (pepper), seeded, membrane removed and
finely chopped
440 g (15½ oz) tinned corn kernels, drained
3 tablespoons finely chopped flat-leaf (Italian) parsley

Preheat the oven to 210°C (415°F/Gas 6–7). Lightly grease
a 12-hole muffin tray. Sift the flour, baking powder and
¼ teaspoon salt into a large bowl. Add the polenta and
sugar. Stir thoroughly until all the ingredients are well
mixed. Make a well in the centre.

Combine the egg, milk, Tabasco and oil in a separate bowl,
then add to the flour mixture all at once. Stir gently with a
fork or spatula until the mixture is just moistened. (Do not
overmix as the batter should look quite lumpy.)

Spoon the mixture evenly into the prepared muffin holes.
Bake for 20 minutes, or until golden. Loosen the muffins
with a flat-bladed knife but leave in the tray for 2 minutes.
Transfer to a wire rack to cool.

Zucchini and carrot muffins

preparation 20 minutes
cooking 20 minutes
makes 12

2 zucchini (courgettes)
2 carrots
250 g (9 oz/2 cups) self-raising flour
1 teaspoon ground cinnamon
½ teaspoon freshly grated nutmeg
60 g (2¼ oz/½ cup) chopped pecans
2 eggs
250 ml (9 fl oz/1 cup) milk
90 g (3¼ oz) butter, melted

Preheat the oven to 210°C (415°F/Gas 6–7). Lightly grease a
12-hole muffin tray. Wash and dry the zucchini and carrots,
then grate them.

Sift the flour, cinnamon, nutmeg and a pinch of salt into a
large mixing bowl. Add the carrot, zucchini and chopped
pecans. Stir thoroughly until all the ingredients are well
combined. Make a well in the centre.

Put the eggs, milk and melted butter in a separate mixing
bowl. Whisk well until combined, then add all at once to
the flour mixture. Stir gently with a fork or spatula until the
mixture is just moistened. (Do not overmix as the batter
should look quite lumpy.)

Spoon the mixture evenly into the prepared muffin holes.
Bake for 15–20 minutes, or until golden. Loosen the muffins
with a flat-bladed knife or spatula and leave in the tin for
2 minutes, before turning out onto a wire rack to cool.

Pumpkin scones

preparation 35 minutes
cooking 12 minutes
makes 12

30 g (1 oz) unsalted butter, chopped
2 tablespoons caster (superfine) sugar
125 g (4½ oz/½ cup) mashed cooked pumpkin (winter squash)
(see Note)
1 egg, lightly beaten
125 ml (4 fl oz/½ cup) milk
340 g (11¾ oz/2¾ cups) self-raising flour
pinch of salt
milk, to glaze
unsalted butter, to serve

Preheat the oven to 210°C (415°F/Gas 6–7). Lightly grease
a baking tray. Using electric beaters, beat the butter and
sugar in a small mixing bowl until the mixture is light and
creamy. Add the pumpkin, egg and milk. Mix until well
combined.

Sift the flour and salt into a large mixing bowl. Make a well
in the centre and add almost all of the mashed pumpkin
mixture. Mix lightly, using a flat-bladed knife, to form a soft
dough, adding more liquid if necessary.

Knead the dough briefly on a lightly floured surface. Roll
dough out to 2 cm (¾ inch) thick.

Cut into rounds using a floured plain 5 cm (2 inch) cutter.
Place the rounds, close together, on the prepared tray and
brush with a little milk. Bake for 10–12 minutes, or until
golden brown. Serve warm with butter.

Note To make 125 g (4½ oz/½ cup) of mashed pumpkin you
will need around 250 g (9 oz) of raw pumpkin.

Top left: Capsicum and corn muffins. Top right: Zucchini and carrot muffins. Bottom right: Pumpkin scones.

Cheese and chive scones

preparation 20 minutes
cooking 12 minutes
makes 9

250 g (9 oz/2 cups) self-raising flour
30 g (1 oz) butter, chopped
60 g (2¼ oz/½ cup) grated cheddar cheese
25 g (1 oz/¼ cup) shredded parmesan cheese
2 tablespoons snipped chives
125 ml (4 fl oz/½ cup) milk
30 g (1 oz/¼ cup) grated cheddar cheese, extra

Preheat the oven to 210°C (415°F/Gas 6–7). Brush a baking tray with melted butter or oil. Sift the flour and a pinch of salt into a bowl. Rub in the butter using your fingertips. Stir in the cheeses and the chives. Make a well in the centre, add the milk and almost all of 125 ml (4 fl oz/½ cup) water. Mix lightly with a flat-bladed knife to form a soft dough, adding more water if the dough is too dry.

Knead the dough briefly on a lightly floured surface until smooth. Press out the dough to 2 cm (¾ inch) thick. Using a floured 5 cm (2 inch) plain round cutter, cut nine rounds from the dough. Place the rounds on the prepared tray and sprinkle with extra cheese. Bake for 12 minutes, or until the cheese is golden.

Potato and olive scones

preparation 25 minutes
cooking 15 minutes
makes 15

250 g (9 oz) potatoes, chopped
125 ml (4 fl oz/½ cup) milk
250 g (9 oz/2 cups) self-raising flour
30 g (1 oz) butter, chopped
30 g (1 oz/¼ cup) black olives, pitted and chopped
3–4 teaspoons chopped rosemary
milk, extra, to glaze

Preheat the oven to 210°C (415°F/Gas 6–7). Brush a baking tray with melted butter or oil. Boil or microwave the potatoes until tender. Mash the potatoes with the milk and season with freshly ground black pepper.

Sift the flour into a large bowl. Rub in the butter, using your fingertips. Add the olives and rosemary and stir until just combined. Make a well in the centre and add the mashed potato and almost all of 125 ml (4 fl oz/½ cup) water. Mix with a flat-bladed knife, using a cutting action, until the mixture forms a soft dough. Add a little more water if the dough is too dry.

Knead the dough briefly on a lightly floured surface until smooth. Press out to a thickness of 2 cm (¾ inch). Using a floured 5 cm (2 inch) plain round cutter, cut 15 rounds from the dough and place them on the prepared tray. Brush the tops with the extra milk and cook for about 10–15 minutes until the scones are golden brown.

Mini onion and parmesan scones

preparation 25 minutes
cooking 12 minutes
makes 24

30 g (1 oz) butter
1 small onion, finely chopped
250 g (9 oz/2 cups) self-raising flour, sifted
50 g (1¾ oz/½ cup) finely shredded parmesan cheese
125 ml (4 oz/½ cup) milk
cayenne pepper, to sprinkle

Preheat the oven to 210°C (415°F/Gas 6–7). Brush a baking tray with a little melted butter or oil.

Melt the butter in a small frying pan, add the onion and cook, over low heat, for 2–3 minutes or until soft. Allow to cool slightly.

Combine the sifted flour, parmesan and a pinch salt in a bowl. Make a well in the centre and add the onion. Combine the milk with 125 ml (4 oz/½ cup) water and add almost all to the bowl. Mix lightly, with a flat-bladed knife, using a cutting action, until the mixture forms a soft dough. Add more liquid if the dough is too dry.

Knead the dough briefly on a lightly floured surface until smooth and press out to 2 cm (¾ inch) thick. Cut the dough into 24 rounds with a 3 cm (1¼ inch) plain round cutter. Place the rounds on the prepared tray and sprinkle each lightly with cayenne pepper. Cook for 10–12 minutes until golden brown.

Note *Handle scone dough with a light touch. Cut the liquid in with a knife and then take care not to over-knead or you'll have tough scones.*

Top left: Cheese and chive scones. Top right: Potato and olive scones. Bottom right: Mini onion and parmesan scones.

breads
and **pizzas**

Grissini

preparation 30 minutes + 1 hour 10 minutes standing
cooking 20 minutes
makes 24

2 teaspoons dried yeast
1 teaspoon sugar
500 g (1 lb 2 oz/4 cups) plain (all-purpose) flour
60 ml (2 fl oz/¼ cup) olive oil
2 small handfuls chopped basil
4 garlic cloves, crushed
50 g (1¾ oz) parmesan cheese, grated
2 teaspoons sea salt flakes
2 tablespoons grated parmesan cheese, extra

Put the yeast, sugar and 310 ml (10 fl oz/1¼ cups) warm water in a small bowl and stir well. Leave in a warm place for 10 minutes, or until bubbles appear on the surface. The mixture should be frothy and slightly increased in volume. If your yeast doesn't foam, it is dead, so you will have to discard it and start again.

Sift the flour and 1 teaspoon of salt into a bowl and stir in the yeast and oil mixture. Add a little more water if the dough is dry.

Gather the dough into a ball and turn out onto a lightly floured surface. Knead the dough for 10 minutes, or until soft and elastic. Divide into two portions and flatten into rectangles. Put the basil and garlic on one portion and the parmesan on the other. Fold the dough to enclose the fillings, then knead for a few minutes to incorporate the flavourings evenly.

Place each dough portion into a separate lightly oiled bowl and cover with plastic wrap. Leave the bowls in a warm place for about 1 hour, or until the dough has doubled in volume. Preheat the oven to 230°C (450°F/Gas 8). Lightly grease two large baking trays.

Punch down the doughs and knead each again for 1 minute. Divide each piece of dough into 12 even portions, and roll each portion into a stick 30 cm (12 inches) long. Place the dough sticks on the baking trays and brush with water. Sprinkle the basil and garlic dough with the sea salt flakes, and the cheese dough with the extra parmesan cheese. Bake for 15 minutes, or until crisp and golden. Transfer to a wire rack to cool.

Storage Grissini can be stored in an airtight container for up to 1 week.

Once the dough has doubled in volume, punch it down before kneading.

Roll each portion of dough into a long, thin sausage shape that is about 30 cm (12 inches) long.

Beer bread rolls

preparation 15 minutes
cooking 20 minutes
makes 4 rolls

405 g (14¼ g/3¼ cups) plain (all-purpose) flour
3 teaspoons baking powder
1 tablespoon sugar
50 g (1¾ oz) butter, chopped
375 ml (13 fl oz/1½ cups) beer

Preheat the oven to 210°C (415°F/Gas 6–7). Process the flour, baking powder, sugar, butter and 1 teaspoon salt in a food processor until crumbly. Add the beer and process in bursts to form a soft dough.

Turn the dough out onto a well-floured surface and knead until smooth, adding extra flour if needed. Divide the dough into four balls, place on greased oven trays and flatten slightly. Brush with a little water and slash the tops with a knife. Bake for 10 minutes. Reduce the oven to 180°C (350°F/Gas 4) and bake for a further 10 minutes, or until cooked. Transfer to a wire rack to cool. Serve with butter.

Onion and buttermilk bread

preparation 15 minutes
cooking 30 minutes
makes 4 small loaves

375 g (13 oz/3 cups) self-raising flour
35 g (1¼ oz) French onion soup powder
2 tablespoons snipped chives
435 ml (15¼ fl oz/1¾ cups) buttermilk, plus a little extra

Preheat the oven to 180°C (350°F/Gas 4). Sift the flour into a large bowl and stir in the dried soup and chives. Mix in the buttermilk with a flat-bladed knife, using a cutting action, until the mixture forms a soft dough. Add extra buttermilk if the mixture is too dry.

Turn the dough out onto a lightly floured surface and quickly knead into a smooth ball. Cut into four even-sized pieces and shape each into a ball. Place on a floured baking tray, allowing room for each to rise. Sift extra flour over the top and make a slash with a sharp knife across the top of each loaf. Bake the loaves for 25–30 minutes, or until cooked and golden. Transfer to a wire rack to cool.

Lemon pepper bread

preparation 20 minutes
cooking 25 minutes
makes 2 loaves

250 g (9 oz/2 cups) self-raising flour
2 teaspoons lemon pepper, or 1 teaspoon grated lemon zest
and 2 teaspoons black pepper
50 g (1¾ oz) butter, chopped
1 tablespoon snipped chives
90 g (3¼ oz/¾ cup) grated cheddar cheese
2 teaspoons white vinegar
185 ml (6 fl oz/¾ cup) milk

Preheat the oven to 210°C (415°F/Gas 6–7). Brush two baking trays with melted butter or oil. Sift the flour and 1 teaspoon salt into a large bowl and add the lemon pepper, or lemon zest and pepper. Using your fingertips, rub in the butter until the mixture resembles coarse breadcrumbs. Stir in the chives and cheese.

In a separate bowl, stir the vinegar into the milk (it should look slightly curdled). Add to the flour mixture and mix to a soft dough, adding more milk if dough is too stiff.

Turn the dough out onto a lightly floured surface and knead until smooth. Divide the dough into two portions. Place on the prepared trays and press each portion out into a circle approximately 2.5 cm (1 inch) thick. Score each with a knife into eight wedges, cutting lightly into the top of the bread. Dust lightly with flour. Bake for 20–25 minutes, or until the bread is a deep golden colour and sounds hollow when tapped on the base. Transfer to a wire rack to cool a little. Serve warm with butter.

Top left: Beer bread rolls. Top right: Onion and buttermilk bread. Bottom right: Lemon pepper bread.

Sourdough rye bread

preparation 20 minutes + overnight standing
cooking 40 minutes
makes 2 loaves

sourdough starter
2 teaspoons dried yeast
1 teaspoon caster (superfine) sugar
200 g (7 oz/2 cups) rye flour

bread dough
100 g (3½ oz/1 cup) rye flour
550 g (1 lb 4 oz/4½ cups) unbleached plain (all-purpose) flour
45 g (1¾ oz/¼ cup) soft brown sugar
3 teaspoons caraway seeds
2 teaspoons dried yeast, extra
60 ml (2 fl oz/¼ cup) oil
rye flour, extra, to sprinkle

To make the sourdough starter, combine the yeast, sugar, rye flour and 435 ml (15¼ fl oz/1¾ cups) warm water in a bowl. Cover with plastic wrap and set aside overnight at room temperature to sour. For a stronger flavour, leave for up to 3 days.

To make the bread dough, brush a large baking tray with oil or melted butter. In a large bowl, combine the rye flour, 440 g (15½ oz/3½ cups) of the plain flour, sugar, caraway seeds and 2 teaspoons salt. Dissolve the yeast in 250 ml (9 fl oz/1 cup) warm water. Make a well in the centre of the dry ingredients and add the sourdough starter, dissolved yeast and oil. Mix, using a wooden spoon then your hands, until the dough forms a rough, slightly sticky ball, which leaves the side of the bowl. Add some of the remaining flour, if necessary—you may not need to use it all.

Turn onto a lightly floured surface. Knead for 10 minutes, or until smooth and elastic. Incorporate the remaining flour, if needed. Place the dough in a large, lightly oiled bowl. Leave, covered with plastic wrap, in a warm place for 45 minutes, or until well risen. Punch down and knead for 1 minute. Divide into two even-sized portions. Shape into round or oblong loaves and place on the baking tray. Sprinkle with rye flour and use the end of a wooden spoon handle to press holes 2 cm (¾ inch) deep in the top, or make three slashes. Leave, covered with plastic wrap, in a warm place for 45 minutes, or until the dough is well risen.

Preheat the oven to 180°C (350°F/Gas 4). Sprinkle the loaves with flour. Bake for 40 minutes, or until a skewer inserted in the centre comes out clean. Transfer to a wire rack to cool.

Chapattis

preparation 40 minutes + 50 minutes standing
cooking 1 hour 25 minutes
makes 14

280 g (10 oz/2¼ cups) atta flour (see Note)
melted ghee or oil, for brushing

Place the flour in a large bowl with a pinch of salt. Slowly add 250 ml (9 fl oz/1 cup) water, or enough to form a firm dough. Place on a lightly floured surface and knead until smooth. Cover with plastic wrap and leave for 50 minutes.

Divide into 14 portions and roll into 14 cm (5½ inch) circles. Heat a frying pan over medium heat and brush with the ghee or oil. Cook the chapattis one at a time over medium heat, flattening the surface, for 2–3 minutes on each side or until golden brown and bubbles appear. Serve with curries.

Note *Atta flour is also known as chapatti flour and is a finely milled, low-gluten, soft-textured, wholemeal (whole-wheat) wheat flour used to make Indian flat breads. If unavailable, use plain wholemeal flour—sift it first and discard the husks. This may result in heavier, coarser bread.*

Naan

preparation 15 minutes + 2 hours standing
cooking 10 minutes
makes 8

500 g (1 lb 2 oz/4 cups) plain (all-purpose) flour
1 teaspoon baking powder
½ teaspoon bicarbonate of soda (baking soda)
1 egg, beaten
125 g (4½ oz/½ cup) plain yoghurt
80 g (2¾ oz) ghee or butter, melted
250 ml (9 fl oz/1 cup) milk

Preheat the oven to 200°C (400°F/Gas 6). Lightly grease two 28 x 33 cm (11¼ x 13 inch) baking trays. Sift together the flour, baking powder, bicarbonate of soda and 1 teaspoon salt. Mix in the egg, yoghurt and 1 tablespoon of the ghee or butter and gradually add enough of the milk to form a soft dough. Cover with a damp cloth and leave in a warm place for 2 hours.

Knead the dough on a well-floured surface for 2–3 minutes, or until smooth. Divide into eight portions and roll each one into an oval 15 cm (6 inches) long. Brush with water and place, wet side down, on the baking trays. Brush with the rest of the melted ghee or butter and bake for 8–10 minutes, or until golden brown. Serve with Indian curries.

Variation *To make garlic naan, crush 6 garlic cloves and sprinkle evenly over the dough prior to baking.*

The chapattis need to be cooked until golden and bubbly on both sides.

Once the dough has rested, knead it for a few minutes until smooth.

Bottom: Naan. Top: Chapattis.

Walnut bread

preparation 45 minutes + 2 hours 40 minutes standing
cooking 50 minutes
makes 1 large loaf

2½ teaspoons dried yeast
90 g (3¼ oz/¼ cup) liquid malt
2 tablespoons olive oil
300 g (10½ oz/3 cups) walnut halves, lightly toasted
540 g (1 lb 3 oz/4⅓ cups) white strong flour
1 egg, lightly beaten

Grease a baking tray. Put the yeast, liquid malt and 330 ml (11¼ fl oz/1⅓ cups) warm water in a small bowl and stir well. Leave in a warm place for 10 minutes, or until bubbles appear on the surface. The mixture should be frothy and slightly increased in volume. If your yeast doesn't foam, it is dead, so you will have to discard it and start again. Stir in the oil.

Process 200 g (7 oz/2 cups) of the toasted walnuts in a food processor until they resemble coarse meal.

In a large bowl, combine 500 g (1 lb 2 oz/4 cups) of the flour with 1½ teaspoons salt and stir in the ground walnuts. Make a well and add the yeast mixture. Mix with a large metal spoon until just combined.

Turn out onto a lightly floured surface and knead for 10 minutes, or until smooth, incorporating enough of the remaining flour to keep the dough from sticking—it should be soft and moist, but it won't become very springy.

Shape the dough into a ball. Place in a lightly oiled bowl, cover with plastic wrap or a damp tea towel (dish towel) and leave in a warm place for up to 1½ hours, or until the dough has doubled in size.

Punch down the dough and turn out onto a lightly floured surface. With very little kneading, shape the dough into a flattened 20 x 25 cm (8 x 10 inch) rectangle. Spread with the remaining walnuts and roll up firmly from the short end. Place the loaf on the baking tray, cover with plastic wrap or a damp tea towel and leave to rise for 1 hour, or until doubled in size.

Preheat the oven to 190°C (375°F/Gas 5). Glaze the loaf with the egg and bake for 45–50 minutes, or until golden and hollow sounding when tapped on the base. Transfer to a wire rack to cool.

Note *Use good-quality pale and plump walnuts for this recipe. Cheap walnuts can taste bitter.*

With the short edge facing towards you, roll the dough up.

Use the beaten egg as a glaze for the loaf—this will give it a lovely finish.

Cottage loaf

preparation 30 minutes + 50 minutes standing
cooking 40 minutes
makes 1 large loaf

2 teaspoons dried yeast
1 tablespoon soft brown sugar
250 g (9 oz/2 cups) white strong flour
300 g (10½ oz/2 cups) wholemeal (whole-wheat) strong flour
1 tablespoon vegetable oil

Put the yeast, 1 teaspoon of the sugar and 125 ml (4 fl oz/ ½ cup) warm water in a small bowl and mix well. Leave in a warm place for 10 minutes, or until bubbles appear on the surface. The mixture should be frothy and slightly increased in volume. If your yeast doesn't foam, it is dead, so you will have to discard it and start again.

Put the flours and 1 teaspoon salt in a large bowl. Make a well in the centre and add the yeast mixture, oil, the remaining sugar and 250 ml (9 fl oz/1 cup) warm water. Mix with a wooden spoon then turn out onto a lightly floured surface. Knead for 10 minutes, or until smooth and elastic. Incorporate a little extra flour into the dough as you knead, to stop the dough from sticking.

Place the dough in an oiled bowl and lightly brush oil over the dough. Cover with plastic wrap or a damp tea towel (dish towel) and leave in a warm place for 45 minutes, or until doubled in size.

Punch down the dough then turn out onto a lightly floured surface and knead the dough for 3–4 minutes. Pull away one-third of the dough and knead both portions into a smooth ball. Place the large ball on a large floured baking tray and brush the top with water. Sit the smaller ball on top and, using two fingers, press down into the centre of the dough to join the two balls together. Cover with plastic wrap or a damp tea towel and set aside in a warm place for 40 minutes, or until well risen.

Preheat the oven to 190°C (375°F/Gas 5). Sift some white flour over the top of the loaf and bake for 40 minutes, or until golden brown and cooked. Leave on the tray for 2–3 minutes to cool slightly, then transfer to a wire rack to cool completely.

Fougasse

preparation 30 minutes + 1 hour 20 minutes standing
cooking 35 minutes
makes 4 small loaves

2 teaspoons dried yeast
1 teaspoon sugar
500 g (1 lb 2 oz/4 cups) white strong flour
60 ml (2 fl oz/¼ cup) olive oil
185 g (6½ oz/1 cup) black pitted olives, chopped, optional
1 handful chopped mixed herbs, such as parsley, oregano and basil, optional

Put the yeast, sugar and 125 ml (4 fl oz/½ cup) warm water in a small bowl and stir until dissolved. Leave in a warm place for 10 minutes, or until bubbles appear on the surface. The mixture should be frothy and slightly increased in volume. If your yeast doesn't foam, it is dead, so you will have to discard it and start again.

Sift the flour and 2 teaspoons salt into a bowl and make a well in the centre. Add the yeast mixture, olive oil and 185 ml (6 fl oz/¾ cup) warm water. Mix to a soft dough and gather into a ball with floured hands.

Turn out onto a floured surface and knead for 10 minutes, or until smooth. Place the dough in a large, lightly oiled bowl, cover loosely with plastic wrap or a damp tea towel (dish towel) and leave in a warm place for 1 hour, or until doubled in size.

Punch down the dough and add the olives and herbs, if desired. Knead for 1 minute. Divide the mixture into four equal portions. Press each portion into a large, oval shape about 1 cm (½ inch) thick and make several cuts on either side of each. Lay the dough on large, floured baking trays, cover with plastic wrap and leave to rise for 20 minutes.

Preheat the oven to 210°C (415°F/Gas 6–7). Bake the fougasse for 35 minutes, or until crisp. To make the crust crispy, spray the inside of the oven with water after 15 minutes cooking. Transfer to a wire rack to cool.

Note *Although fougasse is traditionally made as a plain bread, these days bakeries often incorporate ingredients such as fresh herbs, olives, chopped ham and anchovies into the dough.*

Bottom: Fougasse. Top: Cottage loaf.

Cheese and herb pull-apart

preparation 30 minutes + 1 hour 40 minutes standing
cooking 30 minutes
makes 1 loaf

2 teaspoons dried yeast
1 teaspoon sugar
500 g (1 lb 2 oz/4 cups) plain (all-purpose) flour
2 tablespoons chopped flat-leaf (Italian) parsley
2 tablespoons snipped chives
1 tablespoon chopped thyme
60 g (2¼ oz) cheddar cheese, grated
milk, to glaze

Put the yeast, sugar and 125 ml (4 fl oz/½ cup) warm water in a small bowl and stir well. Leave in a warm place for 10 minutes, or until bubbles appear on the surface. The mixture should be frothy and slightly increased in volume. If your yeast doesn't foam, it is dead, so you will have to discard it and start again.

Sift the flour and 1½ teaspoons salt in a large bowl. Make a well in the centre and add the yeast mixture and 250 ml (9 fl oz/1 cup) warm water. Mix to a soft dough. Turn onto a lightly floured surface and knead for 10 minutes, or until smooth. Place the dough in an oiled bowl, cover with plastic wrap or a damp tea towel (dish towel) and leave for 1 hour, or until doubled in size.

Punch down the dough and knead for 1 minute. Divide the dough in half and shape each half into 10 flat discs, 6 cm (2½ inches) in diameter. Mix the herbs with the cheddar and put 2 teaspoons of the mixture on one of the discs. Press another disc on top, then repeat with the remaining discs and herb mixture.

Grease a 6 x 10.5 x 21 cm (2½ x 4¼ x 8¼ inch) loaf (bar) tin. Stand the filled discs upright in the prepared tin, squashing them together. Cover the tin with plastic wrap or a damp tea towel and leave in a warm place for 30 minutes, or until the dough is well risen.

Preheat the oven to 210°C (415°F/Gas 6–7). Lightly brush the loaf with a little milk and bake for 30 minutes, or until the bread is brown and crusty and sounds hollow when tapped on the base. Transfer to a wire rack to cool.

Pretzels

preparation 50 minutes + 1 hour 40 minutes standing
cooking 15 minutes
makes 12

1 teaspoon dried yeast
¼ teaspoon sugar
150 ml (5 fl oz) warm milk
185 g (6½ oz/1½ cups) white strong flour
30 g (1 oz) butter, melted
1 egg yolk, lightly beaten
coarse sea salt, to sprinkle

Put the yeast, sugar and warm milk in a small bowl and stir well. Leave in a warm place for 10 minutes, or until bubbles appear on the surface. The mixture should be frothy and slightly increased in volume. If your yeast doesn't foam, it is dead, so you will have to discard it and start again.

Put the flour and ¼ teaspoon salt in a large bowl and make a well in the centre. Add the yeast mixture and butter and mix to a rough dough with a wooden spoon. Turn out onto a floured surface and knead for 10 minutes until smooth and elastic.

Place into an oiled bowl, oil the surface of the dough, cover with plastic wrap or a clean tea towel (dish towel) and set aside in a warm place for 1 hour until doubled in size.

Preheat the oven to 190°C (375°F/Gas 5). Line a large baking tray with baking paper. Punch down the dough and knead again for 2–3 minutes. Divide into 12 pieces. Cover the dough while working with each piece. Roll each piece into a long rope 40 cm (16 inches) long. Circle and knot into a pretzel shape. Place well spaced on the tray. Cover with a tea towel. Leave to rise in a warm, draught-free place for 20–30 minutes.

Lightly brush the pretzels with the beaten egg yolk and sprinkle with sea salt. Place the pretzels in the oven and spray them twice with water before baking for 12–15 minutes, or until crisp and golden brown. Transfer to a wire rack to cool.

Bottom: Pretzels. Top: Cheese and herb pull-apart.

Damper

preparation 20 minutes
cooking 25 minutes
makes 1 damper

375 g (13 oz/3 cups) self-raising flour
90 g (3¼ oz) butter, melted
125 ml (4 fl oz/½ cup) milk
milk, extra, to glaze
flour, extra, to dust

Preheat the oven to 210°C (415°F/Gas 6–7). Grease a baking tray. Sift the flour and 1–2 teaspoons salt into a bowl and make a well in the centre. Combine the butter, milk and 125 ml (4 fl oz/½ cup) water and pour into the well. Stir with a knife until just combined. Turn the dough onto a lightly floured surface and knead for 20 seconds, or until smooth. Place the dough on the baking tray and press out to a 20 cm (8 inch) circle.

Using a sharp pointed knife, score the dough into eight sections about 1 cm (½ inch) deep. Brush with milk, then dust with flour. Bake for 10 minutes. Reduce the oven to 180°C (350°F/Gas 4) and bake the damper for another 15 minutes, or until the damper is golden and sounds hollow when the surface is tapped. Transfer to a wire rack to cool a little. Serve with butter.

Note Damper is the Australian version of soda bread. It is traditionally served warm with slatherings of golden syrup. If you prefer, you can make four rounds instead of one large damper and slightly reduce the cooking time.

Unleavened lavash

preparation 40 minutes + 1 hour refrigeration
cooking 35 minutes
makes 4

125 g (4½ oz/1 cup) plain (all-purpose) flour
½ teaspoon sugar
20 g (¾ oz) chilled butter, chopped
80 ml (2½ fl oz/⅓ cup) milk
sesame and poppy seeds, to sprinkle

Put the flour, sugar, butter and ½ teaspoon salt in a food processor. Process in short bursts until the butter is incorporated. With the machine running, gradually pour in the milk and process until the dough comes together—you may need to add an extra 1 tablespoon milk. Turn out onto a lightly floured surface and knead briefly until smooth. Wrap in plastic wrap and refrigerate for 1 hour.

Preheat the oven to 190°C (375°F/Gas 5). Lightly grease a large baking tray. Cut the dough into four pieces. Working with one piece at a time, roll until very thin, into a rough square shape measuring about 20 cm (8 inches) along the sides. Place the dough shapes on the tray, brush the tops lightly with water and sprinkle with the seeds. Roll a rolling pin lightly over the surface of the dough to press in the seeds. Bake for 6–8 minutes, or until golden brown and dry. Transfer to a wire rack until cool and crisp. Break into large pieces. Repeat the process with the remaining dough.

Scottish baps

preparation 40 minutes + 1 hour 25 minutes standing
cooking 30 minutes
makes 12 baps

2 teaspoons dried yeast
1 teaspoon caster (superfine) sugar
440 g (15½ oz/3½ cups) white strong flour
250 ml (9 fl oz/1 cup) lukewarm milk
50 g (1¾ oz) butter, melted
1 tablespoon plain (all-purpose) flour

Lightly dust two baking trays with flour. Put the yeast, sugar and 2 tablespoons of the white strong flour in a small bowl. Gradually add the milk, blending until smooth and dissolved. Leave in a warm place for 10 minutes, or until bubbles appear on the surface. The mixture should be frothy and slightly increased in volume. If your yeast doesn't foam, it is dead, so you will have to discard it and start again.

Sift the remaining flour and 1½ teaspoons salt into a large bowl. Make a well in the centre and add the yeast mixture and butter. Using a flat-bladed knife, mix to form a soft dough. Turn the dough onto a lightly floured surface and knead for 3 minutes, or until smooth. Shape into a ball and place in a large oiled bowl. Cover with plastic wrap or a damp tea towel (dish towel) and leave in a warm place for 1 hour, or until well risen.

Preheat the oven to 210°C (415°F/Gas 6–7). Punch down the dough with your fist. Knead the dough again for 2 minutes, or until smooth. Divide into 12 pieces. Knead one portion of dough at a time on a lightly floured surface for 1 minute, roll into a ball and shape into a flat oval. Repeat with the remaining dough.

Place the baps on the trays and dust with the plain flour. Cover with plastic wrap and leave in a warm place for 15 minutes, or until well risen. Make an indent in the centre of each bap with your finger. Bake for 30 minutes until browned and cooked through. Transfer to a wire rack to cool a little. Serve warm.

Top left: Damper. Top right: Unleavened lavash. Bottom right: Scottish baps.

Mini wholemeal loaves

preparation 40 minutes + 1 hour 55 minutes standing
cooking 45 minutes
makes 4 small loaves

2 teaspoons dried yeast
1 tablespoon caster (superfine) sugar
125 ml (4 fl oz/½ cup) warm milk
600 g (1 lb 5 oz/4 cups) wholemeal (whole-wheat) strong flour
60 ml (2 fl oz/¼ cup) oil
1 egg, lightly beaten

Grease four 13 x 6½ x 5 cm (5 x 2¾ x 2 inch) baking tins. Put the yeast, sugar and milk in a small bowl and mix well. Leave in a warm place for 10 minutes, or until bubbles appear on the surface. The mixture should be frothy and slightly increased in volume. If your yeast doesn't foam, it is dead, so you will have to discard it and start again.

Put the flour and 1 teaspoon salt in a large bowl, make a well in the centre and add the yeast mixture, oil and 250 ml (9 fl oz/1 cup) warm water. Mix to a soft dough and gather into a ball. Turn out onto a floured surface and knead for 10 minutes. Add a little extra flour if the dough is too sticky.

Place the dough in a large oiled bowl, cover loosely with plastic wrap or a damp tea towel (dish towel) and leave in a warm place for 1 hour, or until well risen. Punch down the dough, turn out onto a floured surface and knead for 1 minute, or until smooth. Divide into four portions, knead into shape and put in the tins. Cover loosely with plastic wrap or a damp tea towel and leave in a warm place for 45 minutes, or until risen.

Preheat the oven to 210°C (415°F/Gas 6–7). Brush the loaf tops with the beaten egg. Bake for 10 minutes, then reduce the oven temperature to 180°C (350°F/Gas 4) and bake for a further 30–35 minutes, or until the base sounds hollow when tapped. Cover with foil if the tops become too brown. Transfer to a wire rack to cool.

Malt bread

preparation 45 minutes + 1 hour 50 minutes standing
cooking 40 minutes
makes 1 loaf

2 teaspoons dried yeast
1 teaspoon sugar
300 g (10½ oz/2 cups) plain (all-purpose) wholemeal (whole-wheat) flour
125 g (4½ oz/1 cup) plain (all-purpose) flour
2 teaspoons ground cinnamon
60 g (2¼ oz/½ cup) raisins
30 g (1 oz) butter, melted
1 tablespoon treacle
1 tablespoon liquid malt extract
1 tablespoon hot milk
½ teaspoon liquid malt extract, extra

Brush a 7 x 14 x 21 cm (2¾ x 5½ x 8¼ inch) loaf (bar) tin with oil and line the base with baking paper. Combine 250 ml (9 fl oz/1 cup) lukewarm water, the yeast and sugar in a small bowl. Cover with plastic wrap and set aside in a warm place for 10 minutes, or until bubbles appear on the surface. The mixture should be frothy and slightly increased in volume. If your yeast doesn't foam, it is dead, so you will have to discard it and start again.

Sift the flours and cinnamon into a large bowl, then add the raisins and stir. Make a well in the centre. Add the melted butter, treacle, 1 tablespoon of malt extract and the yeast mixture. Mix to a soft dough using a flat-bladed knife. Turn onto a lightly floured surface and knead for 10 minutes, or until smooth. Shape the dough into a ball and place in a lightly oiled bowl. Set aside, covered with plastic wrap, in a warm place for 1 hour, or until well risen. Punch down the dough, then knead until smooth.

Roll into a 20 cm (8 inch) square and then roll up. Place the dough in the tin, with the seam underneath, and set aside, covered with plastic wrap, in a warm place for 40 minutes, or until well risen.

Preheat the oven to 180°C (350°F/Gas 4). Brush the dough with the combined milk and extra malt. Bake for 40 minutes or until a skewer inserted into the centre of the bread comes out clean. Set aside for 3 minutes in the tin before transferring to a wire rack to cool.

Bottom: Malt bread. Top: Mini wholemeal loaves.

Flatbread with za'atar

preparation 35 minutes + 2 hours standing time
cooking 15 minutes
makes 10

1 tablespoon dried yeast
1 teaspoon sugar
405 g (14¼ oz/3¼ cups) plain (all-purpose) flour
125 ml (4 fl oz/½ cup) olive oil
20 g (¾ oz/⅓ cup) za'atar (see Note)
1 tablespoon sea salt flakes

Put the yeast and sugar in a small bowl with 60 ml (2 fl oz/ ¼ cup) warm water and stir until dissolved. Leave in a warm place for 10 minutes, or until bubbles appear on the surface. The mixture should be frothy and slightly increased in volume. If your yeast doesn't foam, it is dead, so you will have to discard it and start again.

Sift the flour and ½ teaspoon salt into a large bowl. Make a well in the centre and pour in the yeast mixture and 310 ml (10¾ fl oz/1¼ cups) warm water. Gradually combine to form a dough, then knead on a floured surface for 10–15 minutes until smooth and elastic, gradually adding 1 tablespoon olive oil as you knead, until all the oil has been used. Cover and set aside in a warm place for 1 hour, or until risen.

Punch down the dough with your fist and then knead again. Set aside and leave to rise for 30 minutes. Knead briefly and divide into 10 portions. Roll each portion to a smooth circle about 5 mm (¼ inch) thick. Set aside covered with a tea towel (dish towel) for another 20 minutes.

Preheat the oven to 220°C (425°F/Gas 7). Grease two baking trays. Place the rolls on the trays and gently press the surface with your fingers to create a dimpled effect. Brush with the remaining oil and sprinkle with za'atar and sea salt flakes. Bake for 12–15 minutes. Transfer to a wire rack to cool a little. Serve warm.

Note *Za'atar mix is a Middle Eastern spice blend of toasted sesame seeds, dried thyme, dried majoram and sumac. It is available from speciality food stores.*

Ham, cheese and onion quickbread

preparation 25 minutes
cooking 1 hour 5 minutes
makes 1 loaf

1 tablespoon oil
3 onions, thinly sliced into rings
2 teaspoons soft brown sugar
200 g (7 oz) sliced ham, finely chopped
375 g (13 oz/3 cups) self-raising flour
100 g (3½ oz) chilled butter
90 g (3¼ oz/¾ cup) grated cheddar cheese
125 ml (4 fl oz/½ cup) milk

Heat half of the oil in a large, heavy-based frying pan. Add the onion and cook over medium heat for 10 minutes, stirring occasionally. Add the sugar and continue to cook for 10–15 minutes, or until golden. Set aside to cool.

Heat the remaining oil in a small frying pan, add the ham and cook over moderately high heat until golden brown. Drain on crumpled paper towel and add to the onion. Allow to cool slightly.

Preheat the oven to 210°C (415°F/Gas 6–7). Lightly grease a baking tray. Sift the flour into a large bowl and rub in the butter with your fingertips until the mixture resembles fine breadcrumbs.

Add three-quarters of the onion mixture and 60 g (2¼ oz/ ½ cup) of the cheddar to the flour and mix well. Make a well in the centre and add the milk and about 125 ml (4 fl oz/½ cup) of water (add enough water to bring the dough together). Mix with a flat-bladed knife, using a cutting action, until the mixture forms a soft dough. Gently gather together into a ball.

Lay the dough on the tray and press out to form a 22 cm (8½ inch) circle. Using a sharp knife, mark the dough into quarters, cutting two-thirds of the way through. Sprinkle with the rest of the onion mixture and the remaining cheddar. Bake for 15 minutes, then reduce the oven to 180°C (350°F/Gas 4). Cover the top loosely with foil if it starts getting too brown. Bake for another 20 minutes, or until the base sounds hollow when tapped. Transfer to a wire rack to cool.

203

Bottom: Ham, cheese and onion quickbread. Top: Flatbread with za'atar.

Ciabatta

preparation 30 minutes + 6 hours standing
cooking 30 minutes
makes 1 loaf

2 teaspoons dried yeast
1 teaspoon sugar
375 g (13 oz/3 cups) white strong flour
50 ml (1¾ fl oz) olive oil
extra flour, to sprinkle

Put the yeast, sugar and 80 ml (2½ oz/⅓ cup) warm water in a small bowl and stir well. Leave in a warm place for 10 minutes, or until bubbles appear on the surface. The mixture should be frothy and slightly increased in volume. If your yeast doesn't foam, it is dead, so you will have to discard it and start again.

Put 250 g (9 oz/2 cups) of the flour in a large bowl with 2 teaspoons salt and make a well in the centre. Add the yeast mixture, oil and 230 ml (7¾ fl oz) water to the bowl and stir to combine.

Use a cupped hand to knead the wet dough, lifting and stirring for 5 minutes. The dough will be quite wet at this stage, but do not add extra flour. Shape the dough into a ball and put in a clean bowl. Cover with plastic wrap or a damp tea towel (dish towel) and leave in a warm place for 4 hours, or until doubled in size.

Stir in the remaining flour, using a cupped hand, and mix until the flour has been incorporated. Scrape down the side of the bowl. Cover with plastic wrap or a clean tea towel and leave in a warm place for 1–1¼ hours.

Liberally sprinkle a large baking tray with flour. Do not punch down the dough but carefully tip it out onto the tray. Use floured hands to spread the dough into an oval about 12 x 30 cm (4½ x 12 inches). Use heavily floured hands to spread evenly and tuck under the dough edges to plump up the dough. Sprinkle liberally with flour. Cover with plastic wrap and leave for 30 minutes.

Preheat the oven to 210°C (415°F/Gas 6–7). Place a heatproof container of ice on the base of the oven. Bake the ciabatta for 30 minutes, or until puffed and golden. Remove the melted ice after about 20 minutes. The loaf is cooked when it sounds hollow when tapped. Transfer to a wire rack to cool.

Soy and linseed loaf

preparation 30 minutes + 1 hour 55 minutes standing
cooking 50 minutes
makes 1 loaf

110 g (3¾ oz/½ cup) pearl barley
2 teaspoons dried yeast
1 teaspoon caster (superfine) sugar
1 tablespoon linseeds (flax seeds)
2 tablespoons soy flour
2 tablespoons gluten flour
150 g (5½ oz/1 cup) wholemeal (whole-wheat) strong flour
310 g (11 oz/2½ cups) white strong flour
2 tablespoons olive oil

Brush a 10 x 26 cm (4 x 10½ inch) loaf (bar) tin with oil.
Put the barley in a saucepan with 500 ml (17 fl oz/2 cups)
water, bring to the boil and boil for 20 minutes, or until
softened. Drain.

Put the yeast, sugar and 150 ml (5 fl oz) warm water in
a small bowl and mix well. Leave in a warm place for
10 minutes, or until bubbles appear on the surface. The
mixture should be frothy and slightly increased in volume.
If your yeast doesn't foam, it is dead, so you will have to
discard it and start again.

Put the barley, linseeds, soy and gluten flours, wholemeal
flour, 250 g (9 oz/2 cups) of the white flour and 1 teaspoon
salt in a large bowl. Make a well in the centre and add the
yeast mixture, oil and 150 ml (5 fl oz) warm water. Mix with
a wooden spoon to a soft dough. Turn out onto a floured
surface and knead for 10 minutes, or until smooth and
elastic. Incorporate enough of the remaining flour until the
dough is no longer sticky.

Place in an oiled bowl and brush the dough with oil. Cover
with plastic wrap or a damp tea towel (dish towel) and
leave in a warm, draught-free place for 45 minutes, or until
doubled in size. Punch down and knead for 2–3 minutes.

Pat the dough into a 20 x 24 cm (8 x 9½ inch) rectangle. Roll
up firmly from the long side and place, seam side down,
in the loaf tin. Cover with plastic wrap or a damp tea towel
and set aside in a warm, draught-free place for 1 hour, or
until risen to the top of the tin. Preheat the oven to 200°C
(400°F/Gas 6).

Brush the dough with water and make two slits on top.
Bake for 30 minutes, or until golden. Transfer to a wire rack
to cool.

Turkish bread

preparation 30 minutes + 1 hour 40 minutes standing
cooking 30 minutes
makes 3 loaves

1 tablespoon dried yeast
½ teaspoon sugar
60 g (2¼ oz/½ cup) plain (all-purpose) flour
440 g (15½ oz/3½ cups) white strong flour
80 ml (2½ fl oz/⅓ cup) olive oil
1 egg, lightly beaten with 2 teaspoons water
nigella or sesame seeds, to sprinkle

Put the yeast, sugar and 125 ml (4 fl oz/½ cup) warm water
in a small bowl and stir well. Add a little of the flour and
mix to a paste. Leave in a warm place for 10 minutes, or
until bubbles appear on the surface. The mixture should
be frothy and slightly increased in volume. If your yeast
doesn't foam, it is dead, so you will have to discard it and
start again.

Put the remaining flours and 1½ teaspoons salt in a large
bowl and make a well in the centre. Add the yeast mixture,
olive oil and 250 ml (9 fl oz/1 cup) warm water. Mix to a
rough dough, then turn out onto a floured surface and
knead for 5 minutes. Add minimal flour as the dough
should remain damp and springy.

Shape the dough into a ball and place in a large oiled
bowl. Cover with plastic wrap or a damp tea towel (dish
towel) and leave in a warm place for 1 hour to triple in size.
Punch down and divide into three. Knead each portion for
2 minutes and shape each into a ball. Cover with plastic
wrap or a damp tea towel and leave for 10 minutes.

Roll each portion of dough into a rectangle 15 x 35 cm
(6 x 14 inches). Cover with damp tea towels and leave in a
warm place for 20 minutes. Indent all over the surface with
your fingers, brush with the egg glaze and sprinkle with the
seeds. Preheat the oven to 220°C (425°F/Gas 7).

For the best results, bake each loaf separately. Place a
baking tray in the oven for a couple of minutes until hot,
remove and sprinkle lightly with flour. Place one portion
of dough on the hot tray and bake for 10–12 minutes, or
until puffed and golden brown. Wrap in a clean tea towel
to soften the crust and set aside to cool. Meanwhile, repeat
baking the remaining portions of dough.

Bottom: Turkish bread. Top: Soy and linseed loaf.

Bagels

preparation 35 minutes + 12 hours refrigeration
cooking 16 minutes
makes 8

2 teaspoons dried yeast
1 teaspoon sugar
1 tablespoon barley malt syrup or honey
500 g (1 lb 2 oz/4 cups) white strong flour
2 teaspoons salt
coarse polenta, to dust

Put the yeast, sugar and 375 ml (13 fl oz/1½ cups) warm water in a small bowl and stir until dissolved. Leave in a warm place for 10 minutes, or until bubbles appear on the surface. The mixture should be frothy and slightly increased in volume. If your yeast doesn't foam, it is dead, so you will have to discard it and start again.

Put 250 g (9 oz/2 cups) of the flour in a large bowl, make a well in the centre and add the yeast mixture and salt. Stir with a wooden spoon, adding flour as necessary to make a firm dough.

Turn the dough out onto a floured work surface and knead for 10–12 minutes, or until smooth and stiff. Add more flour if necessary, to make the dough quite stiff.

Divide the dough into eight portions and roll them into smooth balls. Cover with plastic wrap or a clean tea towel (dish towel) and leave for 5 minutes.

Roll each ball under your palms to form a rope 28 cm (11¼ inches) long. Do not taper the ends. Dampen the ends slightly, overlap by 4 cm (1½ inches) and pinch firmly together. Place one at a time around the base of your fingers and, with the overlap under your palm, roll the rope several times. Apply firm pressure to seal the seam. It should be the same thickness all the way around. Place all the rings on polenta-dusted baking trays, cover with plastic wrap and refrigerate for 12 hours.

Preheat the oven to 240°C (475°F/Gas 8). Line two baking trays with baking paper. Remove the bagels from the fridge 20 minutes before baking. Bring a large pan of water to the boil and drop the bagels, in two batches into the water for 30 seconds. Remove and drain, base-down, on a wire rack.

Place the bagels on the prepared baking trays and bake for 15 minutes, or until deep golden brown and crisp. Transfer to a wire rack to cool.

When rolling the balls into a rope, it is important not to taper the ends or the bagels will be uneven.

Seal the seam and create an invisible join by rolling the overlap under your hand.

Traditional cornbread

preparation 15 minutes
cooking 25 minutes
makes 1 loaf

150 g (5½ oz/1 cup) polenta
2 tablespoons caster (superfine) sugar
125 g (4½ oz/1 cup) plain (all-purpose) flour
2 teaspoons baking powder
½ teaspoon bicarbonate of soda (baking soda)
1 egg, lightly beaten
250 ml (9 fl oz/1 cup) buttermilk
60 g (2¼ oz) butter, melted

Preheat the oven to 210°C (415°F/Gas 6–7). Brush a 20 cm (8 inch) square cake tin with oil or melted butter and line the base with baking paper.

Put the polenta and sugar in a large bowl. Add the sifted flour, baking powder, bicarbonate of soda and ½ teaspoon salt and mix thoroughly.

In a separate bowl, combine the beaten egg, buttermilk and melted butter. Stir the mixture quickly into the dry ingredients. Stir only until the ingredients are moistened. Pour the mixture into the prepared tin and smooth the surface. Bake for 20–25 minutes, or until a skewer inserted in the centre of the bread comes out clean.

Place on a wire rack and leave to cool for 10 minutes before turning out. Cut into squares and serve warm.

Banana bread

preparation 20 minutes
cooking 45 minutes
makes 1 loaf

250 g (9 oz/2 cups) plain (all-purpose) flour
2 teaspoons baking powder
1 teaspoon mixed (pumpkin pie) spice
150 g (5½ oz) unsalted butter, softened
185 g (6½ oz/1 cup) soft brown sugar
2 eggs, lightly beaten
235 g (8½ oz/1 cup) mashed ripe banana (about 2 bananas)
icing (confectioners') sugar, to dust

Preheat the oven to 180°C (350°F/Gas 4). Grease and line the base of a 6 x 13 x 23 cm (2½ x 5 x 9 inch) loaf (bar) tin. Sift together the flour, baking powder, mixed spice and ¼ teaspoon salt into a bowl.

Using electric beaters, beat the butter and sugar in a mixing bowl until the mixture is light and creamy. Add the eggs a little at a time, beating well after each addition. Mix in the

banana. Gradually add the sifted dry ingredients and mix until smooth. Pour into the loaf tin and bake on the middle shelf for 35–45 minutes, or until the top is nicely coloured and a skewer inserted into the centre of the bread comes out clean. Cool in the tin for 10 minutes before turning out onto a wire rack. Dust with icing sugar.

Moroccan flatbread

preparation 1 hour + 40 minutes standing
cooking time 12 minutes
makes 16

375 g (13 oz/2½ cups) plain (all-purpose)
wholemeal (whole-wheat) flour
1 teaspoon caster (superfine) sugar
2 teaspoons dried yeast
½ teaspoon sweet paprika
50 g (1¾ oz/⅓ cup) cornmeal
1 tablespoon oil
1 egg, lightly beaten
2 tablespoons sesame seeds

Preheat the oven to 180°C (350°F/Gas 4). Lightly grease a baking tray. Put 75 g (2¾ oz/½ cup) of the flour, the sugar, yeast, 1 teaspoon salt and 310 ml (10¾ fl oz/1¼ cups) lukewarm water in a bowl and stir until dissolved. Cover and leave in a warm place for 10 minutes, or until bubbles appear on the surface. The mixture should be frothy and slightly increased in volume. If your yeast doesn't foam, it is dead, so you will have to discard it and start again.

Sift the paprika, cornmeal and remaining flour into a bowl. Add the oil then stir in the yeast mixture. Mix to a firm dough and knead until smooth. Cover and leave in a warm, draught-free place for 20 minutes.

Divide the dough into 16 portions, roll each into a ball then flatten into 8 cm (3¼ inch) rounds. Place on the baking tray, brush with egg and sprinkle with sesame seeds. Cover and set aside for 10 minutes, or until puffed up. Bake for 12 minutes, or until golden. Transfer to a wire rack to cool.

Top left: Traditional cornbread. Top right: Banana bread. Bottom right: Moroccan flatbread.

Pumpernickel

preparation 1 hour + 2 hours 25 minutes standing
cooking 50 minutes
makes 2 loaves

1 tablespoon dried yeast
1 teaspoon caster (superfine) sugar
90 g (3¼ oz/¼ cup) molasses
60 ml (2 fl oz/¼ cup) cider vinegar
90 g (3¼ oz) butter
30 g (1 oz) dark chocolate, chopped
1 tablespoon instant coffee powder
560 g (1 lb 4 oz/4½ cups) unbleached plain (all-purpose) flour
300 g (10½ oz/3 cups) rye flour
75 g (2¾ oz/1 cup) bran
1 tablespoon caraway seeds
2 teaspoons fennel seeds
1 egg white
caraway seeds, extra, to sprinkle

Grease a 20 cm (8 inch) round cake tin and a 12 x 28 cm (4½ x 11¼ inch) loaf (bar) or bread tin, or use any baking tin that has a 1.75 litre capacity. Line the base of each tin with baking paper. Put 125 ml (4 fl oz/½ cup) warm water, the yeast and sugar in a small bowl and stir well. Leave in a warm place for 10 minutes, or until bubbles appear on the surface. The mixture should be frothy and slightly increased in volume. If your yeast doesn't foam, it is dead, so you will have to discard it and start again.

Put the molasses, vinegar, butter, chocolate, coffee powder and 500 ml (17 fl oz/2 cups) cold water into a saucepan and stir over low heat until the butter and chocolate have melted and the mixture is just warmed.

Put the rye flour, bran, caraway and fennel seeds, 440 g (15½ oz/3½ cups) of the plain flour and 1 teaspoon salt in a large bowl. Make a well in the centre and add the yeast and chocolate mixtures. Using a wooden spoon, and then your hands, combine the dough until it leaves the side of the bowl and forms a firm, sticky ball.

Turn out onto a heavily floured surface and knead for 10 minutes. Incorporate enough of the remaining plain flour to make a dense but smooth and elastic dough. Divide in half and place in separate lightly oiled bowls. Brush the surface of the dough with melted butter or oil. Cover with plastic wrap or a damp tea towel (dish towel) and leave in a warm, draught-free place for 1¼ hours, or until well risen. Punch down the dough and knead each portion for 1 minute. Shape each portion to fit a tin and place one in each tin. Cover with lightly oiled plastic wrap or a damp tea towel and leave in a warm place for 1 hour, or until well risen.

Preheat the oven to 180°C (350°F/Gas 4). Glaze the dough with combined egg white and 1 tablespoon water and sprinkle with caraway seeds. Bake for 50 minutes, or until well browned. During the last 15 minutes, cover with foil to prevent excess browning. Leave in the tins for 15 minutes before turning out onto a wire rack to cool.

Note Pumpernickel is a dense rye bread that originated in Germany.

Greek Easter bread

preparation 1 hour + 1 hour 50 minutes standing
cooking 45 minutes
makes 1 loaf

2 teaspoons dried yeast
125 ml (4 fl oz/½ cup) milk
60 g (2¼ oz) butter
55 g (2 oz/¼ cup) caster (superfine) sugar
1 teaspoon grated orange zest
375 g (13 oz/3 cups) white strong flour
1 teaspoon ground anise
1 egg, lightly beaten

topping
1 egg, lightly beaten
1 tablespoon milk
1 tablespoon sesame seeds
1 tablespoon chopped slivered almonds
1 tablespoon caster (superfine) sugar

Place the yeast and 2 tablespoons warm water in a small bowl and stir well. Leave in a warm place for 10 minutes, or until bubbles appear on the surface. The mixture should be frothy and slightly increased in volume. If your yeast doesn't foam, it is dead, so you will have to discard it and start again.

Combine the milk, butter, sugar, orange zest and ½ teaspoon salt in a small saucepan. Heat until the butter has melted and the milk is just warm. Sift 310 g (11 oz/2½ cups) of the flour and the ground anise into a large bowl. Make a well in the centre, add the yeast and the milk mixtures, then the egg. Gradually beat into the flour for 1 minute, or until a smooth dough forms.

Turn out onto a lightly floured surface. Knead, incorporating the remaining flour, for 10 minutes, or until the dough is smooth and elastic. Place in an oiled bowl and brush the surface with oil. Cover with plastic wrap and leave in a warm place for 1 hour, or until well risen.

Lightly grease a baking tray. Punch down the dough and knead for 1 minute. Divide the dough into three equal pieces. Roll each portion into a sausage 35 cm (14 inches) long. Plait the strands and fold the ends under. Place on the tray.

To make the topping, combine the egg and milk and brush over the dough. Sprinkle with the sesame seeds, almonds and sugar (if using dyed eggs, add them at this stage—see Note). Cover with lightly oiled plastic wrap and leave in a warm place for 40 minutes, or until well risen.

Preheat the oven to 180°C (350°F/Gas 4). Bake the bread for 30–40 minutes, or until cooked. The bread should sound hollow when tapped. Transfer to a wire rack to cool.

Note *Decorate with one or two dyed hard-boiled eggs. Push the eggs onto the dough after plaiting. Use Greek red dye, which is available in some Greek speciality food stores, and comes with detailed instructions on how to dye eggs.*

Sprinkle the plaited dough with a topping of sesame seeds, chopped almonds and sugar.

The vibrant red colour of the dyed eggs comes from Greek red dye. Press the eggs into the dough.

breads *and* **pizzas**

Hot cross buns

preparation 30 minutes + 1 hour 10 minutes standing
cooking 25 minutes
makes 12 buns

1 tablespoon dried yeast or 30 g (1 oz) fresh yeast
500 g (1 lb 2 oz/4 cups) white strong flour
2 tablespoons caster (superfine) sugar
1 teaspoon mixed (pumpkin pie) spice
1 teaspoon ground cinnamon
40 g (1½ oz) butter
150 g (5½ oz/1¼ cups) sultanas (golden raisins)

paste for crosses
30 g (1 oz/¼ cup) plain (all-purpose) flour
¼ teaspoon caster (superfine) sugar

glaze
1½ tablespoons caster (superfine) sugar
1 teaspoon powdered gelatine

Lightly grease a baking tray. Put the yeast, 2 teaspoons of the flour, 1 teaspoon of the sugar and 125 ml (4 fl oz/½ cup) warm water in a small bowl and stir well. Leave in a warm place for 10 minutes, or until bubbles appear on the surface. The mixture should be frothy and slightly increased in volume. If your yeast doesn't foam, it is dead, so you will have to discard it and start again.

Sift the remaining flour and spices into a large bowl and stir in the sugar. Using your fingertips, rub in the butter. Stir in the sultanas. Make a well in the centre, stir in the yeast mixture and up to 185 ml (6 fl oz/¾ cup) water to make a soft dough. Turn the dough out onto a lightly floured surface and knead for 5 minutes, or until smooth, adding more flour if necessary, to prevent sticking. Place the dough in a large floured bowl, cover with plastic wrap or a damp tea towel (dish towel) and leave in a warm, draught-free place for 30–40 minutes, or until doubled in size.

Preheat the oven to 200°C (400°F/Gas 6). Turn the dough out onto a lightly floured surface and knead gently to deflate.

Divide into 12 portions and roll each into a ball. Place the balls on the tray, just touching each other, in a rectangle three rolls wide and four rolls long. Cover loosely with plastic wrap or a damp tea towel and leave in a warm place for 20 minutes, or until nearly doubled in size.

To make the crosses for the buns, mix the flour, sugar and 2½ tablespoons water into a paste. Spoon into a paper piping (icing) bag and pipe crosses on top of the buns. Bake for 20 minutes, or until golden brown. To make the glaze, put the sugar, gelatine and 1 tablespoon water in a small saucepan and stir over the heat until dissolved. Brush over the hot buns and leave to cool.

Notes *These spiced, sweet, yeasted traditional Easter buns are heavily glazed and usually served warm or at room temperature. They are split open and buttered, or sometimes toasted.*

The dried fruit in these buns can be varied. Often, currants and chopped candied (glacé) peel are used. The crosses are sometimes made with pastry instead of flour and water paste, or crosses can be scored into the dough prior to proving.

Focaccia

preparation 50 minutes + 2 hours standing time
cooking 25 minutes
makes 1 flat loaf

2 teaspoons dried yeast
1 teaspoon caster (superfine) sugar
2 tablespoons olive oil
405 g (14¼ oz/3¼ cups) white strong flour
1 tablespoon full-cream milk powder

topping

1 tablespoon olive oil
1–2 garlic cloves, crushed
black olives
rosemary sprigs or leaves
1 teaspoon dried oregano
1–2 teaspoons coarse sea salt

Lightly grease an 18 x 28 cm (7 x 11¼ inch) baking tin. Put the yeast, sugar and 250 ml (9 fl oz/1 cup) warm water in a small bowl and stir well. Leave in a warm place for 10 minutes, or until bubbles appear on the surface. The mixture should be frothy and slightly increased in volume. If your yeast doesn't foam, it is dead, so you will have to discard it and start again. Add the oil.

Sift 375 g (13 oz/3 cups) of the flour, the milk powder and ½ teaspoon salt into a large bowl. Make a well in the centre and add the yeast mixture. Beat with a wooden spoon until the mixture is well combined. Add enough of the remaining flour to form a soft dough, and then turn onto a lightly floured surface.

Knead for 10 minutes, or until the dough is smooth and elastic. Place the dough in a large, lightly oiled bowl. Brush the surface of the dough with oil. Cover with plastic wrap or a damp tea towel (dish towel) and leave in a warm place for 1 hour, or until well risen. Punch down the dough and knead for 1 minute. Roll into a rectangle, 18 x 28 cm (7 x 11¼ inches) and place in the prepared tin. Cover with plastic wrap and leave to rise in a warm place for 20 minutes. Using the handle of a wooden spoon, form indents 1 cm (½ inch) deep all over the dough at regular intervals. Cover with plastic wrap and set aside for 30 minutes, or until the dough is well risen. Preheat the oven to 180°C (350°F/Gas 4).

To make the topping, brush the combined olive oil and garlic over the surface of the dough. Top with the olives and rosemary sprigs, then sprinkle with the oregano and salt.

Bake for 20–25 minutes, or until golden and crisp. Cut into large squares and serve warm.

Note *Focaccia is best eaten on the day of baking. It can be reheated if necessary.*

Knead the dough thoroughly for 10 minutes or so until it is smooth and elastic.

Press or roll the dough into a rectangular shape before lifting it into the prepared baking tin.

Potato and rosemary pizzettas

preparation 25 minutes + 1 hour 10 minutes standing
cooking 15 minutes
makes 48

1 teaspoon dried yeast
½ teaspoon sugar
310 g (11 oz/2½ cups) plain (all-purpose) flour
80 ml (2½ fl oz/⅓ cup) olive oil

topping
400 g (14 oz) all-purpose potatoes, unpeeled
2 tablespoons olive oil, extra
1 tablespoon rosemary leaves
sea salt, to sprinkle

To make the bases, place the yeast, sugar and 80 ml (2½ fl oz/⅓ cup) water in a small bowl. Cover and leave in a warm place for 10 minutes, or until bubbles appear on the surface. The mixture should be frothy and slightly increased in volume. If your yeast doesn't foam, it is dead, so you will have to discard it and start again.

Sift the flour and ¼ teaspoon salt into a large bowl. Make a well in the centre and stir in the yeast mixture, the oil and 80 ml (2½ fl oz/⅓ cup) water. Mix to a soft dough. Turn out onto a lightly floured surface and knead for 5 minutes, or until the dough is smooth and elastic. Place the dough in an oiled bowl, cover and leave in a warm place for about 1 hour, or until the dough has doubled in size.

Preheat the oven to 220°C (425°F/Gas 7). Punch down the dough to expel the air. Turn out and knead for 1 minute, or until smooth. Divide into 48 portions and roll each portion to a 5 cm (2 inch) round. Place each round on lightly greased baking trays.

Cut the potatoes into slices. Cover each dough round with a slice of potato, leaving a 1 cm (½ inch) border. Brush the pizzettas with the extra olive oil and sprinkle with rosemary leaves and sea salt. Bake on the highest shelf in the oven for 12–15 minutes, or until the pastry is crisp and lightly browned. Serve immediately.

Note These pizzettas are best made close to serving. The dough can be prepared ahead on the day of serving and refrigerated, covered, up to the point of second kneading. Alternatively, at this stage, the dough can be frozen. When hard, remove from the trays and seal in plastic bags. Place on lightly greased baking trays to thaw. The pizzettas can be baked several hours ahead and reheated in a 180°C (350°F/Gas 4) oven for 5 minutes, or until warmed through.

Ham and pineapple pizza wheels

preparation 25 minutes
cooking 20 minutes
makes 16

250 g (9 oz/2 cups) self-raising flour
40 g (1½ oz) butter, chopped
125 ml (4 fl oz/½ cup) milk

topping
90 g (3¼ oz/⅓ cup) tomato paste (concentrated purée)
2 small onions, finely chopped
4 pineapple slices, finely chopped
200 g (7 oz) sliced ham, shredded
80 g (2¾ oz) cheddar cheese, grated
2 tablespoons finely chopped flat-leaf (Italian) parsley

Preheat the oven to 180°C (350°F/Gas 4). Brush two baking trays with oil. Sift the flour into a bowl. Using your fingertips, rub in the butter until the mixture resembles fine breadcrumbs. Make a well in the centre and add almost all the milk. Mix with a flat-bladed knife, using a cutting action, until the mixture comes together in beads. Gather into a ball and turn out onto a lightly floured work surface.

Divide the dough in half. Roll out each half on baking paper to a 20 x 30 cm (8 x 12 inch) rectangle, about 5 mm (¼ inch) thick. Spread the tomato paste over each rectangle, leaving a 1 cm (½ inch) border.

Mix the onion, pineapple, ham, cheddar and parsley together. Spread evenly over the tomato paste, leaving a 2 cm (¾ inch) border. Using the paper as a guide, roll up the dough from the long side.

Cut each roll into eight even slices. Place the slices on the trays and bake for 20 minutes, or until golden. Serve warm.

Bottom: Ham and pineapple pizza wheels. Top: Potato and rosemary pizzettas.

Pissaladière

preparation 50 minutes + 40 minutes standing
cooking 2 hours
serves 8

2 teaspoons dried yeast
1 teaspoon caster (superfine) sugar
310 g (11 oz/2½ cups) white strong flour
2 tablespoons milk powder
1 tablespoon vegetable oil

topping
80 ml (2½ fl oz/⅓ cup) olive oil
3–4 garlic cloves, finely chopped
6 onions, cut into thin rings
425 g (15 oz) tinned chopped tomatoes
1 tablespoon tomato paste (concentrated purée)
15 g (½ oz) chopped flat-leaf (Italian) parsley
1 tablespoon chopped thyme
3 x 50 g (1¾ oz) tins anchovy fillets, drained and halved lengthways
36 small black olives

Lightly grease two 30 cm (12 inch) pizza trays. To make the bases, put the yeast, sugar and 250 ml (9 fl oz/1 cup) warm water in a small bowl and stir well. Leave in a warm place for 10 minutes, or until bubbles appear on the surface. The mixture should be frothy and slightly increased in volume. If your yeast doesn't foam, it is dead, so you will have to discard it and start again.

Sift 250 g (9 oz/2 cups) of the flour, the milk powder and ½ teaspoon salt into a large bowl and make a well in the centre. Add the oil and yeast mixture and mix thoroughly. Turn out onto a lightly floured surface and knead for 10 minutes, gradually adding small amounts of the remaining flour, until the dough is smooth and elastic.

Place in an oiled bowl and brush the surface with oil. Cover with plastic wrap and leave in a warm place for 30 minutes, or until doubled in size.

To make the topping, heat the oil in a saucepan. Add the garlic and onion and cook, covered, over low heat for about 40 minutes, stirring frequently. The onion should be softened but not browned. Uncover and cook, stirring frequently, for

another 30 minutes, or until lightly golden. Take care not to burn. Allow to cool.

Put the tomatoes in a saucepan and cook over medium heat, stirring frequently, for 20 minutes, or until thick and reduced to about 250 ml (9 fl oz/1 cup). Remove from the heat and stir in the tomato paste and herbs. Season to taste. Cool, then stir into the onion mixture.

Preheat the oven to 220°C (425°F/Gas 7). Punch down the dough, then turn out onto a floured surface and knead for 2 minutes. Divide in half. Return one half to the bowl and cover. Roll the other out to a 30 cm (12 inch) circle and press into the tray. Brush with olive oil. Spread half the onion and tomato mixture evenly over the dough, leaving a small border. Arrange half the anchovy fillets over the top in a lattice pattern and place an olive in each square. Repeat with the rest of the dough and topping. Bake for 15–20 minutes, or until the dough is cooked through and lightly browned.

Note If your oven can accommodate both pissaladière at once and you want to cook them together, the cooking time will be longer. Rotate the trays towards the end of cooking time.

Summer potato pizza

preparation 30 minutes + 10 minutes standing
cooking 40 minutes
serves 6

10 g (¼ oz) dried yeast
½ teaspoon caster (superfine) sugar
310 g (11 oz/2½ cups) plain (all-purpose) flour
2 teaspoons polenta or semolina
2 tablespoons olive oil

topping
2 garlic cloves, crushed
4–5 potatoes, unpeeled, thinly sliced
1 tablespoon rosemary leaves

Preheat the oven to 210°C (415°F/Gas 6–7). To make the base, put the yeast, sugar, ½ teaspoon salt and 250 ml (9 fl oz/1 cup) warm water in a small bowl and stir well. Leave in a warm place for 10 minutes, or until bubbles appear on the surface. The mixture should be frothy and slightly increased in volume. If your yeast doesn't foam, it is dead, so you will have to discard it and start again.

Sift the flour into a bowl, make a well in the centre, add the yeast mixture and mix to a dough.

Turn the dough out onto a lightly floured surface and knead for 5 minutes, or until smooth and elastic. Roll out to a 30 cm (12 inch) circle. Lightly spray a pizza tray with oil and sprinkle with the polenta or semolina.

Place the pizza base on the tray. Mix 2 teaspoons of the oil with the garlic and brush over the pizza base. Gently toss the remaining olive oil, potato slices, rosemary leaves, 1 teaspoon of salt and some pepper in a bowl.

Arrange the potato slices in overlapping circles over the pizza base and bake for 40 minutes, or until the base is crisp and golden.

Neatly lay the potato slices in overlapping circles around the pizza base.

Sour cream and tomato pizzas

preparation 30 minutes + 1 hour 40 minutes standing
cooking 40 minutes
serves 4

1 teaspoon dried yeast
1 teaspoon caster (superfine) sugar
250 g (9 oz/2 cups) plain (all-purpose) flour
125 ml (4 fl oz/½ cup) olive oil

topping
125 g (4½ oz/½ cup) sour cream
90 g (3¼ oz/⅓ cup) ricotta cheese
2 tablespoons chopped herbs (such as basil, lemon thyme, sage)
2 tablespoons oil
2 onions, thinly sliced
5 ripe tomatoes, sliced
2 garlic cloves, thinly sliced
50 g (1¾ oz) marinated niçoise olives
10 lemon thyme sprigs

Preheat the oven to 200°C (400°F/Gas 6). To make the bases, put the yeast, sugar and 170 ml (5½ fl oz/⅔ cup) warm water in a small bowl and stir well. Leave in a warm place for 10 minutes, or until bubbles appear on the surface. The mixture should be frothy and slightly increased in volume. If your yeast doesn't foam, it is dead, so you will have to discard it and start again.

Put the flour and a pinch of salt into a food processor, add the olive oil and the yeast mixture with the motor running and process until it forms a rough dough. Turn out onto a lightly floured surface and knead until smooth. Place into a lightly oiled bowl, cover and allow to rest in a warm area for 1½ hours, or until doubled in size. Punch down the dough and remove from the bowl. Knead and roll out to four 14 cm (5½ inch) circles and place the bases on a non-stick baking tray.

To make the topping, combine the sour cream, ricotta and chopped herbs. Spread over the pizza bases, leaving a 1 cm (½ inch) border.

Heat the oil in a frying pan, add the onions and cook for 10 minutes, or until caramelized. Cool slightly, spoon over the ricotta mixture and top with the tomatoes, garlic, olives, lemon thyme and some freshly cracked black pepper. Bake for 15 minutes, or until the base is crisp and golden.

Note *If you prefer, make this into one 30 cm (12 inch) pizza. It will need to be cooked for 30 minutes.*

Bottom: Sour cream and tomato pizzas. Top: Summer potato pizza.

Potato and onion pizza

preparation 40 minutes + 1 hour 40 minutes standing
cooking 45 minutes
serves 4

2 teaspoons dried yeast
½ teaspoon sugar
185 g (6½ oz/1½ cups) white strong flour
150 g (5½ oz/1 cup) plain (all-purpose)
wholemeal (whole-wheat) flour
1 tablespoon olive oil

topping
1 large red capsicum (pepper)
1 potato
1 large onion, sliced
125 g (4½ oz) soft goat's cheese, crumbled into small pieces
35 g (1¼ oz/¼ cup) capers
1 tablespoon dried oregano
1 teaspoon olive oil

To make the base, put the yeast, sugar, a pinch of salt and 250 ml (9 fl oz/1 cup) warm water in a bowl. Leave in a warm place for 10 minutes, or until bubbles appear on the surface. The mixture should be frothy and slightly increased in volume. If your yeast doesn't foam, it is dead, so you will have to discard it and start again.

Sift both flours into a bowl. Make a well in the centre, add the yeast mixture and mix to a firm dough. Knead on a lightly floured surface for 5 minutes, or until smooth. Place in a lightly oiled bowl, cover with plastic wrap or a damp tea towel (dish towel) and leave in a warm place for 1–1½ hours, or until doubled in size.

Preheat the oven to 200°C (400°F/Gas 6). Brush a 30 cm (12 inch) pizza tray with oil. Punch down the dough and knead for 2 minutes. Roll out to a 35 cm (14 inch) round. Put the dough on the tray and tuck the edge over to form a rim.

To make the topping, cut the red capsicum into large flattish pieces and remove the membrane and seeds. Place, skin side up, under a hot grill (broiler) until blackened. Cool in a plastic bag, then peel away the skin and cut the flesh into narrow strips.

Cut the potato into paper-thin slices and arrange over the base with the capsicum, onion and half the cheese. Sprinkle with the capers, oregano and 1 teaspoon cracked pepper and drizzle with oil. Brush the crust edge with oil and bake for 20 minutes. Add the remaining cheese and bake for a further 15–20 minutes, or until the crust has browned.

Pizza Margherita

preparation 40 minutes + 1 hour standing
cooking 40 minutes
serves 4–6

225 g (8 oz) white strong flour
1 teaspoon sugar
2 teaspoons dried yeast
1 tablespoon olive oil
90 ml (3 fl oz) milk

topping
1 tablespoon olive oil
1 garlic clove, crushed
425 g (15 oz) tinned crushed tomatoes
1 bay leaf
1 teaspoon chopped thyme
6 chopped basil leaves
polenta, to sprinkle
150 g (5½ oz) bocconcini cheese (fresh baby mozzarella cheese), thinly sliced
olive oil, extra, to drizzle

To make the pizza base, put the flour, sugar, yeast and ½ teaspoon salt in a large bowl. Stir the olive oil with the milk and 80 ml (2½ fl oz/⅓ cup) warm water and add to the bowl. Stir with a wooden spoon.

Place on a lightly floured work surface and knead for 5 minutes, or until soft and smooth. Lightly oil a bowl, add the dough and turn to coat in the oil. Leave in a warm place for 1 hour, or until doubled in size. Preheat the oven to 210°C (415°F/Gas 6–7).

To make the topping, heat the oil in a saucepan over medium heat, add the garlic and stir for 30 seconds. Add the tomatoes, bay leaf, thyme and basil and simmer, stirring occasionally, for 20–25 minutes, or until thick. Cool, then remove the bay leaf.

Place the dough on a floured work surface, punch down to expel the air and knead for 5 minutes. Shape into a neat ball and roll to 28–30 cm (11¼–12 inch) diameter. Oil a pizza tray the size of the dough. Sprinkle the tray with polenta and place the dough on top. Spread the sauce over the dough, leaving a 3 cm (1¼ inch) border. Arrange the bocconcini over the top and drizzle with olive oil. Bake for 15 minutes, or until crisp and bubbling.

Bottom: Pizza Margharita. Top: Potato and onion pizza.

Mushroom, ricotta and olive pizza

preparation 30 minutes + 40 minutes standing
cooking 1 hour
serves 6

10 g (¼ oz) dried yeast or 15 g (½ oz) fresh yeast
¼ teaspoon caster (superfine) sugar
125 ml (4 fl oz/½ cup) skim milk
220 g (7¾ oz/1¾ cups) plain (all-purpose) flour

topping
4 roma (plum) tomatoes, quartered
½ teaspoon caster (superfine) sugar
2 teaspoons olive oil
2 garlic cloves, crushed
1 onion, thinly sliced
750 g (1 lb 10 oz) mushrooms, sliced
250 g (9 oz/1 cup) low-fat ricotta cheese
2 tablespoons sliced black olives
small handful basil leaves

Preheat the oven to 210°C (415°F/Gas 6–7). To make the topping, put the tomato on a baking tray covered with baking paper, sprinkle with the sugar and some salt and cracked black pepper and bake for 20 minutes, or until the edges are starting to darken. Set aside.

To make the base, put the yeast, sugar and 60 ml (2 fl oz/¼ cup) warm water in a small bowl and stir well. Leave in a warm place for 10 minutes, or until bubbles appear on the surface. The mixture should be frothy and slightly increased in volume. If your yeast doesn't foam, it is dead, so you will have to discard it and start again. Warm the milk, then stir it into the mixture.

Sift the flour into a large bowl and stir in the yeast and milk. Mix to a soft dough, then turn onto a lightly floured surface and knead for 5 minutes. Leave, covered, in a lightly oiled bowl in a warm place for 40 minutes, or until doubled in size.

Heat the oil in a frying pan and fry the garlic and onion until soft. Add the mushrooms and stir until they are soft and the liquid has evaporated. Leave to cool.

Turn the dough out onto a lightly floured surface and knead lightly. Roll out to a 38 cm (15 inch) circle and transfer to a lightly greased oven or pizza tray. Spread with the ricotta, leaving a border to turn over the filling. Top with the mushrooms, leaving a circle in the centre, and arrange the oven-dried tomatoes and olives in the circle. Fold the dough edge over onto the mushroom and dust the edge with flour. Bake for 25 minutes, or until the crust is golden. Garnish with basil.

The yeast mixture is ready when bubbles appear on the surface and it is foamy.

Use the back of a spoon to spread the ricotta over the base, leaving a border.

Turkish pizzas

preparation 25 minutes + 1 hour 10 minutes standing
cooking 45 minutes
makes 8

1 teaspoon dried yeast
½ teaspoon sugar
225 g (8 oz) plain (all-purpose) flour

topping
80 ml (2½ fl oz/⅓ cup) olive oil
250 g (9 oz) onions, finely chopped
500 g (1 lb 2 oz) minced (ground) lamb
2 garlic cloves
1 teaspoon ground cinnamon
1½ teaspoons ground cumin
½ teaspoon cayenne pepper
60 g (2¼ oz/¼ cup) tomato paste (concentrated purée)
400 g (14 oz) tinned good-quality crushed tomatoes
50 g (1¾ oz/⅓ cup) pine nuts
3 tablespoons chopped coriander(cilantro)
Greek-style yoghurt, to serve

To make the bases, put the yeast, sugar and 60 ml (2 fl oz/ ¼ cup) warm water in a bowl. Leave in a warm place for 10 minutes, or until bubbles appear on the surface. The mixture should be frothy and slightly increased in volume. If your yeast doesn't foam, it is dead, so you will have to discard it and start again.

Sift the flour and 1 teaspoon salt into a bowl, stir in the yeast mixture, 1 tablespoon of the oil and 100 ml (3½ fl oz) warm water. Mix to form a soft dough, then turn onto a floured board and knead for 10 minutes, or until smooth. Place in an oiled bowl, cover and leave in a warm place for 1 hour, or until doubled in size.

Heat 2 tablespoons of the oil in a frying pan over low heat and cook the onion for 5 minutes, or until soft but not golden. Add the lamb and cook for 10 minutes, or until brown. Add the garlic and spices, tomato paste and tomatoes. Cook for 15 minutes, until quite dry. Add half the pine nuts and 2 tablespoons of the coriander. Season, then leave to cool.

Preheat the oven to 210°C (415°F/Gas 6–7). Grease two baking trays.

Knock down the dough, then turn out onto a floured surface. Form into eight portions and roll each into a 12 x 18 cm (4½ x 7 inch) oval. Place on the trays. Divide the lamb mixture evenly among them and spread, leaving a small border. Sprinkle with the remaining pine nuts. Brush the edges with oil. Roll the uncovered dough over to cover the outer edges of the filling. Pinch the sides together at each end. Brush with oil. Bake for 15 minutes, or until golden. Sprinkle with coriander and serve with yoghurt.

savoury pies
and **pastries**

Ham and olive empanadillas

preparation 45 minutes
cooking 15 minutes
makes about 15

2 hard-boiled eggs, roughly chopped
40 g (1½ oz) stuffed green olives, chopped
95 g (3¼ oz) ham, finely chopped
30 g (1 oz/¼ cup) grated cheddar cheese
3 sheets ready-rolled puff pastry
1 egg yolk, lightly beaten

Preheat the oven to 220°C (425°F/Gas 7). Lightly grease two baking trays.

Combine the boiled eggs with the olives, ham and cheese in a bowl. Cut the puff pastry sheets into 10 cm (4 inch) rounds (about five rounds from each sheet). Spoon a tablespoon of the ham and olive mixture into the centre of each round, fold over the pastry to enclose the filling and crimp the edges to seal.

Place the pastries on the trays, spacing them 2 cm (¾ inch) apart. Brush with the egg yolk and bake for 15 minutes, or until brown and puffed, swapping the trays around in the oven after 10 minutes. Cover loosely with foil if browning too much. Serve hot.

Olive twists

preparation 20 minutes
cooking 10 minutes
makes about 50

1 tablespoon capers
4 anchovy fillets
2 tablespoons ready-made olive paste (tapenade)
2 tablespoons finely chopped parsley
oil, to drizzle
2 sheets ready-rolled puff pastry

Preheat the oven to 200°C (400°F/Gas 6). Line a large baking tray with baking paper.

Finely chop the capers and anchovy fillets and mix with the olive paste, parsley and a drizzle of oil, to form a smooth paste. Spread the pastry with the paste and cut into 1.5 cm (⅝ inch) strips. Twist each strip about four times and bake for about 5–10 minutes, or until golden brown.

Borek of asparagus

preparation 20 minutes
cooking 25 minutes
makes 16

16 asparagus spears
2 tablespoons finely grated lemon zest
2 sheets ready-rolled puff pastry
1 egg yolk
1 tablespoon sesame seeds
tzatziki, to serve

Preheat the oven to 200°C (400°F/Gas 6). Lightly grease two baking trays.

Add the asparagus to a large saucepan of lightly salted boiling water and simmer for 3 minutes. Drain and refresh under cold water. Trim to 10 cm (4 inch) lengths.

Combine ½ teaspoon salt, ½ teaspoon pepper and the lemon zest in a shallow dish and roll each asparagus spear in the mixture.

Cut the pastry sheets into sixteen 12 x 6 cm (4½ x 2½ inch) rectangles and put one asparagus spear on each piece of pastry. In a bowl, combine the egg yolk with 2 teaspoons water and brush some on the sides and ends of the pastry. Roll up like a parcel, enclosing the sides so that the asparagus is completely sealed in. Press the joins of the pastry with a fork.

Place the parcels on the prepared trays. Brush with the remaining egg and sprinkle with sesame seeds. Bake for 15–20 minutes, or until golden. Serve warm or cold, with tzatziki on the side.

Top left: Ham and olive empandillas. Top right: Olive twists. . Bottom right: Borek of asparagus.

Spinach and feta triangles

preparation 30 minutes
cooking 45 minutes
makes 8

1 kg (2 lb 4 oz) English spinach (see Variation)
60 ml (2 fl oz/¼ cup) olive oil
1 onion, chopped
10 spring onions (scallions), sliced
20 g (¾ oz/⅓ cup) chopped flat-leaf (Italian) parsley
1 tablespoon chopped dill
large pinch of freshly grated nutmeg
35 g (1¼ oz/⅓ cup) grated parmesan cheese
150 g (5½ oz/1 cup) crumbled feta cheese (see Note)
90 g (3¼ oz/⅓ cup) ricotta cheese
4 eggs, lightly beaten
40 g (1½ oz) butter, melted
1 tablespoon olive oil, extra
12 sheets filo pastry

Trim any coarse stems from the spinach. Wash the leaves thoroughly, roughly chop and place in a large saucepan with just a little water clinging to the leaves. Cover and cook gently over low heat for 5 minutes, or until the leaves have wilted. Drain well and allow to cool slightly before squeezing tightly to remove the excess water. Chop.

Heat the oil in a frying pan. Add the onion and cook over low heat for 10 minutes, or until soft and golden. Add the spring onion and cook for a further 3 minutes. Remove from the heat. Stir in the drained spinach, parsley, dill, nutmeg, cheeses and egg. Season well.

Preheat the oven to 180°C (350°F/Gas 4). Lightly grease two baking trays. Combine the melted butter with the extra oil. Work with three sheets of pastry at a time, keeping the rest covered with a damp tea towel (dish towel). Brush each sheet with butter mixture and lay on top of each other. Cut in half lengthways.

Place 4 tablespoons of the filling on an angle at the end of each strip. Fold the pastry over to enclose the filling and form a triangle. Continue folding over until you reach the end of the pastry. Put on the baking trays and brush with the remaining butter mixture. Bake for 20–25 minutes, or until the pastry is golden brown.

Variation *If you are unable to buy English spinach, silverbeet (Swiss chard) can be used instead. Use the same quantity and trim the coarse white stems from the leaves.*

Note *Feta is a traditional Greek-style salty cheese. Any leftover should be stored immersed in lightly salted water and kept refrigerated. Rinse and pat dry before using.*

Fold the bottom corner of the pastry over the spinach filling to form a triangle.

Continue folding over the pastry until you get to the end of the pastry.

Tomato and eggplant borek

preparation 50 minutes + 1 hour refrigeration
cooking 1 hour
makes 30

80 g (2¾ oz) butter, melted
80 ml (2½ fl oz/⅓ cup) olive oil
185 g (6½ oz/1½ cups) plain (all-purpose) flour

filling
250 g (9 oz) tomatoes
2 teaspoons olive oil
1 small onion, chopped
½ teaspoon ground cumin
300 g (10½ oz) eggplant (aubergine), cut into
2 cm (¾ inch) cubes
2 teaspoons tomato paste (concentrated purée)
1 tablespoon chopped coriander (cilantro)
1 egg, lightly beaten

To make the pastry, put the butter, oil and 80 ml (2½ fl oz/⅓ cup) water into a bowl. Season well with salt. Gradually add the flour in batches, mixing with a wooden spoon to form an oily, lumpy dough that comes away from the side of the bowl. Knead gently to bring the dough together, cover with plastic wrap and refrigerate for 1 hour.

Score a cross in the base of each tomato. Put in a heatproof bowl and cover with boiling water. Leave for 30 seconds, then transfer to cold water, drain and peel away the skin from the cross. Cut the tomatoes in half, scoop out the seeds and chop the flesh.

Heat the oil in a frying pan, add the onion and cook, stirring, over low heat for 2–3 minutes, or until soft. Add the cumin, cook for 1 minute, then add the eggplant and cook, stirring, for 8–10 minutes, or until the eggplant begins to soften. Stir in the tomato and tomato paste. Cook over medium heat for 15 minutes, or until the mixture becomes dry. Stir occasionally. Season and stir in the coriander. Cool.

Preheat the oven to 180°C (350°F/Gas 4). Lightly grease two baking trays.

Roll out half the pastry on a lightly floured surface to 2 mm (1⁄16 inch) thick. Using an 8 cm (3¼ inch) cutter, cut rounds from the pastry. Spoon 2 level teaspoons of the mixture into the centre of each round, lightly brush the edges with water and fold over the filling, expelling any air. Press firmly and crimp the edge with a fork to seal. Place on the trays and brush with the beaten egg. Bake in the top half of the oven for 25 minutes, or until golden brown and crisp.

Vol-au-vents

preparation 20 minutes + 15 minutes refrigeration
cooking 30 minutes
makes 4

250 g (9 oz) block ready-made puff pastry, thawed
1 egg, lightly beaten

sauce and filling
40 g (1½ oz) butter
2 spring onions (scallions), finely chopped
2 tablespoons plain (all-purpose) flour
375 ml (13 fl oz/1½ cups) milk
your choice of filling (see Note)

Preheat the oven to 220°C (425°F/Gas 7). Line a baking tray with baking paper.

Roll out the pastry to a 20 cm (8 inch) square. Cut four circles of pastry with a 10 cm (4 inch) cutter. Place the rounds onto the tray and cut 6 cm (2½ inch) circles into the centre of the rounds with a cutter, taking care not to cut right through the pastry. Place the baking tray in the refrigerator for 15 minutes.

Using a floured knife blade, 'knock up' the sides of each pastry round by making even indentations about 1 cm (½ inch) apart around the circumference. This should allow even rising of the pastry as it cooks. The dough can be made ahead of time up to here and frozen until needed.

Carefully brush the pastry with the egg, avoiding the 'knocked up' edge as any glaze spilt on the sides will stop the pastry from rising. Bake for 15–20 minutes, or until the pastry has risen and is golden brown and crisp. Cool on a wire rack.

Remove the centre from each pastry circle and pull out and discard any partially cooked pastry from the centre. The pastry can be returned to the oven for 2 minutes to dry out if the centre is undercooked. The pastry cases are now ready to be filled with a hot filling before serving.

To make the sauce, melt the butter in a saucepan, add the spring onion and stir over low heat for 2 minutes, or until soft. Add the flour and stir for 2 minutes, or until lightly golden. Gradually add the milk, stirring until smooth. Stir constantly over medium heat for 4 minutes, or until the mixture boils and thickens. Season well. Remove and stir in your choice of filling (see Note).

Note Add 350 g (12 oz) of any of the following to your white sauce: sliced, cooked mushrooms; peeled, deveined and cooked prawns (shrimp); chopped, cooked chicken breast; poached, flaked salmon; cooked and dressed crabmeat; oysters; steamed asparagus spears.

Bottom: Vol-au-vents. Top: Tomato and eggplant borek.

Curried pork and veal sausage roll

preparation 30 minutes
cooking 35 minutes
makes 36

3 sheets ready-rolled puff pastry
2 eggs, lightly beaten
3 dried Chinese mushrooms
1 tablespoon oil
4 spring onions (scallions), finely chopped
1 garlic clove, crushed
1 small red chilli, finely chopped
2–3 teaspoons curry powder
750 g (1 lb 10 oz) minced (ground) pork and veal
80 g (2¾ oz/1 cup) fresh breadcrumbs
1 egg, extra, lightly beaten
3 tablespoons chopped coriander (cilantro)
1 tablespoon soy sauce
1 tablespoon oyster sauce

Preheat the oven to 200°C (400°F/Gas 6). Lightly grease two baking trays.

Cut the pastry sheets in half and lightly brush the edges with some of the beaten egg. Soak the mushrooms in hot water for 30 minutes, squeeze dry and chop finely.

Heat the oil in a frying pan and cook the spring onions, garlic, chilli and curry powder. Transfer to a bowl and mix with the pork and veal, breadcrumbs, mushrooms, extra egg, coriander, soy sauce and oyster sauce.

Divide into six even portions. Pipe or spoon the filling down the centre of each piece of pastry, then brush the edges with some of the egg. Fold the pastry over the filling, overlapping the edges and placing the join underneath. Brush the rolls with more of the egg, then cut each into six short pieces.

Cut two small slashes on top of each roll. Place the rolls on the trays and bake for 15 minutes, then reduce the oven to 180°C (350°F/Gas 4) and bake for another 15 minutes, or until puffed and golden.

Chutney chicken sausage rolls

preparation 30 minutes
cooking 30 minutes
makes 36

3 sheets ready-rolled puff pastry
2 eggs, lightly beaten
750 g (1 lb 10 oz) minced (ground) chicken
4 spring onions (scallions), finely chopped
80 g (2¾ oz/1 cup) fresh breadcrumbs
1 carrot, finely grated
2 tablespoons fruit chutney
1 tablespoon sweet chilli sauce
1 tablespoon grated fresh ginger
sesame seeds, to sprinkle

Preheat the oven to 200°C (400°F/Gas 6). Lightly grease two baking trays.

Cut the pastry sheets in half and lightly brush the edges with some of the beaten egg.

Mix half the remaining egg with the remaining ingredients in a large bowl, then divide the mixture into six even portions. Pipe or spoon the filling down the centre of each piece of pastry, then brush the edges with some of the egg. Fold the pastry over the filling, overlapping the edges and placing the join underneath. Brush the rolls with more egg, then cut each into six short pieces. Sprinkle the rolls with sesame seeds.

Cut two small slashes on top of each roll and place on the trays. Bake for 15 minutes. Reduce the oven to 180°C (350°F/Gas 4) and bake for another 15 minutes, or until puffed and golden.

Bottom: Chutney chicken sausage rolls. Top: Curried pork and veal sausage roll.

Mini spinach pies

preparation 45 minutes + 30 minutes cooling
cooking 35 minutes
makes 24

80 ml (2½ fl oz/⅓ cup) olive oil
2 onions, finely chopped
2 garlic cloves, chopped
150 g (5½ oz) small button mushrooms, roughly chopped
200 g (7 oz) English spinach, chopped
½ teaspoon chopped thyme
100 g (3½ oz) crumbled feta cheese
3–4 sheets ready-rolled shortcrust (pie) pastry
milk, to glaze

Heat 2 tablespoons of the oil in a frying pan over medium heat and cook the onion and garlic for 5 minutes, or until soft and lightly coloured. Add the mushrooms and cook for another 4 minutes, or until softened. Transfer to a bowl.

Heat 1 tablespoon of the oil in the same pan over medium heat, add half the spinach and cook, stirring well, for 2–3 minutes, until softened. Add to the bowl. Repeat with the remaining oil and spinach. Add the thyme and feta to the bowl and mix. Season well and leave to cool.

Preheat the oven to 200°C (400°F/Gas 6). Lightly grease two 12-hole round-based patty pans or mini muffin tins. Roll out the pastry sheets until slightly thinner than they were originally (you may only need to use three sheets). Cut out 24 rounds with a 7.5 cm (3 inch) cutter. Use these to line the patty tins, then add the spinach filling. Cut rounds of 7 cm (2¾ inches) from the remaining pastry to fit the tops of the pies. Press the edges with a fork to seal.

Prick the pie tops once with a fork, brush with milk and bake for 15–20 minutes, or until golden. Serve immediately or leave to cool on a wire rack.

Line the tins with pastry rounds, then fill with the spinach filling.

Potato and goat's cheese pies

preparation 25 minutes
cooking 1 hour
makes 4

4 potatoes, peeled
4 slices prosciutto
150 g (5½ oz) goat's cheese
250 g (9 oz/1 cup) sour cream
2 eggs, lightly beaten
125 ml (4 fl oz/½ cup) pouring cream

Preheat the oven to 180°C (350°F/Gas 4). Brush four 250 ml (9 fl oz/1 cup) ramekins with melted butter.

For each pie, thinly slice a potato and pat dry with paper towel. Line the base of a ramekin with a half slice of prosciutto. Layer half the potato slices neatly into the dishes. Put the other half slice of prosciutto on top and crumble a quarter of the goat's cheese over it. Cover with the remaining potato slices and press down firmly. The potato should fill the dish to the top.

Mix together the sour cream, egg and cream and season well. Pour into the ramekins, allowing it to seep through the layers. Place on a baking tray and bake for 50–60 minutes, or until the potato is soft when tested with a skewer. Leave for 5 minutes, then run a knife around the edge and turn out onto serving plates.

Use the remaining potato slices to cover the top of the goat's cheese.

Bottom: Potato and goat's cheese pies. Top: Mini spinach pies.

Italian zucchini pie

preparation 30 minutes + 30 minutes refrigeration +
30 minutes draining
cooking 1 hour
serves 6

310 g (11 oz/2½ cups) plain (all-purpose) flour
80 ml (2½ fl oz/⅓ cup) olive oil
1 egg, lightly beaten
60–80 ml (2–2½ fl oz/¼–⅓ cup) iced water
600 g (1 lb 5 oz) zucchini (courgettes)
150 g (5½ oz) provolone cheese, grated
120 g (4¼ oz) ricotta cheese
3 eggs
2 garlic cloves, crushed
2 teaspoons finely chopped basil
pinch of freshly grated nutmeg
1 egg, lightly beaten

To make the pastry, sift the flour and ½ teaspoon salt into a large bowl and make a well in the centre. Combine the oil, egg and almost all the water and add to the flour. Mix with a flat-bladed knife, using a cutting action, until the mixture comes together in beads (adding a little water if the mixture is too dry). Turn onto a lightly floured surface and gather together into a smooth ball. Cover with plastic wrap and refrigerate for 30 minutes.

Preheat the oven to 200°C (400°F/Gas 6) and heat a baking tray. Grease an 18 cm (7 inch) pie dish.

Grate the zucchini, toss with ¼ teaspoon of salt and drain in a colander for 30 minutes. Squeeze out any liquid and place in a large bowl with the provolone, ricotta, eggs, garlic, basil and nutmeg. Season well and mix thoroughly.

Roll out two-thirds of the pastry between two sheets of baking paper until large enough to line the base and side of the dish.

Spoon the filling into the pastry case and level the surface. Brush the pastry rim with egg. Roll out two-thirds of the remaining dough between the baking paper to make a lid. Cover the filling and press the edges together firmly. Trim and crimp the rim. Prick the top all over with a skewer and brush with egg.

Roll the remaining dough into a 30 x 10 cm (12 x 4 inch) long strip. Use a long sharp knife to cut this into nine 1 cm (½ inch) wide lengths. Press three ropes together at one end and then press them onto the work surface to secure them. Plait the ropes and make two more plaits. Trim the ends and space the plaits parallel across the centre of the pie. Brush with egg. Bake on the hot tray for 50 minutes, or until golden.

Mediterranean pie

preparation 25 minutes + 20 minutes refrigeration
cooking 35 minutes
serves 4

375 g (13 oz/3 cups) plain (all-purpose) flour
1 egg, lightly beaten
125 ml (4 fl oz/½ cup) buttermilk
100 ml (3½ fl oz) olive oil

filling
2 tablespoons olive oil
100 g (3½ oz) button mushrooms, sliced
400 g (14 oz) tinned tomatoes, drained and roughly chopped
100 g (3½ oz) sliced salami
180 g (6¼ oz) jar artichokes, drained
4 tablespoons basil, torn
100 g (3½ oz) grated mozzarella cheese
30 g (1 oz/¼ cup) grated parmesan cheese
milk, to glaze

To make the pastry, sift the flour into a large bowl and make a well in the centre. Add the egg and buttermilk, then the oil and mix with a large metal spoon until the mixture comes together and forms a soft dough (add a little water if the mixture is too dry). Turn onto a lightly floured surface and gather together into a smooth ball. Cover with plastic wrap and refrigerate for 20 minutes.

Preheat the oven to 210°C (415°F/Gas 6–7). Lightly grease a large baking tray and place in the oven to heat up.

Heat the oil in a large frying pan, add the mushrooms and cook over medium heat for 5 minutes, or until they have softened and browned a little.

Divide the pastry in half and roll out each portion between two sheets of baking paper, into 30 cm (12 inch) rounds. Layer the tomato, salami, mushrooms, artichokes, basil, mozzarella and parmesan on one of the pastry rounds, leaving a narrow border. Season well.

Brush the border with milk. Top with the remaining pastry circle to enclose the filling, then pinch and seal the edges together. Cut three slits in the top. Brush the top with milk. Place on the preheated tray and bake for 30 minutes, or until golden.

Bottom: Mediterranean pie. Top: Italian zucchini pie.

Shepherd's pie

preparation 30 minutes + cooling
cooking 1 hour 35 minutes
serves 6

60 ml (2 fl oz/¼ cup) olive oil
1 large onion, finely chopped
2 garlic cloves, crushed
2 celery stalks, finely chopped
3 carrots, diced
2 bay leaves
1 tablespoon thyme, chopped
1 kg (2 lb 4 oz) minced (ground) lamb
1½ tablespoons plain (all-purpose) flour
125 ml (4 fl oz/½ cup) dry red wine
2 tablespoons tomato paste (concentrated purée)
400 g (14 oz) tinned chopped tomatoes
800 g (1 lb 12 oz) potatoes, chopped
60 ml (2 fl oz/¼ cup) milk
100 g (3½ oz) butter
½ teaspoon freshly grated nutmeg

Heat 2 tablespoons of the oil in a large, heavy-based saucepan and cook the onion for 3–4 minutes, or until softened. Add the garlic, celery, carrot, bay leaves and thyme, and cook for 2–3 minutes. Transfer to a bowl and remove the bay leaves.

Add the remaining oil to the same pan and cook the minced lamb over high heat for 5–6 minutes, or until it changes colour. Mix in the flour, cook for 1 minute, then pour in the red wine and cook for 2–3 minutes. Return the vegetables to the pan with the tomato paste and tomato. Reduce the heat, cover and simmer for 45 minutes, stirring occasionally. Season and transfer to a shallow 3 litre (105 fl oz/12 cup) casserole dish and leave to cool. Preheat the oven to 180°C (350°F/Gas 4).

Boil the potatoes in salted water for 20–25 minutes, or until tender. Drain, then mash with the milk and butter until smooth. Season with nutmeg and black pepper. Spoon over the filling and fluff with a fork. Bake for 40 minutes, until golden and crusty.

Cook the lamb until it changes colour, then return the vegetables to the pan and stir well.

Filo vegetable strudel

preparation 30 minutes + 30 minutes standing
cooking 1 hour
serves 6–8

1 large eggplant (aubergine), thinly sliced
1 red capsicum (pepper)
3 zucchini (courgettes), sliced lengthways
2 tablespoons olive oil
6 sheets filo pastry (see Note)
50 g (1¾ oz) baby English spinach leaves
60 g (2¼ oz) feta cheese, sliced

Preheat the oven to 190°C (375°F/Gas 5). Lightly grease a baking tray. Sprinkle the eggplant slices with a little salt and leave to drain in a colander for 30 minutes. Pat dry with paper towels.

Cut the capsicum into quarters and place, skin side up, under a hot grill (broiler) for 10 minutes, or until the skin blackens. Put in plastic bag and let cool. Peel away the skin. Brush the eggplant and zucchini with olive oil and grill for 5–10 minutes, or until golden brown. Set aside to cool.

Brush one sheet of filo pastry at a time with olive oil, then lay them on top of each other. Place half the eggplant slices lengthways down the centre of the filo and top with a layer of zucchini, capsicum, spinach and feta cheese. Repeat the layers until the vegetables and cheese are used up. Tuck in the ends of the pastry, then roll up like a parcel. Brush lightly with oil and place on the baking tray. Bake for 35 minutes, or until golden brown.

Note *Unopened packets of filo can be stored in the fridge for up to a month. Once opened, use within 2–3 days.*

Once you have formed your layers of filling, neatly tuck in the pastry ends, then roll up like a parcel.

Bottom: Filo vegetable strudel. Top: Shepherd's pie.

Polenta pie

preparation 20 minutes + 15 minutes standing + refrigeration
cooking 50 minutes
serves 6

2 eggplants (aubergines), thickly sliced
330 ml (11¼ fl oz/1⅓ cups) vegetable stock
150 g (5½ oz/1 cup) fine polenta
60 g (2¼ oz/heaped ½ cup) finely grated parmesan cheese
1 tablespoon olive oil
1 large onion, chopped
2 garlic cloves, crushed
1 large red capsicum (pepper), diced
2 zucchini (courgettes), thickly sliced
150 g (5½ oz) button mushrooms, cut into quarters
400 g (14 oz) tinned chopped tomatoes
3 teaspoons balsamic vinegar
olive oil, for brushing

Spread the eggplant in a single layer on a board and sprinkle with salt. Leave for 15 minutes, then rinse, pat dry and cut into cubes.

Line a 23 cm (9 inch) round cake tin with foil. Pour the stock and 330 ml (11¼ fl oz/1⅓ cups) water into a saucepan and bring to the boil. Add the polenta in a thin stream and stir over low heat for 5 minutes, or until the liquid is absorbed and the mixture comes away from the side of the pan.

Remove the pan from the heat and stir in the parmesan cheese until it melts through the polenta. Spread into the prepared tin, smoothing the surface as much as possible. Refrigerate until set.

Preheat the oven to 200°C (400°F/Gas 6). Heat the oil in a large saucepan with a lid and add the onion. Cook over medium heat, stirring occasionally, for about 3 minutes. Add the garlic and cook for a further minute. Add the eggplant, capsicum, zucchini, mushrooms and tomato. Bring to the boil, then reduce the heat and simmer, covered, for about 20 minutes. Stir occasionally to prevent it catching on the bottom of the pan. Stir in the vinegar and season.

Transfer the vegetable mixture to a 23 cm (9 inch) ovenproof pie dish, piling it up slightly in the centre. Turn out the polenta, peel off the foil and cut into 12 wedges. Arrange smooth side down in a single layer, over the vegetables. Brush lightly with a little olive oil and bake for 20 minutes, or until lightly brown and crisp.

Stir the polenta until the liquid has been absorbed and it starts to come away from the side of the pan.

Arrange the wedges of polenta neatly to cover the vegetable filling.

Chicken coriander pie

preparation 40 minutes
cooking 45 minutes
serves 4

50 g (1¾ oz) butter
2 onions, chopped
100 g (3½ oz) button mushrooms, sliced
250 g (9 oz) cooked chicken, chopped
4 hard-boiled eggs
1 tablespoon plain (all-purpose) flour
280 ml (9¾ fl oz) chicken stock
1 egg yolk
3 tablespoons chopped coriander (cilantro) leaves
250 g (9 oz) block ready-made puff pastry, thawed
1 egg, lightly beaten

Preheat the oven to 200°C (400°F/Gas 6). Melt half the butter in a large pan. Add the onion and mushrooms and cook for 5 minutes, or until soft, then stir in the chicken. Spoon half the mixture into a 20 cm (8 inch) round, straight-sided pie dish. Slice the eggs and lay over the chicken, then top with the remaining mixture.

Melt the remaining butter in a saucepan, add the flour and cook for 1 minute. Gradually add the stock and cook for 4 minutes, stirring constantly, then remove from the heat. Stir in the egg yolk and coriander and season. Leave to cool, then pour over the chicken filling in the pie dish.

Roll out the pastry into a square larger than the pie dish. Dampen the rim with water and lay the pastry over the top, pressing down firmly to seal. Trim the edges. Roll the leftover pastry into a long strip. Slice it into three equal lengths and make a plait. Brush the top of the pie with the beaten egg and place the plait around the edge. Brush again with the remaining egg. Make a few slits in the centre and bake for 35 minutes, until golden.

Beef, stout and potato pie

preparation 30 minutes
cooking 3 hours 20 minutes
serves 6

2 tablespoons olive oil
1.25 kg (2 lb 12 oz) chuck steak, cut into small cubes
2 onions, sliced
2 bacon slices, roughly chopped
4 garlic cloves, crushed
2 tablespoons plain (all-purpose) flour
435 ml (15¼ fl oz) tin stout
375 ml (13 fl oz/1½ cups) beef stock
1½ tablespoons chopped thyme
2 large potatoes, thinly sliced

Heat 1 tablespoon of the oil over high heat in a large flameproof casserole dish. Add the beef in batches and cook, stirring, for 5 minutes, or until the meat is browned. Remove from the dish. Reduce the heat to low, add the remaining oil, then cook the onion and bacon for 10 minutes, stirring occasionally. Add the garlic and cook for another minute. Return the beef to the dish.

Sprinkle the flour over the beef, cook for a minute, stirring, and then gradually add the stout, stirring constantly. Add the stock, increase the heat to medium–high and bring to the boil. Stir in the thyme, season well, then reduce the heat and simmer for 2 hours, or until the beef is tender and the mixture has thickened.

Preheat the oven to 200°C (400°F/Gas 6). Lightly grease a 1.25 litre (44 fl oz/5 cup) ovenproof dish and pour in the beef filling. Arrange the potato slices in a single overlapping layer over the top to cover the meat. Brush lightly with olive oil and sprinkle with salt. Bake for 45–50 minutes, or until the topping is golden.

Use the leftover pastry to make a neat plait, then lay it around the edge of the pie.

Lay neat slices of potato in a slightly overlapping layer to cover the beef filling.

Bottom: Beef, stout and potato pie. Top: Chicken coriander pie.

Moroccan beef pies

preparation 45 minutes + 30 minutes refrigeration
cooking 1 hour 30 minutes
makes 4

1 tablespoon oil
2 garlic cloves, crushed
1 onion, cut into thin wedges
2 teaspoons ground cumin
2 teaspoons ground ginger
2 teaspoons paprika
pinch of saffron threads
500 g (1 lb 2 oz) chuck steak, cubed
375 ml (13 fl oz/1½ cups) beef stock
1 small cinnamon stick
100 g (3½ oz) pitted prunes, halved
2 carrots, sliced
1 teaspoon grated orange zest
¼ preserved lemon, rinsed, pith and flesh removed, finely chopped, optional
200 g (7 oz) Greek-style yoghurt, optional

pastry
250 g (9 oz/2 cups) plain (all-purpose) flour
125 g (4½ oz) butter, chilled and cubed
1 egg, lightly beaten
1–2 tablespoons iced water

Heat the oil in a large saucepan, add the garlic and onion and cook for 3 minutes, or until soft. Add the cumin, ginger, paprika and saffron and stir for 1 minute, or until fragrant. Add the meat and toss. Add the stock, cinnamon, prunes and carrot. Bring to the boil, reduce the heat and simmer, covered, for 30 minutes. Increase the heat to medium, add the zest and cook, uncovered, for 20 minutes, or until the liquid has reduced. Remove the cinnamon; cool completely.

To make the pastry, sift the flour into a large bowl. Rub the butter into the flour until it resembles fine breadcrumbs. Make a well in the centre, add the egg and water and mix with a flat-bladed knife, using a cutting action, until the mixture comes together in beads (adding a little more water if necessary). Turn onto a lightly floured surface and gather together into a smooth ball. Cover with plastic wrap and refrigerate for 30 minutes.

Preheat the oven to 200°C (400°F/Gas 6). Lightly grease four 9 cm (3½ inch) pie tins. Divide the dough into four pieces and roll out between two sheets of baking paper to make 20 cm (8 inch) circles. Press into the tins, leaving the excess hanging over the sides.

Divide the filling among the tins. Fold over the excess pastry, pleating as you go. Place on a baking tray and bake for 35–40 minutes, or until golden. If using, combine the preserved lemon and yoghurt and serve with the pies.

Simmer the beef and vegetable mixture until you have a thick, rich sauce.

Pleat the excess pastry around the edge of the pies—there will be a gap in the middle.

Brik a l'oeuf

preparation 30 minutes
cooking 20 minutes
makes 2

6 sheets filo pastry
30 g (1 oz) butter, melted
1 small onion, finely chopped
200 g (7 oz) tinned tuna in oil, drained
6 pitted black olives, chopped
1 tablespoon chopped parsley
2 eggs

Preheat the oven to 200°C (400°F/Gas 6). Lightly grease a baking tray.

Cut the pastry sheets in half widthways. Brush four sheets with melted butter and lay them on top of each other. Place half of the combined onion, tuna, olives and parsley at one end and make a well in the centre. Break an egg into the well, being careful to leave the yolk whole. Season well.

Brush two more sheets with melted butter, place them together and lay them on top of the tuna and egg. Fold in the sides and roll up into a neat firm package, still keeping the egg whole.

Place on the baking tray and brush with melted butter. Repeat with the remaining pastry and filling. Bake for 20 minutes, or until golden.

Note *The yolk will still be soft after 15 minutes cooking. If you prefer a firmer egg, bake for longer. Tuna in oil is preferable to brine as it will keep the filling moist when cooked.*

Cheese and onion pie

preparation 25 minutes + 10 minutes cooling
cooking 45 minutes
serves 4

2 tablespoons olive oil
2 onions, chopped
185 g (6½ oz/1½ cups) grated cheddar cheese
1 tablespoon chopped flat-leaf (Italian) parsley
1 teaspoon English mustard
2 teaspoons worcestershire sauce
2 eggs, lightly beaten
2 sheets ready-rolled puff pastry

Preheat the oven to 190°C (375°F/Gas 5). Line a baking tray with baking paper.

Heat the oil in a large frying pan over medium heat, add the onion and cook for 5–7 minutes, or until soft and golden. Transfer to a bowl and allow to cool for 10 minutes.

Add the cheese, parsley, mustard and worcestershire sauce to the onion and mix well. Add half the egg to the bowl and season well.

Cut each sheet of pastry into a 23 cm (9 inch) circle. Lay one sheet of pastry on the baking tray. Spread the filling over the pastry base, piling it higher in the middle and leaving a narrow border. Lightly brush the border with some of the remaining egg and place the second sheet on top, stretching it slightly to neatly fit. Press and seal the edges well and brush the top with the remaining egg. Cut two slits in the top for steam holes.

Bake for 10 minutes, then reduce the heat to 180°C (350°F/Gas 4) and cook for another 20–25 minutes, or until the pastry is crisp and golden brown.

Carefully break an egg into the well you have made in the filling.

Cover the filling with your second circle of pastry, then press the edges to seal the two layers.

Bottom: Cheese and onion pie. Top: Brik a l'oeuf.

Cornish pasties

preparation 1 hour + refrigeration
cooking 45 minutes
makes 6

310 g (11 oz/2½ cups) plain (all-purpose) flour
125 g (4½ oz) butter, chilled and cubed
4–5 tablespoons iced water
160 g (5½ oz) round steak, diced
1 small potato, finely chopped
1 small onion, finely chopped
1 small carrot, finely chopped
1–2 teaspoons worcestershire sauce
2 tablespoons beef stock
1 egg, lightly beaten

To make the pastry, process the flour, butter and a pinch of salt in a food processor for 15 seconds, or until crumbly. Add the water and process in short bursts until it comes together. Turn onto a lightly floured surface and gather together into a smooth ball. Cover with plastic wrap and refrigerate for 30 minutes.

Preheat the oven to 210°C (415°F/Gas 6–7). Lightly grease a baking tray.

Mix together the steak, potato, onion, carrot, worcestershire sauce and stock. Season well.

Divide the dough into six portions and roll out to 3 mm (⅛ inch) thick. Cut into six 16 cm (6¼ inch) rounds. Divide the filling evenly and put in the centre of each pastry circle.

Brush the pastry edges with the beaten egg and fold over. Pinch to form a frill and place on the tray. Brush with the remaining egg and bake for 15 minutes. Reduce the heat to 180°C (350°F/Gas 4) and bake the pasties for a further 25–30 minutes, or until golden.

To get the traditional appearance of a Cornish pasty, pinch the edges of the dough to form a frill.

Welsh lamb pie

preparation 20 minutes + cooling
cooking 2 hours 35 minutes
serves 6

750 g (1 lb 10 oz) boned lamb shoulder, cubed
90 g (3¼ oz/¾ cup) plain (all-purpose) flour, seasoned
2 tablespoons olive oil
200 g (7 oz) bacon slices, finely chopped
2 garlic cloves, chopped
4 large leeks, sliced
1 large carrot, chopped
2 large potatoes, peeled and diced
310 ml (10¾ fl oz/1¼ cups) beef stock
1 bay leaf
2 teaspoons chopped parsley
375 g (13 oz) block ready-made puff pastry, thawed
1 egg, lightly beaten

Toss the meat in the flour. Heat the oil in a large frying pan over medium heat and brown the meat in batches for 4–5 minutes, then remove from the pan. Cook the bacon for 3 minutes. Add the garlic and leek and cook for 5 minutes, or until soft.

Put the meat in a large saucepan, add the leek and bacon, carrot, potato, stock and bay leaf and bring to the boil, then reduce the heat, cover and simmer for 30 minutes. Uncover and simmer for 1 hour, or until the meat is cooked and the liquid has thickened. Season to taste. Remove the bay leaf, stir in the parsley and set aside to cool.

Preheat the oven to 200°C (400°F/Gas 6). Place the filling in an 18 cm (7 inch) pie dish. Roll out the pastry between two sheets of baking paper until large enough to cover the pie. Trim the edges and pinch to seal.

Decorate the pie with pastry trimmings. Cut two slits in the top for steam to escape. Brush with egg and bake for 45 minutes, or until the pastry is crisp and golden.

To decorate the pie, roll out the pastry trimmings and cut out decorative shapes.

Bottom: Welsh lamb pie. Top: Cornish pasties.

Rich beef pie

preparation 35 minutes + 30 minutes refrigeration
cooking 2 hours 45 minutes
serves 6

filling
2 tablespoons oil
1 kg (2 lb 4 oz) chuck steak, cubed
1 large onion, chopped
1 large carrot, finely chopped
2 garlic cloves, crushed
2 tablespoons plain (all-purpose) flour
250 ml (9 fl oz/1 cup) beef stock
2 teaspoons thyme
1 tablespoon worcestershire sauce

pastry
250 g (9 oz/2 cups) plain (all-purpose) flour
150 g (5½ oz) butter, chilled and cubed
1 egg yolk
60–80 ml (2–2½ fl oz/¼–⅓ cup) iced water
1 egg yolk and 1 tablespoon milk

Heat 1 tablespoon of the oil in a large frying pan and brown the meat in batches. Remove from the pan and set aside. Heat the remaining oil, add the onion, carrot and garlic, and cook over medium heat until browned.

Return all the meat to the pan and stir in the flour. Cook for 1 minute, then remove the pan from the heat and slowly stir in the stock, mixing the flour in well. Add the thyme and worcestershire sauce, and bring to the boil. Season to taste.

Reduce the heat to very low, cover with a lid and simmer for 1½–2 hours, or until the meat is tender. During the last 15 minutes of cooking remove the lid and allow the liquid to reduce until very thick. Cool completely.

To make the pastry, sift the flour into a large bowl. Rub the butter into the flour until it resembles fine breadcrumbs. Make a well in the centre, add the egg yolk and 2 tablespoons of the iced water, and mix with a flat-bladed knife, using a cutting action, until the mixture comes together in beads (adding a little more water if necessary). Turn out onto a lightly floured surface and gently gather together into a smooth ball. Cover in plastic wrap and refrigerate for 30 minutes.

Preheat the oven to 200°C (400°F/Gas 6). Divide the pastry into two pieces and roll out one piece on a sheet of baking paper until large enough to line a 23 cm (9 inch) pie dish. Fill with the cold filling and roll out the remaining piece of pastry until large enough to fully cover the dish. Dampen the edges of the pastry with a little water. Lay the top piece of pastry over the pie and gently press the pastry together. Trim the edges with a sharp knife and re-roll the trimmings to make decorations for the pie top.

Cut a few slits in the top of the pastry to allow the steam to escape. Beat together the egg yolk and milk, and brush over the top of the pie. Bake in the oven for 20–30 minutes, or until the pastry is golden.

Use the sheet of baking paper to help you place the pastry into the pie dish.

Carefully lay the second piece of pastry over the pie filling, then neaten the edges.

Potato filo pies

preparation 1 hour
cooking 1 hour 20 minutes
makes 6

6 roma (plum) tomatoes, halved lengthways
60 ml (2 fl oz/¼ cup) olive oil
50 g (1¾ oz) butter
3 garlic cloves, crushed
800 g (1 lb 12 oz) potatoes, unpeeled and sliced
500 g (1 lb 2 oz) English spinach, trimmed
12 sheets filo pastry
100 g (3½ oz) butter, melted
2 tablespoons sesame seeds

Preheat the oven to 200°C (400°F/Gas 6). Place the tomato halves, cut side up, on a baking tray, drizzle with 1 tablespoon of the oil and sprinkle with a little salt. Bake for 40 minutes.

Heat the butter and remaining oil in a large non-stick frying pan and cook the garlic and potato, tossing occasionally, for 10 minutes, or until the potato is tender. Set aside on paper towel. Cook the spinach in the pan for 1–2 minutes, or until wilted. Cool and then squeeze out any excess moisture.

Preheat the oven to 180°C (350°F/Gas 4). Lightly grease a baking tray.

Work with one sheet of pastry at a time and cover the rest with a damp tea towel (dish towel). Brush the pastry with melted butter and place another sheet on top. Brush with butter and repeat with another two layers. Cut in half widthways. Place a few potato slices at one end of each half, leaving a wide border on each side. Top with two tomato pieces and some spinach.

Fold in the sides of the pastry and roll up. Place on the baking tray, brush with melted butter and sprinkle with some sesame seeds. Use the remaining filo and filling to make another five parcels. Bake for 25–30 minutes, or until lightly golden.

Potato and salmon parcels

preparation 30 minutes
cooking 40 minutes
makes 12

750 g (1 lb 10 oz) floury potatoes, peeled
40 g (1½ oz) butter
60 ml (2 fl oz/¼ cup) pouring cream
125 g (4½ oz/1 cup) grated cheddar cheese
210 g (7½ oz) tinned red salmon, skin and bones removed, flaked
1 tablespoon chopped dill
4 spring onions (scallions), finely chopped
3 sheets ready-rolled puff pastry
1 egg, lightly beaten

Cut the potatoes into small pieces and cook in a saucepan of boiling water until tender. Mash with the butter and the cream until there are no lumps. Add the cheese, salmon, dill and spring onion to the potato and mix well.

Preheat the oven to 200°C (400°F/Gas 6). Lightly grease two baking trays.

Cut each pastry sheet into four squares. Divide the mixture between the squares (approximately ¼ cup in each). Lightly brush the edges with the egg. Bring all four corners to the centre to form a point and press together to make a parcel.

Put the parcels on the greased trays and glaze with the egg. Bake for 15–20 minutes, or until the pastry is golden brown.

Note *Before removing the pastries from the oven, lift them gently off the tray and check that the bottom of the parcels are cooked through. Take care not to overcook the parcels or they may burst open.*

Hint *If you like your puff pastry to taste extra buttery, brush it with melted butter before baking.*

Fold the long edges in towards the middle, then roll up the pastry, starting at the filling end.

Bring each corner of the square into the middle, then pinch them together to make a parcel.

Bottom: Potato and salmon parcels. Top: Potato filo pies.

Steak and kidney pie

preparation 20 minutes
cooking 2 hours
serves 6

750 g (1 lb 10 oz) round steak
4 lamb kidneys
2 tablespoons plain (all-purpose) flour
1 tablespoon oil
1 onion, chopped
30 g (1 oz) butter
1 tablespoon worcestershire sauce
1 tablespoon tomato paste (concentrated purée)
125 ml (4 fl oz/½ cup) red wine
250 ml (9 fl oz/1 cup) beef stock
125 g (4½ oz) button mushrooms, sliced
½ teaspoon dried thyme
20 g (¾ oz/⅓ cup) chopped parsley
375 g (13 oz) block ready-made puff pastry, thawed
1 egg, lightly beaten

Cut the meat into small cubes. Trim the skin from the kidneys. Quarter the kidneys and trim away any fat or sinew. Coat the meat and kidneys with the flour and shake off the excess.

Heat the oil in a pan. Add the onion and cook for 5 minutes, or until soft. Remove with a slotted spoon. Add the butter to the pan. Brown the meat and kidneys in batches and then return all the meat and onion to the pan.

Add the worcestershire sauce, tomato paste, wine, stock, mushrooms, thyme and parsley to the pan. Bring to the boil then simmer, covered, for 1 hour, or until the meat is tender. Season and leave to cool. Spoon the mixture into a 1.5 litre (52 fl oz/6 cup) pie dish.

Preheat the oven to 210°C (415°F/Gas 6–7). Roll out the puff pastry on a lightly floured surface so that it is 5 cm (2 inches) larger than the dish. Cut thin strips from the pastry and press onto the rim, sealing the joins. Place the pastry on top of the pie. Trim the edges and cut steam holes in the top. Decorate with pastry trimmings and brush the top with the egg. Bake for 35–40 minutes, or until golden.

Low-fat spinach pie

preparation 25 minutes
cooking 45 minutes
serves 6

1.5 kg (3 lb 5 oz) English spinach
2 teaspoons olive oil
1 onion, chopped
4 spring onions (scallions), chopped
750 g (1 lb 10 oz) reduced-fat cottage cheese
2 eggs, lightly beaten
2 garlic cloves, crushed
pinch of freshly grated nutmeg
15 g (½ oz/¼ cup) chopped mint
8 sheets filo pastry
30 g (1 oz) butter, melted
40 g (1½ oz/½ cup) fresh breadcrumbs

Preheat the oven to 180°C (350°F/Gas 4). Lightly spray a square 1.5 litre (52 fl oz/6 cup) ovenproof dish with oil.

Trim and wash the spinach, then place in a large saucepan with the water clinging to the leaves. Cover and cook for 2–3 minutes, until just wilted. Drain, cool, then squeeze dry and chop.

Heat the oil in a small pan. Add the onion and spring onion and cook for 2–3 minutes, until softened. Combine in a bowl with the chopped spinach. Stir in the cottage cheese, egg, garlic, nutmeg and mint. Season and mix thoroughly.

Brush a sheet of filo pastry with a little butter. Fold in half widthways and line the base and sides of the dish. Repeat with 3 more sheets. Keep the unused sheets moist by covering with a damp tea towel (dish towel).

Sprinkle the breadcrumbs over the pastry. Spread the filling into the dish. Fold over any overlapping pastry. Brush and fold another sheet and place on top. Repeat with 3 more sheets. Tuck the pastry in at the sides. Brush the top with any remaining butter. Score squares or diamonds on top using a sharp knife. Bake for 40 minutes, or until golden.

Squeeze as much liquid as possible from the spinach, then cut it finely.

Bottom: Low-fat spinach pie. Top: Steak and kidney pie.

Beef and red wine pies

preparation 50 minutes
cooking 2 hours 40 minutes
makes 6

60 ml (2 fl oz/¼ cup) oil
1.5 kg (3 lb 5 oz) chuck steak, cubed
2 onions, chopped
1 garlic clove, crushed
30 g (1 oz/¼ cup) plain (all-purpose) flour
310 ml (10¾ fl oz/1¼ cups) dry red wine
500 ml (17 fl oz/2 cups) beef stock
2 bay leaves
2 thyme sprigs
2 carrots, chopped
4 sheets ready-rolled shortcrust (pie) pastry
1 egg, lightly beaten
4 sheets puff pastry

Heat 2 tablespoons of oil in a large frying pan, add the meat and fry in batches until browned. Remove all the meat from the pan. Heat the remaining oil in the same pan, add the onion and garlic and cook, stirring, until golden brown. Add the flour and stir over medium heat for 2 minutes, or until well browned.

Remove from the heat and gradually stir in the combined wine and stock. Return to the heat and stir until the mixture boils and thickens. Return the meat to the pan with the bay leaves and thyme, and simmer for 1 hour. Add the carrot and simmer for another 45 minutes, until the meat and carrot are tender and the sauce has thickened. Season to taste with salt and freshly ground black pepper, and remove the bay leaves and thyme. Cool.

Preheat the oven to 200°C (400°F/Gas 6). Lightly grease six 9 cm (3½ inch) metal pie tins. Cut the shortcrust pastry sheets in half diagonally. Line the base and side of each pie tin with the pastry and trim the edges. Line each pie with baking paper and fill with baking beads. Place on a baking tray and bake for 8 minutes. Remove the paper and beads and bake for a further 8 minutes, or until the pastry is lightly browned. Cool.

Spoon the filling into the pastry cases and brush the edges with some of the beaten egg. Cut the puff pastry sheets in half diagonally and cover the tops of the pies. Trim the excess, pressing the edges with a fork to seal. Cut a slit in the top of each pie. Brush the tops with the remaining egg, and bake for 20–25 minutes, or until the pastry is golden.

Line the tart tins with the pieces of shortcrust pastry and press into the tins with your fingers.

Trim off the excess puff pastry, then use a fork to seal the edges and make a decorative pattern.

Ham and chicken pie

preparation 40 minutes
cooking 1 hour
serves 8–10

375 g (13 oz/3 cups) plain (all-purpose) flour
180 g (6¼ oz) butter, chilled and cubed
2–3 tablespoons iced water
1 egg, lightly beaten

filling
1 kg (2 lb 4 oz) minced (ground) chicken
1 teaspoon dried mixed herbs
2 eggs, lightly beaten
3 spring onions (scallions), finely chopped
2 tablespoons chopped parsley
2 teaspoons French mustard
80 ml (2½ fl oz/⅓ cup) pouring cream
200 g (7 oz) sliced leg ham

Preheat the oven to 180°C (350°F/Gas 4). Process the flour and butter in a food processor for 15 seconds, or until crumbly. Add the water and process in short bursts until it comes together. Turn onto a lightly floured surface and gather together into a smooth ball. Roll out two-thirds of the pastry to line a 20 cm (8 inch) spring-form tin, leaving some pastry hanging over the side. Cover with plastic wrap and refrigerate until required. Wrap the remaining pastry in plastic wrap and refrigerate.

To make the filling, mix together the chicken, herbs, egg, spring onion, parsley, mustard and cream and season well. Spoon a third of the filling into the pastry-lined tin and smooth the surface. Top with half the ham and then another chicken layer, followed by the remaining ham and then a final layer of chicken filling.

Brush the inside edge of pastry with egg. Roll out the remaining pastry to make the lid, pressing the pastry edges together. Trim the edge. Decorate with pastry trimmings. Brush with beaten egg and bake for 1 hour, or until golden.

Pumpkin, leek and corn pie

preparation 30 minutes + cooling
cooking 1 hour 25 minutes
serves 6

80 ml (2½ fl oz/⅓ cup) olive oil
2 leeks, thinly sliced
2 large garlic cloves, chopped
1 butternut pumpkin (squash), peeled, seeded and diced
3 corn cobs
185 g (6½ oz/1½ cups) grated cheddar cheese
1 teaspoon chopped rosemary
15 g (½ oz/½ cup) chopped flat-leaf (Italian) parsley
12 sheets filo pastry
5 eggs, lightly beaten

Preheat the oven to 180°C (350°F/Gas 4). Lightly grease a 33 x 25 cm (13 x 10 inch) oven dish.

Heat 1 tablespoon of the oil in a small saucepan and cook the leek and garlic for 10 minutes, stirring occasionally, until soft and golden. Transfer to a large bowl and cool.

Meanwhile, cook the pumpkin in boiling water for 5 minutes, or until just tender. Drain and cool. Cook the corn in boiling water for 7–8 minutes, or until tender. Drain and leave until cool enough to handle. Cut the kernels off the cobs and add them to the bowl with the pumpkin, cheese, rosemary and parsley, then season and mix gently.

Cover the filo pastry with a damp tea towel (dish towel) to prevent it drying out. Lightly brush one sheet of filo with oil and place in the dish. Layer five more sheets in the dish, brushing all but the last sheet with oil.

Gently stir the egg into the pumpkin mixture, then spoon into the dish. Cover with the remaining filo pastry, again brushing each layer with oil, and tuck in the edges. Bake for 1 hour, or until the pastry is golden brown and the filling has set.

Layer the slices of ham and the chicken filling, trying to keep each layer neat and even.

Once you have laid the last pastry sheet on the pie, tuck the edges down the side.

Bottom: Pumpkin, leek and corn pie. Top: Ham and chicken pie.

Salmon pie

preparation 25 minutes + refrigeration
cooking 50 minutes
serves 4–6

60 g (2¼ oz) butter
1 onion, finely chopped
200 g (7 oz) button mushrooms, sliced
2 tablespoons lemon juice
220 g (7¾ oz) salmon fillet, boned, skinned and cubed
2 hard-boiled eggs, chopped
2 tablespoons chopped dill
2 tablespoons chopped parsley
185 g (6½ oz/1 cup) cooked rice
60 ml (2 fl oz/¼ cup) pouring cream
375 g (13 fl oz) block ready-made puff pastry, thawed
1 egg, lightly beaten

Lightly grease a baking tray. Melt half the butter in a frying pan and cook the onion for 5 minutes, or until soft but not browned. Add the mushrooms and cook for 5 minutes. Stir in the lemon juice and transfer to a bowl.

Melt the remaining butter in the pan, add the salmon and cook for 2 minutes. Remove from the heat, cool slightly and add the egg, dill, parsley, salt and pepper. Stir gently and set aside. Stir together the rice and cream.

Roll out half the pastry to a rectangle measuring 18 x 30 cm (7 x 12 inches) and place on the tray. Spread with half the rice mixture, leaving a small border all the way around. Top with the salmon mixture, then the mushroom mixture, and finish with the remaining rice.

Roll out the remaining pastry to 20 x 33 cm (8 x 13 inches) to cover the filling. Crimp the edges to seal. Refrigerate for 30 minutes. Preheat the oven to 210°C (415°F/Gas 6–7). Brush with the beaten egg and bake for 15 minutes. Reduce the heat to 180°C (350°F/Gas 4) and bake for a further 15–20 minutes until golden.

Use a rolling pin to help you lay out the second sheet of pastry, lining up the edges with the first.

Chicken and leek pie

preparation 20 minutes
cooking 50 minutes
serves 4–6

60 g (2¼ oz) butter
2 large leeks, thinly sliced
4 spring onions (scallions), sliced
1 garlic clove, crushed
30 g (1 oz/¼ cup) plain (all-purpose) flour
375 ml (13 fl oz/1½ cups) chicken stock
125 ml (4 fl oz/½ cup) pouring cream
1 barbecued chicken, skin and bones removed, chopped
2 sheets ready-rolled puff pastry
60 ml (2 fl oz/¼ cup) milk

Preheat the oven to 200°C (400°F/Gas 6). In a large saucepan, melt the butter and add the leek, spring onion and garlic. Cook over low heat for 6 minutes, or until the leek is soft but not browned. Sprinkle in the flour and mix well. Pour in the stock gradually and cook, stirring well, until thick and smooth. Stir in the cream and add the chopped chicken.

Put the mixture in a shallow 20 cm (8 inch) pie dish and set aside to cool.

Cut a circle out of one of the sheets of pastry to cover the top of the pie. Paint around the rim of the pie dish with a little of the milk. Put the pastry on top and seal around the edge firmly. Trim off any overhanging pastry and decorate the edge with a fork.

Cut the other sheet of pastry into 1 cm (½ inch) strips and loosely roll up each strip like a snail. Arrange the spirals on top of the pie, starting from the middle and leaving gaps between them. The spirals may not cover the whole surface of the pie. Make a few small holes between the spirals to let out any steam and brush the top of the pie lightly with the remaining milk. Bake for 35–40 minutes, or until the top is brown and crispy. Make sure the spirals are well cooked and are not raw in the middle.

Roll up the pastry strips into small scrolls, then place them on the pie.

Bottom: Chicken and leek pie. Top: Salmon pie.

Family-style meat pie

preparation 30 minutes + cooling + 20 minutes refrigeration
cooking 1 hour 45 minutes
serves 6

1 tablespoon oil
1 onion, chopped
1 garlic clove, crushed
750 g (1 lb 10 oz) minced (ground) beef
250 ml (9 fl oz/1 cup) beef stock
250 ml (9 fl oz/1 cup) beer
1 tablespoon tomato paste (concentrated purée)
1 tablespoon yeast extract (e.g. marmite)
1 tablespoon worcestershire sauce
2 teaspoons cornflour (cornstarch)
1 sheet ready-rolled shortcrust (pie) pastry
375 g (13 oz) block ready-made puff pastry, thawed
1 egg, lightly beaten

Heat the oil in a large saucepan over medium heat and cook the onion for 5 minutes, until golden. Increase the heat, add the garlic and beef and cook, breaking up any lumps, for about 5 minutes, until the beef changes colour.

Add the stock, beer, tomato paste, yeast extract, worcestershire sauce and 125 ml (4 fl oz/½ cup) water. Reduce the heat to medium and cook for 1 hour, or until there is little liquid left. Combine the cornflour with 1 tablespoon water, then stir into the meat and cook for 5 minutes, or until thick and glossy. Remove from the heat and cool completely.

Lightly grease an 18 cm (7 inch) pie tin. If necessary, roll out the shortcrust pastry between two sheets of baking paper until large enough to line the base and side of the tin. Use a small ball of pastry to help press the pastry into the tin, allowing any excess to hang over the side.

Roll out the puff pastry between two sheets of baking paper to make a 23 cm (9 inch) circle. Spoon the filling into the pastry case and smooth it down. Brush the pastry edges with the egg, then place the puff pastry over the top. Cut off any excess with a sharp knife. Press the top and bottom pastries together, then scallop the edges with a fork or your fingers. Refrigerate for 20 minutes. Preheat the oven to 200°C (400°F/Gas 6) and heat a baking tray.

Brush the remaining egg over the top of the pie, place on the hot tray on the bottom shelf of the oven and bake for 25–30 minutes, or until golden and well puffed.

Spoon the meat filling into the base of the pie and smooth out the top.

Use a sharp knife to cut around the edge of the pie, slicing off any excess pastry.

savoury pies *and* **pastries**

Chicken and corn pies

preparation 25 minutes + 2 hours refrigeration
cooking 50 minutes
makes 6

1 tablespoon olive oil
650 g (1 lb 7 oz) boneless, skinless chicken thighs,
cut into small pieces
1 tablespoon grated fresh ginger
400 g (14 oz) oyster mushrooms, halved
3 corn cobs, kernels removed
125 ml (4 fl oz/½ cup) chicken stock
2 tablespoons kecap manis (see Note)
2 tablespoons cornflour (cornstarch)
90 g (3¼ oz) coriander (cilantro) leaves, chopped
6 sheets ready-rolled shortcrust (pie) pastry
milk, to glaze

Lightly grease six 10 cm (4 inch) metal pie tins. Heat the oil in a large frying pan over high heat and add the chicken. Cook for 5 minutes, or until golden. Add the ginger, mushrooms and corn and cook for 5–6 minutes, until the chicken is just cooked through. Add the stock and kecap manis. Mix the cornflour with 2 tablespoons water, then stir into the pan. Boil for 2 minutes before adding the coriander. Cool and then chill for 2 hours.

Preheat the oven to 180°C (350°F/Gas 4). Using a saucer as a guide, cut a 15 cm (6 inch) round from each sheet of shortcrust pastry and line the pie tins. Fill the cases with the cooled filling, then cut out another six rounds large enough to make the lids. Trim away any extra pastry and seal the edges with a fork. Decorate with pastry scraps. Prick a few holes in the top of each pie, brush with a little milk and bake for 35 minutes, until golden.

Note *Kecap manis is a thick, sweet soy sauce. If you can't find it, use regular soy sauce mixed with a little soft brown sugar.*

Cottage pie

preparation 30 minutes
cooking 1 hour 45 minutes
serves 6–8

2 tablespoons olive oil
2 onions, chopped
2 carrots, diced
1 celery stalk, diced
1 kg (2 lb 4 oz) minced (ground) beef
2 tablespoons plain (all-purpose) flour
375 ml (13 fl oz/1½ cups) beef stock
1 tablespoon soy sauce
1 tablespoon worcestershire sauce
2 tablespoons tomato sauce (ketchup)
1 tablespoon tomato paste (concentrated purée)
2 bay leaves
2 teaspoons chopped flat-leaf (Italian) parsley

topping
400 g (14 oz) potatoes, peeled and diced
400 g (14 oz) parsnips, peeled and diced
30 g (1 oz) butter
125 ml (4 fl oz/½ cup) milk

Heat the oil in a large frying pan over medium heat and cook the onion, carrot and celery, stirring occasionally, for 5 minutes, until softened and lightly coloured. Add the beef and cook for 7 minutes, then stir in the flour and cook for 2 minutes. Add the stock, soy sauce, worcestershire sauce, tomato sauce and paste and bay leaves and simmer over low heat for 30 minutes, stirring occasionally. Leave to cool. Remove the bay leaves and stir in the parsley.

Preheat the oven to 180°C (350°F/Gas 4). Lightly grease a 2.5 litre (87 fl oz/10 cup) ovenproof dish. To make the topping, boil the potato and parsnip in salted water for 15–20 minutes, or until tender. Drain, return to the pan and mash with the butter and enough milk to make a firm mash.

Spoon the filling into the dish and spread the topping over it. Fluff with a fork. Bake for 40 minutes, or until golden.

Once the pies are filled, top them with the second pastry round.

Spoon the meaty filling into a greased ovenproof dish, then top with the mashed potato and parsnip.

Bottom: Cottage pie. Top: Chicken and corn pies.

Bacon and whole egg filo pies

preparation 30 minutes
cooking 30 minutes
makes 6

1 teaspoon oil
4 spring onions (scallions), chopped
6 lean bacon slices, chopped
125 ml (4 fl oz/½ cup) milk
60 ml (2 fl oz/¼ cup) pouring cream
2 tablespoons chopped parsley
pinch of freshly grated nutmeg
7 eggs
10 sheets filo pastry
melted butter, for brushing

Heat the oil in a frying pan and cook the spring onion and bacon for 2–3 minutes, then set aside to cool. Mix together the milk, cream, parsley, nutmeg and 1 egg and season with salt and cracked pepper.

Brush 1 sheet of filo pastry with the melted butter, then brush another sheet and lay it on top. Repeat until you have a stack of 5 sheets. Cut into 6 squares. Repeat with the remaining 5 sheets of pastry. Place 2 squares together at an angle to form a rough 8-pointed star and place into a 250 ml (9 fl oz/1 cup) muffin tin. Repeat with the remaining pastry squares.

Preheat the oven to 200°C (400°F/Gas 6). Divide the spring onion and bacon mixture evenly between the filo pastry cups. Pour over the cream mixture and carefully break an egg on the top of each pie. Bake for 10 minutes, then reduce the oven to 180°C (350°F/Gas 4) and bake for a further 10–15 minutes, or until the pastry is lightly crisp and golden and the egg is just set. Serve the pies immediately.

Creamy snapper pies

preparation 25 minutes
cooking 1 hour 20 minutes
makes 6

2 tablespoons olive oil
4 onions, thinly sliced
375 ml (13 fl oz/1½ cups) fish stock
875 ml (30 fl oz/3½ cups) pouring cream
1 kg (2 lb 4 oz) skinless snapper fillets, cut into large bite-sized pieces
2 sheets ready-rolled puff pastry
1 egg, lightly beaten

Heat the oil in a large saucepan, add the onion and stir over medium heat for 20 minutes, or until golden brown and slightly caramelised.

Add the stock, bring to the boil and cook for 10 minutes, or until the liquid has nearly evaporated. Stir in the cream, bring to the boil, then simmer for 20 minutes, until the liquid reduces by half or coats the back of a spoon.

Preheat the oven to 220°C (425°F/Gas 7). Divide half the sauce among six 310 ml (10¾ fl oz/1¼ cup) deep ovenproof dishes. Put some fish in each dish and top with the sauce.

Cut the pastry sheets into rounds slightly larger than the tops of the dishes. Brush the edges of the pastry with a little of the egg. Press onto the dishes. Brush lightly with the remaining egg. Bake for 30 minutes, or until the pastry is crisp, golden and puffed.

Carefully crack an egg into each pie, trying to keep the egg yolk intact.

The pastry rounds should be a little larger than the pie dishes.

275

Bottom: Creamy snapper pies. Top: Bacon and whole egg filo pies.

Pumpkin and feta pie

preparation 30 minutes + cooling + 30 minutes refrigeration
cooking 1 hour 35 minutes
serves 6

700 g (1 lb 9 oz) butternut pumpkin (squash), cubed
4 garlic cloves, unpeeled
100 ml (3½ fl oz) olive oil
2 small red onions, halved and sliced
1 tablespoon balsamic vinegar
1 tablespoon soft brown sugar
100 g (3½ oz) feta cheese, broken into small pieces
1 tablespoon chopped rosemary

pastry
250 g (9 oz/2 cups) plain (all-purpose) flour
125 g (4½ oz) butter, chilled and cubed
60 g (2¼ oz/½ cup) grated parmesan cheese
60–80 ml (2–2½ fl oz/¼–⅓ cup) iced water

Preheat the oven to 200°C (400°F/Gas 6). Place the pumpkin and garlic cloves on a baking tray, drizzle with 2 tablespoons of the oil and bake for 25–30 minutes, until the pumpkin is tender. Transfer the pumpkin to a large bowl and the garlic to a plate. Leave to cool.

Meanwhile, heat 2 tablespoons oil in a pan, add the onion and cook over medium heat, stirring occasionally, for 10 minutes. Add the vinegar and sugar and cook for 15 minutes, or until the onion is caramelised. Remove from the heat and add to the pumpkin. Leave to cool.

While the vegetables are cooling, make the pastry. Sift the flour and 1 teaspoon salt into a large bowl. Rub the butter into the flour until the mixture resembles fine breadcrumbs. Stir in the cheese. Make a well in the centre, add most of the water and mix with a flat-bladed knife, using a cutting action, until the mixture comes together in beads (adding a little more water if necessary). Turn onto a lightly floured surface and gather together into a smooth ball. Cover with plastic wrap and refrigerate for 30 minutes.

Add the feta cheese and rosemary to the pumpkin. Squeeze out the garlic flesh and mix it through the vegetables. Season to taste.

Roll out the dough between two sheets of baking paper to a 35 cm (14 inch) circle. Remove the top sheet of paper and place the bottom paper with the pastry on a tray. Arrange the pumpkin and feta mixture on top, leaving a 6 cm (2½ inch) border. Fold over the edges, pleating as you fold. Bake for 40 minutes, or until crisp and golden.

When drizzling the pumpkin with oil, try to cover the pieces evenly.

Roughly pleat the overhanging pastry around the edges of the pie for a rustic look.

Cheese and chive soufflé tart

preparation 40 minutes
cooking 55 minutes
serves 6–8

80 g (2¾ oz) butter
40 g (1½ oz/⅓ cup) plain (all-purpose) flour
250 ml (9 fl oz/1 cup) pouring cream
160 g (5½ oz/⅔ cup) sour cream
4 eggs, separated
130 g (4½ oz/1 cup) grated gruyère cheese
3 tablespoons chopped chives
¼ teaspoon freshly grated nutmeg
pinch of cayenne pepper
12 sheets filo pastry

Preheat the oven to 190°C (375°F/Gas 5). Lightly grease a deep 20 cm (8 inch) loose-based fluted flan (tart) tin or pie dish. Melt half the butter in a saucepan. Sift in the flour and cook, stirring, for 1 minute. Remove from the heat and gradually whisk in the cream and sour cream.

Return to the heat and whisk constantly until the mixture boils and thickens. Remove from the heat and whisk in the egg yolks. Then cover the surface with plastic wrap and set aside to allow to cool slightly. Whisk in the cheese, chives, nutmeg and cayenne pepper.

Melt the remaining butter and brush some over each sheet of pastry. Fold each one in half and use to line the flan tin, allowing the edges to overhang.

Beat the egg whites until stiff peaks form, then stir a spoonful into the cheese mixture to loosen it up. Gently fold in the rest of the beaten egg white. Spoon the mixture into the pastry case and then fold the pastry over the top. Brush the top with the remaining melted butter and bake for 40–45 minutes, or until puffed and golden. Serve immediately.

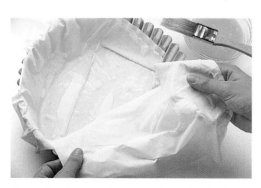

The pastry should be brushed with melted butter before being used to line the tin.

Salami, eggplant and artichoke tart

preparation 20 minutes + 40 minutes refrigeration
cooking 55 minutes
serves 4–6

125 g (4½ oz/1 cup) plain (all-purpose) flour
60 g (2¼ oz) butter, chilled and cubed
1 egg yolk
1–2 tablespoons iced water

filling
2 tablespoons oil
250 g (9 oz) eggplant (aubergine), cubed
110 g (3¾ oz/½ cup) quartered marinated artichokes
125 g (4½ oz) piece salami, cubed
1 tablespoon chopped chives
1 tablespoon chopped parsley
1 egg, lightly beaten
60 ml (2 fl oz/¼ cup) pouring cream

Process the flour, butter and a pinch of salt in a food processor for 15 seconds, or until crumbly. Add the egg yolk and water and process in short bursts until it just comes together (adding a little more water if necessary). Turn onto a lightly floured surface and gather together into a smooth ball. Cover with plastic wrap and refrigerate for 30 minutes. Preheat the oven to 200°C (400°F/Gas 6). Lightly grease a shallow 20 cm (8 inch) loose-based flan (tart) tin.

Roll out the pastry on a sheet of baking paper to line the tin and trim off any excess. Refrigerate for 10 minutes. Prick the pastry with a fork and bake for 10 minutes, until lightly browned. Cool.

Heat the oil and toss the eggplant over high heat until it begins to brown and soften; drain on paper towels. Mix the eggplant, artichokes, salami and herbs and press firmly into the pastry case. Pour over the combined egg and cream and bake for 45 minutes, or until browned and set.

Pour the creamy egg mixture over the vegetables, trying to obtain even coverage.

Bottom: Salami, eggplant and artichoke tart. Top: Cheese and chive soufflé tart.

Asparagus pie

preparation 40 minutes + 45 minutes refrigeration
cooking 30 minutes
serves 6

350 g (12 oz) plain (all-purpose) flour
250 g (9 oz) butter, chilled and cubed
170 ml (5½ fl oz/⅔ cup) iced water

filling
800 g (1 lb 10 oz) asparagus
30 g (1 oz) butter
½ teaspoon chopped thyme
1 French shallot (eschallot), chopped
60 g (2¼ oz) sliced ham
80 ml (2½ fl oz/⅓ cup) pouring cream
2 tablespoons grated parmesan cheese
1 egg
pinch of freshly grated nutmeg
1 egg, extra, lightly beaten

To make the pastry, mix the flour and a pinch of salt in a food processor for 3 seconds. Add the cubes of butter and mix until it is cut finely but not entirely blended into the flour—a few lumps are desirable. With the motor running on the processor, gradually pour in the iced water until the dough comes together. It should still have some small pebbles of butter.

Transfer the dough to a lightly floured work surface and press into a rectangle about 30 x 12 cm (12 x 4½ inches). Fold one end into the centre, then the opposite end over to cover the first. Roll into a rectangle again and repeat the folding three or four times. Wrap in plastic wrap and chill for 45 minutes.

Remove the woody ends from the asparagus and slice the thick spears in half lengthways. Heat the butter in a large frying pan and cook the asparagus, thyme and shallot with a tablespoon of water for 3 minutes, stirring often, until the asparagus is tender. Season well.

Preheat the oven to 200°C (400°F/Gas 6). Lightly grease a 20 cm (8 inch) fluted, loose-based flan (tart) tin. Roll the pastry out to a circle about 30 cm (12 inches) diameter and line the tin, leaving the rest of the pastry hanging over the edge. Place half the asparagus in the dish, top with the ham, then the remaining asparagus.

Combine the cream, parmesan, egg and nutmeg. Season well and pour over the asparagus. Fold the excess pastry over the filling, forming loose pleats. Brush with the beaten egg and bake for 25 minutes, or until golden.

Fold one short end of pastry into the middle, then repeat with the other short end.

Lay out the asparagus pieces facing the same direction, then pour the cream mixture over the top.

Veal pie with Jerusalem artichoke and potato topping

preparation 40 minutes
cooking 1 hour 20 minutes
serves 4–6

1 tablespoon olive oil
500 g (1 lb 2 oz) lean minced (ground) veal
2 onions, finely chopped
3 garlic cloves, crushed
150 g (5½ oz) bacon, diced
½ teaspoon dried rosemary
2 tablespoons plain (all-purpose) flour
pinch of cayenne pepper
125 ml (4 fl oz/½ cup) dry white wine
150 ml (5 fl oz) pouring cream
1 egg, lightly beaten
2 hard-boiled eggs, roughly chopped

topping

500 g (1 lb 2 oz) Jerusalem artichokes
400 g (14 oz) potatoes
100 g (3½ oz) butter

Heat the oil in a large frying pan and cook the veal, onion, garlic, bacon and rosemary, stirring often, for 10 minutes, or until the veal changes colour. Stir in the flour and cayenne pepper and cook for 1 minute. Pour in the wine and 125 ml (4 fl oz/½ cup) water. Season well. Simmer for 5 minutes, or until the sauce is very thick, then stir in the cream, beaten egg and chopped egg.

Preheat the oven to 210°C (415°F/Gas 6–7). Lightly grease a 20 cm (8 inch) spring-form tin. Peel and chop the artichokes and potatoes and boil together for 12–15 minutes, until tender. Drain, add the butter, then mash until smooth.

Spoon the veal filling into the tin then spread with the potato and artichoke topping. Bake for 20 minutes, then reduce the heat to 180°C (350°F/Gas 4) and bake for another 30 minutes, or until golden.

Once the potato and artichoke are tender, use a fork or masher to mash them until smooth.

Bacon and egg pie

preparation 20 minutes
cooking 1 hour 10 minutes
serves 4–6

1 sheet ready-rolled shortcrust (pie) pastry
2 teaspoons oil
4 bacon slices, chopped
5 eggs, lightly beaten
60 ml (2 fl oz/¼ cup) pouring cream
1 sheet puff pastry
1 egg, lightly beaten, extra

Preheat the oven to 210°C (415°F/Gas 6–7). Lightly grease a 20 cm (8 inch) loose-based flan (tart) tin.

Place the shortcrust pastry in the tin and trim the pastry edges. Cover the pastry with baking paper, fill with baking beads or rice and bake for 10 minutes. Remove the baking paper and beads and bake for a further 10 minutes, or until dry. Allow to cool.

Heat the oil in a frying pan. Add the bacon and cook over medium heat for a few minutes, or until lightly browned. Drain on paper towel and allow to cool slightly. Arrange the bacon over the pastry base and pour the mixed eggs and cream over the top.

Brush the edges of the pastry with the egg glaze, cover with puff pastry and press on firmly to seal. Trim the pastry edges and decorate the top with trimmings. Brush with remaining egg glaze and bake for 40 minutes, or until puffed and golden brown.

Spread the bacon out evenly over the pastry base, then fill with the filling.

Bottom: Bacon and egg pie. Top: Veal pie with Jerusalem artichoke and potato topping.

Salmon filo pie with dill butter

preparation 25 minutes + cooling
cooking 1 hour
serves 6–8

150 g (5½ oz/¾ cup) medium-grain white rice
90 g (3¼ oz) butter, melted
8 sheets filo pastry
500 g (1 lb 2 oz) fresh salmon fillet, cut into small cubes
2 French shallots (eschallots), finely chopped
1½ tablespoons baby capers
150 g (5½ oz) Greek-style yoghurt
1 egg
1 tablespoon grated lemon zest
3 tablespoons chopped dill
30 g (1 oz/¼ cup) dry breadcrumbs
1 tablespoon sesame seeds
2 teaspoons lemon juice

Put the rice in a large saucepan and add enough water to cover it by 2 cm (1 inch). Bring to the boil over medium heat, then reduce the heat to low, cover and cook for 20 minutes, or until all the water has been absorbed and tunnels appear on the surface of the rice. Set aside to cool.

Preheat the oven to 180°C (350°F/Gas 4). Lightly grease a 20 x 30 cm (8 x 12 inch) baking tin with melted butter.

Cover the filo pastry with a damp tea towel (dish towel). Mix the salmon with the shallots, capers, rice, yoghurt and egg. Add the lemon zest, 1 tablespoon of the dill and season well.

Layer four sheets of pastry in the base of the tin, brushing each one with melted butter and leaving the sides of the pastry hanging over the edge of the tin. Spoon in the salmon filling and pat down well. Fold the pastry over the filling.

Top with four sheets of filo, brushing each one with melted butter and sprinkling all but the top layer with a tablespoon of breadcrumbs. Sprinkle the top with sesame seeds.

Score the top of the pie into diamonds without cutting right through the pastry. Bake for 35–40 minutes on the lowest shelf until golden brown. Reheat the remaining butter, add the lemon juice and remaining dill and pour a small amount over each portion of pie.

Mix the cooked rice with the other filling ingredients until evenly distributed.

Use a sharp knife to score the pastry into diamond patterns, but don't cut through the pastry.

Roasted tomato and zucchini tartlets

preparation 45 minutes
cooking 1 hour 20 minutes
makes 6

3 roma (plum) tomatoes, halved lengthways
1 teaspoon balsamic vinegar mixed with 1 teaspoon olive oil
3 small zucchini (courgettes), sliced
3 sheets ready-rolled puff pastry
1 egg yolk, lightly beaten
12 small black olives
24 capers, rinsed and drained

pistachio mint pesto
75 g (2½ oz/½ cup) unsalted shelled pistachio nuts
40 g (1½ oz/2 cups) firmly packed mint leaves
2 garlic cloves, crushed
80 ml (2½ fl oz/⅓ cup) olive oil
50 g (1¾ oz/½ cup) grated parmesan cheese

Preheat the oven to 150°C (300°F/Gas 2). Lay the tomatoes, cut side up, on a baking tray. Roast for 30 minutes, then brush with some of the combined vinegar and oil. Roast for a further 30 minutes. Increase the temperature to 210°C (415°F/Gas 6–7).

To make the pesto, put the pistachios, mint and garlic in a food processor and process for 15 seconds. With the motor running, slowly pour in the olive oil. Add the parmesan and process briefly.

Preheat the grill (broiler) and line with foil. Lay the zucchini in a single layer on the foil and brush with the remaining balsamic vinegar and oil. Grill for 5 minutes, turning once.

Roll out the pastry to 25 x 40 cm (10 x 16 inches) and cut out six 12 cm (4 inches) circles. Put the circles on a greased baking tray and brush with egg yolk. Spread a tablespoon of pesto on each, leaving a 2 cm (¾ inch) border. Divide the zucchini among the pastries and top with tomatoes. Bake for 15 minutes, or until golden. Top with olives and capers.

Leave a border around the pesto, then neatly arrange the zucchini slices on top.

Mediterranean ricotta tarts

preparation 20 minutes + 20 minutes cooling
cooking 30 minutes
makes 6

30 g (1 oz/⅓ cup) dry breadcrumbs
2 tablespoons olive oil
1 garlic clove, crushed
½ red capsicum (pepper), quartered and cut into thin strips
1 zucchini (courgette), cut into thin strips
3 slices prosciutto, cut into thin strips
375 g (13 oz) firm ricotta cheese (see Note)
40 g (1½ oz/⅓ cup) grated cheddar cheese
30 g (1 oz/⅓ cup) grated parmesan cheese
2 tablespoons shredded basil
4 black olives, pitted and sliced

Preheat the oven to 180°C (350°F Gas 4). Lightly grease six 10 cm (4 inch) fluted flan (tart) tins. Lightly sprinkle 1 teaspoon breadcrumbs over the base and side of each tin.

Heat half the oil in a frying pan, add the garlic, capsicum and zucchini and cook, stirring, over medium heat for 5 minutes, or until the vegetables are soft. Remove from the heat and add the prosciutto. Season to taste.

Place the ricotta in a large bowl and add the other cheeses and remaining breadcrumbs. Season. Press the mixture into the tins and smooth the surface.

Bake for 20 minutes, or until the tarts are slightly puffed and golden. Cool completely (the tarts will deflate on cooling) and remove from the tins. Do not refrigerate.

Sprinkle the bases with basil and divide the vegetable mixture between them. Top with the olives then drizzle with the remaining oil.

Note *Use firm ricotta or very well-drained ricotta, or the tarts will be difficult to remove from the tins.*

Rotate the tart tins so the breadcrumbs evenly cover the base and side of the tins.

Bottom: Mediterranean ricotta tarts. Top: Roasted tomato and zucchini tartlets.

Beef and caramelized onion pie

preparation 40 minutes + 20 minutes cooling
cooking 2 hours 30 minutes
serves 6–8

80 ml (2½ fl oz/⅓ cup) oil
2 large red onions, thinly sliced
1 teaspoon dark brown sugar
1 kg (2 lb 4 oz) lean rump steak, diced
30 g (1 oz/¼ cup) plain (all-purpose) flour, seasoned
2 garlic cloves, crushed
225 g (8 oz) button mushrooms, sliced
250 ml (9 fl oz/1 cup) beef stock
150 ml (5 fl oz) stout
1 tablespoon tomato paste (concentrated purée)
1 tablespoon worcestershire sauce
1 tablespoon chopped thyme
350 g (12 oz) potatoes, diced
2 carrots, diced
375 g (13 oz) block ready-made puff pastry, thawed
1 egg, lightly beaten

Heat 2 tablespoons of the oil in a frying pan over medium heat and cook the onion for 5 minutes, or until light brown. Add the sugar and cook for another 7–8 minutes, or until the onion caramelizes. Remove from the pan, set aside and wipe the pan clean.

Toss the beef in the flour and shake off the excess. Heat the remaining oil in the same pan and cook the meat in batches over high heat until browned. Return all the meat to the pan, add the garlic and mushrooms and cook for 2 minutes. Add the stock, stout, tomato paste, worcestershire sauce and thyme. Bring to the boil, then reduce the heat and simmer, covered, for 1 hour. Add the potato and carrot and simmer for 30 minutes. Remove from the heat and allow to cool.

Preheat the oven to 190°C (375°F/Gas 5). Lightly grease a 1.25 litre (44 fl oz/5 cup) pie dish.

Pour in the filling and top with the onion. Roll the pastry out between two sheets of baking paper until it is 2.5 cm (1 inch) wider than the pie dish. Cut a 2 cm (¾ inch) strip around the edge of the pastry, brush with water and then place damp side down on the rim of the dish.

Cover with the remaining pastry and press the edges together. Knock up the rim by making small slashes in the edges of the pastry with the back of a knife. Re-roll the trimmings and use them to decorate the pie. Brush with egg and bake for 35 minutes, or until golden.

Once the filling is in the pie dish, evenly top it with the caramelized onion.

Use a thin strip of pastry to lay around the rim of the pie dish.

savoury tarts
and **quiches**

Spicy chicken tarts

preparation 50 minutes
cooking 55 minutes
makes 8

2 large onions, finely chopped
400 g (14 oz) eggplant (aubergine), cubed
2 garlic cloves, crushed
800 g (1 lb 12 oz) tinned chopped tomatoes
1 tablespoon tomato paste (concentrated purée)
3 teaspoons soft brown sugar
1 tablespoon red wine vinegar
3 tablespoons chopped parsley
4 sheets ready-rolled shortcrust (pie) pastry
2 teaspoons ground cumin seeds
2 teaspoons ground coriander
1 teaspoon paprika
400 g (14 oz) skinless, boneless chicken breast
olive oil
sour cream and coriander (cilantro) leaves, to serve

Fry the onion in a little oil until golden. Add the eggplant and garlic and cook for a few minutes. Stir in the tomato, tomato paste, sugar and vinegar. Bring to the boil, reduce the heat, cover and simmer for 20 minutes. Uncover and simmer for 10 minutes, or until thickened. Add the parsley and season. Preheat the oven to 190°C (375°F/Gas 5).

Grease eight 7.5 cm (3 inch) pie tins, line with the pastry and decorate the edges with a spoon. Prick the bases with a fork. Bake for 15 minutes, or until golden.

Mix the cumin seeds, coriander and paprika on baking paper. Coat the chicken breasts in the spices. Heat some oil in a frying pan and cook the chicken for 10 minutes, turning regularly, or until brown and cooked through. Slice the chicken diagonally.

Fill the pie cases with the eggplant mixture and decorate with the sliced chicken, sour cream and coriander leaves.

Pesto and anchovy tart

preparation 35 minutes
cooking 30 minutes
serves 6

pesto
75 g (2½ oz/1½ cups firmly packed) basil leaves
2 garlic cloves
50 g (1¾ oz/½ cup) grated parmesan cheese
80 g (2¾ oz/½ cup) pine nuts, toasted
60 ml (2 fl oz/¼ cup) olive oil

375 g (13 oz) block ready-made puff pastry, thawed
1 egg yolk, lightly beaten
45 g (1½ oz) tin anchovies, drained
50 g (1¾ oz/⅓ cup) grated mozzarella cheese
35 g (1¼ oz/⅓ cup) grated parmesan cheese

To make the pesto, put the basil, garlic, parmesan and pine nuts in a food processor and chop finely. With the motor running, slowly add the oil and process until well combined.

Preheat the oven to 200°C (400°F/Gas 6). Roll the pastry into a rectangle 18 x 35 cm (7 x 14 inches), and 5 mm (¼ inch) thick. Cut a 2 cm (¾ inch) strip from all the way round the edge of the pastry. Combine the egg yolk with 1 teaspoon water and brush the edge of the pastry. Trim the pastry strips to fit around the rectangle and attach them to form a crust. Place on a lightly floured baking tray and, using the tip of a sharp knife, make small cuts all over the base. Bake for 15 minutes. Press the centre of the pastry down with the back of a spoon and bake for a further 5 minutes, or until lightly golden. Allow to cool.

Spread the pesto evenly over the base of the pastry. Cut the anchovies into strips and arrange over the pesto. Sprinkle the grated mozzarella and parmesan over the top and bake for 10 minutes, or until golden.

Combine the spices on a piece of baking paper, then coat the chicken in the spice mixture.

Cut a thin strip of pastry and use it to create a border all the way around the pastry rectangle.

293

Bottom: Pesto and anchovy tart. Top: Spicy chicken tarts.

Italian summer tart

preparation 40 minutes + 50 minutes refrigeration
cooking 1 hour
serves 4–6

185 g (6½ oz/1½ cups) plain (all-purpose) flour
90 g (3¼ oz) butter, chilled and cubed
1 egg yolk
2–3 tablespoons iced water

filling

1 tablespoon olive oil
2 small red onions, sliced
1 tablespoon balsamic vinegar
1 teaspoon soft brown sugar
1 tablespoon thyme leaves
170 g (6 oz) jar marinated quartered artichokes, drained
4 slices prosciutto, cut into strips
12 black olives

To make the pastry, place the flour, butter and a pinch of salt in a food processor and process for 15 seconds, or until crumbly. Add the egg yolk and water and process in short bursts until it comes together (adding a little more water if necessary). Turn onto a lightly floured work surface and gather together into a smooth ball. Cover with plastic wrap and refrigerate for at least 30 minutes.

Roll the pastry between two sheets of baking paper until large enough to fit a 35 x 10 cm (14 x 4 inch) loose-based flan (tart) tin. Press it well into the sides and trim off the excess. Cover and refrigerate for 20 minutes.

Preheat the oven to 190°C (375°F/Gas 5). Cover the pastry case with baking paper and fill evenly with baking beads or rice. Bake for 15 minutes. Remove the paper and beads and bake for a further 15 minutes, or until the pastry is golden and dry. Cool on a wire rack.

To make the filling, heat the oil in a saucepan, add the onion slices and cook, stirring occasionally, for 15 minutes. Add the vinegar and sugar and cook for a further 15 minutes. Remove from the heat, stir through the thyme leaves and set aside to cool.

Spread the onion mixture evenly over the pastry case. Arrange the quartered artichoke pieces on top, then fill the spaces between the artichokes with neatly rolled-up pieces of prosciutto and the black olives. This tart is best served at room temperature.

Once the flour and butter have been processed until crumbly, add the water and egg yolk.

Fill any gaps in between the other ingredients with black olives.

Sweet potato, potato and onion tart

preparation 45 minutes + 15 minutes refrigeration
cooking 1 hour 20 minutes
serves 4–6

125 g (4½ oz/1 cup) plain (all-purpose) flour
90 g (3¼ oz) butter, chilled and cubed
1–2 tablespoons iced water

filling
400 g (14 oz) orange sweet potato, peeled
400 g (14 oz) potatoes, peeled
1 onion, thinly sliced
250 ml (9 fl oz/1 cup) pouring cream
2 eggs
1 tablespoon wholegrain mustard

To make the pastry, process the flour and butter in a food processor for 15 seconds, or until crumbly. Add the water and process in short bursts until it comes together. Turn onto a lightly floured surface and gather into a smooth ball.

Roll out the pastry on a sheet of baking paper large enough to fit the base and sides of a 23 cm (9 inch) flan (tart) tin. Trim away the excess and chill for 15 minutes. Preheat the oven to 190°C (375°F/Gas 5).

Cover the pastry with baking paper, fill with baking beads or rice and bake for 10 minutes. Remove the baking paper and beads and bake for a further 10 minutes, or until dry. Cool the pastry case.

Thinly slice the sweet potato and potato. Cook in a steamer for 15 minutes, or until just tender. Drain off any liquid, cover and set aside.

Layer the sweet potato and potato in the pastry case, in an overlapping pattern, with the onion, gently pushing the layers in to compact them, finishing with onion. Combine the cream, eggs and mustard, season and pour over the tart. Bake for 45 minutes, or until golden.

Neatly lay the sweet potato, potato and onion in the pastry case, then pour in the creamy filling.

Tomato, parmesan and anchovy tart

preparation 10 minutes + cooling
cooking 1 hour 45 minutes
serves 6–8

60 ml (2 fl oz/¼ cup) olive oil
1 onion, finely chopped
2 tablespoons chopped parsley
1 teaspoon dried basil
1 teaspoon sugar
2 x 800 g (1 lb 12 oz) tins tomatoes, drained
2 sheets ready-rolled shortcrust (pie) pastry
2 teaspoons chopped anchovy fillets
2 tablespoons grated parmesan cheese
3 eggs, lightly beaten

Heat the oil in a frying pan and gently fry the onion for 15 minutes, or until golden. Add the parsley, basil and sugar and cook for 20–30 seconds, stirring constantly.

Drain the tomatoes and chop into a pulp. Add to the pan, then reduce the heat and simmer for 30 minutes, or until dark and quite dry. Cool.

Preheat the oven to 180°C (350°F/Gas 4) and grease a 23 cm (9 inch) shallow fluted loose-based flan (tart) tin. Roll the pastry sheets together, one on top of the other, to 3 mm (⅛ inch) thick. Line the tin with the pastry and prick with a fork. Cover with baking paper, fill with baking beads or rice and bake for 10 minutes. Remove the baking paper and beads and bake for a further 10 minutes, or until dry. Cool the pastry case.

Stir the anchovies, parmesan cheese and eggs through the filling, then spoon into the pastry case and level the surface. Bake for 40 minutes, or until set.

Line a flan (tart) tin with pastry, then prick it all over with a fork.

Bottom: Tomato, parmesan and anchovy tart. Top: Sweet potato, potato and onion tart.

Caramelized onion, rocket and blue cheese tarts

preparation 30 minutes + 30 minutes refrigeration
cooking 1 hour 10 minutes
makes 6

250 g (9 oz/2 cups) plain (all-purpose) flour
125 g (4½ oz) butter, chilled and cubed
30 g (1 oz/¼ cup) grated parmesan cheese
1 egg, lightly beaten
60 ml (2 fl oz/¼ cup) iced water

filling
2 tablespoons olive oil
3 onions, thinly sliced
100 g (3½ oz) baby rocket (arugula) leaves
100 g (3½ oz) blue cheese, crumbled
3 eggs, lightly beaten
60 ml (2 fl oz/¼ cup) pouring cream
60 g (2¼ oz/½ cup) grated parmesan cheese
pinch of freshly grated nutmeg

To make the pastry, sift the flour into a large bowl. Rub the butter into the flour until it resembles fine breadcrumbs. Stir in the parmesan. Make a well in the centre, add the egg and water and mix with a flat-bladed knife, using a cutting action, until the mixture comes together in beads (adding a little more water if necessary). Turn onto a lightly floured surface and gather together into a smooth ball. Cover with plastic wrap and refrigerate for 30 minutes.

Preheat the oven to 200°C (400°F/Gas 6). Divide the pastry into six portions. Roll the dough out between two sheets of baking paper to fit six 8 cm (3¼ inch) fluted loose-based flan (tart) tins, trimming off the excess.

Cover the pastry cases with baking paper, fill with baking beads or rice and bake for 10 minutes. Remove the baking paper and beads and bake for a further 10 minutes, or until dry. Cool slightly. Reduce the oven to 180°C (350°F/Gas 4).

Heat the oil in a large frying pan, add the onion and cook over medium heat for 20 minutes, or until the onion is caramelized. Add the rocket and stir until wilted. Remove from the pan and cool.

Divide the mixture between the tart bases and sprinkle with the blue cheese. Whisk together the eggs, cream, parmesan and nutmeg and pour evenly over each of the tarts. Place on a baking tray and bake for 20–30 minutes. Serve hot or cold.

Using your fingertips, rub the butter into the flour until it is fine and crumbly.

Line the tins with pastry, then use a small ball of excess pastry to press it into the base.

Tomato and thyme tart

preparation 35 minutes + 15 minutes refrigeration
cooking 30 minutes
serves 6–8

250 g (9 oz/2 cups) plain (all-purpose) flour
125 g (4½ oz) butter, chilled and cubed
125 g (4½ oz) cream cheese, chopped
1 tablespoon thyme leaves

filling
40 g (1½ oz/½ cup) fresh breadcrumbs
30 g (1 oz/¼ cup) grated parmesan cheese
2 tablespoons lemon thyme leaves
6 roma (plum) tomatoes, sliced
3 spring onions (scallions), sliced
1 egg yolk, lightly beaten with 1 teaspoon of water

To make the pastry, process the butter, cream cheese
and thyme in a food processor. Add 2 tablespoons water
and process in short bursts until the mixture just comes
together (adding a little more water if necessary). Turn onto
a floured surface and gather together into a ball. Press into
a large triangle, cover with plastic wrap and refrigerate for
15 minutes. Place on a greased baking tray and prick all
over with a fork.

Preheat the oven to 210°C (415°F/Gas 6–7). Place the
breadcrumbs, most of the parmesan and 1 tablespoon of
the lemon thyme on the pastry, leaving an 8 cm (3¼ inch)
border. Overlap the tomatoes and scatter some of the
spring onions on top, maintaining the border. Add freshly
ground black pepper, the remaining spring onions,
parmesan cheese and lemon thyme. Fold the pastry border
over the filling, pleating as you go, and press to seal. Brush
with the egg and water glaze and bake for 10 minutes.
Reduce the oven temperature to 180°C (350°F/Gas 4) and
cook for a further 15–20 minutes, or until golden.

Fold the excess pastry over the filling, pleating it so
it looks neat and tidy.

French shallot tatin

preparation 45 minutes + 20 minutes refrigeration
cooking 1 hour
serves 4–6

750 g (1 lb 10 oz) French shallots (eschallots)
50 g (1¾ oz) butter
2 tablespoons olive oil
60 g (2¼ oz/⅓ cup lightly packed) soft brown sugar
60 ml (2 fl oz/¼ cup) balsamic vinegar
125 g (4½ oz/1 cup) plain (all-purpose) flour
60 g (2¼ oz) butter, chilled and cubed
2 teaspoons wholegrain mustard
1 egg yolk
1–2 tablespoons iced water

Peel the shallots, leaving the bases intact and tips exposed.
Heat the butter and oil in a large saucepan and cook the
shallots over low heat for 15 minutes, then remove. Add
the sugar, vinegar and 60 ml (2 fl oz/¼ cup) water and stir
to dissolve the sugar. Return the shallots to the pan and
simmer over low heat for 15 minutes, turning occasionally.

Preheat the oven to 200°C (400°F/Gas 6). To make the
pastry, process the flour and butter in a food processor for
15 seconds, or until crumbly. Add the mustard, egg yolk
and most of the water and process in short bursts until
the mixture comes together (adding a little more water if
necessary). Turn onto a lightly floured surface and gather
together into a smooth ball. Cover with plastic wrap and
refrigerate for 30 minutes.

Grease a shallow 20 cm (8 inch) round sandwich tin. Tightly
pack the shallots into the tin and pour over syrup from the
pan. Roll out the pastry on a sheet of baking paper to a
circle, 1 cm (½ inch) larger than the tin. Lift the pastry into
the tin and lightly push it down so it is slightly moulded
over the shallots. Bake for 20–25 minutes, or until golden
brown. Cool for 5 minutes on a wire rack. Place a plate over
the tin and turn the tart out.

Hint *Put the unpeeled shallots in boiling water for 30 seconds
to make them easier to peel.*

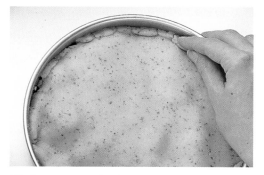

Lift the pastry into the tin over the shallots, then
push the edges down.

Bottom: French shallot tatin. Top: Tomato and thyme tart.

Mushroom and ricotta filo tart

preparation 35 minutes
cooking 40 minutes
serves 6

60 g (2¼ oz) butter
270 g (9½ oz) field mushrooms, sliced
2 garlic cloves, crushed
1 tablespoon Marsala
1 teaspoon thyme leaves
½ teaspoon chopped rosemary leaves
pinch of freshly grated nutmeg
5 sheets filo pastry
75 g (2½ oz) butter, melted
200 g (7 oz) ricotta cheese
2 eggs, lightly beaten
125 g (4½ oz/½ cup) sour cream
1 tablespoon chopped flat-leaf (Italian) parsley

Preheat the oven to 180°C (350°F/Gas 4). Melt the butter in a frying pan and cook the mushrooms over high heat for a few minutes, until they begin to soften. Add the garlic, cook for another minute, then stir in the Marsala, thyme, rosemary and nutmeg. Remove the mushrooms from the pan and drain off any liquid.

Work with 1 sheet of filo pastry at a time, keeping the rest covered with a damp tea towel (dish towel) to stop them drying out. Brush the sheets with melted butter and fold in half. Place on top of each other to line a shallow 23 cm (9 inch) loose-based flan (tart) tin, allowing the pastry to hang over the rim.

Beat the ricotta, eggs and sour cream together and season to taste. Spoon half the mixture into the tin, then layer the mushrooms. Top with the rest of the ricotta mixture. Loosely fold the overhanging pastry over the filling. Bake for 35 minutes, or until firm. Sprinkle with the parsley.

Fried green tomato tart

preparation 35 minutes + 15 minutes refrigeration
cooking 40 minutes
serves 6

4 green tomatoes
1 tablespoon olive oil
20 g (¾ oz) butter
1 teaspoon ground cumin
2 garlic cloves, crushed
1 sheet ready-rolled puff pastry
60 g (2¼ oz/¼ cup) sour cream
1 tablespoon chopped basil
2 tablespoons chopped parsley
60 g (2¼ oz/½ cup) grated cheddar cheese

Cut the tomatoes into thin slices. Heat the oil and butter in a frying pan and fry the cumin and garlic for 1 minute. Fry the tomatoes in batches for 2–3 minutes, until slightly softened. Drain on paper towels.

Preheat the oven to 200°C (400°F/Gas 6). Cut a 24 cm (9½ inch) round from the puff pastry and place on a greased baking tray. Make a 2 cm (¾ inch) border by scoring gently around the edge. Make small cuts inside the border. Refrigerate for 15 minutes, then bake for 10–15 minutes.

Combine the sour cream, basil and half the parsley. Sprinkle the cheddar cheese over the centre of the pastry. Arrange a layer of tomatoes around the inside edge of the border and then add the rest. Bake for 20 minutes, or until the pastry is golden. Spoon the cream mixture into the middle and sprinkle over the remaining parsley.

Use half the ricotta filling as the base of the tart, top with all the mushrooms, then another layer of filling.

Neatly arrange the slices of tomato over the tart tin so they are slightly overlapping.

Bottom: Fried green tomato tart. Top: Mushroom and ricotta filo tart.

Vegetable tart with salsa verde

preparation 30 minutes + 30 minutes refrigeration
cooking 50 minutes
serves 6

215 g (7¾ oz/1¾ cups) plain (all-purpose) flour
120 g (4¼ oz) butter, chilled and cubed
60 ml (2 fl oz/¼ cup) pouring cream
1–2 tablespoons iced water

salsa verde

1 garlic clove
40 g (1½ oz/2 cups) flat-leaf (Italian) parsley
80 ml (2½ fl oz/⅓ cup) extra virgin olive oil
3 tablespoons chopped dill
1½ tablespoons dijon mustard
1 tablespoon red wine vinegar
1 tablespoon drained baby capers

filling

1 large (250 g/9 oz) waxy potato, cut into 2 cm (¾ inch) cubes
1 tablespoon olive oil
2 garlic cloves, crushed
1 red capsicum (pepper), cut into cubes
1 red onion, sliced
2 zucchini (courgettes), sliced
2 tablespoons chopped dill
1 tablespoon chopped thyme
1 tablespoon drained baby capers
150 g (5½ oz) marinated quartered artichoke hearts, drained
30 g (1 oz/⅔ cup) baby English spinach leaves

To make the pastry, sift the flour and ½ teaspoon salt into a large bowl. Rub the butter into the flour until it resembles fine breadcrumbs. Make a well in the centre, add the cream and most of the water and mix with a flat-bladed knife, using a cutting action, until the mixture comes together in beads (adding a little more water if necessary). Turn onto a lightly floured surface and gather together into a smooth ball. Cover with plastic wrap and refrigerate for 30 minutes.

Preheat the oven to 200°C (400°F/Gas 6) and grease a 27 cm (10¾ inch) loose-based flan (tart) tin. Roll the dough out between two sheets of baking paper until large enough to line the tin, trimming off the excess. Cover with baking paper, fill with baking beads or rice and bake for 15–20 minutes. Remove the baking paper and beads,

reduce the heat to 180°C (350°F/Gas 4) and bake for a further 20 minutes, or until golden. Cool the pastry case.

Mix all the salsa verde ingredients in a food processor until almost smooth.

Boil the potato until just tender. Drain. Heat the oil in a large frying pan and cook the garlic, capsicum and onion for 3 minutes, stirring often. Add the zucchini, dill, thyme and capers and cook for 3 minutes. Reduce the heat, add the potato and artichokes, and heat through. Season to taste.

Spread 3 tablespoons of the salsa verde over the pastry. Spoon the filling into the case and drizzle with half the remaining salsa. Pile the spinach leaves in the centre and drizzle over the last of the salsa verde.

Goat's cheese and sweet potato tart

preparation 30 minutes + 40 minutes refrigeration
cooking 40 minutes
serves 2–3

2 teaspoons fine semolina
125 g (4½ oz/1 cup) self-raising flour
60 g (2¼ oz) butter, chilled and cubed
1 egg yolk
2 tablespoons iced water

filling
2 tablespoons olive oil
1 small leek, chopped
50 g (1¾ oz) goat's cheese, crumbled
1 egg, lightly beaten
2 tablespoons pouring cream
150 g (5½ oz) sweet potato, thinly sliced
½ teaspoon cumin seeds

To make the pastry, process the flour and butter in a food processor for 15 seconds, or until crumbly. Add the yolk and water and process in short bursts until the mixture just comes together (adding more water if necessary). Turn onto a lightly floured surface and gather together into a smooth ball. Cover with plastic wrap and refrigerate for 30 minutes.

Lightly grease a 25 cm (10 inch) pizza tray or baking tray and sprinkle with the semolina. Roll out the dough to a 20 cm (8 inch) circle. Lift onto the tray and roll over the outside edge to make a small rim; pinch this decoratively. Prick the base with a fork and refrigerate for 10 minutes. Preheat the oven to 200°C (400°F/Gas 6). Bake for 12 minutes, or until just brown.

To make the filling, heat half the oil in a saucepan and cook the leek until soft; cool. Spread the leek then cheese over the pastry case and season. Pour over the combined egg and cream; top with the sweet potato. Brush with the rest of the oil and scatter with cumin. Bake for 20–25 minutes, or until set. Stand for 5 minutes before cutting.

Use the tips of your finger to create a decorative pattern in the pastry rim.

Fresh herb tart

preparation 40 minutes + 40 minutes refrigeration
cooking 1 hour 10 minutes
serves 4–6

150 g (5½ oz/1¼ cups) plain (all-purpose) flour
100 g (3½ oz) butter, chilled and cubed
1–2 tablespoons iced water
250 g (9 oz/1 cup) light sour cream
125 ml (4 fl oz/½ cup) thick (double/heavy) cream
2 eggs, lightly beaten
1 tablespoon chopped thyme
2 tablespoons chopped parsley
1 tablespoon chopped oregano

To make the pastry, process the flour, butter and a pinch of salt in a food processor for 15 seconds, or until crumbly. Add most of the water and process in short bursts until the mixture just comes together (adding a little more water if necessary). Turn onto a lightly floured surface and gather together into a smooth ball. Cover with plastic wrap and refrigerate for 30 minutes.

Roll out the pastry on a sheet of baking paper to line a 35 x 10 cm (14 x 4 inch) loose-based flan (tart) tin and trim away the excess pastry. Refrigerate for 10 minutes. Preheat the oven to 200°C (400°F/Gas 6).

Cover the pastry with baking paper, fill with baking beads or rice and bake for 20 minutes. Remove the paper and beads and reduce the oven temperature to 180°C (350°F/Gas 4). Bake for a further 15–20 minutes, or until golden and dry. Cool the pastry case.

Whisk together the sour cream, thickened cream and eggs until smooth. Then stir in the herbs and season.

Place the pastry case on a baking tray and pour in the filling. Bake for 25–30 minutes, or until set. Allow to stand for 15 minutes before serving and cutting.

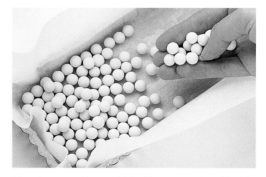

Line the pastry base with baking paper, then fill with baking beads or dried beans.

Bottom: Fresh herb tart. Top: Goat's cheese and sweet potato tart.

Roasted tomato and garlic tart

preparation 40 minutes
cooking 1 hour 10 minutes
serves 4

4 roma (plum) tomatoes, halved
1 tablespoon olive oil
1 teaspoon balsamic vinegar
1 teaspoon salt
5–10 garlic cloves, unpeeled
2 sheets ready-rolled puff pastry
1 egg, lightly beaten
10 bocconcini (fresh baby mozzarella cheese), halved

Preheat the oven to 200°C (400°F/Gas 6). Put the tomatoes, cut side up, on a baking tray and drizzle with the olive oil, balsamic vinegar and salt. Bake for 20 minutes. Add the garlic and bake for a further 15 minutes. Cool and squeeze or peel the garlic from its skin.

Grease a 35 x 10 cm (14 x 4 inch) loose-based fluted flan (tart) tin. Lay a sheet of pastry over each end of the tin, so that they overlap in the middle and around the edges. Seal the sheets together with egg and trim the edges. Cover with baking paper, fill with baking beads or rice and bake for 15 minutes. Remove the baking paper and beads and bake for a further 10 minutes, or until dry.

Place the roasted tomatoes along the centre of the tart and fill the gaps with the garlic and bocconcini. Bake for a further 10 minutes and serve.

Feta tart with beetroot

preparation 40 minutes + 15 minutes refrigeration
cooking 1 hour
serves 6

110 g (3¾ oz/¾ cup) plain wholemeal (whole-wheat) flour
90 g (3½ oz/¾ cup) plain (all-purpose) flour
125 g (4½ oz) butter, chilled and cubed
1 egg yolk
1–2 tablespoons iced water
300 g (10½ oz) ricotta cheese
300 g (10½ oz) crumbled feta cheese
3 eggs, lightly beaten
300 g (10½ oz) baby beetroot (beets), with short stalks attached
1 tablespoon walnut or olive oil
1 tablespoon red wine vinegar
30 g (1 oz/¼ cup) chopped pecans
2 tablespoons coriander (cilantro) leaves

To make the pastry, process the flours, butter and a pinch of salt in a food processor for 15 seconds, or until crumbly. Add the egg yolk and most of the water and process in short bursts until it comes together. Turn onto a lightly floured surface and gather together into a smooth ball. Cover with plastic wrap and refrigerate for 15 minutes. Preheat the oven to 180°C (350°F/Gas 4).

Mix the cheeses together with a fork. Add the eggs and mix well. Grease a 23 cm (9 inch) loose-based flan (tart) tin. Roll out the pastry on a floured surface to line the tin, press it into the sides and trim off any excess pastry. Cover with baking paper, fill with baking beads or rice and bake for 10 minutes. Remove the paper and beads and bake for a further 10 minutes, or until dry.

Spoon the filling into the base and bake for 30 minutes, or until the filling is firm and puffed (the filling will flatten slightly when removed from the oven).

Cook the beetroots until tender, then peel and cut in half. Drizzle with the combined oil and vinegar, and season. Serve the beetroot, pecans and coriander with the tart.

You will need to overlap two sheets of pastry to cover the tin.

Baby beetroots look good with a small amount of stalk still attached to their tops.

Bottom: Feta tart with beetroot. Top: Roasted tomato and garlic tart.

Spinach and ricotta lattice tart

preparation 50 minutes + 30 minutes refrigeration
cooking 40 minutes
serves 6

250 g (9 oz/2 cups) plain (all-purpose) flour
125 g (4½ oz) butter, chilled and cubed
1 egg
2 tablespoons sesame seeds
2–3 tablespoons iced water

filling
50 g (1¾ oz) butter
120 g (4¼ oz/1 cup) finely chopped spring onions (scallions)
2 garlic cloves, crushed
500 g (1 lb 2 oz) English spinach, trimmed, washed and roughly shredded
2 tablespoons chopped mint
185 g (6½ oz) ricotta cheese
50 g (1¾ oz) grated parmesan cheese
3 eggs, lightly beaten
milk, to glaze

To make the pastry, process the flour, butter and a pinch of salt in a food processor for 15 seconds, or until crumbly. Add the egg, sesame seeds and most of the water and process in short bursts until the mixture just comes together (adding a little more water if necessary). Turn onto a lightly floured surface and gather together into a smooth ball. Cover with plastic wrap and refrigerate for 30 minutes. Place a baking tray in the oven and preheat the oven to 180°C (350°F/Gas 4).

To make the filling, melt the butter in a large saucepan, add the spring onion and garlic and cook until soft. Add the spinach a little at a time, then stir in the mint. Remove from the heat and allow to cool slightly before stirring in the cheeses and the egg. Season and mix well.

Grease a shallow 23 cm (9 inch) round or 22 cm (8½ inch) square loose-based flan (tart) tin. Roll out two-thirds of the pastry to thinly line the tin, pressing it well into the sides. Spoon the filling into the pastry case.

Roll out the remaining pastry and cut into 1.5 cm (⅝ inch) strips. Interweave the strips in a lattice pattern over the top of the tart. Dampen the edge of the pastry base and gently press the strips down. Trim the edges of the pastry by pressing down with your thumb or by rolling a rolling pin across the top of the tin. Brush with milk. Place on the baking tray and bake for about 40 minutes, or until the pastry is golden.

Note Depending on how thick you like to roll your pastry, there may be about 100 g (3½ oz) of pastry trimmings left over. It is easier to have this little bit extra when making the lattice strips as they will be long enough to cover the top of the pie. The extra pastry can be covered and frozen for future use as decorations, or made into small tart cases.

Use a ruler and a pastry cutter to form neat strips of pastry to act as the tart top.

Interweave the pastry strips to form a lattice pattern over the top of the tart.

Blue cheese and onion quiche

preparation 40 minutes + 30 minutes refrigeration
cooking 1 hour 40 minutes
serves 8

250 g (9 oz/2 cups) plain (all-purpose) flour
100 g (3½ oz) butter, chilled and cubed
1–2 tablespoons iced water

filling
2 tablespoons olive oil
1 kg (2 lb 4 oz) red onions, very thinly sliced
1 teaspoon soft brown sugar
185 ml (6 fl oz/¾ cup) pouring cream
3 eggs
100 g (3½ oz) blue cheese, crumbled
1 teaspoon chopped thyme

Heat the oil in a pan over low heat and cook the onion and sugar, stirring regularly, for 45 minutes, or until the onion is lightly golden.

To make the pastry, process the flour, butter and a pinch of salt in a food processor for 15 seconds, or until crumbly. Add most of the water and process in short bursts until the mixture just comes together (adding more water if necessary). Turn onto a lightly floured surface and gather together into a smooth ball. Cover with plastic wrap and refrigerate for 15 minutes.

Preheat the oven to 180°C (350°F/Gas 4). Roll out the pastry thinly on a lightly floured surface to fit a greased 22 cm (8½ inch) loose-based flan (tart) tin. Trim away the excess pastry. Refrigerate for 15 minutes.

Cover the pastry case with baking paper, fill with baking beads or rice and bake for 10 minutes. Remove the baking paper and beads and bake for a further 10 minutes, or until dry. Cool the pastry case.

Gently spread the onion in the pastry case. Whisk together the cream, eggs, blue cheese, thyme and some freshly ground black pepper to taste. Pour into the base and bake for 35 minutes, or until firm.

Artichoke and provolone quiches

preparation 40 minutes + 30 minutes refrigeration
cooking 35 minutes
makes 6

250 g (9 oz/2 cups) plain (all-purpose) flour
125 g (4½ oz) butter, chilled and cubed
1 egg yolk
60 ml (2 fl oz/¼ cup) iced water

filling
1 small eggplant (aubergine), sliced
olive oil
6 eggs, lightly beaten
3 teaspoons wholegrain mustard
150 g (5½ oz) provolone cheese, grated
200 g (7 oz) marinated artichokes, sliced
125 g (4½ oz) semi-dried (sun-blushed) tomatoes

To make the pastry, process the flour, butter and a pinch of salt in a food processor for 15 seconds, or until crumbly. Add the egg yolk and most of the water and process in short bursts until the mixture just comes together (adding more water if necessary). Turn onto a lightly floured surface and gather together into a smooth ball. Cover with plastic wrap and refrigerate for 30 minutes.

Preheat the oven to 190°C (375°F/Gas 5) and grease six 11 cm (4¼ inch) oval or round pie tins.

To make the filling, brush the eggplant with olive oil and grill (broil) until golden. Mix together the egg, mustard and cheese in a bowl.

Roll out the pastry to line the tins. Trim away the excess pastry and decorate the edges. Place one eggplant slice in each tin and top with the artichokes and tomatoes. Pour the egg mixture over the top and bake for 25 minutes, or until golden and cooked.

Use your rolling pin to help you position the pastry into the base of the tin.

Lay one slice of eggplant into the base of each tart, then top with artichokes and tomatoes.

Bottom: Artichoke and provolone quiches. Top: Blue cheese and onion quiche.

Quiche lorraine

preparation 35 minutes + 35 minutes refrigeration
cooking 1 hour 5 minutes
serves 4–6

185 g (6½ oz/1½ cups) plain (all-purpose) flour
90 g (3¼ oz) butter, chilled and cubed
1 egg yolk
2–3 tablespoons iced water

filling
20 g (¾ oz) butter
1 onion, chopped
4 bacon slices, cut into thin strips
2 tablespoons chopped chives
2 eggs
185 ml (6 fl oz/¾ cup) pouring cream
60 ml (2 fl oz/¼ cup) milk
100 g (3½ oz) Swiss cheese, grated

To make the pastry, process the flour, butter and a pinch of salt in a food processor for 15 seconds, or until crumbly. Add the egg yolk and water and process in short bursts until it comes together (adding a little more water if necessary). Turn onto a lightly floured surface and gather together into a smooth ball. Cover with plastic wrap and refrigerate for at least 15 minutes.

Roll the pastry between two sheets of baking paper until large enough to line a shallow 25 cm (10 inch) loose-based flan (tart) tin. Press well into the side of the tin and trim off any excess pastry. Refrigerate the pastry-lined tin for 20 minutes. Preheat the oven to 190°C (375°F/Gas 5).

Cover the pastry case with baking paper, fill with baking beads or rice and bake for 15 minutes. Remove the baking paper and beads and bake for a further 10 minutes, or until dry. Cool the pastry case. Reduce the oven temperature to 180°C (350°F/Gas 4).

To make the filling, heat the butter in a frying pan. Add the onion and bacon and cook for 10 minutes, stirring frequently, until the onion is soft and the bacon is cooked. Stir through the chives and leave to cool.

Beat together the eggs, cream and milk. Season with freshly ground black pepper. Spread the filling evenly into the pastry case. Pour the egg mixture over the top and sprinkle with the cheese. Bake for 30 minutes, or until the filling is set and golden.

Rolling the pastry out between two layers of baking paper can make the job easier.

When filling the tart case with the creamy filling, make sure you achieve even coverage.

Feta, basil and olive quiche

preparation 40 minutes + 25 minutes refrigeration
cooking 40 minutes
serves 6

150 g (5½ oz/1¼ cups) plain (all-purpose) flour
90 g (3¼ oz) butter, melted and cooled
60 ml (2 fl oz/¼ cup) milk

filling
200 g (7 oz) feta cheese, cubed
15 g (½ oz/¼ cup) basil leaves, shredded
30 g (1 oz/¼ cup) sliced black olives
3 eggs, lightly beaten
80 ml (2½ fl oz/⅓ cup) milk
90 g (3¼ oz/⅓ cup) sour cream

Grease a deep 23 cm (9 inch) loose-based flan (tart) tin. To make the pastry, sift the flour into a large bowl. Add the butter and milk and stir until the mixture comes together to form a dough. Turn out onto a floured surface and gather into a ball. Refrigerate for 5 minutes. Roll out the pastry and place in the tin, press it well into the sides and trim the edge. Refrigerate for 20 minutes. Preheat the oven to 200°C (400°F/Gas 6).

To make the filling, spread the feta evenly over the base of the pastry and top with the basil and olives.

Whisk the eggs, milk and sour cream until smooth, then pour into the pastry case. Bake for 15 minutes, then reduce the oven temperature to 180°C (350°F/Gas 4) and cook for a further 25 minutes, or until the filling is firmly set. Serve at room temperature.

Tomato and thyme quiche

preparation 35 minutes + 30 minutes refrigeration
cooking 45 minutes
serves 8

185 g (6½ oz/1½ cups) plain (all-purpose) flour
125 g (4½ oz) butter, chilled and cubed
1 egg yolk
2–3 tablespoons iced water

filling
400 g (14 oz) tinned tomatoes
4 eggs
300 g (10½ oz) sour cream
25 g (1 oz/¼ cup) grated parmesan cheese
2 spring onions (scallions), finely chopped
1–2 tablespoons chopped thyme

Preheat the oven to 210°C (415°F/Gas 6–7). To make the pastry, sift the flour into a large bowl. Rub the butter into the flour until it resembles fine breadcrumbs. Make a well in the centre, add the combined egg yolk and most of the water and mix to a soft dough, adding more water if necessary. Turn onto a lightly floured surface and gather together into a smooth ball. Cover with plastic wrap and refrigerate for 30 minutes.

Roll out the pastry to line a shallow 23 cm (9 inch) flan (tart) tin, trimming off the excess. Cover with baking paper, fill with baking beads or rice and bake for 10 minutes. Remove the baking paper and beads and bake for a further 5 minutes, or until dry.

Drain the tomatoes and halve lengthways. Place, cut side down, on paper towels to drain. Beat together the eggs and sour cream and stir in the cheese and spring onion.

Pour the filling into the pastry case. Arrange the tomatoes, cut side down, over the filling. Sprinkle with thyme and black pepper. Reduce the oven to 180°C (350°F/Gas 4) and bake for 30 minutes, or until the filling is set and golden.

Storage *The pastry case can be blind-baked a day in advance and stored in an airtight container.*

Sprinkle the feta, basil and olives evenly over the pastry base.

Blind bake the pastry case first before pouring in the filling, otherwise the base will be too wet.

Bottom: Tomato and thyme quiche. Top: Feta, basil and olive quiche.

Eggplant and sun-dried capsicum quiches

preparation 30 minutes + 45 minutes refrigeration
cooking 1 hour
makes 6

185 g (6 oz/1½ cups) plain (all-purpose) flour
125 g (4½ oz) butter, chilled and cubed
1 egg yolk
1 tablespoon iced water

filling
100 g (3½ oz) slender eggplant (aubergine), thinly sliced
30 g (1 oz) butter
4 spring onions (scallions), finely chopped
1–2 garlic cloves, crushed
½ small red capsicum (pepper), finely chopped
40 g (1½ oz/¼ cup) sun-dried capsicums (peppers), drained and chopped
2 eggs, lightly beaten
185 ml (6 fl oz/¾ cup) pouring cream

To make the pastry, process the flour, butter and a pinch of salt in a food processor for 15 seconds, or until crumbly. Add the egg yolk and water. Process in short bursts until the mixture comes together (adding a little extra water if necessary). Turn onto a lightly floured surface and gather together into a smooth ball. Cover with plastic wrap and refrigerate for 30 minutes.

Brush the eggplant slices with olive oil and grill (broil) until browned. Heat the butter in a pan and cook the spring onion, garlic and capsicum for 5 minutes, stirring frequently, until soft. Add the sun-dried capsicum and leave to cool. Combine egg and cream in a bowl and season well.

Grease six 8 cm (3 inch) fluted tart tins. Roll out the pastry thinly to line the tins, and trim. Cover and refrigerate for 15 minutes. Preheat the oven to 190°C (375°F/Gas 5). Cover the pastry cases with baking paper, fill with baking beads or rice and bake for 10 minutes. Remove the baking paper and beads and bake for a further 10 minutes, or until dry.

Divide the filling among the pastry cases, top with the eggplant and pour over the cream and egg mixture. Bake for 25–30 minutes, or until set.

Smoked salmon and caper quiche

preparation 25 minutes + 40 minutes refrigeration
cooking 1 hour 10 minutes
serves 6–8

185 g (6½ oz/1½ cups) plain (all-purpose) flour
90 g (3¼ oz) butter, chilled and cubed
2 teaspoons cracked black pepper
1 egg yolk
2 tablespoons iced water

filling
1 tablespoon olive oil
1 small leek, chopped
½ teaspoon sugar
200 g (7 oz) sliced smoked salmon
50 g (1¾ oz/⅓ cup) frozen peas
2 tablespoons baby capers
75 g (2½ oz) cream cheese
2 eggs
2 teaspoons dijon mustard
185 ml (6 fl oz/¾ cup) pouring cream

To make the pastry, process the flour, butter and a pinch of salt in a food processor for 15 seconds, or until crumbly. Add the pepper, egg yolk and most of the water. Process in short bursts until the mixture comes together (adding more water if necessary). Turn onto a lightly floured surface and gather together into a smooth ball. Cover with plastic wrap and refrigerate for 30 minutes. Preheat the oven to 200°C (400°F/Gas 6). Grease a 17 cm (6½ inch) deep loose-based fluted flan (tart) tin.

Lay the pastry in the tin, place on a baking tray and refrigerate for 10 minutes. Prick the base with a fork and bake for 12 minutes.

To make the filling, heat the oil in a pan and cook the leek and sugar over low heat for 15 minutes. Cool, then spoon into the pastry. Scrunch up the salmon slices and lay around the edge. Put the peas and capers in the centre.

Process the cream cheese, eggs and mustard in a food processor until smooth. Add the cream and pour into the pastry case. Bake for 40 minutes, or until set.

Bottom: Smoked salmon and caper quiche. Top: Eggplant and sun-dried capsicum quiches.

Corn and bacon crustless quiches

preparation 30 minutes
cooking 35 minutes
makes 4

4 corn cobs
2 teaspoons olive oil
2 bacon slices, cut into thin strips
1 small onion, finely chopped
3 eggs, lightly beaten
2 tablespoons chopped chives
2 tablespoons chopped parsley
60 g (2½ oz) fresh white breadcrumbs
80 ml (2½ fl oz/⅓ cup) pouring cream

Preheat the oven to 180°C (350°F/Gas 4) and lightly grease four 185 ml (6 fl oz/¾ cup) ramekins or dariole moulds.

Remove the husks from the corn and, using a coarse grater, grate the corn kernels into a deep bowl—there should be about 1½ cups corn flesh and juice. Heat the oil in a saucepan and cook the bacon and onion for 3–4 minutes, or until the onion softens. Transfer to a bowl. Stir in the corn, egg, chives, parsley, breadcrumbs and cream and season well. Spoon into the ramekins.

Put the ramekins in a large baking dish. Add enough hot water to the baking dish to come halfway up the sides of the ramekins. Lay foil loosely over the top. Bake for 25–30 minutes, or until just set.

Seafood quiche

preparation 20 minutes + 20 minutes refrigeration
cooking 1 hour
serves 4–6

2 sheets ready-rolled shortcrust (pie) pastry
30 g (1 oz) butter
300 g (10½ oz) mixed raw seafood
90 g (3¼ oz/¾ cup) grated cheddar cheese
3 eggs
1 tablespoon plain (all-purpose) flour
125 ml (4 fl oz/½ cup) pouring cream
125 ml (4 fl oz/½ cup) milk
1 small fennel, finely sliced
1 tablespoon grated parmesan cheese

Grease a 23 cm (9 inch) loose-based fluted flan (tart) tin. Lay the pastry sheets so that they slightly overlap and roll out until large enough to fit the tin. Press well into the sides and trim off the excess pastry. Refrigerate for 20 minutes. Preheat the oven to 190°C (375°F/Gas 5).

Cover the pastry case with baking paper and spread with a layer of baking beads or rice. Bake for 15 minutes. Remove the paper and beads and bake for 10 minutes, or until golden. Cool on a wire rack.

Heat the butter in a pan and cook the seafood for 2–3 minutes. Leave to cool. Arrange in the pastry case and sprinkle with the cheddar cheese.

In a bowl, beat the eggs together and whisk in the flour, ¼ teaspoon salt, ½ teaspoon freshly ground black pepper, cream and milk. Pour over the seafood filling. Sprinkle the fennel and parmesan cheese over the top. Bake for 30–35 minutes. Leave to cool slightly before serving.

You need to pour in enough hot water to come halfway up the sides of the ramekins.

Sprinkle the fennel and parmesan evenly over the other ingredients in the quiche.

Bottom: Seafood quiche. Top: Corn and bacon crustless quiches.

Mediterranean quiche

preparation 50 minutes + 15 minutes refrigeration
cooking 1 hour 25 minutes
serves 6–8

2 sheets ready-rolled shortcrust (pie) pastry
60 ml (2 fl oz/¼ cup) olive oil
2 garlic cloves, crushed
1 onion, diced
1 small chilli, seeded and finely chopped
1 red capsicum (pepper), cut into bite-sized pieces
1 yellow capsicum (pepper), cut into bite-sized pieces
400 g (14 oz) tinned tomatoes, drained and chopped
2 tablespoons chopped oregano
4 eggs, lightly beaten
35 g (1¼ oz/⅓ cup) grated parmesan cheese

Grease a 23 cm (9 inch) loose-based fluted flan (tart) tin. Place the sheets of pastry so that they are slightly overlapping and roll out until large enough to fit the tin. Press well into the sides and trim off the excess pastry. Cover and refrigerate for 15 minutes. Preheat the oven to 190°C (375°F/Gas 5).

Cover the pastry case with baking paper and spread with a layer of baking beads or rice. Bake for 10 minutes. Remove the paper and beads and bake for another 10 minutes, or until golden. Cool on a wire rack.

Heat the oil in a frying pan and cook the garlic and onion until soft. Add the chilli, red and yellow capsicum and cook for 6 minutes. Stir in the tomatoes and oregano and simmer, covered, for 10 minutes. Remove the lid and cook until the liquid has evaporated. Remove from the heat and leave to cool.

Stir the egg and cheese into the tomato mixture and spoon into the pastry case. Bake for 35–45 minutes, or until the filling has set.

Asparagus and artichoke quiches

preparation 40 minutes + 30 minutes refrigeration
cooking 40 minutes
makes 6

150 g (5½ oz/1¼ cups) plain (all-purpose) flour
90 g (3¼ oz) butter, chilled and cubed
60 g (2¼ oz/½ cup) grated cheddar cheese
2–3 tablespoons iced water

filling
155 g (5½ oz) asparagus, trimmed and cut into bite-sized pieces
2 eggs
80 ml (2½ fl oz/⅓ cup) pouring cream
40 g (1½ oz/⅓ cup) grated gruyère cheese
150 g (5½ oz) marinated artichoke hearts, quartered
1 tablespoon rosemary leaves

To make the pastry, process the flour, butter and a pinch of salt in a food processor for 15 seconds, or until crumbly. Add the cheese and water. Process in short bursts until the mixture just comes together (adding a little more water if necessary). Turn onto a lightly floured surface and gather together into a smooth ball. Cover with plastic wrap and refrigerate for 30 minutes.

Preheat the oven to 190°C (375°F/Gas 5) and grease six 8 cm (3¼ inch) loose-based fluted flan (tart) tins. Roll out the pastry to fit the tins, trimming away excess. Prick the pastry bases with a fork, place on a baking tray and bake for 10–12 minutes, or until the pastry is light and golden.

To make the filling, blanch the asparagus pieces in boiling water. Drain and refresh in iced water. In a bowl, lightly beat the eggs, cream and half the cheese together and season.

Divide the artichoke and asparagus among the pastry cases, pour the egg and cream mixture over the top and sprinkle with the remaining cheese. Bake for 25 minutes, or until the filling is set and golden. If the pastry is over-browning, cover with foil.

Cook the capsicum and pepper for long enough that all the liquid has evaporated.

Neatly arrange the artichokes and asparagus pieces into the pastry cases.

Bottom: Asparagus and artichoke quiches. Top: Mediterranean quiche.

Tomato and bacon quiche

preparation 45 minutes + 1 hour refrigeration
cooking 1 hour 10 minutes
serves 6

185 g (6 oz/1½ cups) plain (all-purpose) flour
pinch of cayenne pepper
pinch of mustard powder
125 g (4½ oz) butter, chilled and cubed
40 g (1½ oz/⅓ cup) grated cheddar cheese
1 egg yolk

filling
25 g (1 oz) butter
100 g (3½ oz) lean bacon, chopped
1 small onion, finely sliced
3 eggs
185 ml (6 fl oz/¾ cup) pouring cream
½ teaspoon salt
2 tomatoes, peeled, seeded and chopped into chunks
90 g (3¼ oz/¾ cup) grated cheddar cheese

To make the pastry, process the flour, pepper, mustard and butter together until crumbly. Add the cheese and egg yolk and process in short bursts until the mixture comes together. Add 1–2 tablespoons of cold water if needed. Turn onto a lightly floured surface and gather together into a smooth ball. Cover with plastic wrap and refrigerate for 30 minutes. Grease a 23 cm (9 inch) loose-based deep flan (tart) tin.

To make the filling, melt the butter in a frying pan and cook the bacon for a few minutes until golden. Add the onion and cook until soft. Remove from the heat. In a bowl, lightly beat the eggs, cream and salt together. Add the bacon and onion, then fold in the tomato and cheese.

Roll out the pastry on a floured surface until large enough to fit the tin. Trim the excess pastry and refrigerate for 30 minutes. Preheat the oven to 180°C (350°F/Gas 4). Cover the pastry with baking paper, fill with baking beads or rice and bake for 10 minutes. Remove the baking paper and beads and bake for a further 10 minutes, or until dry.

Pour the filling into the pastry case and bake for 35 minutes, or until golden and set.

Caramelized onion quiche

preparation 45 minutes + 20 minutes refrigeration
cooking 1 hour 45 minutes
serves 6

185 g (6½ oz/1½ cups) plain (all-purpose) flour
125 g (4½ oz) butter, chilled and cubed
1 egg yolk
1–2 tablespoons iced water
800 g (1 lb 12 oz) onions, thinly sliced
75 g (2½ oz) butter
1 tablespoon soft brown sugar
185 g (6½ oz/¾ cup) sour cream
2 eggs
40 g (1½ oz) prosciutto, cut into strips
40 g (1½ oz) grated cheddar cheese
2 teaspoons thyme leaves

To make the pastry, process the flour, butter and a pinch of salt in a food processor for 15 seconds, or until crumbly. Add the egg yolk and most of the water. Process in short bursts until the mixture comes together (adding more water if necessary). Turn onto a lightly floured surface and gather together into a smooth ball. Cover with plastic wrap and refrigerate for 30 minutes.

Blanch the onion in boiling water for 2 minutes, then drain. Melt the butter in a saucepan and cook the onion over low heat for 25 minutes, or until soft. Stir in the sugar and cook for 15 minutes, stirring occasionally. Preheat the oven to 200°C (400°F/Gas 6). Grease a 23 cm (9 inch) loose-based flan (tart) tin.

Roll out the pastry until large enough to fit the tin and trim off the excess. Cover the pastry case with baking paper, fill with baking beads or rice and bake for 10 minutes. Remove the baking paper and beads and bake for a further 10 minutes, or until dry.

Lightly beat the sour cream and eggs together. Add the prosciutto, cheese and thyme. Stir in the onion and pour the mixture into the pastry case. Bake for 40 minutes, or until set. If the pastry starts to over-brown, cover with foil.

Once the onion is tender but not browned, add the brown sugar.

Bottom: Caramelized onion quiche. Top: Tomato and bacon quiche.

Roasted pumpkin and spinach quiche

preparation 20 minutes
cooking 1 hour 50 minutes
serves 6

500 g (1 lb 2 oz) butternut pumpkin (squash)
1 red onion, cut into small wedges
2 tablespoons olive oil
1 garlic clove, crushed
1 teaspoon salt
4 eggs
125 ml (4 fl oz/½ cup) pouring cream
125 ml (4 fl oz/½ cup) milk
1 tablespoon chopped parsley
1 tablespoon chopped coriander (cilantro) leaves
1 teaspoon wholegrain mustard
6 sheets filo pastry
50 g (1¾ oz) English spinach, blanched
1 tablespoon grated parmesan cheese

Preheat the oven to 190°C (375°F/Gas 5).Cut the pumpkin into 1 cm (½ inch) slices, leaving the skin on. Place the pumpkin, onion, 1 tablespoon of the oil, garlic and salt in a baking dish. Roast for 1 hour, or until lightly golden and cooked.

Whisk together the eggs, cream, milk, herbs and mustard. Season with salt and freshly ground black pepper.

Grease a 23 cm (9 inch) loose-based fluted flan (tart) tin. Brush each sheet of filo pastry with oil and then line the tin with the six sheets. Fold the sides down, tucking them into the tin to form a crust.

Heat a baking tray in the oven for 10 minutes. Place the tart tin on the tray and arrange the vegetables over the base. Pour the egg mixture over the vegetables and sprinkle with the parmesan cheese.

Bake for 35–40 minutes, or until the filling is golden brown and set.

Gently pour the egg mixture over the vegetables, making sure to obtain even coverage.

Zucchini and prosciutto quiche

preparation 35 minutes + 20 minutes refrigeration
cooking 1 hour 15 minutes
serves 6

2 sheets ready-rolled shortcrust (pie) pastry
2 tablespoons olive oil
100 g (3½ oz) prosciutto
1 onion, chopped
4 zucchini (courgettes), thinly sliced
4 eggs
170 ml (5½ fl oz/⅔ cup) pouring cream
60 ml (2 fl oz/¼ cup) milk
25 g (¾ oz/¼ cup) grated parmesan cheese

Place the two sheets of pastry together, slightly overlapping, and roll out until large enough to line a shallow 25 cm (10 inch) loose-based fluted flan (tart) tin. Trim off the excess pastry and refrigerate for 20 minutes. Preheat the oven to 200°C (400°F/Gas 6).

Cover the pastry case with baking paper, fill with baking beads or rice and bake for 15 minutes. Remove the baking paper and beads and bake for a further 10 minutes, or until dry. Cool the pastry case.

To make the filling, heat the olive oil in a frying pan. Cut the prosciutto into thin strips and cook until it is crisp. Remove from the pan with a slotted spoon and drain on paper towel. Cook the onion until soft and remove from the pan. Cook the zucchini and, when almost cooked, season well. Remove from the heat.

In a bowl, mix together the eggs, cream, milk and most of the parmesan cheese.

Lay the prosciutto, onion and zucchini in the pastry case, then pour in the egg and milk mixture. Sprinkle with the remaining parmesan cheese. Bake for 35–40 minutes, until the filling has set and is golden.

To make a neat edge, run a knife around the top of the tart tin to rim away excess pastry.

Bottom: Zucchini and prosciutto quiche. Top: Roasted pumpkin and spinach quiche.

Peach pie

preparation 35 minutes + 40 minutes refrigeration
cooking 1 hour
serves 6–8

250 g (9 oz/2 cups) plain (all-purpose) flour
30 g (1 oz/¼ cup) icing (confectioners') sugar, sifted
125 g (4½ oz) unsalted butter, chilled and cubed
1 egg yolk
2 tablespoons iced water

filling
2 x 825 g (1 lb 13 oz) tins peach slices, drained
125 g (4½ oz/½ cup) caster (superfine) sugar
30 g (1 oz/¼ cup) cornflour (cornstarch)
¼ teaspoon almond essence
20 g (¾ oz) unsalted butter, chopped
1 tablespoon milk
1 egg, lightly beaten
1 tablespoon caster (superfine) sugar, extra, to sprinkle

To make the pastry, sift the flour and icing sugar into a large bowl. Rub the butter into the flour until it resembles fine breadcrumbs. Make a well in the centre, add the egg yolk and water and mix with a flat-bladed knife, using a cutting action, until the mixture comes together in beads (adding a little more water if necessary). Turn onto a lightly floured work surface and gather together into a smooth ball. Cover with plastic wrap and refrigerate for at least 20 minutes.

Preheat the oven to 200°C (400°F/Gas 6). Roll out two-thirds of the dough between two sheets of baking paper until large enough to line an 18 cm (7 inch) pie tin, pressing it firmly into the side and trimming away the excess. Refrigerate for 20 minutes.

Cover the pastry case with baking paper, fill with baking beads or rice and bake for 10 minutes. Remove the baking paper and beads and bake for a further 10 minutes, or until dry. Cool the pastry case.

Mix the peaches, caster sugar, cornflour and almond essence and spoon into the pastry case. Dot with butter and moisten the edge with milk.

Roll out the remaining dough to a 25 cm (10 inch) square. Using a fluted pastry cutter, cut the pastry into ten strips, each 2.5 cm (1 inch) wide. Lay the strips in a lattice pattern over the filling. Press firmly on the edges and trim. Brush the lattice with egg and sprinkle with the extra sugar. Bake for 10 minutes, reduce the oven to 180°C (350°F/Gas 4) and bake for another 30 minutes, or until the top is golden.

Nutty fig pie

preparation 40 minutes + 40 minutes refrigeration
cooking 1 hour
serves 8

200 g (7 oz/1⅔ cups) plain (all-purpose) flour
85 g (3 oz/⅔ cup) icing (confectioners') sugar
100 g (3½ oz) unsalted butter, chilled and cubed
1 egg yolk
1 tablespoon iced water

filling
150 ml (5 fl oz) pouring cream
60 g (2¼ oz) unsalted butter
90 g (3¼ oz/¼ cup) honey
95 g (3¼ oz/½ cup lightly packed) soft brown sugar
200 g (7 oz) hazelnuts, toasted and skins removed
100 g (3½ oz/⅔ cup) pine nuts, toasted
100 g (3½ oz) flaked almonds, toasted
100 g (3½ oz) blanched almonds, toasted
150 g (5½ oz) dessert figs, quartered

To make the pastry, sift the flour and icing sugar into a large bowl. Rub the butter into the flour until it resembles fine breadcrumbs. Make a well in the centre, add the egg yolk and water and mix with a flat-bladed knife, using a cutting action, until the mixture comes together in beads (adding a little more water if necessary). Turn onto a lightly floured work surface and gather together into a smooth ball. Cover with plastic wrap and refrigerate for at least 20 minutes.

Preheat the oven to 200°C (400°F/Gas 6) and grease a 20 cm (8 inch) pie tin. Roll the pastry out between two sheets of baking paper until large enough to line the tin, trimming away the excess. Use a fork to prick the base several times and score the edge. Refrigerate for 20 minutes, then bake for 15 minutes, or until dry and golden. Allow to cool.

Place the cream, butter, honey and sugar in a saucepan and stir over medium heat until the sugar dissolves and the butter melts. Remove from the heat and stir in the nuts and figs. Spoon into the pastry case and bake for 30 minutes. Remove and cool before slicing.

Spoon the buttery nut filling into the pastry shell, then smooth it out evenly.

333

Apple and pecan filo pie

preparation 25 minutes
cooking 50 minutes
serves 8

60 g (2¼ oz/½ cup) pecans
50 g (1¾ oz) unsalted butter
55 g (2 oz/¼ cup) caster (superfine) sugar
1 teaspoon finely grated lemon zest
1 egg, lightly beaten
2 tablespoons plain (all-purpose) flour
3 green apples
10 sheets filo pastry
40 g (1½ oz) unsalted butter, melted
icing (confectioners') sugar, to dust

Preheat the oven to 180°C (350°F/Gas 4). Lightly grease a 35 x 11 cm (14 x 4¼ inch) tin. Spread the pecans in a single layer on a baking tray and bake for 5 minutes to lightly toast. Leave to cool, then chop finely.

Beat the butter, sugar, lemon zest and egg with electric beaters until creamy. Stir in the flour and nuts.

Peel, core and thinly slice the apples. On a flat surface, layer 10 sheets of the filo pastry, brushing each sheet with melted butter before laying the next sheet on top. Fit the layered pastry loosely into the prepared tin. Spread the nut mixture evenly over the pastry base and lay the apple slices on top.

Fold the overhanging pastry over the filling and brush with butter. Trim one side of the pastry lengthways and crumple it over the top of the tart. Bake for 45 minutes, or until brown and crisp. Before serving, dust with sifted icing sugar. Serve hot or cold.

Storage *This tart is best eaten on the day it is made.*

Variation *Thinly sliced pears can be used instead of apples. Walnuts can replace the pecans. Toasting the nuts improves their flavour and makes them a little more crunchy.*

Neatly arrange the slices of apple into the tart tin before folding over the overhanging pastry.

Mango and passionfruit pies

preparation 25 minutes + 20 minutes refrigeration
cooking 25 minutes
makes 6

335 g (11¾ oz/2⅔ cups) plain (all-purpose) flour
2 tablespoons icing (confectioners') sugar
125 g (4½ oz) unsalted butter, chilled and cubed
150 ml (5 fl oz) iced water
1 egg, lightly beaten
icing (confectioners') sugar, to dust

filling
3 ripe mangoes, peeled and sliced or chopped
60 g (2¼ oz/¼ cup) passionfruit pulp
1 tablespoon custard powder (if unavailable, substitute with instant vanilla pudding mix)
90 g (3¼ oz/⅓ cup) caster (superfine) sugar

To make the pastry, sift the flour and icing sugar into a large bowl. Rub the butter into the flour until it resembles fine breadcrumbs. Make a well in the centre, add the water and mix with a flat-bladed knife, using a cutting action, until the mixture comes together in beads (adding a little more water if necessary). Turn onto a lightly floured work surface and gather together into a smooth ball. Cover with plastic wrap and refrigerate for at least 20 minutes.

Preheat the oven to 190°C (375°F/Gas 5). Grease six 8 cm (3¼ inch) fluted flan (tart) tins. Roll out two-thirds of the pastry between two sheets of baking paper until 3 mm (⅛ inch) thick. Cut out six 13 cm (5 inch) circles. Line the tins with the circles; trim. Refrigerate until needed.

Combine the fruit, custard powder and sugar.

Roll out the remaining pastry between baking paper to 3 mm (⅛ inch) thick. Cut out six 11 cm (4¼ inch) circles. Re-roll the trimmings and cut out shapes for decorations. Fill the pastry cases with the mango mixture and brush the edges with egg. Top with the pastry circles, press the edges to seal and trim. Decorate with the shapes. Brush the tops with beaten egg and dust with sifted icing sugar. Bake for 20–25 minutes, or until golden.

Use your fingers to press the pastry into the base and side of the tin.

Bottom: Mango and passionfruit pies. Top: Apple and pecan filo pie.

Farmhouse rhubarb pie

preparation 40 minutes + refrigeration
cooking 50 minutes
serves 6

185 g (6½ oz/1½ cups) plain (all-purpose) flour, sifted
125 g (4½ oz) unsalted butter, chilled and cubed
2 tablespoons icing (confectioners') sugar
1 egg yolk
1 tablespoon iced water

filling
250 g (9 oz/1 cup) sugar
750 g (1 lb 10 oz) chopped rhubarb
2 large apples, peeled, cored and chopped
2 teaspoons grated lemon zest
3 pieces preserved ginger, sliced
2 teaspoons sugar
sprinkle of ground cinnamon

To make the pastry, process the flour, butter and icing sugar in a food processor for 15 seconds, or until crumbly. Add the yolk and water and process in short bursts until the dough comes together. Cover in plastic wrap and refrigerate for 15 minutes.

Preheat the oven to 190°C (375°F/Gas 5). Roll out the pastry to a rough 35 cm (14 inch) circle and line a greased 20 cm (8 inch) pie plate, leaving the extra pastry to hang over the edge. Refrigerate while you prepare the filling.

Heat the sugar and 125 ml (4 fl oz/½ cup) water in a pan for 4–5 minutes or until syrupy. Add the rhubarb, apple, lemon zest and ginger. Cover and simmer for 5 minutes, until the rhubarb is cooked but still holds its shape.

Drain off the liquid and cool the rhubarb. Spoon into the pastry base and sprinkle with the sugar and cinnamon. Fold the overhanging pastry roughly over the fruit and bake for 40 minutes, or until golden.

Key lime pie

preparation 25 minutes + 2 hours refrigeration
cooking 25 minutes
serves 8

125 g (4½ oz) sweet wheatmeal biscuits
90 g (3¼ oz) unsalted butter, melted
4 egg yolks
400 g (14 oz) tin condensed milk
125 ml (4 fl oz/½ cup) lime juice
2 teaspoons finely grated lime zest
250 ml (9 fl oz/1 cup) pouring cream, to serve

To make the pie base, finely crush the biscuits in a food processor for 30 seconds. Transfer to a bowl, add the melted butter and mix thoroughly. Press into a 23 cm (9 inch) pie dish and refrigerate until firm. Preheat the oven to 180°C (350°F/Gas 4).

Beat the egg yolks, condensed milk, lime juice and zest with electric beaters for 1 minute. Pour into the crust and smooth the surface. Bake for 20–25 minutes, or until set.

Refrigerate the pie for 2 hours or until well chilled. Serve with cream.

Don't worry about being too neat when folding over the pastry—this is a rustic pie.

Press the crushed biscuit mixture into the base of the pie dish—this will act as the pie base.

Bottom: Key lime pie. Top: Farmhouse rhubarb pie.

Freeform blueberry pie

preparation 30 minutes + 20 minutes refrigeration
cooking 30 minutes
serves 6–8

185 g (6½ oz/1½ cups) plain (all-purpose) flour
100 g (3½ oz) unsalted butter, chilled and cubed
2 teaspoons grated orange zest
1 tablespoon caster (superfine) sugar
2–3 tablespoons iced water

filling
40 g (1½ oz/⅓ cup) crushed amaretti biscuits (cookies),
or almond bread
60 g (2¼ oz/½ cup) plain (all-purpose) flour
1 teaspoon ground cinnamon
90 g (3¼ oz/⅓ cup) caster (superfine) sugar
500 g (1 lb 2 oz/3¼ cups) blueberries
milk, for brushing

To make the pastry, sift the flour into a large bowl. Rub the butter into the flour until it resembles fine breadcrumbs. Stir in the orange zest and sugar. Make a well in the centre, add almost all the water and mix with a flat-bladed knife, using a cutting action, until the mixture comes together in beads (adding a little more water if necessary). Turn onto a lightly floured surface and gather together into a smooth ball. Cover with plastic wrap and refrigerate for 20 minutes.

Preheat the oven to 200°C (400°F/Gas 6). For the filling, combine the crushed biscuit, flour, cinnamon and 1½ tablespoons sugar. Roll the pastry out to a 36 cm (14 inch) circle and sprinkle with the biscuit mixture, leaving a 4 cm (1½ inch) border. Arrange the blueberries evenly over the biscuit base, then bring up the edges of the pastry to make a crust.

Brush the side of the pie with the milk. Sprinkle with the remaining sugar and bake for 30 minutes, or until the sides are crisp and brown. Serve at room temperature.

Cherry pie

preparation 25 minutes + 15 minutes refrigeration
cooking 40 minutes
serves 6–8

150 g (5½ oz/1¼ cups) plain (all-purpose) flour
30 g (1 oz/¼ cup) icing (confectioners') sugar
60 g (2¼ oz) ground almonds
100 g (3½ oz) unsalted butter, chilled and cubed
60 ml (2 fl oz/¼ cup) iced water
2 x 700 g (1 lb 9 oz) tins pitted morello cherries, drained
1 egg, lightly beaten
caster (superfine) sugar, to sprinkle

Sift the flour and icing sugar into a bowl and then stir in the ground almonds. Rub the butter into the flour until it resembles fine breadcrumbs. Make a well in the centre, add almost all the water and mix with a flat-bladed knife, using a cutting action, until the mixture comes together in beads (adding a little more water if necessary).

Turn the dough out onto a lightly floured surface and press together until smooth. Roll out the dough to a 25 cm (10 inch) circle. Cover with plastic and refrigerate for about 15 minutes.

Preheat the oven to 200°C (400°F/Gas 6). Spoon the cherries into a 23 cm (9 inch) round pie dish. Cover the pie dish with the pastry top and trim away the excess. Roll out the trimmings to make decorations. Brush the pastry top with beaten egg to secure the decorations and sprinkle lightly with caster sugar. Place the pie dish on baking tray and bake for 35–40 minutes, or until golden.

Fold the pastry border over the edge of the
blueberries to hold the blueberries in place.

Use your fingertips to rub the butter into the flour
and icing sugar mixture until it looks crumbly.

339

Bottom: Cherry pie. Top: Freeform blueberry pie.

Pecan pie

preparation 30 minutes + 20 minutes refrigeration
cooking 1 hour 10 minutes
serves 6

185 g (6½ oz/1½ cups) plain (all-purpose) flour
125 g (4½ oz) unsalted butter, chilled and cubed
2–3 tablespoons iced water

filling
200 g (7 oz/12 cups) pecans
3 eggs, lightly beaten
50 g (1¾ oz) unsalted butter, melted and cooled
140 g (5 oz/¾ cup lightly packed) soft brown sugar
170 ml (5½ fl oz/⅔ cup) light corn syrup
1 teaspoon natural vanilla extract
icing (confectioner's) sugar, to dust

To make the pastry, process the flour and butter in a food processor for 20 seconds, or until crumbly. Add almost all the water and process in short bursts until the mixture comes together (adding a little more water if necessary). Turn onto a lightly floured surface and gather together into a smooth ball.

Roll the pastry out to a large rectangle and line a fluted 35 x 11 cm (14 x 4¼ inch) flan (tart) tin. Refrigerate for 20 minutes.

Preheat the oven to 180°C (350°F/Gas 4). Cover the pastry with baking paper, fill with baking beads or rice and bake for 10 minutes. Remove the baking paper and beads and bake for a further 10 minutes, or until dry. Cool the pastry case completely.

Spread the pecans over the pastry base. Whisk together the egg, butter, sugar, corn syrup, vanilla and a pinch of salt, then pour carefully over the nuts. Decorate with pastry trimmings, then put the tin on a baking tray and bake for 45 minutes. Lightly dust with sifted icing sugar and allow to cool before serving at room temperature.

Apple strudel

preparation 20 minutes
cooking 30 minutes
serves 8–10

4 green cooking apples
30 g (1 oz) unsalted butter
2 tablespoons orange juice
1 tablespoon honey
55 g (2 oz/¼ cup) sugar
90 g (3 oz/¾ cup) sultanas (golden raisins)
2 sheets ready-rolled puff pastry
25 g (1 oz/¼ cup) ground almonds
1 egg, lightly beaten
2 tablespoons soft brown sugar
1 teaspoon ground cinnamon

Preheat the oven to 220°C (425°F/Gas 7). Lightly grease two baking trays. Peel, core and thinly slice the apples. Heat the butter in a pan and cook the apples for 2 minutes until lightly golden. Add the orange juice, honey, sugar and sultanas and stir until the sugar dissolves and the apples are just tender. Leave to cool completely.

Place a sheet of pastry on a flat work surface. Fold in half and make small cuts in the folded edge at 2 cm (¾ inch) intervals. Open out the pastry and sprinkle with half of the ground almonds. Drain the cooked apple and place half of the apple in the centre of the pastry. Brush the edges with egg and fold together, pressing firmly.

Place the strudel on one of the baking trays, seam side down. Brush with egg and sprinkle with half of the combined sugar and cinnamon. Make another strudel with the other sheet of pastry and remaining apple filling. Bake for 20–25 minutes, or until the pastry is golden and crisp.

Variation *Many types of fresh or tinned fruit, such as pears, cherries and apricots, can be used for strudel.*

Uncooked rice, dried beans or baking beads can be used to weigh down the pastry when blind baking.

Use scissors or a knife to make small incisions into the folded pastry edge.

Bottom: Apple strudel. Top: Pecan pie.

Rhubarb pie

preparation 40 minutes + 30 minutes refrigeration + cooling
cooking 1 hour
serves 6

335 g (11¾ oz/2⅔ cups) plain (all-purpose) flour
40 g (1½ oz) unsalted butter, chilled and cubed
85 g (3 oz) white vegetable shortening, chilled and cubed
2 tablespoons icing (confectioners') sugar
150 ml (5 fl oz) iced water

filling
1.5 kg (3 lb 5 oz) rhubarb, trimmed and chopped
250 g (9 oz/1 cup) caster (superfine) sugar
½ teaspoon ground cinnamon
2½ tablespoons cornflour (cornstarch)
30 g (1 oz) unsalted butter, cubed
1 egg, lightly beaten
icing (confectioners') sugar, to dust

Grease a 20 cm (8 inch) ceramic pie dish. To make the pastry, sift the flour and ½ teaspoon salt into a large bowl. Rub the butter and shortening into the flour until the mixture resembles fine breadcrumbs. Stir in the icing sugar. Make a well in the centre, add almost all the water and mix with a flat-bladed knife, using a cutting action, until it comes together in beads (adding a little more water if necessary).

Turn onto a lightly floured surface and gather together into a smooth ball. Cover with plastic wrap and refrigerate for 30 minutes.

To make the filling, put the rhubarb, sugar, cinnamon and 2 tablespoons water in a saucepan and stir over low heat until the sugar is dissolved. Cover and simmer for 5–8 minutes, stirring occasionally, until the rhubarb is tender. Mix the cornflour with 60 ml (2 fl oz/¼ cup) water and add the mixture to the pan. Bring to the boil, stirring until thickened. Allow to cool.

Preheat the oven to 180°C (350°F/Gas 4) and heat a baking tray. Roll out two-thirds of the dough to a 30 cm (12 inch) circle to line the pie dish. Spoon the rhubarb into the dish and dot with butter.

Roll out the remaining pastry to form a lid. Moisten the pie rim with egg and press the top in place. Trim the edges and make a slit in the top. Decorate with pastry trimmings. Brush with egg and bake on the hot tray for 35–40 minutes, or until golden. Dust with sifted icing sugar to serve.

Cook the rhubarb until it is soft, then use cornflour to thicken the sauce.

Carefully lay the second sheet of pastry over the filling to create a lid for the pie.

Almond pies

preparation 20 minutes
cooking 25 minutes
makes 8

30 g (1 oz) flaked almonds
60 g (2 oz) unsalted butter, softened
60 g (2 oz/½ cup) icing (confectioners') sugar
60 g (2 oz/¾ cup) ground almonds
30 g (1 oz/¼ cup) plain (all-purpose) flour
1 egg
½ tablespoon rum or brandy
¼ teaspoon natural vanilla extract
4 sheets ready-rolled puff pastry
1 egg, lightly beaten
1 tablespoon sugar, to sprinkle

Preheat the oven to 200°C (400°F/Gas 6). Toast the flaked almonds on a baking tray for 2–3 minutes, or until just golden. Remove the almonds and return the tray to the oven to keep it hot.

Beat together the butter, icing sugar, ground almonds, flour, eggs, rum and vanilla with electric beaters for 2–3 minutes, until smooth and combined. Fold in the flaked almonds.

Cut out eight 10 cm (4 inch) rounds and eight 11 cm (4¼ inch) rounds from the puff pastry. Spread the smaller rounds with the filling, leaving a small border. Brush the borders with beaten egg and cover with the tops. Seal the edges with a fork. Pierce the tops to make steam holes. Brush with egg and sprinkle with the sugar. Bake on the hot tray for 15–20 minutes, or until the pastry is puffed and golden brown.

Raspberry lattice pies

preparation 50 minutes
cooking 25 minutes
makes 8

125 g (4½ oz/½ cup) cream cheese
125 g (4½ oz) unsalted butter
185 g (6½ oz/1½ cups) plain (all-purpose) flour
1 egg, lightly beaten
1 tablespoon caster (superfine) sugar

filling
250 g (9 oz/2 cups) raspberries
70 g (2½ oz) unsalted butter, softened
90 g (3¼ oz/⅓ cup) caster (superfine) sugar
1 egg
70 g (2½ oz/⅔ cup) ground almonds

To make the cream cheese pastry, beat the cream cheese and butter until soft. Stir in the sifted flour with a knife and mix to a dough. Press together to form a ball. Lightly grease eight small pie dishes or eight 125 ml (4 fl oz/½ cup) muffin holes. Roll out the pastry to 3 mm (⅛ inch) thick between two sheets of baking paper. Cut out eight rounds with a 10 cm (4 inch) cutter and ease into the tins.

Divide the raspberries among the pastry cases. Cream together the butter and sugar and then beat in the egg. Fold in the almonds and spoon on top of the raspberries.

Preheat the oven to 180°C (350°F/Gas 4). Roll out the pastry scraps and cut into 5 mm (¼ inch) wide strips. Weave into a lattice on a board, lightly press down with the palm of your hand and cut into rounds with the 10 cm (4 inch) cutter. Brush the pastry rims of the tartlets with beaten egg, put the lattice rounds on top and gently press down the edges to seal. Re-roll the scraps until all the tartlets are topped. Glaze with beaten egg, sprinkle with caster sugar and bake for 20–25 minutes, or until golden.

Leave a small border around the edge of the pastry so the second pastry round can be neatly joined.

Interweave pastry strips into a lattice, then cut out into rounds large enough to fit the top of the pies.

Bottom: Raspberry lattice pies. Top: Almond pies.

Plum cobbler

preparation 25 minutes
cooking 40 minutes
serves 6

750 g (1 lb 10 oz) plums
90 g (3¼ oz/⅓ cup) sugar
1 teaspoon natural vanilla extract

topping
125 g (4½ oz/1 cup) self-raising flour
60 g (2¼ oz) unsalted butter, chilled and cubed
60 g (2¼ oz/⅓ cup lightly packed) soft brown sugar
60 ml (2 fl oz/¼ cup) milk
1 tablespoon caster (superfine) sugar

Preheat the oven to 200°C (400°F/Gas 6). Cut the plums into quarters and remove the stones. Put the plums, sugar and 2 tablespoons water in a saucepan and bring to the boil, stirring, until the sugar dissolves.

Reduce the heat, then cover and simmer for 5 minutes, or until the plums are tender. Remove the skins if you prefer. Add the vanilla and spoon the mixture into a 750 ml (26 fl oz/3 cup) ovenproof dish.

To make the topping, sift the flour into a large bowl and add the butter. Rub in the butter with your fingertips until the mixture resembles fine breadcrumbs. Stir in the brown sugar and 2 tablespoons of the milk. Stir with a knife to form a soft dough, adding more milk if necessary.

Turn out onto a lightly floured surface and gather together to form a smooth dough. Roll out until 1 cm (½ inch) thick and cut into rounds with a 4 cm (1½ inch) cutter.

Overlap the rounds around the inside edge of the dish over the filling. Lightly brush with milk and sprinkle with sugar. Bake on a tray for 30 minutes, or until the topping is golden and cooked through.

Roll out the pastry, then use a cutter to cut out rounds from it.

Pear and apple crumble pie

preparation 20 minutes + 20 minutes refrigeration
cooking 1 hour 10 minutes
serves 8

1 sheet ready-rolled shortcrust (pie) pastry
3 pears
4 green apples
60 g (2½ oz/¼ cup) caster (superfine) sugar
2 teaspoons grated orange zest
90 g (3¼ oz/¾ cup) raisins
60 g (2¼ oz/¼ cup) plain (all-purpose) flour
60 g (2¼ oz/¼ cup firmly packed) soft brown sugar
½ teaspoon ground ginger
60 g (2¼ oz) unsalted butter

Lightly grease an 18 cm (7 inch) pie dish. Line the pie dish with the pastry sheet, trimming away the excess. Wrap in plastic wrap and refrigerate for 20 minutes.

Meanwhile, peel, core and slice the pears and apples and place in a large saucepan. Add the sugar, orange zest and 2 tablespoons water and cook over low heat, stirring occasionally for 20 minutes, or until the fruit is tender but still holding its shape. Remove from the heat, add the raisins and a pinch of salt, mix and leave to cool completely. Spoon into the pie dish.

Preheat the oven to 200°C (400°F/Gas 6) and preheat a baking tray. To make the topping, put the flour, brown sugar and ginger in a bowl and rub in the butter with your fingertips until the mixture resembles coarse breadcrumbs. Sprinkle over the fruit.

Put the dish on the hot baking tray and bake for 10 minutes, then reduce the oven temperature to 180°C (350°F/Gas 4) and bake for another 40 minutes, or until browned. Check the pie after 20 minutes and cover with foil if the topping is over-browning.

The crumble topping should resemble coarse breadcrumbs; sprinkle it over the fruit filling.

347

Bottom: Pear and apple crumble pie. Top: Plum cobbler.

Lemon meringue pie

preparation 30 minutes + 20 minutes refrigeration
cooking 1 hour
serves 6–8

200 g (7 oz/1⅔ cups) plain (all-purpose) flour
85 g (3 oz/⅔ cup) icing (confectioners') sugar
100 g (3½ oz) unsalted butter, chilled and cubed
1 egg yolk
1 tablespoon iced water

filling
30 g (1 oz/¼ cup) plain (all-purpose) flour
30 g (1 oz/¼ cup) cornflour (cornstarch)
230 g (8 oz/1 cup) caster (superfine) sugar
185 ml (6 fl oz/¾ cup) lemon juice
1 tablespoon grated lemon zest
50 g (1¾ oz) unsalted butter, chopped
6 egg yolks

meringue
4 egg whites
345 g (12 oz/1 cup) caster (superfine) sugar
pinch of cream of tartar

To make the pastry, sift the flour and icing sugar into a large bowl. Rub the butter into the flour until it resembles fine breadcrumbs. Make a well in the centre, add the egg yolk and water and mix with a flat-bladed knife, using a cutting action, until the mixture comes together in beads (adding a little more water if necessary). Turn onto a lightly floured surface and gather together into a smooth ball. Cover with plastic wrap and refrigerate for 20 minutes.

Lightly grease an 18 cm (7 inch) pie plate. Roll out the pastry between two sheets of baking paper into a 30 cm (12 inch) circle to line the pie plate, and trim away the excess. Press a teaspoon into the pastry rim to make a decorative edge. Prick all over the base with a fork. Cover and refrigerate for 20 minutes. Preheat the oven to 180°C (350°F/Gas 4).

Cover the pastry case with baking paper, fill with baking beads or rice and bake for 10 minutes. Remove the baking paper and beads and bake for a further 10 minutes, or until dry. Cool the pastry case completely. Increase the oven to 200°C (400°F/Gas 6).

To make the filling, put the flours, sugar, juice and zest in a saucepan. Gradually add 310 ml (10¾ fl oz/1¼ cups) water and whisk over medium heat until smooth. Cook, stirring, for another 2 minutes, or until thickened. Remove from the heat and vigorously whisk in the butter and yolks. Return to low heat and stir for 2 minutes, or until the filling is very thick.

To make the meringue, in a clean, dry bowl beat the egg whites, sugar and cream of tartar with electric beaters for 10 minutes, until thick and glossy.

Spread the filling over the pastry base, then spread the meringue over the top, piling it high in the centre. Use a knife to form peaks. Bake for 12–15 minutes, or until golden.

Press the tip of a teaspoon into the pastry edge to create a decorative pattern.

The meringue topping should be thick, glossy and form tall peaks on the pie.

Banoffie pie

preparation 35 minutes + 1 hour 15 minutes refrigeration
cooking 40 minutes
serves 8

150 g (5½ oz/1¼ cups) plain (all-purpose) flour
2 tablespoons icing (confectioners') sugar
90 g (3¼ oz) ground walnuts
80 g (2¾ oz) unsalted butter, chilled and cubed
2–3 tablespoons iced water

filling
400 g (14 oz) tin condensed milk
30 g (1 oz) unsalted butter
1 tablespoon golden syrup (if unavailable, use half honey and
half dark corn syrup)
4 bananas, sliced
375 ml (13 fl oz/1½ cups) whipping cream

To make the pastry, sift the flour and icing sugar into a large bowl. Add the walnuts. Rub the butter into the flour until it resembles fine breadcrumbs. Make a well in the centre, add the water and mix with a flat-bladed knife, using a cutting action, until the dough comes together in beads (adding a little more water if necessary). Turn onto a lightly floured surface and gather together into a smooth ball. Cover with plastic wrap and refrigerate for 15 minutes. Roll out until large enough to line a 23 cm (9 inch) fluted flan (tart) tin, trimming away the excess. Refrigerate for 20 minutes.

Preheat the oven to 180°C (350°F/Gas 4). Cover the pastry with baking paper and spread with a layer of baking beads or rice. Bake for 15 minutes, then remove the paper and beads. Bake the pastry for another 20 minutes, or until dry and lightly golden. Leave to cool completely.

Heat the condensed milk, butter and golden syrup in a small saucepan for 5 minutes, stirring constantly until it boils, thickens and turns a light caramel colour. Cool slightly. Arrange half the banana over the pastry and pour the caramel over the top. Refrigerate for 30 minutes.

Whip the cream and spoon over the caramel. Top with more banana before serving.

Top the caramel with cream; either in small mounds like here or in a smooth layer.

Bramble pie

preparation 30 minutes + 30 minutes refrigeration
cooking 40 minutes
serves 4–6

125 g (4½ oz/1 cup) self-raising flour
125 g (4½ oz/1 cup) plain (all-purpose) flour
125 g (4½ oz) unsalted butter, chilled and cubed
2 tablespoons caster (superfine) sugar
1 egg, lightly beaten
60–80 ml (2–2½ fl oz/¼–⅓ cup) milk

filling
2 tablespoons cornflour (cornstarch)
2–4 tablespoons caster (superfine) sugar, to taste
1 teaspoon grated orange zest
1 tablespoon orange juice
600 g (1 lb 5 oz) brambles (see Note)
1 egg yolk, mixed with 1 teaspoon water

To make the pastry, process the flours, butter and sugar in a food processor for 30 seconds, or until crumbly. Add the egg and almost all the milk and process in short bursts until the mixture comes together (adding more milk if necessary). Turn onto a lightly floured surface and gather into a ball. Refrigerate for 30 minutes.

Put the cornflour, sugar, orange zest and juice in a saucepan and mix well. Add half the brambles and stir over low heat for 5 minutes until the mixture boils and thickens. Cool, then add the remaining brambles. Pour into a 750 ml (26 fl oz/3 cup) pie dish.

Preheat the oven to 180°C (350°F/ Gas 4). Divide the dough in half and roll out one half large enough to cover the dish. Trim away the excess. Roll out the other half and use cutters of various sizes to cut out enough hearts to cover the top. Brush the pie top with egg glaze. Bake for 35 minutes or until golden brown.

Note *Brambles include any creeping stem berries, such as boysenberries, blackberries, loganberries and youngberries. Use one variety or a combination.*

It can look very effective to top the pie with hearts of varying sizes.

Bottom: Bramble pie. Top: Banoffie pie.

351

Apple pie

preparation 45 minutes + 20 minutes refrigeration
cooking 1 hour
serves 6–8

310 g (11 oz/2½ cups) plain (all-purpose) flour
40 g (1½ oz/⅓ cup) self-raising flour
185 g (6½ oz) unsalted butter, chilled and cubed
2½ tablespoons caster (superfine) sugar
6–7 tablespoons iced water

filling

6 large green apples, peeled, cored and cut into wedges
2 tablespoons caster (superfine) sugar
1 teaspoon finely grated lemon zest
pinch of ground cloves
2 tablespoons apricot jam
1 egg, lightly beaten
1 tablespoon sugar

To make the pastry, sift the flours into a bowl. Rub the butter into the flour with your fingertips until the mixture resembles fine breadcrumbs. Add the sugar, mix well and make a well in the centre. Add most of the water and mix with a flat-bladed knife, using a cutting action, until the mixture comes together in beads, adding water if needed. Gather the pastry together on a floured surface. Divide into two, making one half a little bigger. Wrap in plastic and refrigerate for 20 minutes.

Meanwhile, put the apples in a large heavy-based saucepan with the sugar, lemon zest, cloves and 2 tablespoons water. Cover and simmer for 8 minutes, or until just tender, shaking the pan occasionally. Drain and cool. Preheat the oven to 200°C (400°F/Gas 6).

Roll out the larger piece of pastry between two sheets of baking paper and line a 23 cm (9 inch) pie plate, trimming away the excess pastry. Brush the jam over the base and spoon in the apple filling. Roll out the remaining piece of pastry between two sheets of baking paper until large enough to cover the pie. Brush a little water around the rim to secure the top. Trim off the excess pastry, pinch the edges together and cut steam holes in the top.

Roll out the pastry trimmings to make leaves to decorate the pie. Brush the top lightly with egg and sprinkle with sugar. Bake for 20 minutes, then reduce the oven temperature to 180°C (350°F/Gas 4) and bake for 30–35 minutes, or until golden brown.

It can be easier to roll the pastry out if you do it between two sheets of baking paper.

Use the baking paper to help you lift the pastry into the pie plate.

Chocolate tart

preparation 30 minutes + 30 minutes refrigeration
cooking 30 minutes
serves 12

200 g (7 oz/1⅔ cups) plain (all-purpose) flour
85 g (3 oz/⅔ cup) icing (confectioners') sugar
100 g (3½ oz) unsalted butter, chilled and cubed
1 egg yolk
1 tablespoon iced water

filling
50 g (1¾ oz/⅓ cup) chopped dark chocolate
400 g (14 oz/2⅔ cups) chopped milk chocolate
300 ml (10½ fl oz) thick (double/heavy) cream

To make the pastry, sift the flour and icing sugar into a large bowl. Rub the butter into the flour until it resembles fine breadcrumbs. Make a well in the centre, add the egg yolk and water and mix with a flat-bladed knife, using a cutting action, until the mixture comes together in beads (adding a little more water if necessary). Turn onto a lightly floured surface and gather together into a smooth ball. Cover with plastic wrap and refrigerate for 30 minutes.

Preheat the oven to 200°C (400°F/Gas 6). Grease a 35 x 11 cm (14 x 4¼ inch) loose-based rectangular tart tin.

Roll out the pastry on a lightly floured work surface until 3 mm (⅛ inch) thick, to fit the base and sides of the tin. Roll the pastry onto the rolling pin, then lift and ease it into the tin, gently pressing to fit into the corners. Trim the edges, cover with plastic wrap and refrigerate for 30 minutes.

Cover the pastry case with baking paper, fill with baking beads or rice and bake for 10 minutes. Remove the baking paper and beads and bake for a further 10 minutes, or until dry. Cool the pastry case.

Place the dark chocolate in a heatproof bowl and sit it over a saucepan of barely simmering water, making sure the base of the bowl does not touch the water. Stir until the chocolate has melted. Brush the base of the pastry with the melted chocolate.

Put the milk chocolate and cream in a small heatproof bowl. Sit the bowl over a small saucepan of simmering water, stirring until the chocolate has melted and the mixture is smooth. Allow the chocolate to cool slightly, then pour into the pastry case. Refrigerate overnight, or until the chocolate filling has set. Serve the tart in small slices as it is very rich.

Chocolate orange tarts

preparation 45 minutes
cooking 50 minutes
serves 6

90 g (3¼ oz/¾ cup) plain (all-purpose) flour
50 g (1¾ oz/¼ cup) rice flour
55 g (2 oz/½ cup) ground almonds
1 tablespoon sugar
125 g (4½ oz) unsalted butter, chopped
1 egg yolk, at room temperature

filling
100 g (3½ oz/⅔ cup) chopped dark chocolate
110 g (3¾ oz/¾ cup) chopped milk chocolate
1 teaspoon grated orange zest
2 tablespoons orange juice
310 ml (10¾ fl oz/1¼ cups) pouring cream
2 eggs, at room temperature
3 egg yolks, at room temperature, whisked
whipped cream and candied (glacé) orange zest, to serve
icing (confectioners') sugar, to dust

To make the pastry, process the flours, a pinch of salt, the ground almonds, sugar and butter in a food processor for 20 seconds, or until crumbly. Add the egg yolk and 1–2 tablespoons cold water and process in short bursts until the dough comes together. Divide the dough into six even portions then roll out between two sheets of baking paper to a 6 mm (¼ inch) thickness. Line the tart tins with the dough, and trim the edges with a sharp knife. Refrigerate for 20 minutes.

Preheat the oven to 180°C (350°F/Gas 4). Brush six 12 cm (4 inch) individual fluted flan tins with melted butter.

Cover the pastry cases with baking paper, fill with baking beads or rice and bake for 15 minutes. Remove the baking paper and beads and bake for a further 5 minutes, or until dry. Cool the pastry cases.

To make the filling, place the chocolate in a heatproof bowl and sit it over a saucepan of barely simmering water, making sure the base of the bowl does not touch the water. Stir until the chocolate has melted.

Whisk together the orange zest, juice, cream, eggs and egg yolks. Gradually add to the melted chocolate, whisking constantly. Pour the mixture into the pastry cases and bake for 20–25 minutes, or until just set (the filling will set more as the tarts cool). Serve warm with whipped cream and candied orange zest and dust with sifted icing sugar.

Bottom: Chocolate orange tarts. Top: Chocolate tart.

Tarte tatin

preparation 15 minutes
cooking 1 hour 10 minutes
serves 6

100 g (3½ oz) unsalted butter
185 g (6½ oz/¾ cup) sugar
6 large pink lady or fuji apples, peeled, cored and quartered
(see Note)
1 sheet ready-rolled puff pastry

Preheat the oven to 220°C (425°F/Gas 7). Lightly grease a 23 cm (9 inch) shallow cake tin. Melt the butter in a frying pan, add the sugar and cook, stirring, over medium heat for 4–5 minutes, or until the sugar starts to caramelize and turn brown. Continue to cook, stirring, until the caramel turns golden brown.

Add the apple to the pan and cook over low heat for 20–25 minutes, or until it starts to turn golden brown. Carefully turn the apple over and cook the other side until evenly coloured. If a lot of liquid comes out of the apple, increase the heat until it has evaporated—the caramel should be sticky rather than runny. Remove from the heat. Using tongs, arrange the hot apple in circles in the tin and pour the sauce over the top.

Place the pastry over the apple, tucking the edge down firmly with the end of a spoon. Bake for 30–35 minutes, or until the pastry is cooked. Leave for 15 minutes before inverting onto a serving plate.

Note *The moisture content of apples varies quite a lot, which affects the cooking time. Golden delicious, pink lady or fuji apples are good to use because they don't break down during cooking.*

Use the end of a spoon to push the pastry down around the edge of the tin.

Treacle tart

preparation 30 minutes + 40 minutes refrigeration
cooking 35 minutes
serves 4–6

150 g (5½ oz/1¼ cups) plain (all-purpose) flour
90 g (3¼ oz) unsalted butter, chilled and cubed
2–3 tablespoons iced water
1 egg, lightly beaten, to glaze

filling
350 g (12 oz/1 cup) golden syrup or dark corn syrup
25 g (1 oz) unsalted butter
½ teaspoon ground ginger
140 g (5 oz/1¾ cups) fresh white breadcrumbs
icing (confectioners') sugar, to dust, optional

To make the pastry, sift the flour into a large bowl. Rub the butter into the flour until it resembles fine breadcrumbs. Make a well in the centre, add almost all the iced water and mix with a flat-bladed knife, using a cutting action, until the mixture comes together in beads (adding a little more water if necessary). Turn onto a lightly floured surface and gather together into a smooth ball. Cover with plastic wrap and refrigerate for 20 minutes.

Brush a 20 cm (8 inch) diameter flan (tart) tin with melted butter or oil. Roll out the pastry large enough to fit the base and side of the tin, allowing a 4 cm (1½ inch) overhang. Ease the pastry into the tin and trim by running a rolling pin firmly across the top of the tin. Re-roll the trimmed pastry to a rectangle 10 x 20 cm (4 x 8 inches). Using a sharp knife or fluted pastry wheel, cut into long 1 cm (½ inch) strips. Cover the pastry-lined tin and strips with plastic wrap and refrigerate for 20 minutes. Preheat the oven to 180°C (350°F/Gas 4).

To make the filling, combine the golden syrup, butter and ginger in a small saucepan and stir over low heat until the butter melts. Stir in the breadcrumbs until combined. Pour the mixture into the pastry case. Lay half the pastry strips over the tart, starting at the centre and working outwards. Lay the remaining strips over the tart to form a lattice pattern. Brush the lattice with beaten egg. Bake for 30 minutes, or until the pastry is lightly golden. Serve warm or at room temperature. You can dust the top with icing sugar and serve with ice cream or cream.

356

Bottom: Treacle tart. Top: Tarte tatin.

Filo peach tartlets

preparation 40 minutes
cooking 25 minutes
makes 8

6 sheets filo pastry
60 g (2¼ oz) unsalted butter, melted
90 g (3¼ oz/¾ cup) slivered almonds
1½ teaspoons ground cinnamon
90 g (3¼ oz/½ cup lightly packed) soft brown sugar
185 ml (6 fl oz/¾ cup) orange juice, strained
4 peaches

Preheat the oven to 180°C (350°F/Gas 4). Cut each sheet of pastry into eight squares. Line eight large muffin holes with three layers of filo pastry, brushing between layers with melted butter and overlapping the sheets at angles.

Mix together the almonds, cinnamon and half the sugar. Sprinkle into the pastry cases, then cover with three final squares of filo brushed with butter. Bake for 10–15 minutes.

Meanwhile, dissolve the remaining sugar in the orange juice in a saucepan, bring to the boil, reduce the heat and simmer. Halve the peaches and slice thinly. Add to the syrup and stir gently to coat the fruit. Simmer for 2–3 minutes then lift from the pan with a slotted spoon. Arrange the peaches on the pastries and serve.

Variation *You can use tinned peaches if fresh are not available.*

The slivered almond mixture will act as the base for the peaches.

Lime and blueberry tart

preparation 30 minutes + 40 minutes refrigeration
cooking 1 hour
serves 8

200 g (7 oz/1⅔ cups) plain (all-purpose) flour
85 g (3 oz/⅔ cup) icing (confectioners') sugar
100 g (3½ oz) unsalted butter, chilled and cubed
1 egg yolk
1 tablespoon iced water

filling

3 eggs
125 g (4½ oz/½ cup) caster (superfine) sugar
60 ml (2 fl oz/¼ cup) buttermilk
1 tablespoon lime juice
2 teaspoons finely grated lime zest
2 tablespoons custard powder (if unavailable,
substitute with instant vanilla pudding mix)
250 g (9 oz) blueberries
icing (confectioner's) sugar, to dust

To make the pastry, sift the flour and icing sugar into a large bowl. Rub the butter into the flour until it resembles fine breadcrumbs. Make a well in the centre, add the egg yolk and water and mix with a flat-bladed knife, using a cutting action, until the mixture comes together in beads (adding a little more water if necessary). Turn onto a lightly floured surface and gather together into a smooth ball. Cover with plastic wrap and refrigerate for 20 minutes.

Roll out the pastry between two sheets of baking paper to line a 23 cm (9 inch) pie tin, trimming away the excess pastry. Refrigerate for 20 minutes. Preheat the oven to 200°C (400°F/Gas 6).

Cover the pastry with baking paper, fill with baking beads or rice and bake for 10 minutes. Remove the baking paper and beads and bake for a further 5 minutes, or until dry. Cool the pastry case. Reduce the oven to 180°C (350°F/Gas 4).

To make the filling, beat the eggs and sugar with electric beaters until thick and pale. Add the buttermilk, lime juice and zest, and sifted custard powder. Stir together, then spoon into the pastry case. Bake for 15 minutes, then reduce the oven to 160°C (315°F/Gas 2–3) and cook for another 20–25 minutes, or until the filling has coloured slightly and is set. Leave to cool (it will sink a little), then top with the blueberries. Dust with sifted icing sugar.

Bottom: Lime and blueberry tart. Top: Filo peach tartlets.

Chocolate-almond tarts

preparation 40 minutes + 20 minutes refrigeration
cooking 15 minutes
makes 18 tarts

125 g (4½ oz/1 cup) plain (all-purpose) flour
60 g (2¼ oz) unsalted butter, chilled and cubed
1 tablespoon icing (confectioners') sugar
1 tablespoon lemon juice

filling
1 egg
90 g (3¼ oz/⅓ cup) caster (superfine) sugar
2 tablespoons unsweetened cocoa powder
90 g (3¼ oz/½ cup) ground almonds
60 ml (2 fl oz/¼ cup) pouring cream
80 g (2¾ oz/¼ cup) apricot jam
18 blanched almonds
icing (confectioner's) sugar, to dust

Preheat the oven to 180°C (350°F/Gas 4). Lightly grease two 12-cup shallow patty pans or mini muffin tins. To make the pastry, process the flour, butter and icing sugar in a food processor for 15 seconds, or until crumbly. Add the juice and process in short bursts until it comes together.

Roll out the dough between two sheets of baking paper to 6 mm (¼ inch) thick. Cut rounds with a 7 cm (2¾ inch) fluted cutter to line the tins and refrigerate for 20 minutes.

Beat the egg and sugar with electric beaters until thick and pale. Sift the cocoa over the top. With a flat-bladed knife, stir in the ground almonds and cream.

Place a dab of jam in the centre of each pastry base. Spoon the filling over the jam and place an almond in the centre of each one. Bake for 15 minutes, or until puffed and set on top. Leave in the tins for 5 minutes, then cool on a wire rack. Dust with sifted icing sugar to serve.

Use a flat-bladed knife to stir the ground almonds and cream into the creamed egg and sugar.

Low-fat fruit tarts

preparation 25 minutes + 30 minutes refrigeration
cooking 20 minutes
makes 6

125 g (4½ oz/1 cup) plain (all-purpose) flour
30 g (1 oz/¼ cup) custard powder (if unavailable,
substitute with instant vanilla pudding mix)
30 g (1 oz/¼ cup) icing (confectioners') sugar
40 g (1½ oz) unsalted butter
2 tablespoons skim milk
2 x 125 g (4½ oz) tubs low-fat fromage frais
100 g (3½ oz) ricotta cheese
strawberries, hulled and halved; blueberries; and kiwi fruit,
peeled and sliced
80–105 g (2¾–3½ oz/¼–⅓ cup) redcurrant jelly

Lightly grease six 7 cm (2¾ inch) shallow loose-based flan (tart) tins. To make the pastry, process the flour, custard powder, icing sugar and butter in a food processor for 15 seconds, or until crumbly. Add the skim milk and process in short bursts until it comes together into a soft dough. Turn onto a lightly floured surface and gather together into a smooth ball. Cover with plastic wrap and refrigerate for 30 minutes. Preheat the oven to 200°C (400°F/Gas 6).

Divide the dough into six portions and roll out to fit the tins. Cover with baking paper and spread with a layer of baking beads or rice. Bake for 10 minutes, remove the paper and beads and bake for another 10 minutes, or until golden. Allow to cool before removing from the tins.

Mix the fromage frais and ricotta together until smooth. Spread over the pastry bases and top with the fruit. Heat the redcurrant jelly until liquid in a small saucepan and brush over the fruit.

Line the pastry cases with baking paper and use rice, dried beans or baking beads as a weight.

Bottom: Low-fat fruit tarts. Top: Chocolate-almond tarts.

Berry ricotta cream tartlets

preparation 1 hour + 1 hour refrigeration
cooking 40 minutes
serves 6

185 g (6½ oz/1½ cups) plain (all-purpose) flour
90 g (3¼ oz/½ cup) ground almonds
40 g (1½ oz/⅓ cup) icing (confectioners') sugar
125 g (4½ oz) unsalted butter, chilled and cubed
1 egg, lightly beaten

filling
200 g (7 oz) ricotta cheese
1 teaspoon natural vanilla extract
2 eggs
160 g (5¾ oz/⅔ cup) caster (superfine) sugar
125 ml (4 fl oz/½ cup) pouring cream
60 g (2¼ oz/½ cup) raspberries
80 g (2¾ oz/½ cup) blueberries
icing (confectioners') sugar, to dust

To make the pastry, sift the flour into a large bowl, then add the ground almonds and icing sugar. Rub the butter into the flour until it resembles fine breadcrumbs. Make a well in the centre, add the egg and mix with a flat-bladed knife, using a cutting action, until the mixture comes together in beads. Turn onto a lightly floured work surface and gather into a ball. Wrap in plastic wrap and refrigerate for 30 minutes.

Grease six 8 cm (3¼ inch) deep loose-based flan (tart) tins. Roll out the pastry between two sheets of baking paper to fit the base and side of the tins, trimming away the excess. Prick the bases with a fork, then refrigerate for 30 minutes. Preheat the oven to 180°C (350°F/Gas 4).

Line the pastry bases with baking paper and cover with baking beads or rice. Bake for 8–10 minutes, then remove the paper and beads. Mix the ricotta cheese, vanilla, eggs, sugar and cream in a food processor until smooth. Divide the berries among the tarts and pour over the filling. Bake for 25–30 minutes, or until just set—the top should be soft but not too wobbly. Cool. Dust with sifted icing sugar.

Once the berries have been divided among the tart shells, pour in the ricotta filling.

Pear and almond flan

preparation 15 minutes + 2 hours 30 minutes refrigeration
cooking 1 hour 10 minutes
serves 8

150 g (5 oz/1¼ cups) plain (all-purpose) flour
90 g (3¼ oz) butter, chilled and cubed
60 g (2¼ oz/¼ cup) caster (superfine) sugar
2 egg yolks
1 tablespoon iced water

filling
165 g (5¾ oz) unsalted butter, softened
160 g (5¾ oz/⅔ cup) caster (superfine) sugar
3 eggs
230 g (8¼ oz/2¼ cups) ground almonds
1½ tablespoons plain (all-purpose) flour
2 ripe pears

Grease a shallow 24 cm (9½ inch) loose-based flan (tart) tin. To make the pastry, process the flour, butter and sugar in a food processor for 15 seconds, or until crumbly. Add the egg yolks and water and process in short bursts until the dough just comes together. Turn out onto a lightly floured surface and gather into a ball. Wrap in plastic wrap and refrigerate for 30 minutes. Preheat the oven to 180°C (350°F/Gas 4).

Roll the pastry between baking paper until large enough to line the tin, trimming any excess. Sparsely prick the base with a fork. Line with baking paper and a layer of baking beads or rice and bake for 10 minutes. Remove the paper and beads and bake for another 10 minutes.

Mix the butter and sugar with electric beaters for 30 seconds (do not cream the mixture). Add the eggs one at a time, beating after each addition. Fold in the ground almonds and flour and spread smoothly over the cooled pastry base.

Peel and halve the pears lengthways and remove the cores. Cut them crossways into 3 mm (⅛ inch) slices. Separate the slices slightly, then place each half on top of the tart to form a cross. Bake for 50 minutes, or until the filling has set (the middle may still be soft). Cool in the tin and refrigerate for at least 2 hours before serving.

Bottom: Pear and almond flan. Top: Berry ricotta cream tartlets.

Golden pine nut tarts

preparation 25 minutes
cooking 20 minutes
makes 24

60 g (2¼ oz/½ cup) plain (all-purpose) flour
60 g (2¼ oz) unsalted butter, chilled and cubed
40 g (1½ oz/¼ cup) pine nuts
20 g (¾ oz) unsalted butter, melted
180 g (6¼ oz/½ cup) golden syrup (if unavailable, substitute
with half honey and half dark corn syrup)
2 tablespoons soft brown sugar

Preheat the oven to 180°C (350°F/Gas 4) and brush two
12-hole patty pans or mini muffin tins with melted butter.

To make the pastry, mix the flour and butter in a food
processor for 20–30 seconds or until the mixture comes
together. Turn out onto a lightly floured surface and press
into a smooth ball. Roll out to a thickness of 3 mm (⅛ inch).
Cut out rounds with a 5 cm (2 inch) fluted scone cutter.
Lift rounds gently with a flat-bladed knife and line each
muffin hole.

Spread the pine nuts on a baking tray and toast in the oven
for 1–2 minutes, until just golden. Cool a little, then divide
among the pastry cases.

Whisk together the melted butter, golden syrup and sugar.
Pour over the pine nuts. Bake for 15 minutes, until golden.
Leave the tarts in the trays for 5 minutes before cooling on
a wire rack.

The pine nuts only need to be toasted briefly before
being spooned into the pastry cases.

Little lemon tarts

preparation 40 minutes + 10 minutes refrigeration
cooking 20 minutes
makes 24

250 g (9 oz/2 cups) plain (all-purpose) flour
125 g (4 oz) unsalted butter, chilled and cubed
2 teaspoons caster (superfine) sugar
1 teaspoon finely grated lemon zest
1 egg yolk
2–3 tablespoons iced water

filling
125 g (4½ oz/½ cup) cream cheese, softened
125 g (4½ oz/½ cup) caster (superfine) sugar
2 egg yolks
2 tablespoons lemon juice
125 ml (4 fl oz/½ cup sweetened condensed milk
icing (confectioner's) sugar, to dust

Preheat the oven to 180°C (350°F/Gas 4) and lightly grease
two 12-hole patty pans or mini muffin tins.

To make the pastry, sift the flour into a large bowl. Rub
the butter into the flour until the mixture resembles fine
breadcrumbs. Make a well in the centre, add the sugar,
lemon zest, egg yolk and water and mix with a flat-bladed
knife, using a cutting action, until the mixture comes
together in beads. Turn out onto a lightly floured surface
and gently gather into a smooth ball. Wrap in plastic wrap
and refrigerate for 10 minutes.

Beat the cream cheese, sugar and yolks until smooth and
thickened. Add the juice and condensed milk and beat well.

Roll out the dough between two sheets of baking paper to
3 mm (⅛ inch) thick. Cut into rounds with a 7 cm (2¾ inch)
fluted cutter and line the patty pans. Lightly prick each base
several times with a fork and bake for 10 minutes, or until
just starting to turn golden.

Spoon 2 teaspoons of filling into each case and bake for
8–10 minutes, or until the filling has set. Cool slightly before
removing from the tins. Dust with sifted icing sugar.

Prick the bases of the pastry cases with a fork
before baking.

Bottom: Little lemon tarts. Top: Golden pine nut tarts.

Summer berry tart

preparation 35 minutes + 20 minutes refrigeration
cooking 35 minutes
serves 4–6

125 g (4½ oz/1 cup) plain (all-purpose) flour
90 g (3 oz) unsalted butter, chilled and cubed
2 tablespoons icing (confectioners') sugar
1–2 tablespoons iced water

filling
3 egg yolks
2 tablespoons caster (superfine) sugar
2 tablespoons cornflour (cornstarch)
250 ml (9 oz/1 cup) milk
1 teaspoon natural vanilla extract
250 g (9 oz) strawberries, hulled and halved
125 g (4½ oz) blueberries
125 g (4½ oz) raspberries
1–2 tablespoons redcurrant jelly

To make the pastry, process the flour, butter and icing sugar in a food processor for 15 seconds, or until crumbly. Add some of the water and process in short bursts until it comes together (adding more water if necessary) Turn onto a lightly floured surface and gather together into a smooth ball. Roll out to line a 20 cm (8 inch) fluted flan (tart) tin, trimming away the excess. Refrigerate for 20 minutes. Preheat the oven to 180°C (350°F/Gas 4).

Cover the pastry with baking paper, fill with baking beads or rice and bake for 15 minutes. Remove the baking paper and beads and bake for a further 15 minutes, or until dry.

Whisk the egg yolks, sugar and cornflour until pale. Heat the milk in a small pan to almost boiling, then pour gradually into the egg mixture, beating constantly. Strain back into the pan. Stir over low heat for 3 minutes or until the custard boils and thickens. Remove from the heat and add the vanilla. Transfer to a bowl, lay plastic wrap directly on the surface to prevent a skin forming, and leave to cool.

Spread the custard in the pastry case and top with the berries. Heat the jelly until liquid and brush over the fruit.

Arrange the fruit in a decorative pattern over the custard filling, then glaze with the jelly.

Low-fat banana and blueberry tart

preparation 30 minutes
cooking 25 minutes
serves 6–8

125 g (4½ oz/1 cup) plain (all-purpose) flour
60 g (2¼ oz/½ cup) self-raising flour
1 teaspoon ground cinnamon
1 teaspoon ground ginger
40 g (1½ oz) unsalted butter, chilled and cubed
95 g (3¼ oz/½ cup lightly packed) soft brown sugar
125 ml (4 fl oz/½ cup) buttermilk

filling
200 g (7 oz/1¼ cups) blueberries
2 bananas
2 teaspoons lemon juice
1 tablespoon raw (demerara) sugar
icing (confectioner's) sugar, to dust

Preheat the oven to 200°C (400°F/Gas 6). Lightly grease a baking tray or pizza tray. Sift the flours and spices into a bowl. Add the butter and sugar and rub in until the mixture resembles fine breadcrumbs. Make a well in the centre and add enough buttermilk to mix to a soft dough.

Roll the dough on a lightly floured surface into a 23 cm (9 inch) circle. Place on the tray and roll the edge into a lip to hold in the fruit.

Spread the blueberries over the dough. Slice the bananas, toss them in the lemon juice, and arrange over the top. Sprinkle with the sugar, and bake for 25 minutes, until the base is browned. Dust with sifted icing sugar to serve..

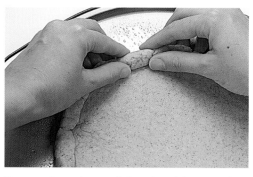

Use your fingertips to roll the edge of the pastry into a lip that will hold the filling in place.

Bottom: Low-fat banana and blueberry tart. Top: Summer berry tart.

Orange macadamia tarts

preparation 40 minutes + 15 minutes refrigeration
cooking 55 minutes
makes 6

185 g (6½ oz/1½ cups) plain (all-purpose) flour
100 g (3½ oz) unsalted butter
60–80 ml (2–2½ fl oz/¼–⅓ cup) iced water

filling
240 g (8 oz/1½ cups) macadamia nuts
55 g (2 oz/¼ cup firmly packed) soft brown sugar
2 tablespoons light corn syrup
20 g (¾ oz) unsalted butter, melted
1 egg, lightly beaten
2 teaspoons finely grated orange zest
icing (confectioner's) sugar, to dust

Preheat the oven to 180°C (350°F/Gas 4). Spread the nuts on a baking tray and bake for 8 minutes, or until lightly golden. Leave to cool.

To make the pastry, process the flour and butter in a food processor for 15 seconds, or until crumbly. Add almost all the water and process in short bursts until the dough just comes together (adding more water if necessary). Turn out onto a lightly floured surface and gather together into a smooth ball. Divide into six portions and roll out to line six 8 cm (3¼ inch) fluted flan (tart) tins. Refrigerate the lined tins for 15 minutes.

Cover the pastry cases with baking paper, fill with baking beads or rice and bake for 10 minutes. Remove the baking paper and beads and bake for a further 10 minutes, or until dry. Cool the pastry case

Divide the nuts among the tarts. Use a wire whisk to beat together the sugar, corn syrup, butter, egg, orange zest and a pinch of salt. Pour over the nuts and bake for 20 minutes, until set and lightly browned. Dust with sifted icing sugar.

Transfer the syrup to a jug to help you pour it into the tart cases.

Low-fat passionfruit tart

preparation 25 minutes + 30 minutes refrigeration
cooking 1 hour
serves 8

90 g (3¼ oz/¾ cup) plain (all-purpose) flour
2 tablespoons icing (confectioners') sugar
2 tablespoons custard powder (if unavailable,
    substitute with instant vanilla pudding mix)
30 g (1 oz) unsalted butter, chilled and cubed
60 ml (2 fl oz/¼ cup) light evaporated milk

filling
125 g (4½ oz/½ cup) ricotta cheese
1 teaspoon natural vanilla extract
30 g (1 oz/¼ cup) icing (confectioners') sugar
2 eggs, lightly beaten
4 tablespoons passionfruit pulp (about 8 passionfruit)
185 ml (6 fl oz/¾ cup) light evaporated milk
icing (confectioner's) sugar, to dust

Preheat the oven to 200°C (400°F/Gas 6) and lightly grease a 23 cm (9 inch) loose-based flan (tart) tin.

To make the pastry, sift the flour, icing sugar and custard powder into a large bowl. Rub the butter into the flour until it resembles fine breadcrumbs. Make a well in the centre, add enough evaporated milk to form a soft dough and mix with a flat-bladed knife, using a cutting action, until the mixture comes together in beads (adding more milk if necessary). Turn onto a lightly floured surface and gather together into a smooth ball. Cover with plastic wrap and refrigerate for 15 minutes.

Roll the pastry out on a floured surface, to fit the tin, and trim the excess. Refrigerate for 15 minutes. Cover with baking paper, fill with baking beads or rice and bake for 10 minutes. Remove the baking paper and beads and bake for a further 5–8 minutes, or until dry. Cool the pastry case. Reduce the oven to 160°C (315°F/Gas 2–3).

Beat the ricotta cheese with the vanilla and icing sugar until smooth. Add the egg, passionfruit pulp and evaporated milk, and beat well. Put the tin on a baking tray and gently pour in the mixture. Bake for 40 minutes, or until set. Allow to cool in the tin. Dust with sifted icing sugar to serve.

Bottom: Low-fat passionfruit tart. Top: Orange macadamia tarts.

Tarte au citron

preparation 1 hour + 30 minutes refrigeration
cooking 1 hour 40 minutes
serves 6–8

125 g (4½ oz/1 cup) plain (all-purpose) flour
80 g (2¾ oz) unsalted butter, softened
1 egg yolk
2 tablespoons icing (confectioners') sugar, sifted

filling
3 eggs
2 egg yolks
175 g (6 oz/¾ cup) caster (superfine) sugar
125 ml (4 fl oz/½ cup) pouring cream
185 ml (6 fl oz/¾ cup) lemon juice
1½ tablespoons finely grated lemon zest
2 small lemons
140 g (5 oz/⅔ cup) sugar

To make the pastry, sift the flour and a pinch of salt into a large bowl. Rub the butter into the flour until it resembles fine breadcrumbs. Make a well in the centre, add the egg yolk and mix with a flat-bladed knife, using a cutting action, until the mixture comes together in beads (adding a little iced water if necessary). Turn onto a lightly floured surface and gather together into a smooth ball. Cover with plastic wrap and refrigerate for 20 minutes.

Preheat the oven to 200°C (400°F/Gas 6). Lightly grease a shallow loose-based flan (tart) tin, about 2 cm (¾ inch) deep and 21 cm (8¼ inches) across the base.

Roll out the pastry between two sheets of baking paper until it is 3 mm (⅛ inch) thick, to fit the base and side of the flan tin. Trim the edge. Refrigerate for 10 minutes.

Cover the pastry with baking paper, fill with baking beads or rice and bake for 10 minutes. Remove the baking paper and beads and bake for a further 6–8 minutes, or until dry. Cool the pastry case. Reduce the oven to 150°C (300°F/Gas 2).

Whisk the eggs, egg yolks and sugar together, add the cream and lemon juice and mix well. Strain and then add the lemon zest. Place the flan tin on a baking sheet on the middle shelf of the oven and carefully pour in the filling right up to the top. Bake for 40 minutes, or until it is just set—it should wobble in the middle when the tin is firmly tapped. Cool the tart before removing from its tin.

Meanwhile, wash and scrub the lemons well. Slice very thinly (2 mm/¹⁄₁₆ inch thick). Combine the sugar and 200 ml (7 fl oz) water in a small frying pan and stir over low heat until the sugar has dissolved. Add the lemon slices and simmer over low heat for 40 minutes, or until the peel is very tender and the pith looks transparent. Lift out of the syrup and drain on baking paper. If serving the tart immediately, cover the surface with the lemon slices. If not, keep the slices covered and decorate the tart when ready to serve. Serve warm or chilled, with a little cream.

The tart is cooked if the filling wobbles in the middle when the tin is tapped on the side.

Cook the lemon slices in the sugary syrup until the peel becomes very soft.

Date and mascarpone tart

preparation 50 minutes + 15 minutes refrigeration
cooking 45 minutes
serves 6–8

90 g (3¼ oz/½ cup) rice flour
60 g (2¼ oz/½ cup) plain (all-purpose) flour
100 g (3½ oz) unsalted butter, chilled and cubed
2 tablespoons icing (confectioners') sugar
25 g (1 oz/¼ cup) desiccated coconut
100 g (3½ oz) marzipan, grated

filling
8 fresh dates (about 200 g/7 oz), stoned and quartered, lengthways
2 eggs
2 teaspoons custard powder (if unavailable,
substitute with instant vanilla pudding mix)
125 g (4½ oz) mascarpone cheese
2 tablespoons caster (superfine) sugar
80 ml (2½ fl oz/⅓ cup) pouring cream
2 tablespoons flaked almonds

Preheat the oven to 180°C (350°F/Gas 4). Grease a shallow, 10 x 34 cm (4 x 13½ inch) fluted loose-based flan (tart) tin. To make the coconut pastry, sift the flours into a large bowl. Rub the butter into the flour until it resembles fine breadcrumbs, then press the mixture together gently. Stir in the icing sugar, coconut and marzipan. Turn onto a lightly floured surface and gather together into a smooth ball. Cover with plastic wrap and refrigerate for 15 minutes.

Roll out the pastry between two sheets of baking paper until large enough to line the tin. Ease the pastry into the tin and trim the edges. Refrigerate for 5–10 minutes. Cover the pastry with baking paper, fill with baking beads or rice and bake for 10 minutes. Remove the baking paper and beads and bake for a further 5 minutes, or until dry. Cool the pastry case.

Arrange the date quarters over the pastry. Whisk together the eggs, custard powder, mascarpone, caster sugar and cream until smooth. Pour the mixture over the dates, then sprinkle with the flaked almonds. Bake for 25–30 minutes, or until golden and just set, then allow to cool slightly. Serve the tart warm.

Neaten the edges of the tart by running a rolling pin over the top of the tin.

Lay the date pieces over the tart base then pour the filling evenly over the top.

Mince pies

preparation 40 minutes + 40 minutes refrigeration
cooking 25 minutes
makes 12

250 g (9 oz/2 cups) plain (all-purpose) flour
½ teaspoon ground cinnamon
125 g (4½ oz) unsalted butter, chilled and cubed
1 teaspoon finely grated orange zest
30 g (1 oz/¼ cup) icing (confectioners') sugar, sifted
1 egg yolk
60–80 ml (2–2½ fl oz/¼–⅓ cup) iced water

filling

60 g (2¼ oz/½ cup) raisins, chopped
60 g (2¼ oz/⅓ cup lightly packed) soft brown sugar
40 g (1½ oz/⅓ cup) sultanas (golden raisins)
45 g (1½ oz/¼ cup) mixed peel (mixed candied citrus peel)
1 tablespoon currants
1 tablespoon chopped blanched almonds
1 small green apple, grated
1 teaspoon lemon juice
1 teaspoon finely grated lemon zest
1 teaspoon finely grated orange zest
½ teaspoon mixed (pumpkin pie) spice
¼ teaspoon grated ginger
pinch of ground nutmeg
25 g (1 oz) unsalted butter, melted
1 tablespoon brandy
icing (confectioners') sugar, to dust

To make the pastry, sift the flour, cinnamon and ¼ teaspoon salt into a large bowl. Rub the butter into the flour with your fingertips until it resembles fine breadcrumbs. Stir in the orange zest and icing sugar and mix. Make a well in the centre and add the egg yolk and most of the water. Mix with a flat-bladed knife, using a cutting action, until the mixture comes together in beads (adding more water if necessary). Turn onto a lightly floured surface and gather together into a smooth ball. Cover with plastic wrap and refrigerate for 20 minutes.

Mix together all the filling ingredients in a large bowl.

Preheat the oven to 180°C (350°F/Gas 4). Grease a 12-hole shallow patty pan or mini muffin tin. Roll out two-thirds of the pastry between two sheets of baking paper until 3 mm

(⅛ inch) thick. Use an 8 cm (3¼ inch) round cutter to cut out rounds to line the patty pans.

Divide the filling among the patty cases. Roll out the remaining pastry and cut out 12 rounds with a 7 cm (2¾ inch) cutter. Using a 2.5 cm (1 inch) star cutter, cut a star from the centre of each. Use the outside part to top the tarts, pressing the edges together to seal. Refrigerate for 20 minutes.

Bake for 25 minutes, or until golden. Leave in the pan for 5 minutes before cooling on a wire rack. Dust with icing sugar to serve.

Note *Any extra fruit mince (mincemeat) can be stored in a sterilised jar in a cool, dark place for 3 months.*

Sicilian cannoli

preparation 40 minutes
cooking 10 minutes
makes 18

250 g (9 oz/2 cups) plain (all-purpose) flour
2 teaspoons instant coffee
2 teaspoons unsweetened cocoa powder
2 tablespoons caster (superfine) sugar
60 g (2¼ oz) unsalted butter, chilled and cubed
80–125 ml (2½–4 fl oz/⅓–½ cup) iced water

filling
250 g (9 oz) ricotta cheese
185 g (6½ oz/1½ cups) icing (confectioners') sugar
1 teaspoon orange flower water
30 g (1 oz/¼ cup) grated dark chocolate
60 g (2¼ oz) candied (glacé) citrus peel
icing (confectioners') sugar, to dust

To make the pastry, sift the flour, coffee and cocoa into a large bowl, then add the sugar and a pinch of salt. Rub the butter into the flour until it resembles fine breadcrumbs. Make a well in the centre then add enough of the water to make a soft dough by mixing together.

Knead lightly and divide in two. Roll each half out between two sheets of baking paper until about 3 mm (⅛ inch) thick. Cut into 18 (7.5 cm/2¾ inch) squares. Place metal cannoli moulds or cannelloni pasta tubes diagonally across the squares and fold the corners across to overlap in the middle. Moisten the overlapping dough, then press firmly to seal. (If you use cannelloni pasta tubes, discard them after frying.)

In a saucepan, deep-fry the tubes, a few at a time, in hot oil deep enough to cover them. When golden and crisp, remove and leave to cool, still on their moulds.

To make the filling, beat the ricotta, icing sugar and orange flower water until smooth. Fold in the chocolate and candied peel. Refrigerate until set.

Slide the pastry tubes off the moulds. Using a piping (icing) bag or a spoon, stuff the tubes with filling, leaving some exposed at each end. Dust the cannoli with sifted icing sugar before serving.

Portuguese custard tarts

preparation 40 minutes
cooking 40 minutes
makes 12

150 g (5½ oz/1¼ cups) plain (all-purpose) flour
25 g (1 oz) white vegetable shortening, chopped and softened
30 g (1 oz) unsalted butter, chopped and softened
220 g (7¾ oz/1 cup) sugar
500 ml (17 fl oz/2 cups) milk
30 g (1 oz/¼ cup) cornflour (cornstarch)
1 tablespoon custard powder (if unavailable,
substitute with instant vanilla pudding mix)
4 egg yolks
1 teaspoon natural vanilla extract

Sift the flour into a large bowl and add about 185 ml (6 fl oz/¾ cup) water, or enough to form a soft dough. Gather the dough into a ball, then roll out on baking paper to form a 24 x 30 cm (9½ x 12 inch) rectangle. Spread the shortening over the surface. Roll up from the short edge to form a log. Roll the dough out into a rectangle again and spread with the butter. Roll up again into a roll and slice into 12 even pieces. Working from the centre outwards, use your fingertips to press each round out to a circle large enough to cover the base and side of twelve 80 ml (2½ fl oz/⅓ cup) muffin holes. Press into the holes and refrigerate while preparing the filling.

Put the sugar and 80 ml (2½ fl oz/⅓ cup) water in a saucepan and stir over low heat until the sugar dissolves. Stir a little of the milk with the cornflour and custard powder in a small bowl to form a smooth paste. Add to the pan with the remaining milk, egg yolks and vanilla. Stir over low heat until the mixture thickens. Transfer to a bowl, cover and cool.

Preheat the oven to 220°C (425°F/Gas 7). Divide the filling among the pastry bases and bake for 25–30 minutes, or until the custard is set and the tops have browned. Cool in the tins, then transfer to a wire rack.

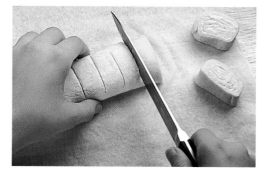

Roll the mixture into a neat log, mark out 12 even slices, then cut them with a sharp knife.

Bottom: Portuguese custard tarts. Top: Sicilian cannoli.

Chocolate éclairs

preparation 20 minutes
cooking 40 minutes
makes 18

125 g (4½ oz) unsalted butter
125 g (4½ oz/1 cup) plain (all-purpose) flour, sifted
4 eggs, at room temperature, lightly beaten
300 ml (10 fl oz) cream, whipped
150 g (5½ oz/1 cup) chopped dark chocolate

Preheat the oven to 210°C (415°F/Gas 6–7). Grease two baking trays. Combine the butter and 250 ml (9 fl oz/1 cup) water in a saucepan. Stir over medium heat until the butter melts. Increase the heat, bring to the boil, then remove from the heat.

Add the flour to the saucepan and quickly beat into the butter mixture with a wooden spoon. Return to the heat and continue beating until the mixture leaves the side of the pan and forms a ball. Transfer to a large bowl and cool slightly. Beat the mixture to release any remaining heat. Gradually add the egg, about 3 teaspoons at a time. Beat well after each addition until all the egg has been added and the mixture is glossy (a wooden spoon should stand upright). It will be too runny if the egg is added too quickly. If this happens, beat for several more minutes, or until thickened.

Spoon into a piping (icing) bag fitted with a 1.5 cm (⅝ inch) plain nozzle. Sprinkle the baking trays lightly with water. Pipe 15 cm (6 inch) lengths onto the trays, leaving room for expansion. Bake for 10–15 minutes, then reduce the heat to 180°C (350°F/Gas 4) and bake for another 15 minutes, or until golden and firm. Cool on a wire rack. Split each éclair, and remove any uncooked dough. Fill the éclairs with cream.

Place the chocolate in a heatproof bowl and sit it over a saucepan of barely simmering water, making sure the base of the bowl does not touch the water. Stir until the chocolate has melted. Spread over the top of each éclair.

Baklava fingers

preparation 30 minutes
cooking 25 minutes
makes 24

filling
90 g (3¼ oz/¾ cup) walnut pieces, finely chopped
1 tablespoon soft brown sugar
1 teaspoon ground cinnamon
20 g (¾ oz) unsalted butter, melted

8 sheets filo pastry
50 g (1¾ oz) unsalted butter, melted

syrup
220 g (7¾ oz/1 cup) sugar
2 tablespoons honey
2 teaspoons orange flower water, optional

Preheat the oven to 210°C (415°F/Gas 6–7). Lightly grease a baking tray.

To make the filling, put the walnuts, sugar, cinnamon and butter in a small bowl and stir until combined.

Remove one sheet of filo and cover the rest with a damp tea towel (dish towel) to prevent them from drying out. Place the sheet of filo pastry on a work bench, brush with melted butter and fold in half. Cut the sheet into three strips and place a heaped teaspoon of filling close to the front edge of the pastry. Roll up, tucking in the edges. Place on the prepared tray and brush with melted butter.

Repeat with the remaining pastry sheets. Bake for 15 minutes, or until golden brown.

To make the syrup, combine the sugar, honey and 125 ml (4 fl oz/½ cup) water in a small saucepan. Stir over low heat, without boiling, until the sugar has completely dissolved. Bring to the boil, reduce the heat and simmer for 5 minutes. Remove from the heat and add the orange flower water.

Transfer to a wire rack over a tray and spoon the syrup over the pastries while both the pastries and syrup are still warm.

Note Store in an airtight container for up to 2 days.

Millefeuille

preparation 30 minutes
cooking 1 hour 30 minutes
serves 6–8

600 g (1 lb 5 oz) block ready-made puff pastry or 3 sheets ready-rolled, thawed
625 ml (21½ fl oz/2½ cups) thick (double/heavy) cream
500 g (1 lb 2 oz) small strawberries, halved
70 g (2½ oz) blueberries, optional
icing (confectioners') sugar, to dust

Preheat the oven to 220°C (425°F/Gas 7). Line a baking tray with baking paper. If using a block of puff pastry, cut the pastry into three and roll out to 25 cm (10 inch) squares. Place one sheet of puff pastry on the tray, prick all over and top with another piece of baking paper and another baking tray and bake for 15 minutes. Turn the trays over and bake on the other side for 10–15 minutes, or until golden brown. Allow to cool and repeat with the remaining pastry.

Trim the edges of each pastry sheet and cut each one in half. Pour the cream into a large bowl and whisk to firm peaks. Place two of the pastry pieces on a serving dish and spoon some of the cream on top. Carefully arrange some of the strawberries and blueberries over the cream, pressing them well down. Top each one with another pastry sheet and repeat with the cream, strawberries and blueberries. Top with a final layer of pastry and dust with icing sugar.

Bottom: Millefeuille. Top: Baklava fingers.

Shredded pastries with almonds

preparation 45 minutes + 2 hours resting
cooking 50 minutes
makes 40 pieces

500 g (1 lb 2 oz) kataifi pastry (see Notes)
250 g (9 oz) unsalted butter, melted
125 g (4½ oz) ground pistachio nuts
200 g (7 oz) ground almonds
575 g (1 lb 4½ oz/2½ cups) caster (superfine) sugar
1 teaspoon ground cinnamon
¼ teaspoon ground cloves
1 tablespoon brandy
1 egg white
1 teaspoon lemon juice
5 cm (2 inch) strip lemon zest
4 whole cloves
1 cinnamon stick
1 tablespoon honey

Allow the kataifi pastry to come to room temperature, still in its packaging. This will take about 2 hours and makes the pastry easier to work with.

Preheat the oven to 170°C (325°F/Gas 3). Brush a 20 x 30 cm (8⅓ x 12 inch) ovenproof dish or tray with some melted butter.

Put the nuts in a bowl with 115 g (4 oz/½ cup) of the caster sugar, the ground cinnamon, ground cloves and brandy. Lightly beat the egg white and add to the mixture. Stir to make a paste. Divide the mixture into eight portions and form each into a sausage shape about 18 cm (7 inches) long.

Take a small handful of the pastry strands and spread them out fairly compactly with the strands running lengthways towards you. The pastry should measure 18 x 25 cm (7 x 10 inches). Brush the pastry with melted butter. Place one of the 'nut' sausages along the end of the pastry nearest to you and roll up into a neat sausage shape. Repeat with the other pastry portions.

Place the rolls close together in the dish and brush them again with melted butter. Bake for 50 minutes, or until golden brown.

While the pastries are cooking, put the remaining sugar in a small saucepan with 500 ml (17 fl oz/2 cups) water and stir over low heat until dissolved. Add the lemon juice, lemon zest, whole cloves and cinnamon stick and boil together for 10 minutes. Stir in the honey, then set aside until cold.

When the pastries come out of the oven, pour the syrup over the top. Leave them to cool completely before cutting each roll into five pieces.

Notes *Kataifi, a shredded pastry, is available from Greek delicatessens and other speciality food stores.*

It is very important that the syrup is cold and the kataifi hot when pouring the syrup over, otherwise the liquid will not be absorbed as well or as evenly.

These pastries keep for up to a week if you cover them. Don't refrigerate them.

Apple turnovers

preparation 40 minutes
cooking 25 minutes
makes 12 pieces

500 g (1 lb 2 oz) block ready-made puff pastry, thawed
1 egg white, lightly beaten
caster (superfine) sugar, to sprinkle

filling
200 g (7 oz/1 cup) tinned pie or stewed apple
1–2 tablespoons caster (superfine) sugar
30 g (1 oz/¼ cup) raisins, chopped
30 g (1 oz/¼ cup) walnut pieces, chopped

Preheat the oven to 210°C (415°F/Gas 6–7). Lightly grease a baking tray. Roll the pastry on a lightly floured surface to 35 x 45 cm (14 x 17¾ inches). Cut out twelve 10 cm (4 inch) pastry rounds.

To make the apple filling, mix together all the ingredients.

Divide the filling among the pastry rounds, then brush the edges with water. Fold in half and pinch firmly together to seal. Use the back of a knife to push up the pastry edge at intervals. Brush the tops with egg white and sprinkle with caster sugar. Make two small slits in the top of each turnover. Bake for 15 minutes, then lower the oven to 190°C (375°F/Gas 5) and bake for 10 minutes, or until golden.

Jalousie

preparation 40 minutes
cooking 45 minutes
serves 4–6

30 g (1 oz) unsalted butter
50 g (1¾ oz/¼ cup lightly packed) soft brown sugar
500 g (1 lb 2 oz) apples, peeled, cored and cubed
1 teaspoon grated lemon zest
1 tablespoon lemon juice
¼ teaspoon freshly grated nutmeg
¼ teaspoon ground cinnamon
30 g (1 oz/¼ cup) sultanas (golden raisins)
375 g (13 oz) block ready-made puff pastry, thawed
1 egg, lightly beaten, to glaze

Preheat the oven to 220°C (425°F/Gas 7). Lightly grease a baking tray and line with baking paper.

Melt the butter and sugar in a frying pan. Add the apple, lemon zest and lemon juice. Cook over medium heat for 10 minutes, stirring occasionally, until the apples are cooked and the mixture is thick and syrupy. Stir in the nutmeg, cinnamon and sultanas. Cool completely.

Cut the block of puff pastry in half. On a lightly floured surface roll out one half of the pastry to an 18 x 24 cm (7 x 9½ inch) rectangle. Spread the fruit mixture onto the pastry, leaving a 2.5 cm (1 inch) border. Brush the edges lightly with the beaten egg.

Roll the second half of the pastry on a lightly floured surface to a 18 x 25 cm (7 x 10 inch) rectangle. Using a sharp knife, cut slashes in the pastry across its width, leaving a 2 cm (¾ inch) border around the edge. The slashes should open slightly and look like a venetian blind (jalousie in French). Place over the fruit and press the edges together. Trim away any extra pastry. Knock up the puff pastry (brush the sides upwards) with a knife to ensure rising during cooking. Glaze the top with egg. Bake for 25–30 minutes, or until puffed and golden.

Cook the apple mixture until soft, then add the spices and sultanas.

Bottom: Jalousie. Top: Apple turnovers.

Danish pastries

preparation 40 minutes +
cooking 25 minutes
makes 12

2 teaspoons dried yeast
125 ml (4 fl oz/½ cup) warm milk
1 teaspoon caster (superfine) sugar
250 g (9 oz/2 cups) plain (all-purpose) flour
55 g (2 oz/¼ cup) caster (superfine) sugar, extra
1 egg, lightly beaten
1 teaspoon natural vanilla extract
250 g (9 oz) unsalted butter, chilled

pastry cream
2 tablespoons caster (superfine) sugar
2 egg yolks
2 teaspoons plain (all-purpose) flour
2 teaspoons cornflour (cornstarch)
125 ml (4 fl oz/½ cup) hot milk

425 g (15 oz) tinned apricot halves, drained
1 egg, lightly beaten
40 g (1½ oz) flaked almonds
80 g (2¾ oz/¼ cup) apricot jam, to glaze

Put the yeast, milk and sugar in a small bowl and stir until the sugar has dissolved. Leave in a warm place for 10 minutes, or until bubbles appear on the surface. The mixture should be frothy and slightly increased in volume. If your yeast doesn't foam, it is dead, so you will have to discard it and start again.

Sift the flour and ½ teaspoon salt into a large bowl and stir in the extra sugar. Make a well in the centre and add the yeast, egg and vanilla. Mix to a firm dough. Turn out onto a lightly floured surface and knead for 10 minutes to form a smooth, elastic dough. Place the dough in a lightly greased bowl, cover and set aside in a warm place for 1 hour, or until doubled in size. Meanwhile, roll the cold butter between two sheets of baking paper to a 15 x 20 cm (6 x 8 inch) rectangle and then refrigerate until required.

Punch down the dough (one punch with your fist) and knead for 1 minute. Roll out to a rectangle measuring 25 x 30 cm (10 x 12 inches). Put the butter in the centre of the dough and fold up the bottom and top of the dough over the butter to join in the centre. Seal the edges with a rolling pin. Give the dough a quarter turn clockwise then roll out to a 20 x 45 cm (8 x 17¾ inch) rectangle. Fold over the top third of the pastry, then the bottom third and then give another quarter turn

clockwise. Cover and refrigerate for 30 minutes. Repeat the rolling, folding, turning and chilling four more times. Wrap in plastic wrap and chill for at least another 2 hours.

To make the pastry cream, put the sugar, egg yolks and flours in a saucepan and whisk to combine. Pour the hot milk over the flour and whisk until smooth. Bring to the boil over moderate heat, stirring all the time, until the mixture boils and thickens. Cover and set aside.

Preheat the oven to 200°C (400°F/Gas 6) and line two baking trays with baking paper. On a lightly floured surface, roll the dough into a rectangle or square 3 mm (⅛ inch) thick. Cut the dough into 10 cm (4 inch) squares and place on the baking trays. Spoon 1 tablespoon of pastry cream into the centre of each square and top with two apricot halves. Brush one corner with the beaten egg and draw up that corner and the diagonally opposite one to touch in the middle between the apricots. Press firmly in the centre. Leave in a warm place to prove for 30 minutes. Brush each pastry with egg and sprinkle with almonds. Bake for 15–20 minutes, or until golden. Cool on wire racks. Melt the apricot jam with 1 tablespoon water in a saucepan and then strain. Brush the tops of the apricots with the hot glaze and serve.

glossary *and* index

Glossary

Terms used in recipes for baking sometimes seem mysterious but once understood, help you cook with confidence. Knowing the function of common ingredients also helps you on your way.

Bake blind means to partially or totally cook a pastry case before filling it. This prevents the pastry going soggy. The uncooked pastry is lined with baking paper or foil and, to prevent it rising, it is filled with dried beans, uncooked rice or special-purpose beads.

Baking powder is a leavener used to aerate cakes, bread and buns. It is a mixture of bicarbonate of soda (baking soda), cream of tartar (an acid) and usually cornflour.

Batter is an uncooked mixture of flour, liquid and sometimes a leavener such as baking powder.

Beat means to briskly combine ingredients, usually with electric beaters but sometimes with a wooden spoon, to introduce air into a mixture to make it smooth and light.

Bicarbonate of soda, or baking soda, is both a component of baking powder and a leavener in its own right, one that gets its leavening power with the aid of acid in yoghurt, sour cream, crème fraîche, molasses or buttermilk.

Biscuit base or crumb crust This is crushed bought biscuits (cookies) combined with melted butter and sometimes spices. The mixture is pressed onto the base and/or sides of a cake or tart tin. It can be baked or unbaked.

Bread dough is a mixture of flour, liquid, leaven (yeast) and sometimes other flavouring and enriching ingredients.

Butter is produced when the fat content of milk (the sweet cream) is separated from the liquid (the buttermilk). The fat globules are churned until they combine and become solid, forming butter. Butter is the most commonly used fat for cake-making as it creams well and has an acceptable flavour. We specify unsalted butter (also known as sweet butter) for use in baking biscuits, slices, cakes and sweet pastries.

Buttermilk is traditionally the liquid that is left after cream is churned into butter. It has a tangy flavour. Because of its acidic content it is used as a raising agent.

Chocolate is made from components extracted from cocoa beans which grow in pods on the cacao tree. Couverture chocolate is considered the best.

Cinnamon is the dried aromatic bark from the laurel family of trees native to Asia. The paper-thin inner bark is rolled and dried to form quills or sticks. The sticks are used as a flavour infusion in syrups and poached fruits. Ground cinnamon adds flavour to cakes, puddings, biscuits and yeast breads.

Cinnamon sugar is used to decorate cakes, before or after baking, and to flavour buttered toast. Caster (superfine) sugar and ground cinnamon are combined in a proportion of four sugar to one (or more, to taste) cinnamon.

Cloves are the strongly scented flower buds of the clove tree which are sun-dried until hard. They contain essential oils and are used whole or ground in baking. The flavour marries especially well with apple.

Cocoa is ground into a powder from the dry solids left when the cocoa butter (the fat) is removed. It is used extensively in baking. Cocoa is usually sifted in with the dry ingredients so it is distributed evenly. Sweetened cocoa powder is sold as drinking chocolate. Dutch cocoa, available from delicatessens, is considered to be the best flavoured cocoa for baking. It is rich, dark in colour and unsweetened.

Copha, or white vegetable shortening, is made from purified coconut oil that is processed into a white solid. Copha is generally used in making uncooked confections and slices or bar cookies.

Corn syrup is a liquid form of sugar refined from corn. A variety of corn syrups are produced, from light, which is less sweet, to dark, which has flavour added.

Cornflour or cornstarch is a fine white powder made from maize or corn (gluten-free) or from wheat. It is used in small quantities in baking, such as in sponges and shortbread, to produce a lighter texture. It is also used to thicken sauces and fillings because it forms a gel when heated. Cornflour is usually mixed to a paste with a small amount of cold liquid before being added to the remaining liquid.

Cream is the fat globules that rise to the top of milk. The fat content determines the type of cream. Cream is used extensively in baking, either as part of the mixture or whipped to decorate. For successful whipping, cream must have a fat content of at least 30 per cent and if the fat content is higher than this, a lighter foam results when the cream is whipped.

Cream of tartar is a component of baking powder. It acts as a raising agent when combined with bicarbonate of soda. Sometimes it is used to help stabilise the beating of egg whites, as in meringue.

Cream together means to beat one or more ingredients, usually butter and sugar, until light and fluffy. Electric beaters or a whisk can be used. The creaming process dissolves the sugar.

Crème fraîche is a naturally soured cream with a nutty, slightly sour taste. It is available at delicatessens.

Dust means to cover lightly, usually referring to icing (confectioners') sugar or cocoa powder that is sifted over the top of a cake or pie for presentation.

Eggs In baking, eggs enrich and also add flavour, moisture, nutritive value and yellow colour. They have three main functional properties in cooking—coagulation, emulsification and foaming ability. Eggs should be refrigerated. Bring them to room temperature before using in baking.

Egg whites increase in volume when whisked, due to the entrapment of air. There are four stages in the whisking of whites. The first is the large bubble stage where the foam is frothy and unstable. The soft peak stage is where the whites form a glossy mass and just hold shape (folded into creams and cake mixtures). The next stage is medium peaks where the foam is very white and glossy—the peaks are soft and the tip falls a little (used for soufflés, mousses and ice creams). The final stage is stiff peaks where the bubbles are very fine and the peaks hold their shape (as in meringue). Make sure all utensils are clean and free of grease and that the bowl is deep enough to hold the volume of whisked whites. Egg whites also act as leaveners, adding volume and texture to soufflés, flourless cakes and sponge cakes. The whisked whites are folded into the mixture just before baking. When cooked, the air is trapped and the mixture expands and coagulates.

Essences and extracts are flavourings that enhance the taste of food. Vanilla extract is used extensively in the baking of cakes and biscuits. Almond extract is also used to boost chopped or ground almond flavour in cakes. An extract is a stronger, purer concentration.

Evaporated milk is canned milk with most of its water removed. Diluted, it can be used as milk. Undiluted, it can replace cream. It is used to enrich sauces and moisten food. With the addition of lemon juice, chilled evaporated milk will whip to form a stable foam.

Fat or shortening contributes flavour, colour and shortness (tenderness) to shortcrust (pie) pastries, cakes and biscuits, and flakiness to layered pastries such as flaky and puff. Lard, butter, margarine and half butter/half lard are all suitable fats for baking. Shredded suet is used in traditional pie crusts. Oils are sometimes used in one-bowl or quick-mix cake mixtures, resulting in a heavier texture. Oil or butter is added to bread dough to add flavour and tenderness. Fat can be creamed with sugar, rubbed into the dry ingredients, melted and mixed into the dry ingredients, or kneaded into bread doughs.

Flour provides the basic structure of bread, cakes, batters and pastry. The process of manufacturing the whole grain where the grain is converted into a variety of flours is called milling. Wheat flour is the most versatile of all the flours. Roller milling produces all white flours and most wholemeal (whole-wheat) flours. Some wholemeal flours are produced by stone milling. Other non-wheat cereals are milled and used in cooking, for example cornflour (cornstarch), cornmeal, potato flour, rice flour and rye flour. These are not termed high-quality flours because, unlike wheat flour, they lack the protein gluten (the strength, elasticity and structure) necessary for baking. However, they are useful for people who are intolerant to wheat products. Bread dough made with non- or low-gluten flour does not have the elasticity of dough made with wheat-based flour so the bread will be dense. Plain white flour, also called all-purpose flour, has a medium protein content of about 10 per cent. Most baked goods use this flour. Self-raising flour has the same protein qualities as plain flour but has baking powder added to it. Self-raising flour can be made by adding 2 teaspoons of baking powder to 150 g (5½ oz/1 cup) of plain flour and then sifting thoroughly several times. Wholemeal flours are coarsely milled or finely ground and can be used instead of plain white flour. If you do use wholemeal, the baked product will have a denser crumb and less volume. Bread flour is produced from hard wheat that has a higher protein (gluten) content, about 12 per cent, than all-purpose bleached or white flour. It is smoother in texture and is used to ensure that the dough is elastic and strong so that the bread has structure, strength and elasticity. It is available in supermarkets and health food stores. Sometimes it is called strong flour.

391

Frangipane is creamed butter and sugar with eggs, ground almonds and a liqueur. It is used to fill a pastry or tart case.

Galettes are small open fruit tarts. They have a thin pastry base topped with raw sliced or halved fruit that is sprinkled with sugar, then dotted with butter and baked.

Gelatine is extracted from collagen, the connective tissue present in the bones and cartilage of animals. Gelatine is a setting agent available in powdered form and as leaves. 3 teaspoons of gelatine powder is equivalent to 6 leaves, which will set 500 ml (17 fl oz/2 cups) of liquid to a light jelly. To dissolve gelatine leaves, soften them in a bowl of cold water for 5 minutes, then remove and squeeze well. Next, dissolve them in warm to hot liquid. To dissolve gelatine powder, sprinkle the powder over a small bowl of water. Sit the bowl in a larger bowl of hot water and leave to dissolve. Agar-agar is a substitute suitable for vegetarian people.

Ginger Native to Southeast Asia, ginger is the rhizome or root of the ginger plant. It is available fresh or dried (ground). Fresh ginger should be bought while plump and firm with a pale outer skin. The powder is used in baking to flavour cakes, biscuits, puddings and gingerbread. Crystallised fresh ginger is used in cakes, desserts and as decoration.

Glacé fruit is fruit that is preserved in sugar. The fruit, usually citrus or pineapple slices, or cherries, is cooked in a strong syrup solution until the fruit is impregnated by the sugar. Cherries are often coloured with various food dyes.

Glaze is a liquid such as milk, sugar syrup, melted butter, softened and sieved jam, beaten whole egg, egg yolk and water, or egg white that is brushed onto food, often before baking to give colour and shine.

Gluten, a protein found in wheat flour, is the muscular substance of great elasticity that strengthens the cellular structure of bread dough. Without the elasticity qualities of gluten, bread is flat and heavy. Gluten flour or powder is often added to bread dough to provide more protein and therefore improved volume, structure and texture. Non-wheat flours, notably rye, oat, barley and corn, lack gluten. If volume is wanted, these flours require added gluten in the form of gluten flour or the addition of some wheat flour. Breads made without the addition of gluten are heavy and dense, as in German rye bread, corn breads and oatcakes. Gluten flour or powder is available at health food shops and some supermarkets.

Golden syrup is a by-product of sugar refining. It is a thick sticky syrup with a deep golden colour and distinctive flavour. It is used in the baking of gingerbread, tarts and some breads to give flavour and moisture. It can be substituted for treacle in baked goods.

Icing sugar Pure icing (confectioners') sugar is powdered white sugar used in the making of icings (frostings) including buttercreams, glacé and royal, and fondants, to decorate cakes. It should be sifted before use to remove lumps and to obtain a smooth finish.

Icing sugar mixture is icing sugar to which a small amount of starch has been added to prevent lumping during storage. It is used in the making of icings such as buttercreams and glacé, but is not suitable for royal icing. It is also known as confectioners' sugar.

Jams are traditionally made from whole ripe fruit that has been cooked to a pulp with sugar until it gels or sets. Jam heated and strained through a sieve, then brushed over the top of baked goods like cakes makes an attractive finish. Small amounts of jam or marmalade blended into a cake mixture add extra flavour and moisture.

Knead This means to work a bread dough with your hands on a flat floured surface. The dough is rhythmically pushed, stretched and folded in order to develop the gluten in the flour. It takes about 10 minutes for the gluten to be fully developed.

Knock back After the first rising, bread dough is 'knocked back' or punched down. This allows all the bubbles of carbon dioxide to be expelled, thus preventing the gluten walls from overstretching and collapsing. The dough is then ready to be shaped and left to rise a second time.

Lard is purified fat from pork. It is sold in solid form in packets and can be refrigerated for weeks. It is traditionally used in pastry-making. Lard is a good shortening (tenderising) agent but lacks flavour and colour, so a blend of butter and lard will produce the most tender pastry with more flavour.

Leavened is a term describing baked products such as breads and cakes that contain a raising agent, usually yeast or baking powder, to increase the volume of the goods.

Malt extract is produced from grain, a process that converts grain starch to a sugar called maltose. The resulting powder or syrup is used widely in baking, brewing and distilling. It retains moisture, thus giving malted breads their distinctive flavour and moist texture. It also aids in the rising of the bread dough.

Maple syrup is a light brown syrup processed from the sap of the maple tree. It is often used as a topping for pancakes.

Marzipan is a mixture of almond paste (meal), egg white and icing sugar. It is mainly used by rolling out thinly to cover fruit cakes before they are finished with a layer of royal icing. Marzipan can be shaped, then tinted with food dyes to resemble fruits, and used to decorate cakes.

Meringue is stabilised egg-white foam and dissolved sugar crystals, brought about by whisking. The quantity of sugar required per egg white in order to form a stable meringue varies from 50 to 75 g (1¾–2½ oz). There are three types of meringue. Swiss meringue produces an externally crisp and dry texture usually with a dry centre. It is suitable for piping, pie toppings and pavlovas. The standard proportion is 50 to 60 g (1¾–2¼ oz) of sugar per egg white.

Soft and creamy in texture, Italian meringue is more stable than the Swiss and is used as a frosting, for Baked Alaska, and sometimes in ice creams. The basic proportion is 50 to 60 g (1¾–2¼ oz) of sugar per egg white—a sugar syrup is first made, then slowly poured onto the beaten white.

Meringue cuite (cooked) is a very firm dry meringue mostly used by pastry cooks in the making of meringue baskets and meringue decorations that can be stored for a length of time. About 75 g (2½ oz) of icing sugar per egg white is used for this.

Meringues need to be baked at a very low temperature, preferably in an electric oven, as they need to dry out and maintain their white colour.

Mixed peel (mixed candied citrus peel) is a mixture of chopped citrus fruit peel preserved in sugar and glucose syrup.

Mixed spice is a blend of ground spices, usually allspice, cinnamon, nutmeg, cloves and ginger. It adds a lightly spicy flavour to cooked fruit such as apples, and to cakes, fruit cakes, puddings and biscuits.

Nutmeg is the dried kernel or seed of the fruit of an evergreen tree native to Southeast Asia. The nutmeg kernel is grated whole or used in powder form to flavour cakes and desserts. Freshly grated nutmeg gives a much superior flavour than powdered nutmeg.

Nuts are formed after a tree or plant has flowered. They are the hardened and dried fruit encased in tough shells that have to be cracked to open (such as macadamias and chestnuts). However, the term 'nut' is also used to describe any seed or fruit with an edible kernel in a hard or brittle shell (almonds, walnuts and coconuts). Nuts are used extensively in baking. Because of their high fat content it is advisable to refrigerate nuts in an airtight container to prevent them turning rancid.

Oils are similar to fats but differ in their physical state. Oils are liquid at room temperature and fats are solid. Animal fats (i.e. saturated fats) that are used in baking include butter, cream, ghee, lard and suet. Vegetable oils (i.e. polyunsaturated and monounsaturated fats), include fruit oils (olive oil), nut oils (walnut, hazelnut), seed oils (sesame, sunflower), pulse oils (soybean) and cereal oils (corn). All are used in one form or the other for the baking of cakes, biscuits, desserts, puddings and breads. Oils enhance the flavour and moistness in baked products.

Organic ingredients have generally been produced without the use of pesticides, insecticides, herbicides, fungicides or artificial fertilisers.

Powdered milk is milk from which most of the moisture has been removed. The resulting milk powder can be stored in airtight tins or foil bags for up to a year. It is reconstituted to milk by adding water, or can be used in its powder form to enrich baked products, especially bread doughs. Powdered milks are made from both full-fat and non-fat (skim) milk.

Proving (also called the second rise) describes the process of the bread dough being knocked back, then shaped and left to rise on its baking tray until doubled in bulk, before baking.

Ribbon stage Eggs and sugar are beaten, either with an electric beater or a hand whisk, until the sugar has dissolved and the egg becomes pale with small bubbles. The beater or whisk will leave a raised mark on top of the mixture when the ribbon stage is reached. The term is used when sponge cakes are being made. The result of the beating is a very light aerated sponge cake.

Salt is used as a seasoning, preservative and flavour enhancer. Salt improves the balance of flavours in sweet baking goods. Iodised salt, often used as table salt, has a trace element of iodine added. Maldon salt, or sea salt, is produced in Essex in the UK and is made by extracting sea salt by natural means. Rock salt is mined from under the ground. In baking, salt is often added even to sweet foods to enhance flavour.

Suet is the fat that surrounds the kidneys of beef cattle. It is often used in dried fruit puddings. Fresh suet can be bought from a butcher. Dried, shredded suet can be found at supermarkets. Butter can be used instead.

Sugar is the common name for sucrose, the simplest form of carbohydrate. There are several types of sugar. The most widely used is white sugar (granulated, caster, cubed and icing sugar). It is usually manufactured from sugar cane or sugar beet and is used extensively in baking and general table use.

Coloured sugars, also manufactured from sugar cane, include brown sugar, often known as soft brown sugar, a golden brown refined sugar, which is used in baked goods. These sugars add colour and flavour and help create a moist texture. Brown sugar is also available as dark brown sugar. The colour in these sugars comes from the molasses content.

Raw sugar, coarse straw-coloured crystals, is also produced from sugar cane. It can be substituted for white sugar to add texture, but is difficult to dissolve. Demerara sugar, a coarse amber-coloured crystal, similar to raw sugar, is also used in baking, especially in crumble topping.

Treacle is a blend of concentrated refinery syrups and extract molasses. It is used in baking to give a distinctive colour and flavour. It also adds moistness and keeping qualities to a baked product. Golden syrup can be substituted in baking.

Vanilla is extracted from the pods of a climbing orchid plant native to South America. The pods or beans are dried and cured. For use in cooking, the pod is split open and infused with the food to allow for maximum flavour. Vanilla is also available as pure essence or extract, which has a more concentrated flavour and is widely used in cakes, biscuits and desserts.

Vanilla sugar is made by placing a whole vanilla pod or bean in a jar of caster sugar and leaving it to stand so the flavour can be absorbed into the sugar.

Yeast is a biological (naturally occurring) raising agent. Fresh yeast (compressed) needs to be blended with water to form a smooth cream, then added to any remaining liquid and left to foam before being added to the dry ingredients. Dried yeast, available in long-life sachets from supermarkets, can be added to liquid or mixed straight into the dry ingredients. For fermentation of the yeast to take place, it needs the right conditions of food (sugar), warmth (26–29°C/79–84°F) and moisture (liquid).

Zest or rind is the outside rind of any citrus fruit. The rind contains all the essential oils and therefore the flavour. Grated or shredded rind is used to flavour cakes, biscuits, syrups and doughs.

393

Index

index

Published in 2011 by Murdoch Books Pty Limited

Murdoch Books Australia
Pier 8/9, 23 Hickson Road
Millers Point NSW 2000
Phone: +61 (0) 2 8220 2000
Fax: +61 (0) 2 8220 2558
www.murdochbooks.com.au

Murdoch Books UK Limited
Erico House, 6th Floor
93–99 Upper Richmond Road
Putney, London SW15 2TG
Phone: +44 (0) 20 8785 5995
Fax: +44 (0) 20 8785 5985
www.murdochbooks.co.uk

Chief Executive: Juliet Rogers
Publishing Director: Chris Rennie

Publisher: Lynn Lewis
Design Concept and Senior Designer: Heather Menzies
Designer: Susanne Geppert
Editor: Zoë Harpham
Production: Alexandra Gonzalez
Index: Jo Rudd

National Library of Australia Cataloguing-in-Publication Data:
The Baking Bible
ISBN: 978-1-74196-991-7 (pbk.)
Includes index.
Cookery. Baking
641.71

PRINTED IN CHINA